Smart Homes For Dummies
3rd Edition

W9-BOO-246

Smart Home A/V Needs

Video-Distribution Network

Stuff You Need	Quantity You Need
RG-6 coaxial cable with F connectors	For a two-way network, two runs from each viewing room to the central distribution point
Wall outlets	One per remote viewing room housing two female connectors
Video distribution panel	One, located in the central wiring closet
Cable set-top box/satellite receiver	One per TV location is typical

Audio-Distribution Network (Single Amplifier)

Stuff You Need	Quantity You Need
Single-zone or multizone integrated amplifier or receiver	One (multizone systems contain one stereo amplifier per zone)
Impedance-matching system	One
Speakers	Two per room (can be in-wall or free-standing speakers)
In-wall speaker cable (16 AWG minimum)	One run between the media room and each remote location
RCA audio patch cords	(Usually) one set per audio component
In-wall speaker wire outlets	Two per remote area (if in-wall speakers aren't being used)
IR control network (using CAT-5e/6 cabling and keypad/controllers)	One controller per room

For Dummies: Bestselling Book Series for Beginners

Smart Homes For Dummies, 3rd Edition

Cheat Sheet

Smart Home Communication Network Needs

Remote Control Network for A/V Equipment

Stuff You Need	Quantity You Need
CAT-5e/6 cabling	One run from each remote location to the media room
Wall-mounted IR sensors or remote keypads	One sensor or keypad per remote location
CAT-5e/6 A/V control system	One installed in wiring closet or media room
IR emitters	One per audio source device being controlled in media room

Telephone Network

Stuff You Need	Quantity You Need
4-pair CAT-5e/6 UTP cabling	One run from wiring closet to each outlet
Modular wall outlets with female RJ-45 jacks	One per telephone extension
Telephone patch cords with male RJ-45 plugs	One per telephone extension
Telephone patch panel mounted in wiring closet	One
CAT-5e/6 UTP cable to connect patch panel	One run per incoming line to incoming lines from telephone company NID
Key Service Unit (KSU) (optional)	One

Computer LAN

Stuff You Need	Quantity You Need
4-pair CAT-5e/6 UTP cabling	One run from wiring closet to each outlet (put extra runs in the home office and home theater/media room)
Modular wall outlets with female RJ-45 jacks	One jack per computer or networked device, and one extra for your broadband modem
CAT-5e/6 UTP patch cords with male RJ-45 plugs	One patch cord per computer or network printer
CAT-5e/6 rated patch panel mounted in wiring closet	One (can be the same one that works with the phone network)
Home router/Ethernet switch	Minimum of one router/switch in your wiring closet (additional hubs can be installed at remote outlets to allow connection of several computers to a single outlet)
Wireless LAN access point (optional)	One or more in larger homes
Cable modem or DSL modem (optional)	One

Wiley, the Wiley Publishing logo, For Dummies, the Dummies Man logo, the For Dummies Bestselling Book Series logo and all related trade dress are trademarks or registered trademarks of John Wiley & Sons, Inc. and/or its affiliates. All other trademarks are property of their respective owners.

Copyright © 2007 Wiley Publishing, Inc. All rights reserved. Item 6567-6.

For more information about Wiley Publishing, call 1-800-762-2974.

For Dummies: Bestselling Book Series for Beginners

Smart Homes

FOR

DUMMIES®

3RD EDITION

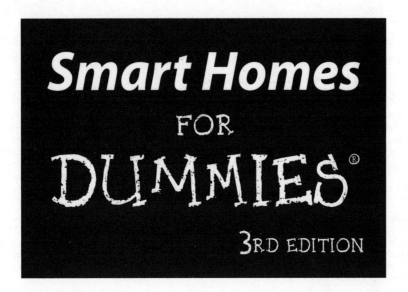

Smart Homes

FOR

DUMMIES®

3RD EDITION

by Danny Briere and Pat Hurley

Wiley Publishing, Inc.

Smart Homes For Dummies®, 3rd Edition

Published by
Wiley Publishing, Inc.
111 River Street
Hoboken, NJ 07030-5774
www.wiley.com

Copyright © 2007 by Wiley Publishing, Inc., Indianapolis, Indiana

Published by Wiley Publishing, Inc., Indianapolis, Indiana

Published simultaneously in Canada

No part of this publication may be reproduced, stored in a retrieval system or transmitted in any form or by any means, electronic, mechanical, photocopying, recording, scanning or otherwise, except as permitted under Sections 107 or 108 of the 1976 United States Copyright Act, without either the prior written permission of the Publisher, or authorization through payment of the appropriate per-copy fee to the Copyright Clearance Center, 222 Rosewood Drive, Danvers, MA 01923, (978) 750-8400, fax (978) 646-8600. Requests to the Publisher for permission should be addressed to the Legal Department, Wiley Publishing, Inc., 10475 Crosspoint Blvd., Indianapolis, IN 46256, (317) 572-3447, fax (317) 572-4355, or online at http://www.wiley.com/go/permissions.

Trademarks: Wiley, the Wiley Publishing logo, For Dummies, the Dummies Man logo, A Reference for the Rest of Us!, The Dummies Way, Dummies Daily, The Fun and Easy Way, Dummies.com, and related trade dress are trademarks or registered trademarks of John Wiley & Sons, Inc. and/or its affiliates in the United States and other countries, and may not be used without written permission. All other trademarks are the property of their respective owners. Wiley Publishing, Inc., is not associated with any product or vendor mentioned in this book.

LIMIT OF LIABILITY/DISCLAIMER OF WARRANTY: THE PUBLISHER AND THE AUTHOR MAKE NO REPRESENTATIONS OR WARRANTIES WITH RESPECT TO THE ACCURACY OR COMPLETENESS OF THE CONTENTS OF THIS WORK AND SPECIFICALLY DISCLAIM ALL WARRANTIES, INCLUDING WITHOUT LIMITATION WARRANTIES OF FITNESS FOR A PARTICULAR PURPOSE. NO WARRANTY MAY BE CREATED OR EXTENDED BY SALES OR PROMOTIONAL MATERIALS. THE ADVICE AND STRATEGIES CONTAINED HEREIN MAY NOT BE SUITABLE FOR EVERY SITUATION. THIS WORK IS SOLD WITH THE UNDERSTANDING THAT THE PUBLISHER IS NOT ENGAGED IN RENDERING LEGAL, ACCOUNTING, OR OTHER PROFESSIONAL SERVICES. IF PROFESSIONAL ASSISTANCE IS REQUIRED, THE SERVICES OF A COMPETENT PROFESSIONAL PERSON SHOULD BE SOUGHT. NEITHER THE PUBLISHER NOR THE AUTHOR SHALL BE LIABLE FOR DAMAGES ARISING HEREFROM. THE FACT THAT AN ORGANIZATION OR WEBSITE IS REFERRED TO IN THIS WORK AS A CITATION AND/OR A POTENTIAL SOURCE OF FURTHER INFORMATION DOES NOT MEAN THAT THE AUTHOR OR THE PUBLISHER ENDORSES THE INFORMATION THE ORGANIZATION OR WEBSITE MAY PROVIDE OR RECOMMENDATIONS IT MAY MAKE. FURTHER, READERS SHOULD BE AWARE THAT INTERNET WEBSITES LISTED IN THIS WORK MAY HAVE CHANGED OR DISAPPEARED BETWEEN WHEN THIS WORK WAS WRITTEN AND WHEN IT IS READ.

For general information on our other products and services, please contact our Customer Care Department within the U.S. at 800-762-2974, outside the U.S. at 317-572-3993, or fax 317-572-4002.

For technical support, please visit www.wiley.com/techsupport.

Wiley also publishes its books in a variety of electronic formats. Some content that appears in print may not be available in electronic books.

Library of Congress Control Number: 2007930401

ISBN: 978-0-470-16567-6

Manufactured in the United States of America

10 9 8 7 6 5 4 3 2 1

About the Authors

Danny Briere founded TeleChoice, Inc., a telecommunications consulting company, in 1985 and now serves as CEO of the company. Widely known throughout the telecommunications and networking industry, Danny has written more than one thousand articles about telecommunications topics and has authored or edited ten books, including *Internet Telephony For Dummies*, *Wireless Home Networking For Dummies* (now in its second edition), *Wireless Hacks and Mods for Dummies*, *Windows XP Media Center Edition 2004 PC For Dummies*, and *Home Theater For Dummies*. He is frequently quoted by leading publications on telecommunications and technology topics and can often be seen on major TV networks, providing analysis on the latest communications news and breakthroughs. Danny splits his time between Mansfield Center, Connecticut, and his island home on Great Diamond Island, Maine, with his wife and four children.

Pat Hurley is Director of Research with TeleChoice, Inc., and specializes in emerging telecommunications and digital home technologies, particularly in all the latest consumer electronics, access gear, and home technologies, including wireless LANs, DSL, cable modems, satellite services, and home-networking services. Pat frequently consults with the leading telecommunications carriers, equipment vendors, consumer goods manufacturers, and other players in the telecommunications and consumer electronics industries. Pat is the coauthor of *Internet Telephony For Dummies*, *Smart Homes For Dummies*, *Wireless Home Networking For Dummies*, *Wireless Hacks and Mods for Dummies*, *Windows XP Media Center Edition 2004 PC For Dummies*, and *Home Theater For Dummies*. He lives in San Diego, California, with his wife, a fiery red-headed toddler named Annabel, and two smelly dogs.

Dedication

I dedicate this book to my wife, Holly, and publicly and officially confess that she has a better memory and is smarter than I. Plus, she's usually right. I thank her dearly for putting up with me while I put in long hours at the office to finish this book, including the 19 times that I was late for dinner. Okay, so that's a low number. Okay, so Holly also doesn't exaggerate as much as I do. In any case, I hope that she will continue to let me infiltrate the home with smart-home techniques (which she secretly likes but won't say) and at least once say that she likes ONE thing I've installed.

— Danny

I dedicate this book to my wife, Christine, for allowing me to bore her nearly to death with long, breathless discussions of networking toys that no normal person wants to spend more than three minutes talking about, and for letting me scare the living daylights out of the dogs with remote-controlled gizmos. To thank her more completely, I promise to not bring a robot into the home — thus avoiding all those dog psychiatrist bills — well, unless it's a robotic dog poop picker-upper!

— Pat

Authors' Acknowledgments

It takes a lot of effort by a lot of people to put a book together. We probably can't give proper acknowledgment to everyone who's given us advice, opinions, and guidance as we've worked on this project, but we'd like to try.

For this third edition, we'd like to specifically thank the following folks for sharing their knowledge and providing their extremely helpful insights into the world of the smart home. To name just a few, we'd like to thank Ian Hendler, Grant Sullivan, Marc Ceraculo, Mara White, and Jack Merrow at Leviton (sorry for leaving you guys at the dinner table during that work crisis!), Gordon Sell at Gordon Sell PR for Canton, Alex Elliot at NextAlarm, Joelle Kenealey at Coltrin Associates for Control4, Eric Smith at Control4, Julie Stern at LEGO Systems, Karl Pawlewicz from Griffin PR for Middle Atlantic, Michael Cukrow and Mark Tracy at Middle Atlantic Products, Barry Haaser at Echelon, Ralph Maniscalco at Honeywell, Michelle Laird at SmartLabs, Brad Kayton at 4HomeMedia, Casey Munck and Frank Sterns at Niles Audio, Roger Dressler and Jeanne Alford at Dolby Labs, Adam Weissman and Jeff Talmadge at Denon, Ted White at the Green Glue Company, Joel Sider at Microsoft, Dave Gilbert at Sound Seal, Steve Muellner and Andrew Corkill at Meade, and Melanie Jensen and Colleen Logan at iFit. And to all the others we forgot — thank you too!

For our earlier editions of the book, Sandy Daniels kept us organized, connected, and sane. She prodded us along, set up interviews, found people we couldn't find ourselves, and generally acted like a bulldog in breaking through corporate mazes to find the right people to interview for the book. If you ever meet her, you'll wonder how such a nice person can be so effective.

We also have built on the help of literally dozens of vendors during our research in previous editions of this book. Special thanks go to Keith Smith at Siemon, David Allred at DirecTV DSL, Jeff Denenholz at X10 Wireless Technologies, Mike Hernandez at ChannelPlus, Peter Radscliff and Jim Gist at Monster Cable, Doug Hagan at Netgear, Matt Graves and Sean Ryan at Listen.com, Nick Smith and Vanessa Tuell at Request, Tom Reed of the HomePlug Powerline Alliance, Dave Thompson of CopperGate Communication, Brian McLeod at Harmony, Andrew Liu at Intel, Mel Richardson and his team at BellSouth, Lawrence Cheng at XM Radio, Tom Lucke, Fred Bargetzi, and Ray O'Sullivan at Crestron, Paul Cunningham at Cunningham Security in Portland, Maine, and George Snyder at Home Automated Living.

Finally, we want to thank the Wiley team who (once again!) bought into our vision of a smart home, and made sure we crossed our *i*'s and dotted our *t*'s (or something like that). Thanks especially to Susan Pink, our project editor, and Melody Layne, our acquisitions editor.

Publisher's Acknowledgments

We're proud of this book; please send us your comments through our online registration form located at www.dummies.com/register/.

Some of the people who helped bring this book to market include the following:

Acquisitions, Editorial, and Media Development

Project Editor: Susan Pink

Acquisitions Editor: Melody Layne

Copy Editor: Susan Pink

Technical Editor: Allen Wyatt, DCI

Editorial Manager: Jodi Jensen

Media Development and Quality Assurance: Angela Denny, Kate Jenkins, Steven Kudirka, Kit Malone

Media Development Coordinator: Jenny Swisher

Media Project Supervisor: Laura Moss-Hollister

Media Development Associate Producer: Richard Graves

Editorial Assistant: Amanda Foxworth

Sr. Editorial Assistant: Cherie Case

Cartoons: Rich Tennant (www.the5thwave.com)

Composition Services

Project Coordinator: Patrick Redmond

Layout and Graphics: Claudia Bell, Stacie Brooks, Denny Hager, Joyce Haughey, Stephanie D. Jumper, Jennifer Mayberry, Barbara Moore, Alicia B. South

Proofreaders: Todd Lothery, Dwight Ramsey, Charles Spencer, Evelyn W. Still

Indexer: Aptara

Anniversary Logo Design: Richard Pacifico

Publishing and Editorial for Technology Dummies

Richard Swadley, Vice President and Executive Group Publisher

Andy Cummings, Vice President and Publisher

Mary Bednarek, Executive Acquisitions Director

Mary C. Corder, Editorial Director

Publishing for Consumer Dummies

Diane Graves Steele, Vice President and Publisher

Joyce Pepple, Acquisitions Director

Composition Services

Gerry Fahey, Vice President of Production Services

Debbie Stailey, Director of Composition Services

Contents at a Glance

Table of Contents

Introduction

Welcome to *Smart Homes For Dummies*, 3rd Edition. This book is the first to specifically tell you how to futureproof your home to take advantage of the present and upcoming gee-whiz things that can make your home a 21st century castle.

Very few things can prepare you for the massive changes that are taking place due to the innovations offered by an interconnected world. The Internet and electronic commerce are changing the way we live, the way we work, and the way we play. (We hope there's more of the last one!)

We're so used to going to stores and buying things. To calling toll-free numbers so we can ask questions and order products. To going to school to learn. To going to the movies to watch the latest *Harry Potter* release. To going to the music store to buy the top-of-the-charts CDs.

Now it can all come to us. We can buy things through our TV sets. We can ask questions and videoconference through our computers. We can attend classes through computer-based training. We can click our remote controls to get video-on-demand. We can download new CDs, live, over the Internet.

It's at our doorstep. The question is, "Can you let it in?" Without a home network, all this might stay outside, or in the TV room, or trapped in that attic office of yours. A home network opens the world to your entire household, and now more than ever is the time to plan.

That's what *Smart Homes For Dummies*, 3rd Edition, provides — a plan for your networked future.

If you plan nothing and simply go with the flow, ordering new capabilities from your cable or telephone company when available, you'll find that they'll start deciding how your home network should be built and operated. This is dangerous because they will not think about what's best for your home — rather, they'll install whatever gets their technicians in and out of your home the fastest. These companies are also not looking at your big picture. In this book, we help you understand how your home can be compatible with what they want, and still keep your vision of a whole-home network too. Read on!

About This Book

Within these pages, you'll find a number of technologies and issues relating to developing digital smart-home technologies. Following are some of the things you discover:

- What a home network is, and what it takes to build one
- The key points to think about before starting to conceptualize a home-network design
- What the various home-network devices and services do
- What's involved in making a home-entertainment center accessible throughout the house
- What you need to create a home-security network
- Your options for dressing up your home-telephone capabilities
- The best way to design a home-data local area network (LAN)
- The ways to boost your in-home wireless LAN and cell phone signals
- The best way to connect your home to the Internet
- What's coming down the road and into your home in the future

Some of the networks and issues that we cover in *Smart Homes For Dummies* are in the realm of the do-it-yourselfer, so we present the big-picture stuff for those readers and give high-level instructions. These instructions don't go into stuff such as removing your drywall and running cables through your house. We recommend *Home Improvement For Dummies* by Gene Hamilton, Katie Hamilton, and the editors of HouseNet (published by Wiley Publishing, Inc.) if you need help with that stuff. And if you don't feel comfortable running cables through your house, hire a professional!

If you're renovating a home, building a new home, or trying to figure out how to connect anything with anything else in your home, you need *Smart Homes For Dummies* to make sure you're getting what you need — not what your builder happens to be selling.

What You're Not to Read

Smart Homes For Dummies isn't a novel. You don't have to read page 1 before going to page 2. So that means that you can just flip around through the book and start wherever you like. You won't feel lost.

You can use the Table of Contents at the front of the book to find out where to look for a topic that interests you, whether it's distributing a DVD signal from your home-entertainment center to your bedroom, or making your lights go on and off by themselves. Or you can search the index for a particular term that interests you. However you find the information, read it and then put the book back on the shelf. That's how this book is meant to be used.

Foolish Assumptions

This book is for everyone. Few people don't have a TV, radio, or some sort of computing device that would benefit from being networked in the future. Although it's easy to say now that computers are only for families in certain financial brackets, within a few years, many TV sets will start shipping with Internet connectivity options on-board. So, if you want to make the most of your home's electronic systems by networking them, you need to read this book or one like it.

You'll get the most out of this book if you're remodeling or building a home, because you're in a position to run wires through your walls. Apartment dwellers can do some of the stuff that we outline in this book (using wireless technologies), and they can get cool ideas for when they do buy their homes.

One big assumption that we (and many in the industry) have had to get out of our heads over the past few years regards wireless technologies. Some folks have taken the position that today's wireless technologies (and no-new-wires technologies that leverage existing phone and power lines) have eliminated the requirement to put network wiring in your walls. Well, wireless is great — it can be an invaluable complement to a wired network. If you live in an apartment or condo and can't get inside the walls to run new wire, wireless may even be good enough to build your entire network around. But if you live in a typical home, we think you're going to find that a wired network is more capable, more reliable, and more flexible. And a wired infrastructure can be a good investment that pays you back if you sell your home.

How This Book Is Organized

We realize that not everyone is going to want to do everything we discuss in the book. So we broke the book down into distinct parts, each of which tackles a different aspect of building a smart-home infrastructure. Part I is the high-level, 50,000-foot view — describing why you might want to create a smart home. Parts II through V look in depth at how to design your home and home network to take advantage of all the neat things coming down the road in each of the major zones, and Part VI tells you how to interconnect them all.

Part 1: Future-Perfect Homes

Part I describes where we're trying to get to: our future-proofed home. We talk about the different major network zones of your home: your entertainment system, your security system, your phone system, and your computer system. We talk about all the other things that you might want to link and why you'd want to do that. And finally, we talk about how you can start thinking about the various things you could accomplish with a fully networked home — your smart home.

Part 11: Making Your Home an Entertainment Center

Part II looks at how to make your home an entertainment center. You find out about creating not merely a home theater, but a true home-wide entertainment complex. How do you listen to your favorite CD from anywhere in the house? How do you share a satellite dish among multiple TVs. How do you watch your napping baby from your living room TV?

We tell you how to sensibly build a media backbone in your home without breaking your bank account. We help you plan for things such as flat-screen TVs, intercom systems, whole-home audio systems, gaming consoles, and satellite systems. We talk about your wiring (and wireless) options for communicating with each part of your home-entertainment complex.

Part 111: Now We're Communicating!

Part III delves into the world of telephones. Life used to be simple in this area. If you wanted a new phone, you could go to the local department store or Radio Shack and buy one. Now you have all sorts of complications in this area. You can choose a multiline phone, a 2.4-GHz or 5-GHz cordless, a VoIP phone, a Skype phone, a screen phone, a combined phone-fax-printer-scanner, an answering machine, central-office-based voice-mail services, and a whole lot more. We help you craft your home-telephone network so that you can communicate with anyone from anywhere — without all that scratchy static, we hope.

Part IV: Livin' Off the Fat of the LAN

Part IV looks at your computer zone. A smart home has a high-bandwidth backbone connection running throughout the house, so you can tap into your data autobahn wherever you like. We help you understand how you can play networked games, share files between computers, print or fax from any computer in the home, or even get the whole family on the Net, at the same time! We look at the world of DSL, cable modems, HughesNet dishes, wireless Internet connections, electrical data connections, and more. Wired or wireless, we help you plan and design a computer LAN for your home. We guide you through the maze of wiring options to make sure that if you want to surf the Net while mowing the lawn, you can.

Part V: Keeping the Bad Guys at Bay — Security

Part V takes you through our home-security boot camp and looks at everything you'd want to do to secure and protect your home. We describe not just fire and burglar alarms, but also video doorbells, closed-circuit TV, driveway sensors, and ways to watch out for your kids. We help you plan your way to a more secure and protected home.

Part VI: Putting It All Together — Home Automation and Control

Part VI brings it all together — the ultimate guide to home networking. We walk you through a whole-home approach to network design. We provide home-design and home-layout tips and expose you to the various products on the market for centralized home networking.

Want to fire up that coffee pot while you're still asleep? Or how about setting the mood with automated lighting? We look at all the latest trends and gadgets governing home automation, including the details about X10, ZigBee, Z-Wave, and Insteon.

Part VII: The Part of Tens

Part VII is the infamous Part of Tens, where we give you ten common pitfalls to avoid when automating your smart home and the top ten toys of the future.

Icons Used in This Book

We use helpful graphical icons to point out items of interest — sort of like Kodak Picture Spots at Disney World. These icons are meant to encourage you to pause and take in what we're saying at that point. Following are the icons we use.

This is the fun stuff. This icon highlights neat new technical and other advances that are just arriving or not too far away. It's like a free pass to the World's Fair and a glimpse at the World of the Future.

This is a helpful reminder to do certain things, which translates to "we've forgotten to do this so often that we put it here just to remind ourselves."

When you see this icon, you may want to wait to make a decision until the industry decides which way it wants to go. Remember the Betamax VCR?

A few people in every crowd raise their hands and ask what's underneath the hood, so every now and then we stop to point out some of the neat stuff that makes the technology work. (We say *neat* because we're nerdy enough to enjoy writing about it.)

This icon highlights a shortcut or timesaving secret that we wished someone had told us before we learned the hard way.

This is never a good icon to see. It means you're working in a part of the Internet or your computer that's dangerous. It's like knowing the Wicked Witch of the West is in your neighborhood and you're wearing the ruby slippers. Be careful.

This icon tells you about a wireless technology that you can use instead of ripping your walls out.

Where to Go from Here

To help you keep up with the latest and greatest in smart-home devices and technologies, we created a companion Web site. Just type `www.digital-dummies.com` in your favorite Web browser, and you can catch up on the latest smart home news, find bonus material that we just couldn't fit into the book, and read our reviews of the coolest new gadgets.

See something that is not quite right? A typo? Something we should correct in the next edition? Drop us an e-mail at `dummies@telechoice.com`.

Whew! As Willy Wonka says, "So much time, so little to do . . . reverse that." Let's get going!

Part I
Future-Perfect Homes

The 5th Wave   By Rich Tennant

"Roger! Check the sewing machine's connection to the PC. I'm getting e-mails stitched across my curtains again."

In this part . . .

In the olden days, your home network was basically comprised of electrical wires and phone lines, with a smattering of alarm wiring here and there. Now your home network covers all sorts of wiring and wireless options, to connect any of a number of different devices — including your car and your microwave.

You can connect home-entertainment systems, security systems, computer networks, telephone systems, and appliances and come up with all sorts of neat applications to help make your home living simpler and more enjoyable.

In this part, we tell you all about the potential of a home network. We discuss the major elements of a whole-home network and describe the advantages of connecting them together. We also give you some advice on how much everything will cost, and show you what the finished product (a networked home) will look like — inside the walls! By the end of this part, you'll be more excited than ever about hooking everything together.

Chapter 1

Mi Casa, Cool Casa

*I*f you stop the average person on the street and start talking about home networks, he or she would probably make references to ABC, CBS, NBC, and FOX, or mention the Home Shopping Network or some other cable network show. *Network,* until recently, has meant little else to most people.

But times, they are a changin'. The invasion of telecommunications into all aspects of life is creating a different meaning of the word *network.* Most people have had some contact with a network through their work environment — computer local area networks (LANs) in the office, control networks in factories, telephone networks in many mid-sized or larger businesses . . . heck, the Internet is a huge network.

You can think of networks simply as things that help you do your work. As you concentrate on printing a document, calling up a database, or checking out the price of a product online, the network is invisible (that is, until it's broken).

The network concept has begun to move from the workplace to the home, and smart home builders and remodelers (and forward-looking owners of otherwise perfect existing homes) are starting to think in terms of wiring (or *wirelessing*) their homes both to make use of a network today and to future-proof against upcoming requirements.

Before you go any further, do this little exercise (don't worry, we won't grade you): Write down all the things in your house that you think you may want to network. Be as creative as you can. Think about your lifestyle and the way your house is set up. When you finish, put the list aside and continue to read this chapter. Toward the end, we'll share our list with you.

Living in Your Smart Home

Your smart home can seep into all aspects of your life. It helps you do those day-to-day tasks that can take up so much time, such as opening the draperies, dimming the lights, and flipping on the Weather Channel to see whether the kids have a snow day. How far you go with your smart home depends on your lifestyle, budget, and tastes.

This section spends a virtual day in a fictitious smart home. Here's the scenario: You, the reader, are part of a family of six, plus the requisite pets (we prefer dogs). You and your spouse both work, and the kids range in age from 8 to 17.

Starting your day

Anyone with kids knows the importance of keeping on a schedule. Your home network helps you do just that, in style.

At first light, you wake to your home-controlled alarm — a stream of pleasant classical music coming over your home-audio network into your bedroom. After a preset length of time, the music fades out and the TV kicks on to your favorite local station, where you can get the weather and traffic reports and information about any school closings or delays. Down the hall, the kids awaken to the music of their choice.

In the kitchen, the coffeemaker starts brewing your morning caffeine requirements. Select shades and drapes throughout the house open to let the day's light stream in. It's winter, so the towel warmers and the radiant heat in the bathrooms' floors are turned on. The automatic pet door out back opens and lets the dog out for his morning constitutional.

By this time, you're already in the kitchen making school lunches. Being the nice person you are, you take a cup of coffee to your spouse, who is listening to National Public Radio in the bathroom. As you finish setting out breakfast for the kids, a glance at the upstairs monitors shows that two of your four kids are still in bed. Your eldest son is videoconferencing with his girlfriend on his computer. You punch the intercom and tell them all to get a move on.

As the children cycle into and out of the bathroom, the home-control system times their showers to make sure no one hogs the bathroom. The shower's water temperature is just to their liking, but that's hardly a surprise — it's the same setting they use each day this time of year.

As you sit down to breakfast, your spouse comes running through, late for the office. A printout of major headlines and personal stock standings sits waiting in the printer, having been created and downloaded from the Internet overnight.

Your spouse works down the street (we did tell you that you work at home, didn't we?), and your smart home knows that you both like a warm car when you get into a 15-degree garage, so the home controller starts the car 15 minutes before the scheduled departure time. Before your spouse climbs inside the toasty car, the home-control system gives a verbal reminder to put the bottles and cans next to the curb because today is recycling day.

As your spouse leaves the garage, your home-control system talks to your phone system and redirects all of your spouse's home-business line calls to the car phone. Once at work, a simple push of a speed dial button on the office phone dials in and redirects the calls again to your spouse's office.

Back at home, you confirm that the kids caught the bus by using the video monitor in the kitchen, and then you get ready for work. You ask the home controller to put the house in your personal mode — in terms of temperature, music, lighting, drape settings, and anything else you may have set.

Getting down to work

You get a second cup of coffee and decide to work for a while in the sunroom. You tell the home controller where you are, and the controller transfers all your business calls to the extension near the table. Your laptop is wirelessly connected to your server and the Internet. You check your various e-mail accounts and voice mail and make a few conference calls on the multiline home-telephone system. While you're on one phone call, you turn on the TV to access the local online directory and navigate to the ordering page for that posh take-out shop down the street. Twenty minutes later, the delivery person arrives at the front door; you take your wireless two-line headset phone — conference call and all — to the door, where you tip the delivery person (you paid over the TV set) and retreat back to the sunroom for lunch.

For a midafternoon break, you head for the exercise room to work off some of that lunch. When you enter, you announce yourself to your voice-activated home-automation system, and it automatically sets the music and other environmental settings to your previously defined preferences. You sit down at your rowing machine, which has a large monitor that shows real-life settings of popular rowing locales.

Halfway through your workout session, a delivery person shows up at your door. An announcement that someone is at the door interrupts the music, and the nearest video display shows a picture of who it is. You don't want to stop mid-workout, so you reply that you are busy and ask him to leave the package inside the door. You prompt for the control system to unlock the front door, and watch as the front door unlocks itself and the delivery person places the packages in the foyer. He leaves, and you start rowing again along Boston's Charles River.

It's your turn for a temperature-controlled shower, where you listen to CNN from the TV set, via moisture-resistant speakers mounted in the bath. Squeaky clean, you go back to work. At 3:00, you have your first videoconference of the day from your office downstairs. While in the basement, you call up your home-control system and start the roast cooking in the oven.

The kids drift home in the afternoon and spread out across the house. While you access your corporation's data network, your kids take advantage of the computers. The youngest kids — twins — play multiplayer games on the home's high-speed Internet connection. Your eldest daughter logs onto the school's educational network to do research for the midterm paper due next week. And your son, when home from football practice, logs onto his school's network to collaboratively work with three others on a joint presentation for the next day. Instant messages, e-mails, and file transfers all flow with ease.

The home controller's voice enunciator reminds you that the roast should be done by now, and you head upstairs.

Dinner time

Meanwhile, at work, your spouse glances at the clock and remembers in a panic that the family needs groceries. A quick dial into the home LAN yields the grocery list on the computerized message board in the kitchen. On the way home, a phone call into the home controller redirects calls back to the car phone in case someone tries to call.

The magnetic driveway sensor tells the home-control system to announce your spouse's arrival. As your spouse enters the house from the garage, the home controller again redirects all calls to the home office, completing the day's cycle. As your spouse brings the groceries into the kitchen, you receive a kiss (sorry, not automated).

Ready to eat, you ask the home controller to set dinner mode in the dining room. A microphone in the light switch hears the command and dims the lights and turns on the gas-driven fireplace. The home-control system selects some family-oriented music from the MP3 server and plays it over the in-wall speakers in the dining room.

After dinner, you start cleaning up as your kids race to their rooms to finish their homework. Later, they watch a TV special in the living room, while you take in an old Spencer Tracy movie in your bedroom. In the meantime, your spouse has a late videoconference in the home office downstairs with clients in Japan. Occasionally, you access the picture-in-picture (PIP) capability on your TV set to check around the house, making sure that no one is getting into any trouble. After the movie, you give a simple command to the home controller and the lights are dimmed, the temperature in select zones is lowered, shades and draperies close, nightlights come on, and the intercom goes into monitor mode for the youngest kids, in case they're sick during the night. (The sound from those monitors plays only in the master bedroom area.)

Peace at last!

With the kids asleep for the night, you decide to take a nice relaxing bath. You instruct your home-control system to prepare the bathroom — dim the lights, open the skylight, run the bath at your favorite temperature, turn off the telephone extensions nearby (route them to voice mail instead), and play your favorite album on the bathroom speakers.

While lounging in bed watching the wide-screen TV, your spouse tells the home-entertainment system's *PVR* (personal video recorder, a hard-drive-based system that can record video digitally) to search the shows it has been archiving every day and play the most recent *Enterprise!* episode.

Your house is in off-hours mode. The dog is inside, and the doggy door is secure. All phones have muted ringing volumes; some don't ring at all. All drapes are closed. The temperature is lower to save energy when your family is tucked in tight under the covers. All security systems are now alert, looking for movement outside the house.

After your bath, you climb in bed and read for a while. You finish your electronic book and decide you want to read the sequel right away. You surf the Web from your TV set, find the book, buy it, download it to the home LAN and thus to your electronic book via a wireless connection.

Your dishwasher kicks on at midnight when the rates are low (you loaded it at dinnertime and turned it on, but the home controller activates it when rates drop). All night long, your home controller and its various sensors keep an eye on everything for you. You sleep peacefully.

The home-network revolution

What's brought about this progression of intelligent home networks into everyday life? One word: computers. And when we say computers, we don't mean only the PC sitting on a desk in a spare bedroom in 60 percent of American homes (although that's an important part of it). We mean also those little blobs of silicon that reside in so many things in your house, such as phones, televisions, refrigerators, and even the car in the garage.

Most of these systems are islands of computing power plugged into the power outlets of your home. The computer chips have no way of talking to each other or sharing the information that they gather and control. The network revolution — the home-network revolution — is taking place as these things begin to talk to each other. Imagine a refrigerator that talks to your electrical utility and goes into its power-hungry defrost mode when the electricity rates are lowest. Or suppose after a power outage that all your clocks reset themselves automatically because they're set to "network time."

Home networks aren't as advanced as the Jetsons' home, but they will be soon. And you'll be missing the boat if you build a new home or remodel your existing one without taking this kind of future into account. Although you can't know today exactly what will be connected to what (and how) tomorrow, you can design a wiring system for your home that will enable you to do the most you can today and be ready for tomorrow's needs.

What's in a Smart Home?

A smart home is a harmonious home, a conglomeration of devices and capabilities working according to the Zen of Home Networking. At the beginning of this chapter, we suggested that you make a list of all the things you might want to network. Following is our list. Notice that practically anything in your home can be, and ultimately will be, networked. That's the whole point of whole-house networking:

✔ **Household items:** Drapes and shades, gates, garage doors, door locks, doorbells, lights, dishwasher, refrigerator, heaters, alarm clocks, washer, dryer, microwave, coffeemaker, hot water system, air conditioners, central vacuum system, water controls (shower, sink, and so on), pool cover, fireplaces, toys, e-books, lawnmower, cars and other vehicles, piano, weather station, furniture

- ✓ **Audio and video:** Receivers, amplifiers, speakers, VCRs, CD players, DVD players, PVR players, TVs, WebTV devices, Apple TV devices, DSS dish, radios, remote controls, gaming consoles, cable TV devices, TV videoconferencing devices

- ✓ **Security:** Baby monitor, video cameras, surveillance monitors, motion detectors, smoke detectors, occupancy sensors, pressure sensors, infrared sensors, intercoms, voice enunciators

- ✓ **Phones:** Corded phones, cordless phones, 900-MHz phones, 2.4-GHz phones, 5.8-GHz phones, fax machine, answering machine, PDAs, screen phone, video phone, cell phones

- ✓ **Computers:** PCs, Macs, laptops, modems, scanners, printers, home servers

The key is getting information to and from each of these devices. That takes a network. Your home network is actually a collection of networks. Communications in and among different devices travel over various network layers, such as your home-telephone network, your computing network, your security network, your electrical communications network (yes, you can talk over your electrical lines, believe it or not), and so on. These collectively are what we call your *home network,* and you mix, match, and jump among these network layers as you communicate throughout your household.

History of home wiring

Traditionally, homes have been wired for only two things: power and telephones. Add a few haphazardly run cable-TV outlets and some doorbells, and you have the sum of the wiring in most homes. Some people put in an alarm system or an intercom system, each with its own set of wires. The result is a house with an expensive bunch of wires that don't talk to each other and aren't good for anything else.

Even more important than the quantity of wires is the quality, especially when it comes to home automation and high-speed data services. Wiring systems that are inadequate for the needs of today's wired citizens occur not only in homes wired 50 years ago but also in many new homes. Older low-voltage wires (telephone and cable TV wires, for example) don't have

adequate capacity for high-speed data use or for multiple lines. They don't go to enough places in the house, and they have no flexibility of configuration. When your needs change, you'll probably have to rewire.

Even electrical power cables may be inadequate (and not just because you don't have enough outlets) for home-automation and control systems to do such tasks as turn on lights and start the coffeemaker. These systems require a power system that is adequately isolated from interference and line noise, which is not the case in many homes.

Luckily, overcoming these problems isn't difficult — or even that expensive. All you need is a little knowledge and a good plan!

Home servers

Traditionally, you buy a lot of boxes for your house, such as VCRs, DVD players, and CD players. As the movement towards digital storage has blossomed, you find VCRs with hard disks and CD jukeboxes that can store hundreds of CDs. We call these boxes *servers* because they mimic the role of computer servers in a corporate environment.

There's a movement afoot to merge all of these servers into a *home server* that stores CDs, DVDs, games, software, and more and "serves" its content to devices that want to play that information. These also will access the Internet for easy access to online content such as iTunes (www.itunes.com) or YouTube (www.youtube.com). Gaming consoles such as the PlayStation 3 and Xbox 360 are trying to become such central repositories, and Microsoft has launched a new product called (not surprisingly) Windows Home Server (in beta at the time of this writing at (http://connect.microsoft.com/WindowsHomeServer). You'll also see home media centers in PC and standalone stereo gear that target the same market. Home servers will range in price from $400 to more than $25,000, depending on what and how much you are trying to store.

We think every home should have a home server of some sort. A home server makes finding things less difficult and creating backups easier, and certain programs such as iTunes run better when everything is in one place. Our approach to home networking in this book enables you to connect a home server whenever you decide to get one.

Why Network Your Home?

A network allows you to do a bevy of things. For instance, you can

✔ **Access the Internet from anywhere in your house:** A home network lets everyone share in the broadband wealth, so you can stop fighting over the one computer with the high-speed connection. What's more, by having a communications *backbone* (wiring infrastructure) in your house, you can let anything — from your TV set to your car — tap in and make use of that connectivity.

✔ **Remotely control your home:** After your home network is connected to your other networks, such as the Internet, you can suddenly do amazing things from almost any interconnected spot. The capability to control a device after it is hooked up to the network is limited only by the openness of the device itself. (In other words, the only limit is the degree of controllability of the device — your home's infrastructure won't hold you back.) Want to turn off the lights downstairs from the bedroom? Click your remote control, and out go the lights. Want to check the babysitter while you're at your neighbor's July 4th bash? Just use the neighbor's computer to log into your home's controller and check up on things. (You can even use your cell phone to do this!)

✔ **Save time:** Think about how much time it takes every day to open the shades, turn on the morning news, let the dog out, and so on. Wouldn't you like to do all that (and more) with one command? By programming these chores into task profiles, you can.

✔ **Save money on electronics:** With a true home network, you have to buy fewer devices to outfit your home. Instead of having a VCR hooked to every TV set, for instance, you can centralize this functionality and distribute the signal around the house through remote control as you need it. The same is true of almost any network-connected device, such as a DSS satellite receiver, PVR, and cable box.

✔ **Save money on communications costs:** By centralizing access to certain telecommunications services, you can cut monthly service costs. For instance, with a home-network backbone, both you and your spouse can connect to the Internet on separate computers while sharing one line and one account. What's more, you can share a high-bandwidth option — such as a cable modem, DSL link, or HughesNet-type satellite service — with the entire family.

You might be ahead of the pack and already have a single broadband link to share with everyone at home. But if your connection is like ours, it can go down a lot. We're seeing the movement towards homes with *two* broadband connections (one as a backup). Being able to have the kids do homework and mom and dad do their necessary browsing is starting to become mission-critical. So a home network will help you share this backup line too!

✔ **Save money on your home expenses:** A wired home can turn back those thermostats when you're away on vacation or cuddled under your blankets at night. It can turn lights off automatically, too. Over time, you may save a surprising amount in heating, cooling, and electricity costs.

✔ **Save money on the future:** At different times in your life, you may find yourself changing the way you use certain rooms — a guest room becomes a nursery or the garage becomes an office, for example. Changes like these can be expensive if you try to bring your network along for the ride. Instead, have a flexible home-network design — one that's futureproofed for all sorts of contingencies — and save money down the road.

✔ **Be more flexible and comfortable with your technological assets:** A home network frees you from being tied to one spot for one activity. For instance, when working late at night, you might want to move the laptop to a comfy recliner instead of a damp basement office. And you can with a distributed means to access the Internet — and therefore your centralized e-mail, calendar, and contact database. The latest home networking technology will route your HDTV signals around your house, freeing your TV set to be anywhere a wireless signal can reach!

✔ **Lose more fat:** A smart home won't stop you from eating chocolate cake, but it will spice up the exercise room. You can run Internet access, CNN, or exercise videos over your home network to help you keep pace and pass the time on a treadmill or bicycle. And, with Internet access, you can access many of the neat new software programs that combine with new exercise equipment to provide passing scenery or live competitors as you row, row, row your rowing machine!

What Does It Take to Network Your Home?

Okay, so you have the big picture: A networked home is a happy home. What does it take to get there? Surprisingly little, or surprisingly a lot. (Can you tell we make good consultants?) It depends on whether you do baby steps or go whole hog.

You can make a home network based on the existing wiring in the walls or using the airwaves in your house, with wireless options. No cost for infrastructure there. Is it as powerful as an installed system? No, but for many it will do the trick.

Alternatively, you can install a whole system from scratch. The cost varies, just like the cost of building a house. The more you put in, the more it costs.

We've used both approaches, wired and wireless. We put investment upfront into our transport layer — the wiring and connectivity in the walls — and less on the things we connect to that layer, to give us more flexibility as things change. For instance, at Danny's house in Maine, rather than design for a big 32" TV, he left the living room unfinished because he knew that the price of flat-screen plasma TVs would plummet. He waited patiently for prices to drop. He's still waiting. So is his wife.

Table 1-1 shows you some of the rough costs for getting into a smart home, with reasonable expectations set forth in this book. These are the costs of the components and the installation — you'll have some additional ongoing costs for services such as Internet and cable TV and for your computing hardware.

Table 1-1	The Cost of It All!			
Expense Area	*Low*	*Midrange*	*High*	*Obscene*
Wired infrastructure	$1000	$2500	$4000	$6000
Wireless infrastructure	$50	$150	$200	$500
Home theater (TV + surround)	$1000	$3000	$25,000	$200,000
Whole-home audio	$1000	$2000	$6000	$30,000
Phone system	$150	$500	$1000	$2000
Intercom system (standalone)	$100	$500	$1000	$2000
Data system	$50	$150	$500	$1500
Security system	$200	$500	$2000	$20,000
Home automation	$50	$1000	$10,000	$30,000
Total	*$3600*	*$10,300*	*$49,700*	*$292,000*

In this book, you'll go through the following process of thinking smartly:

1. Finding out all you can about your options

2. Putting your thoughts on paper

3. Figuring out the costs of your desired options

4. Refining your thoughts based on cost

5. Getting help where needed

6. Installing the systems in a methodical and somewhat structured process

7. Adding all the cool devices that put your smart home to use

8. Sitting back and enjoying yourself. (We'd like to stress this one, but the reality is that you'll enjoy your smart home for a moment and then go back to the first step and start over, because you'll want more.)

We provide detailed steps as well as more budgeting information in Chapter 4.

Chapter 2

Zen and the Art of Whole-Home Networking

As you think about your home network, think in terms of the big picture. Instead of talking about how to link one computer to another, think about a computer network that extends to every room. Instead of trying to extend your cable TV signal from one room to another, think about a video-distribution strategy for the whole house. Instead of discussing your home-entertainment center, map out a media backbone for your entire home.

In this chapter, you look at networks in a broad, whole-home sense. We tell you how all the networks in your home fit together physically and how you can make home networking easier by designing a central location (or two) to house all of your networking equipment. We also discuss some *structured cabling* solutions, which are packages of bundled cabling and distribution panels that can take care of most home-networking infrastructure needs in one easy-to-buy-and-install single-vendor system.

All Together Now!

Your home infrastructure may consist of one or more of the following networks:

✔ A phone network

✔ A data network (often called a *local area network,* or LAN)

- An electrical network

- A security network

- An intercom network (may be part of your phone network)

- An entertainment network

- A home-automation and -control capability that allows your house to do common tasks on its own

- Access to the Internet and other external programming sources (such as satellite broadcasts, cable, and telephone services)

Now, you may not want or need all these different types of networks in your home. However, if you're at a point in the construction or remodeling of your home where running cables is easy, consider providing the cables so that you (or someone who owns your home after you) can add these capabilities later.

We're not implying that you physically need to wire each of these networks separately. When we wrote the first edition of this book, lots of vendors of security, intercom, phone, home-control, and other network gear had their own proprietary wiring that they *required* you to install if you didn't want to void the warranty on the gear. Well, the market voted with their pocketbooks and started buying nonproprietary solutions, and the explosion of broadband and home networking is pushing standards across the whole home — in the form of *Internet protocol,* or *IP,* networking. With applications in the home converging on IP networking, wiring your home is easier. In fact, for most applications, you need to use only one type of cabling: twisted-pair cabling. That solution is so much better than running lots of proprietary cables around the house. Believe us.

One of the difficulties when thinking about home networking is that different networks sometimes do the same thing. To simplify, you can think of your home network in three ways:

- **Physical configuration:** The cables, connections, and specific pieces of equipment that make up the physical aspects of your network. This is where all the detail work comes in.

- **Logical configuration:** Each network is viewed as a single object (such as a phone network) or as a model. Most of the networks we discuss in this book use a star model, in which all the cables meet at a single junction point, just as the spokes of a wheel meet at the hub.

- **Applications:** The network's purpose, or application, and connections. Your entertainment network, for example, may represent a combination of different physical components and logical entities aimed at distributing audio and video around your house. A typical system might include audio and video devices such as a video switch (often part of your home theater receiver), gaming consoles and DVD players, a broadcast satellite that runs to receivers that require phone line access, and home-management software to control the network's functionality.

Although it's easiest to discuss the building of home networks by talking about the cables and connectors (as we do throughout the book), the beginning phases of conceptualizing a home network start from the opposite end. You usually begin by thinking of what you want to accomplish (the applications), move on to considering each individual network and its layout (the logical configuration), and then get to the nitty-gritty of cables, connectors, and specific hardware components (the physical configuration).

Thinking of networks by application, logically, and physically can reveal ways to save money, time, and headaches. For example, if you think strictly in terms of the phone network and data network being logically different networks, you could overlook that these networks may be able to transmit over the same in-wall cables.

As mentioned, we're getting closer to the time when homeowners will be able to install an integrated, unified network that carries voice, video, data, audio, and home-control signals over a single kind of cabling infrastructure. When that day comes, we'll write a really short version of *Smart Homes For Dummies* and spend more time on the golf course or basketball court. Unfortunately (for Pat's jump shot and Danny's swing), that day is still quite a ways off. Today's home network still consists of a number of independent networks, each doing its own thing over its own set of wires and cables. That's not to say that there aren't places where today's individual home networks come together and work together. A typical house has a whole bunch of network interconnection points, making these separate networks behave somewhat like a unified, single network.

Networks can physically interconnect in a home in three ways:

- ✓ **Networks can share the same media (or cables) to carry different kinds of signals.** For example, telephone wiring might be used to carry both telephone service and data networking at different frequencies using a phone-line networking system. Another example: The IP (Internet Protocol) allows many disparate types of signals — voice, data, video, and so on — to peacefully coexist in the same data stream running over common data-networking wiring.

- ✓ **Specific devices can connect to multiple networks.** A DSS satellite receiver, for example, connects to both video and telephone networks. A media server such as a PVR could connect to your video network and your data network.

- ✓ **Incoming service provider feeds can carry multiple services and connect to different networks in the home.** For example, a cable company might provide television, Internet access, and telephone service over three different home networks.

Moving Your Network into the Closet

When integrating a home network in your home design or remodeling plans, the following two points are key:

 ✔ Designate an appropriate location for all your network's central distribution equipment.

 ✔ Make sure that you have an adequate quality and quantity of network cabling running to each potential network outlet in your home.

Wireless disclaimer: It's tempting to believe everything you read about how wireless is going to make wired networks in the home redundant. We wish this were true. We're enamored with the promise of meshed high bandwidth wireless that connects everything in the home under one power of unwired Zen. Unfortunately, we're still a long ways away from this, and every time we think we're getting close, new applications and requirements come along that make the wireless options inadequate or unreliable — for example, just as soon as Wi-Fi got fast enough to support television, high-definition television came along and blew that proposition out the window. So while we wait for wireless to fulfill its promise, we recommend an environment that consists of a wired backbone with wireless endpoints, to provide whole-home wired and wireless support. You can't lose in that environment.

In this section, we discuss the first of these points — designing a central location for your network components. In the following section, we discuss the pieces and parts — the cables and connectors that make up the physical network.

Talk to your builder or remodeler about designating a space as a *central wiring closet.* (For a remodel, it often makes sense to have multiple locations.) The wiring closet should be out of sight but easily accessible, with plenty of space and adequate power to run a great deal of equipment.

By designating a central wiring closet, you gain the following benefits:

 ✔ **Hidden wires:** The walls of a truly wired home contain lots of cables: wires for a phone network, a video network, an audio network, a computer network, a security network, and a remote-control network. Add the connections to the outside phone lines, cable TV, and satellite feeds, and it can quickly become a bowl of spaghetti. You don't want to have to tuck these wires behind your furniture. In a wiring closet, these cables are neatly terminated in a series of wiring panels.

✔ **Hidden hardware:** Much of the hardware that facilitates home networking, such as distribution panels and punchdown blocks (these panels and blocks are special *wiring-termination* devices that connect all the cables running to remote locations in your house), is designed for function rather than form. A central wiring closet puts this hardware out of view.

✔ **Single point of connection:** Most networks we describe in this book connect to the outside world at a single, central location. Why not have the wires of all these networks terminate in the same area to make it easier to do things such as connect your Internet line to your computer network?

✔ **Easy access:** When you want to change the capabilities of your networks or troubleshoot a problem, having everything neatly arranged and easily accessible can eliminate a source of frustration.

Larger homes might have more than one wiring closet. In the simpler olden days of smart home yore, the massive expense of components and the lack of peer-to-peer communications technologies forced a smart home owner to consolidate things in one place. This situation is beginning to change. With a strong networking backbone in the home, and the right architecture and design for that backbone (we've got your back here), devices and applications can hop on and off at will. This allows you to distribute (or cluster) groups of equipment around the home. Danny, for instance, has a main wiring closet in his basement where his satellite receiver, cable modem, telephone, security, and main power connections are consolidated into a Leviton smart wiring panel. But he also has subpanels set up in the back of his main home office, where more specialized forms of equipment for networking, e-mail, wireless connections, backup drives, and such are found, and another in his third-floor entertainment area, again anchored by another Leviton wiring panel, where the audio, video, data, telephone, security, and home-automation equipment is located. All three are interconnected to take advantage of the functionality in the other places, in a whole-home fashion.

The contents of your wiring closet

Most of the cabling and infrastructure components of a home's networks should be installed in the area of your home designated as your wiring closet. A few items — mainly parts of your home-entertainment network — are better located in complementary wiring closets elsewhere (we get to the concept of a *media center* later in this chapter). In addition, a few systems in a home network are inherently decentralized, such as home-control components, security systems, and wireless phone or data network systems. These devices don't necessarily have central control units, or they have control units that should be out in the open and readily accessible, not hidden away in a wiring closet.

The devices that *should* go in a central wiring closet include

- ✔ The coaxial video-distribution panel (see Chapter 6)
- ✔ Patch panels for CAT-5e/6 rated phone and data wiring (see Chapter 11)
- ✔ Central controllers (called ATAs) for VoIP telephone systems (see Chapter 10)
- ✔ Cable, satellite, and DSL modems and routers (see Chapter 13)
- ✔ Ethernet switches (see Chapter 15)
- ✔ Stand-alone home-automation control units (see Chapter 19)

You can also put home servers and some of your central media equipment in the wiring closet if you don't need to physically access them frequently and you need the extra space elsewhere. Some of your wireless (Wi-Fi) capability may be here as well, depending on its location relative to the structure of your home. More on these centralized devices later in the chapter.

Some cable and DSL modems utilize a USB instead of an Ethernet interface. This simplifies connecting one of these modems to a single computer, but it makes it just about impossible to directly connect it to a centralized LAN hub. If your service provider leases or sells you one of these modems, it must be installed next to a server computer in your home office or other location. Most providers give you the choice of USB or Ethernet, but the offer may not be advertised. So ask the question upfront, and ask for an Ethernet modem.

If you are building a new house, take a lot of pictures after the wiring is roughed in. Then, if you need to cut a hole in a wall later on (say, for a new cabinet), you'll know what's behind it.

The location of your wiring closet

In the best-case scenario, you can create a dedicated room for your networking equipment — a central wiring closet just like those in modern offices and other commercial buildings. If we were starting a home from scratch, we'd design the wiring closet as follows:

- ✔ On the main floor of the house.
- ✔ Near an outside wall for easy interconnection to incoming service feeds.
- ✔ Above an accessible part of the basement (if we have a basement).

- ✔ With adequate lighting, ventilation, and climate protection (not in the garage, in other words). Electronic gear generates heat, so if you live south of the Arctic Circle, it's a good idea to have air-conditioning vents in the wiring closet.

- ✔ With adequate AC power-line receptacles to power devices such as video amplifiers, Ethernet hubs, and VoIP phone systems.

Such a closet needn't be too large — something between a standard coat closet and a small walk-in closet. A lot of your gear will go in a wall-mounted structured wiring system — what most manufacturers call the *panel*. Some, however, might go on shelving or in a rack. A typical rack has a 2-by-2-foot footprint.

Of course, the vast majority of home builders or remodelers don't have the luxury of adding this kind of dedicated space for a network wiring closet. In these cases, some other part of the house has to do double duty as your wiring closet. Here are some locations to consider:

- ✔ **The utility room or laundry room:** The biggest disadvantage of this location is the potential for high humidity, so make sure your clothes dryer is well ventilated to the outdoors. (And take steps to keep all the dryer lint from building up on your equipment!)

- ✔ **A protected garage:** The potential for dust and extreme temperatures may make this location less than optimal for some homes.

- ✔ **The basement:** A basement can be a good location because it's easy to run wires through a drop ceiling, but keep in mind that basements can be both dusty and damp.

- ✔ **A weather-protected outdoor closet:** This location is a last resort, but it could be acceptable if you live in a mild climate. However, we don't recommend putting any active electronics, such as Ethernet hubs or phone systems, out here.

The natural enemies of electrical and electronic equipment are moisture, dust, and temperature extremes, so locations that may work for someone in Florida or California may not make sense for those in North Dakota or Arizona.

Feeding Audio and Video from the Media Center

Most network systems in your house — specifically, the data wiring, phone wiring, and coaxial video-distribution wiring — are best located in a wiring closet. The parts of your network that provide the audio and video signals that you send through your house, however, are more appropriately centralized in the room where you use them the most. We call this area the *media center*.

For most people, the media center is also their home theater, the place where the fancy surround-sound audio receiver, the biggest and best TV monitor, and the handcrafted, wood-veneered, titanium-woofer speakers all live.

The contents of your media center

Chances are, you want to be able to quickly access your CD/DVD player (unless it's one of those DVD jukeboxes that holds 200 DVD/CDs or an MP3 home server) and your video source equipment (such as the VCR and DVD player) to change discs or tapes and for local (in-room) listening and viewing. So it makes sense to locate your audio network and the source equipment for your video network in a different place than the rest of your wiring closet. We like to call this location *the media center*, but if that sounds a bit too much like CNN Central in Atlanta, you can call it the "room with all the fun toys."

What goes into a media center? All your audio and video equipment:

- ✔ Video source devices: set-top boxes, VCRs, DVDs, PVRs, and laserdisc players — and Internet-based devices such as an Apple TV (see Chapter 7)

- ✔ Audio source devices: CD players, MP3 players such as iPods, radio tuners, satellite radio receivers such as XM or Sirius, and turntables (see Chapter 8)

- ✔ Audio amplifiers and controllers for your whole-home audio system (see Chapter 8)

- ✔ Impedance-matching panels for audio amplifiers (see Chapter 8)

- ✔ Connecting blocks and emitters from your IR control network or centralized controller panels for a CAT-5e/6 audio/video controller system (see Chapter 19)

Your main video-distribution panel doesn't go in the media center — just the source equipment and a modulator or other distribution device that can distribute signals back over your two-way coaxial or other cabling network (such as a CAT-5e/6 video distribution system) to the panel in the wiring closet.

In addition to the audio/video equipment that you're distributing across your network, you want to have all the stuff needed to do local listening and viewing in your media center. In other words, a television or video monitor, speakers, and a surround-sound receiver or a controller/amplifier system should also be in this room.

Other central hubs

With the explosion of PCs and other computing gear in the home, you might want to create a computing epicenter around which you'll gather your key centralized computing devices. Your home server might go here, as well as specialized backup gear, switching for local multiple PCs, special audio gear for these PCs, and more. For instance, Danny's attic has four PCs for multiplayer gaming, and he uses a local hub to optimize the communications among these four machines while efficiently linking to the central hub in the basement as well as to the Media Center hub. You can create a localized hub just about anywhere in your home where you'll have a big concentration of networked gear. Most manufacturers of home cabling systems (discussed in the "Makers of all-in-one systems" section) offer smaller versions of their panels and other gear designed for such applications. Remember, you don't *have* to subdivide your wiring, but if you have specialized needs (like Danny's computer lab) you might want to.

Setting up your media center

Locating all this gear and related wiring discreetly in your media center can be a bit problematic. This room, unlike a wiring closet, is a public space in your house, not necessarily a place where you can hide unsightly bundles of wire and racks of equipment. So your aesthetic requirements will be a bit higher.

The best solution is to design the room with an enclosed equipment-and-connection area. This is where you would put your *whole-home equipment* — the equipment that you don't need to access to watch a program or listen to something — such as impedance-matching equipment and modulators. Your equipment-and-connection area could be a well-ventilated closet. We've seen sophisticated setups with a false wall behind the TV and equipment racks to allow access to the backs of all of the gear. If you can't find a separate space for your whole-home equipment, you can connect all your outgoing speaker wires and IR or CAT-5e/6 control cables to wall outlets behind your equipment rack, and then use short cables to connect these outlets to the equipment itself.

 If you can't find an aesthetically pleasing way of getting all this stuff in your media center, you might consider putting the audio-amplification and impedance-matching equipment in your wiring closet (along with your whole-house speaker wire connections). Use the shortest run possible of high-quality, shielded audio interconnects to connect these amps to the audio source equipment back in your media center.

Fiber-optic faux pas?

Perhaps you've been skipping around the book, reading up on the stuff that goes into all the different networks in a home, and you've been scratching your head and wondering why you can't find any mention about installing fiber-optic cabling in the home.

Well . . . we didn't forget about it. We don't recommend installing fiber in the home, mainly because somewhere around zero applications for fiber are available among all the thousands of consumer electronics devices sold today. The only place that fiber ever comes into play is for some specialized digital audio interconnects, the kind used to connect CD and DVD players to external digital-to-analog converters (such as the ones inside fancy home-theater receivers).

But isn't fiber the future — and isn't this book all about taking a long-term view? The answers to those questions are "Yes" and "Yes, but . . ." Someday, fiber-optic cable may be the most common cabling for connecting home audio, video, data, and phone networks.

We *do* recommend that you give yourself a head start by designing your home in such a way that adding new cable types such as fiber will be easier when the time comes. But for now, we think that running fiber in a home is a waste of time and money.

Choosing Cables

After electrical wiring, telephone-type wiring (called *twisted pair*) is the most common type of wire in home networks. This category of cabling does more than just carry telephone signals. Twisted-pair cabling is the basis of most computer LANs and can be used to carry other data, such as audio and video signals, in your home network. (The wires are twisted inside a sheath — you can't see the twisting except to note slight bumps at regular intervals in the cabling.)

The wiring in modern phone and LAN systems is twisted for a reason (besides the fact that colored wires woven together look pretty). Through some magical properties of physics, the interweaving of the wires protects against electrical interference. No interference means no *cross talk*, which occurs when, for example, the fax transmission on line one bleeds through to the voice call on line two.

You usually find twisted-pair phone and data wiring in a cable jacket that has no electrical shielding. Those in the know refer to it as *UTP*, or unshielded twisted pair.

Older homes were usually wired with *quad cable*, a flat, untwisted cable that contains two pairs of wires, sufficient for carrying two phone lines. This type of wiring is much more susceptible to interference and cross talk and is ill-suited for modern, high-speed communications and networking. If you currently have quad cable, our advice is to replace it.

Newer homes are generally wired for telephone service with a round cable (usually in a gray jacket) that contains two twisted pairs of wires (four conductors). This cabling is much less prone to interference problems, and most types can carry up to two POTS or ISDN phone lines (described in more detail in Chapter 10) in their native mode. In general, this type of cable is not adequate for truly high-speed data networks but is perfectly adequate for distributing telephone and low-speed analog data service throughout your house. Although these cables are just fine for telephone service, they might not support the most sophisticated phone systems, such as a VoIP PBX or a digital key phone system. In these cases, you'll want to use CAT-5e/6 cabling (which we discuss in the next section) rather than your old phone wires.

Cable categories

UTP cables are rated by their *category,* or the measure of the cable's bandwidth capacity, as shown in Table 2-1. Higher-rated cables can handle higher-speed data networks. Rated cables are usually referred to as CAT-*x,* where *x* is the category rating. For example, Category 5e cable is CAT-5e.

Table 2-1	Category Ratings of UTP Cabling
Cable Rating	*Performance Rating*
Category 1	No performance criteria
Category 2	Rated to 1 MHz (used for telephone wiring)
Category 3	Rated to 16 MHz (used for Ethernet 10BaseT)
Category 4	Rated to 20 MHz (used for 10BaseT)
Category 5	Rated to 100 MHz (used for 100BaseT, 10BaseT)
Category 5e	Rated to100 MHz (used for 1000 BaseT, 100BaseT, 10BaseT)
Category 6	Rated to100 MHz (used for 1000 BaseT, 100BaseT, 10BaseT)

As a baseline for any "smart home" we recommend that you choose Category 5e (CAT-5e) or Category-6 (CAT-6) UTP data-grade wiring. This wire doesn't cost much more than the nonrated variety, and it's better suited to the high-speed technologies that your phone lines may carry, such as *digital subscriber line* (DSL) data connections (see Chapter 13 for more about DSL). CAT-5e and CAT-6, the highest-rated UTP cabling systems generally available on the market as we write, can carry Fast and Gigabit Ethernet networks capable of data rates of 100 Mbps and 1000 Mbps, respectively. This cable can also handle anything a lower-rated UTP cable does, such as carrying telephone signals.

As we write this book, CAT-5e is being supplanted by CAT-6 in the market-place, but for your typical home applications either one will do. Smart people use nothing less than CAT-5e/6 in their homes — even if they are only running a regular phone line. Don't go cheap and get CAT-3 or another lesser-grade wiring.

If you peruse the brochures and Web sites of cable manufacturers and resellers, you may run across someone who is selling UTP cables that appear to have a higher rating than CAT-5e or CAT-6. Some cable manufacturers are selling proprietary CAT-7 cabling systems that promise even greater performance. These higher-rated cables may indeed be capable of carrying even higher-speed networks than CAT-6, but right now no standard ensures that one company's CAT-7 — or whatever they may call it — will carry the same amount of data as another company's.

A final comment: Although your house has other cables, especially the RG-6 cabling we discuss in Chapters 6 and 7, UTP cabling gets most of the attention because there are so many types and because the trend in home-networking circles is to use CAT-5e/6 for just about everything. As the Ethernet and IP protocols continue to penetrate the home, more and more applications will ride on this CAT-5e/6 backbone. Other forms of cabling have different classes and performance characteristics but are more application specific. Coaxial cabling, for instance, is used by many telephone companies to route video around the home. We discuss these cables in turn in their respective sections in this book.

While the trend is to use more UTP telephone/data cabling for everything in your home, we're still far from that. Here are some ideas about other cabling you'll need to complete your home networking layout:

- ✔ **Coaxial cabling:** This is the cabling used for TV antennas, cable TV, and satellite TV. The two most common types of cabling are RG-6 and RG-59, with RG-59 being the lesser grade. We recommend RG-6 throughout the house to maximize your options. RG-59 is typically used for very short connections, such as from your VCR to your TV.

- ✔ **Security cabling:** Most security (alarm) systems use their own special cabling to connect sensors back to the alarm panel. We discuss this cabling in Chapter 18.

- ✔ **Audio speaker cabling:** We'll get into the specifics of all sorts of audio cables in Chapter 9, but when you are putting audio cabling in the walls, look to use at least 16 gauge speaker wires rated for in-wall usage.

The NID

When you're talking telephone cabling, you might hear someone mention NID (network interface device), SID (service interface device), or some other similar term. A *network interface device* is a small plastic box that serves as the point of demarcation between your home's telephone networks and your service provider's network. Incoming phone lines connect to one side of the NID, terminating within a locked portion of the box (only the phone company's techs are allowed in there). This side of the NID is electrically connected to the consumer side of the NID, where your internal phone wiring begins.

The NID is part of a standard telephone-company line installation. Its demarcation function makes the NID a significant part of a phone network. Everything on the telephone company's side of the NID (all the way back to their central telephone-switching office) is their responsibility to maintain and repair. The consumer side of the NID is your inside wiring, and if something goes awry, you pay for its repair.

Many local telephone companies offer inexpensive inside-wiring-repair policies that they tack onto your phone bill every month. If something goes wrong with your inside wiring, the phone company sends someone out to troubleshoot and repair the problem for free. This service can be a good deal if you have an older house.

As cable and telephone companies bundle more services, this clean demarcation is going away because they are managing more things inside the home, such as the cabling for Internet Protocol TV (IPTV) and wireless/wireline combined products.

Patch me in!

The many cables that run through your house can be a big mess when you get to the point where you want to hook them up with the telephone company, the cable company, or something else. Fortunately, you can use a *patch panel* (also called a terminal block or punchdown block) to neatly patch together telephone, data, security and other application lines.

A patch panel is a wall-mounted piece of equipment that serves as a junction point for lines. Inbound lines from various outside-of-house sources are connected to terminals in the patch panel. For instance, you connect telephone lines from your NID into one side of the patch panel. Then, all your in-home distribution lines are connected to another set of terminals. To connect a particular in-house line to your home telephone line, for instance, you would "patch" the two terminals with — you guessed it — a *patch cable*, a process known as *bridging,* or *cross-connecting.*

For video cable wiring (typically RG-6 coaxial cable), the patch panel is usually called a *distribution hub.* But the principles are the same: lines in and lines out. We discuss distribution hubs in detail in Chapter 6.

Patch panels come in all sorts of styles. If you purchase one of the modular distribution systems we discuss later in this chapter, you are likely to have an RJ-11, RJ-45, F-connector or other common cable plug. This makes it easy for you to cross link your sources with your destinations. Some ports on your patch panel may support combinations of lines. For instance, if you have four telephone lines coming into your home, you might have one jack that you can plug a patch cable into a jack that combines all four pairs in one eight-conductor connection. Note that you'll hear us discuss *home runs* throughout the book. This means that the cable is run directly from the remote jack back to this centrally homed location.

You can get patch panels for lots of varied cables or ones for a specific type of cable (say for telephone or data applications). Depending on your installer and how much you want to spend, a patch panel can have the following interfaces:

- **Pole and nut terminal interfaces:** You unscrew the nut, put the wire in, and screw the nut back in.

- **Port interfaces:** You plug the individual runs of phone wire directly into modular jacks, or screw your F-connector from your coax into a female F-connector endpoint.

- **Punchdown interface:** You push the wire into the receptacles by using a *punchdown tool*. This tool simultaneously strips the wire of its insulation and connects the wire electrically to the panel.

Some patch panels could have combinations of the preceding. Figure 2-1 shows a Leviton patch panel with RJ-11, RJ-45, and F-connectors.

 CAT-5e/6 cable can be used for many things (such as phones, computer networks, and audio/video networks). We — and just about everyone else in the home-networking world — recommend that you run at least two CAT-5e/6 cables to every significant room in your house (every place but bathrooms and closets). This setup gives you flexibility because each cable can be reconnected to different networks back at the patch panel. So a cable that today provides extra voice outlets in a bedroom can be reconfigured to connect to your data LAN by simply changing the termination of the cable in your panel from the phone network to the data network.

Unlike the main network UTP cabling, which you buy in bulk and run inside your walls, *patch cables* are usually purchased in precut lengths (of a few feet) with the connectors already attached. If you use a structured prewiring system, such as those offered by Leviton (www.leviton.com), the patch panels and distribution panels are housed in the central wiring hub. These wiring hubs are modular, so you can easily add patch panels or distribution panels as you expand your network. We talk more about these systems shortly.

Figure 2-1:
A patch
panel
dramatically
neatens up
your wiring
hub.

Jacks and plugs for everyone

For the past 30 years or so, telephone and coaxial cable wires have been using standardized connectors — plugs and jacks — to connect equipment to the wiring infrastructure. For UTP cables, these modular connectors come in three physical variants, which look basically the same but come in different widths to accommodate more wires (or positions):

- **Four-position jack and plug:** Connects handsets to telephones.

- **Six-position jack and plug:** Handles one, two, or three lines, which means that two, four, or six wires, respectively, terminate in the jack. Most of these jacks on our phones have only four wires used in the six positions, but you can see six positions if you look closely.

- **Eight-position jack and plugs:** Used for data applications such as Ethernet and other computer LANs; not normally used for phones.

Businesses sometime use 25-pair jack and plugs as well, but you're not likely to need or see these in your house.

We recommend that you use eight-position jacks — not six — throughout your home so that the jacks can be used for voice or data or whatever. Most consumer phone equipment, whether it be one-, two-, or three-line capable, can use RJ-45 outlets for these RJ-11 standard connectors.

Beyond physical size, the communications industry also differentiates jacks by their *configuration* (how many wires are connected to them). You may see documentation referring to jacks and plugs as

- **RJ-11:** Two wires connected for a single-line connection

- **RJ-14:** Four wires connected for a two-line connection

- **RJ-25:** Six wires connected for a three-line connection

- **RJ-45:** Eight wires connected for data LAN (wider than phone jacks)

The RJ-45 jack/plug is the one you will use for most smart home applications such as computer networks (LANs), Voice over IP (VoIP) phones, Ethernet-based audio- and video-distribution systems, and remote-control keypads for your audio/video system. You can also plug phones (with their smaller RJ-11 or RJ-14 jacks) into an RJ-45 outlet.

Security systems use a special kind of RJ jack called the RJ-31X. We talk about this jack in Part V, which covers home-security systems.

All of this "RJ-this" and "RJ-that" talk quickly gets confusing. Even the experts get confused because an RJ-11 can mean different things, depending on whether you're following an old Bell Telephone standard, a Telecommunications

Industry Association (TIA) standard, or something else. We usually refer to six-position phone jacks as RJ-11s, regardless of how many wires are connected, and eight-position jacks as RJ-45s. That's the way most people talk, regardless of what the standards say.

Like all cable connectors, RJ-connectors come in both male and female varieties. We leave the reasons for naming each variety to your own imagination, but we will tell you that you find the male version of the connector on the end of a cable and the female connector on wall outlets or inside equipment such as your PC.

You'll also run into some similar video-cable options — there are cable connectors, but far fewer of them, and we discuss those in Chapter 6.

Modular wall outlets

The *endpoints* of your telephone network are the wall outlets in each room. These wall plates have holes that are populated with modular connections corresponding to what you want to terminate — such as a phone, data, or cable connection.

Although you can find wall plates equipped with RJ-11 modular jacks (and you can plug any of your old telephone equipment into these), RJ-11 jacks are not going to be much good if you want to change the use of the outlets. We recommend that you install RJ-45 outlets everywhere — remember that your standard RJ-11 modular phone connectors will work fine in them.

Accessorize your phone network

A range of small, useful accessories are handy with your home-wiring network, including the following:

✔ **1-to-2 splitter jack:** This jack takes a single RJ-14 or RJ-45 connection (which has two pairs of wire) and splits it into two single-pair RJ-11 or RJ-45 connections so that you can connect two devices.

✔ **2-jack modular adapter:** This adapter takes a single RJ-14 or RJ-45 connection and splits it into two RJ-14 or RJ-45 connections, allowing you to have two two-line phones sharing the same wall jack, for

instance. You can readily find three- and five-jack versions as well.

✔ **Inline coupler:** This accessory connects two four-wire phone cords, which is great when you have to run an extra-long distance across the room. For example, you can use an inline coupler to connect two six-foot telephone cords to get one twelve-foot cord.

These gadgets offer more flexibility when you find that your wired network doesn't quite give you exactly what you want. Grab a handful and keep them in your toolbox — you'll need them.

When you're choosing phone wall outlets for a room, consider what other home-network outlets you'll need in the same location. You can find many modular outlets that take up a double- or triple-gang-sized junction box (a single gang, which we talk about in Chapter 7, is the size of a standard light switch or wall outlet) and allow you to connect data and video networks all in one large outlet.

Investigating All-in-One Wiring Solutions

We believe that most homeowners want to install a home network that can handle, at a minimum, the three main types of network applications: telephone, data, and video. Most major wiring and network infrastructure vendors believe this, too, and offer all-in-one *structured cabling systems*. With these systems, a single vendor supplies (and in many cases, installs) a complete, integrated home-networking infrastructure.

Structured cabling systems

Most structured cabling systems for the home are offshoots of similar (and more complicated) packages of hardware and wiring that networking system vendors have been offering their corporate customers for years. The concept is simple: go to the vendor, tell them your requirements, and get an off-the-shelf, soup-to-nuts system ready for installation.

For the most part, structured cabling systems are made up of the same parts that you'd use if you were building separate home networks by yourself. Specifically, you'll find that most contain the following components:

- **A service center:** Combines phone and data patch panels and a video distribution center in a single unit — making for a neater installation. Service centers are usually modular, wall-mounted components.

- **All-in-one cables:** Cabling that combines telephone and data cabling and coaxial cable for video in a single cable jacket. Some systems even include fiber-optic cables in the same jacket. (See the "Fiber-optic faux pas?" sidebar for our opinion on the matter.)

- **Customized wall outlet plates:** Matched up with the all-in-one cable, these faceplates provide modular connectors for your phone, data, and video outlets.

As you can see, nothing about these systems is different than the pieces you'd install if you were designing your own home networks. They're simply put together in one big kit to facilitate buying, designing, and installing your network infrastructure.

Where all-in-one systems work (and don't work)

If you read the product literature from most manufacturers (we tell you where to find it in just a moment), you get the impression that a structured cabling system can do everything but clean the kitchen sink. However, some of the capabilities and applications listed for these systems are based on forward-looking marketing projections rather than on what you can actually do now.

We mention this not to disparage the structured cabling system but to warn you that installing one may not take care of all your home-networking needs. For example, the following applications are usually *not* easily supported by most structured systems:

- ✔ **Alarm systems:** Although some security features, such as security cameras, can fit in a structured cabling system, a full-featured, monitored, hardwired security system requires its own wiring — usually installed by a registered professional installer. Structured wiring systems allow you to interface the alarm to an outgoing telephone system for monitoring.

- ✔ **Whole-home multizone hi-fi audio:** You can add components to your structured wiring system to distribute *single-zone* audio throughout your home (meaning everyone hears the same thing everywhere), but many don't include the speaker wiring and distribution systems to get hi-fi multizone audio around your home (which allows you to send different audio sources to different parts of the house simultaneously).

So, you're probably thinking, what *do* these systems support? Quite a lot, actually. At a bare minimum, a structured cabling system should provide:

- ✔ **A flexible telephone network** using high-quality, unshielded twisted-pair (UTP) phone cabling and a modular, configurable termination system at the service center.

- ✔ **A computer network** of CAT-5e/6 UTP cabling for data networking.

- ✔ **A centrally distributed coaxial cable (usually RG6) network** for distributing video signals.

- ✔ **An all-in-one modular termination panel** to neatly terminate all this network wiring in your wiring closet.

You'll find structured systems capable of handling additional applications such as alarms, hi-fi audio, and infrared networking as standards supporting such connections become popular.

Makers of all-in-one systems

Just about every company that specializes in network cabling offers a residential structured cabling system. Those that don't are sure to begin soon. Keeping in mind the fact that this is a growing marketplace, here's a list of some of the major vendors and their Web pages:

- ✔ ChannelPlus: www.channelplus.com

- ✔ Elk Products: www.elkproducts.com

- ✔ GE Smart: http://www.geindustrial.com/cwc/products?id=il-pmsw

- ✔ Honeywell FutureSmart: www.futuresmart.com

- ✔ Hubbel netSELECT: http://www.hubbell-premise.com/homenetworking.asp

- ✔ Leviton: www.leviton.com

- ✔ Monster Cable Products: www.monstercable.com

- ✔ On-Q/Legrand: www.onqlegrand.com

- ✔ Unicom: www.unicomlink.com

- ✔ USTec: www.ustecnet.com

Hints for Designing a Futureproofed Home

Here's a collection of some of our best tips for your home adventure:

- ✔ **Anticipate your needs:** You need to think, think, think when planning your home network. A smart home is only as good as your design. And it will cost you a bundle to add something later that you forgot. We know it's hard — you never know where you're going to end up. (Ask Danny, he has *two* sets of twins.)

- ✔ **Read everything:** Different publications and books have different perspectives and goals, and they each add a different aspect to your planning. So, read . . . a lot.

- ✔ **Overdo it:** You start working at home and need a home office. So does your spouse. You have more kids. You need more computers. You add a wing to the house. Running the bare minimum of wires only to rooms that you're sure will need them is not always enough. We admit that we overbuilt our houses. There, we said it. We overbuilt. Why? Because we believe in futureproofing our homes. Can you get by with other options? Yes. Can you add later? Yes, at more cost. Is it easier to do it up front? Oh yes! So overdo it. Run that extra wire.

✔ **Leave room for expansion:** No matter how much you believe that you'll think of everything upfront, you won't. Plan for expansion. If you have a choice of two models, and one is slightly larger, go with the larger one. Will this add cost up front? Absolutely — but it will save you money down the road.

✔ **Run conduits:** Think about access and flexibility for future growth when you run your wires. You never know when you're going to have to run more cable for some reason or another. Run PVC conduits between floors and in the walls, instead of just running wire, so you can add more cable in the future if you need to. Be cognizant of elbows in these PVC runs — cable, especially thicker cable, does not travel well around corners. Figure 2-2 shows how this might work. Leave pull cords in the conduit. (*Pull cords* are cords that you use to pull cables through that conduit.) Also be careful about what you run in the same conduit — some signals running inside cables can interfere with each other. Never run electrical wiring inside these PVC conduits no matter how much money it saves you.

If you're planning on blowing foam insulation into your house, running conduits is even more critical. Most foam insulation is blown into the wall space after the wiring is completed, so you don't get a lot of second chances if you don't run PVC.

Figure 2-2:
Running
PVC pipe in
the wall.

Stud wall (before drywall)

Empty conduit

✔ **Don't forget the power:** Nothing's worse than buying the latest and greatest telephone, bringing it home, plugging the telephone cable in, and then realizing there's no electrical outlet anywhere nearby. Argh! When you renovate your house or build your new home, you need to talk to your electrician and cabling contractor about the location of electrical outlets. Most electrical outlets are installed every so many feet along the wall (per electrical regulations) and aren't coordinated with your phone lines or other smart devices.

In areas that will have lots of electronic gear, such as the home office or home theater, have your electrician run dedicated circuits. There's nothing worse than finding out — a month after you've finished your network — that plugging the vacuum cleaner into that outlet in the foyer knocks out the circuit breaker in your home office because the electrician put them on the same circuit.

✔ **Don't get fooled by all-in-one, all the time:** A big theme in home networking, particularly home automation, is to find a single solution that does everything. True, integration is good and something to look at seriously. But all-in-one solutions are also sometimes the lowest common denominator. Hard-core stereo buffs tend to go with the best-of-breed approach. They buy a tuner from one manufacturer, a CD/DVD player from another, and an amplifier from yet another for a reason: The individual elements have enough to offer on their own to make the hassle of interconnecting them worthwhile. So look at individual options as well as overall solutions in your buying process.

✔ **Be creative:** Planning a smart home is an opportunity to have fun and be creative. The infrastructure you put in place will enable the fun stuff, but it won't create it. Only by hanging neat technologies off the endpoints of that infrastructure will you see the fruits of your efforts. You're creating an investment. When you go to sell your home, its unique attributes will provide value for the buyer.

Racking It Up

Some things about your smart home you won't appreciate fully until you use them over and over. Equipment racks are like that — they sound metallic and boring, but you will be oh so glad you bought one.

An equipment rack complements your wiring hub. The structured wiring solutions we discuss in this book give you a means to manage all the wires coming in to, out of, and around your house. However, wiring panels can house only a few very small pieces of networking gear, such as routers or switches — these panels were not made to house a DirecTV receiver or a home server or other large devices.

That chore falls to an equipment *rack*. If you've ever seen a computer room or a high-end home theater, you've probably seen a vertical bank of computers and other gear housed in an equipment rack. The boom of home entertainment has presented an opportunity for equipment rack vendors to enter the consumer space with racking options for residential use.

As the types of gear become more complex and as new wiring options come on the market, you're going to have to access the rear panels of your equipment and move wiring around. Home equipment racks help you store your equipment, keep it cool, and manage all the wiring behind the gear. Don't be fooled by cheap racks. You are going to place a lot of expensive gear in this rack, and a rack should last you a lifetime.

It used to be that you could stack all your equipment. That was okay until equipment started having more energy-hogging processors and other components that generate a lot of heat. Now if you stack your gear, you will burn out components, particularly if you put a PC in your cabinet. (DVD players are especially susceptible to heat damage.) You need to space the equipment and you need a cooling strategy for your gear. The right rack can solve these problems.

Get a rack that does the following:

- ✔ **Slides:** Unless you have a special situation where you have rear access to your rack, say from a side room, changing cables in the back of your equipment is complicated. You'll have to pull equipment forward to reconfigure jacks, and this can disconnect your other lines at the same time. A sliding rack brings the equipment forward, out of your cabinet, so you can access the rear panels.

- ✔ **Rotates:** A bonus is if the rack rotates once out of the cabinet, so you can maintain your connections. Once you've owned a rotating rack, you'll never go back!

- ✔ **Cools:** Don't buy a racking system without a built-in cooling system. Some offer the ability to connect several fans to the rack's power system, and automatically turn them on and off based on temperature.

- ✔ **Powers:** Your racking system should have a means to connect to multiple power bars so all your power cables can be nicely managed. The best power bars have slide-on stabilizing clips that make sure your power plugs don't come out of the power bar. Note: These power bars typically are not surge protectors — they are power-cable-management devices designed to help you keep all your cables in order. You will still want to route these into a surge protector at some point. You can buy high-end rack-mounted power protection that makes sure your power levels remain constant in your entertainment center.

TIP

If you have a small space that's shared with other things and you need to be able to move around equipment, consider putting the rack on wheels.

When Danny was outfitting his new home theater, he asked a lot of people about racking because the market for residential racking systems was still new. Everyone pointed him to Middle Atlantic Products, Inc. (www.middle atlantic.com). Danny got a Middle Atlantic ASR-HD-42 system, which can hold up to 350 pounds of equipment, has adjustable shelves, and rotates 60º when extended out from the cabinet. (See Figure 2-3.) It has ventilated shelves, power and cooling management options, and — if you believe Danny's raves — is the best-looking, best-made residential equipment rack on the market (which Pat believes, but never wants to give in so easily to Danny on such things).

Figure 2-3:
Danny's rack allows access to his back panels without disconnecting wires.

Racks can be pricey — you can spend more than $1000 on a high-end racking system. But if you go cheap here, you could lose much more than that in equipment. This is simply one area to invest in for the long haul.

Chapter 3

Cool Stuff Home Networks Can Do

· ·

· ·

"I am platform neutral — it doesn't matter to me whether people receive telecommunication services by cable, satellite, streaming, wires, wireless cable, or mental telepathy."

— Rep. Tom Bliley, Chairman, Senate Commerce Committee
regarding 1999 telecommunications network regulation

*W*e can't help you create a futureproofed plan for mental telepathy, but we certainly can help you with the rest of the telecommunication services that Representative Bliley referred to. (We'll just assume that mental telepathy falls into the wireless category.) Soon, your home network will enable you to do numerous things that you never thought were possible.

Neat Phone Tricks

When you define a phone in its historical sense — that is, a device with a handset and a base unit — lots of options are available to the home networker. You can

- ✔ **Go multiline:** Why install a second home-phone line that goes only to one phone? With the proper wiring, you could access that second line from any outlet in the house. Two lines not enough? How about three, four, or more lines?

- ✔ **Get distinctive:** How about giving all the members of the household their own distinctive ringing tones so that they know who the call is for when the phone rings? You can use certain phone company features along with your home-phone network to avoid buying extra phone lines for your household.

- ✔ **Get conferenced:** Although it may sound corporate, consumer-grade conferencing systems make sense if the speakerphones of most phones don't do the trick.

- ✔ **Get transferred:** With a home-phone system, you can transfer calls around the house. Know that your spouse is in the garage? Send the call there.

- ✔ **Intercom someone:** A home-phone system is a great way to get a home-wide intercom system. You can access different rooms by entering different extensions. And you can monitor rooms, too. By tying the system to your front door, you can have visitors leave a message on your phone system when you're not home.

- ✔ **Answer the door:** Use one of the new Doorcom systems to answer the door when you're away. These systems have a doorbell, speakerphone, and microphone — and with a smart home, they can call you where you're vacationing to let you speak with the person at the door through the telephone.

- ✔ **Get video:** With a videophone, you can see who you're talking to. (Depending on the time of day, that may or may not be a good thing.) Some videophones link up with your TV set for even better viewing but still use regular phone lines.

- ✔ **Go wireless:** A home phone is only as good as the length of its cord, but cordless phones give you freedom when you need to run all over the house. That's not new. But what is new is the convergence of cordless base stations with cellular or digital mobile phones. These so-called dual-mode phones allow you to talk all you want for free (at least no airtime charges) when you're near your base station, but they switch over to cellular or PCS frequencies when you leave your home. The phone — and your phone number — goes with you wherever you go. And lately, with the emergence of a lot of Wi-Fi (wireless computer network system) hot spots around the country and in homes, new multi-mode phones enable you to make free or low-cost calls over the Wi-Fi connection (and the Internet) when they're in range — including at home.

✔ **Control your home network:** Some of the leading home-automation systems use the telephone as the interface to their system, using voice recognition and tone input to drive things around your house. Imagine calling your house and telling it to turn on the fire, turn down the lights, and let your spouse figure out the rest!

✔ **Get some sleep:** You can program your home-telephone system to automatically route inbound calls to an answering machine without ringing any of the phones in the house. Or you can selectively ring only certain phones in certain places.

With the convergence of the computer and telephone realms, telephones look and act more like computers, and computers work more like phones. Some phones can send and receive e-mail as well as send faxes. Screen phones allow you to do everything from home banking to grocery shopping from the comfort of your nearest phone outlet. You can make phone calls from your PC through a microphone and a headset, or watch the called party on your computer screen. A properly designed home network will let you do whatever you want with any of these devices.

Entertainment Everywhere

Your home-entertainment system can cost a lot of money, but when you go to your bedroom at night, that stack of electronics equipment in the living room is pretty much useless. A home network allows you to tap into that media complex instead of duplicating it in each room. A great home network will take that showcase of an entertainment center and distribute it around the house. That makes each room a showcase.

A smart home allows you to

✔ **Roam the house:** Want to watch a movie stored on your Media Center PC in your bedroom or watch CNN while cooking dinner? By running your home network to these rooms, you can distribute the audio and video signals to these locations as easily as you route the signal to your TV set in the living room.

✔ **Be flexible:** Want to watch the beginning of a DVD in the living room but watch the end of the movie in the bedroom? No longer are you a slave to where a particular device (such as a DVD player) is located.

✔ **Be creative:** How about using the picture-in-picture capability of your TV set to monitor the kids in the playroom while you're watching HBO? By linking your video-monitoring capability with your television systems, you can have the best of both worlds.

✔ **Stay sane:** Want to listen to holiday music over your intercom system, instead of blasting the stereo loud enough on the first floor so that you can hear it in your office on the third floor?

✔ **Focus your investments:** By making the most use of the devices you have, you can focus future investments on only those pieces that enable you to take maximum advantage of your existing equipment. Already have a DVD player, Blu-Ray player, DSS receiver, tape deck, CD player, and receiver? Great. Put your money into a great display or widescreen TV, and let those other devices drive the new video capabilities over the home network.

Because video is such a critical feature of most households, it makes sense to make sure that you can maximize your pleasure through an entertainment network in your home.

Save Energy — and Money Too

When you network devices in your home, you build value. Part of that value is saving money. Following are some tasks that a smart home can perform that will save you money over the long term:

✔ **Motorize window coverings:** Large picture windows can hike the temperature of your house by several degrees, making the air conditioning work more often and harder — thus boosting bills. Motorized window coverings help keep your utility bills under control. Window coverings also save money by blocking out ultraviolet rays, which fade your upholstery and carpeting. You can control your coverings in many ways, including handheld remote controls, manual control from wall switch locations, timer controls, and even weather controls (for example, temperature sensors that close the blinds when it's hot or cold).

✔ **Control thermostats:** You can save a significant amount on your heating and cooling bills if you better coordinate your heating and air-conditioning systems. You can set up thermostats so that temperature settings change based on the time of day and the day of the week. You can also change settings based on factors such as energy costs, the weather, and occupancy.

✔ **Control heaters and water pumps:** Hot-water heaters and hot-water circulation pumps are big consumers of power. To save power, turn them on and off according to a schedule.

✔ **Control gas usage:** If you're like Danny, you forget to turn off your gas grill, and it runs all night until the tank runs out of gas sometime during the next few days. Some advanced built-in outdoor grills have sophisticated controls. If the grill has an electric component, it can be controlled. The same is true for gas fireplaces.

✔ **Manage when you're away:** When you go to work, you can tell your house to go into a user-defined away mode. This can mean closing drapes, lowering (or raising) temperatures, shutting off lights, and more. If you go away on vacation, your smart home can turn lights on and off to better simulate someone being home.

Internet Outlets

For years, *getting connected* meant that you were having a phone line installed. Today, it means getting hooked up to the Internet. We probably don't need to tell you how important having a connection to the online world has become to most people. And it's not just for Web surfing or e-mail these days. Tens of millions of people use Instant Messaging (IM) programs on a daily basis, millions more use the Internet for making phone calls, and still millions more use social networking sites (such as Facebook.com and Myspace.com) for keeping in touch with friends around the world. Communications aren't the only thing people are using the Internet for — more and more entertainment content (such as music, TV, and movies) come into our homes over the Internet connection as well.

A smart home turns electrical, telephone, cable, and other wired interfaces into Internet outlets — tunnels through your brick and mortar to the wired world beyond. And smart homes don't use just wireline access. They can be wireless, too.

With a smart home, you can

✔ **Network your computing resources:** Why have a printer at each home workstation when printers are not used that much? Share one printer, one scanner, and Internet access among multiple devices to save money and make your overall data LAN simpler.

✔ **Simultaneously access the Internet:** Work in your office downstairs, accessing the corporate internal network (intranet). Your spouse could be in the living room on the couch ordering groceries from the local grocery store's online Web site. Your 12-year-old son could be upstairs in his bedroom playing Everquest on a multiplayer Internet network. And your studious 10-year-old daughter might be accessing her school's extranet, working on homework with other kids. All this could happen at the same time, over the same network.

✔ **Make and receive phone calls through the Internet:** With the right end-point equipment, you can send and receive phone calls over the Internet. You make Internet phone calls with your PC, an adapter for your phone, an adapter for your fax machine, a videophone, or a special Internet telephony appliance (that essentially looks like a phone). Any of these things will allow you to communicate over the Internet, for free (or nearly so), with parties conceivably very far away.

The true benefits of Internet connectivity come later, when all sorts of devices expect Internet connectivity. More on this in Chapter 4.

Remote Control of Almost Everything

Another great thing about a smart home is the control that you have. Depending on the complexity of your home-automation system, you could control everything from the drapes to the heating system. A smart home allows you to add control later by tapping the endpoints, so you can start modestly.

With a home network, you can

✔ **Control your lights:** Simple home-automation systems attach to the electrical system and allow you to control your electrical devices from a common computing platform. You can turn lights on and off and check out the heating levels in different zones.

✔ **Control your remote controls:** We hate to admit it, but one of us (we won't tell who) has *seven* remote controls in one room. Extending remote control over all your components to other rooms in the house would require a lot of extra remote controls. But with a truly smart home, you can extend control over those devices to other rooms by radio frequency or infrared extension units, so that you maintain the same level of control that you'd have if you were in the same room. We recommend (at least one of us does) that you get a universal remote control for those rooms, however.

GPS: Where the boys are

Global Positioning System (GPS) is a location-finding system that can tell you where you are based on its capability to triangulate signals from three or more satellites that orbit the Earth. It can usually spot you within 10 to 100 meters of your location.

GPS capability is now being built into cars, cell phones, clothing, and more. GPS equipment and chips are used in amusement parks to help keep track of your kids. There are even fun games for kids based on GPS; for information about a treasure hunt game, for example, check out www.geocaching.com.

✔ **Control your computers:** One of the benefits of having connectivity to your various computers on the same network is that you can do things in a coordinated way. For instance, suppose you wanted to back up your computers on a regular basis. You can create a schedule on one computer and have it access the hard disks of the other computers on the LAN and create a copy of key files. A truly wired user will store these files off site, in case of fire or the theft of the machines. You can also coordinate new software upgrades as well as virus and junk e-mail protection. Being connected makes a lot of functionality possible in the computer realm.

✔ **Control your life:** Some home-management systems have automated enunciators that can tell you things you ought to know, such as today is your mother's birthday or the day to take out the trash. Linked with the Internet, telephone, or intercom systems, these commands can be sent to specific locations — such as catching you as you walk out the door.

"I've Fallen and I Can't Get Up!"

You don't just have to keep a smart home for yourself; you can share it with others. A smart home has something for everyone and can be tailored to the needs of special interests, such as the elderly, families with young children, or family members with specific disabilities. The great thing about having a strong smart-home foundation is that you can make it flex in many ways depending on what you want to do. Here are some examples:

✔ **Turn on lights:** We joke about "Clap on, clap off," but we have to give the nod to the Clapper as one of the early moves toward home automation — after all, it's merely an occupancy sensor switch based on sound. The familiar Clapper has gone high-tech over the years and now includes clap indication lights to aid with proper clapping and a sensitivity dial to increase or decrease the Clapper's sensitivity to your unique clap. You can also program it to turn on when it hears any sound at all. This isn't good when you're home, but it's a great theft deterrent when you're at work or on vacation.

✔ **Watch your grandkids:** It's never been easier to have a video chat with your kids. No more fancy phone lines, special devices, and expensive software. All you need is a standard broadband connection (you can use dial-up lines, but you won't be satisfied), a $50 to $100 Web camera (we like www.logitech.com), and free software from any of a range of players, including Yahoo (messenger.yahoo.com). With Yahoo's Super Webcam mode, for instance, you can have great quality pictures.

The video picture frames refresh up to 20 frames a second, and the maximum resolution is 320 x 240. This is not quite TV-picture resolution, but it's getting there.

✔ **Talk to your doctor:** One of the leading manufacturers of implanted medical device, Medtronic, Inc. (www.medtronic.com), has developed a service that allows doctors to monitor patients at home. At the core of this offering is the Medtronic Monitor, a small, easy-to-use device that allows patients to collect information by holding a small "antenna" over their implanted device. The monitor automatically downloads the data and sends it through a standard telephone connection from anywhere in the 50 states directly to the secure Medtronic CareLink Network. Clinicians access their patients' data by logging onto the clinician Web site and make decisions at any time and from anywhere through an Internet-connected computer or laptop. Patients can view information about their devices and conditions on their own personalized Web site, and family members or other caregivers also can view this information if granted access by the patient. The Medtronic CareLink Network is intended to support a wide range of implanted cardiac devices — including Medtronic pacemakers, heart failure devices, and monitoring and diagnostic devices — as they become available following FDA approvals.

✔ **Get help now!** Surely you've seen the "I've fallen and can't get up!" commercials. This cuts to the heart of a major issue for those who are often alone at home: What if something happens and no one is around to help? Various firms (www.seniorsafety.com, for one) have put together a service that links a waterproof wireless transceiver (worn around your neck or wrist) with a central unit plugged into your phone jack and electrical outlet. When the button is pushed on the receiver, it contacts the central unit, which calls a 24-hour monitoring center. In about 40 seconds, they open a voice-to-voice channel to the central unit, which means they can speak back and forth with you from basically wherever you are in your home; you don't even have to touch the phone. (The central unit usually has a very loud speaker and supersensitive microphone).

✔ **See who's outside, and then let them in:** With a simple wireless camera and a link to your TV set, you can see who's knocking at the door, so you don't have to get up. And if you want to let them in without getting up, combine your intercom or home-phone system (like those sold by Panasonic, www.panasonic.com) with a door opener contact and just "buzz" someone in.

"Sit, Ubu. Sit!"

Pets are a big part of any family. (If you ask us, they're just *one of* the family.) A smart home doesn't care what species you are. Here are some neat things you can do for your pets. Some are networked; others are smart on their own:

✔ **Feed your pets when you're away:** From fish to cats to dogs, you can program automatic pet feeders to dispense food up to eight times a day, 7 days a week, 365 days a year. It's perfect for anyone who is not always on time to feed Rover, or who suddenly needs to take a trip.

✔ **Keep your pet wet:** Automatic drinking fountains continuously circulate and filter your pet's water, making it more appealing than standing bowl water. A charcoal filter absorbs tastes and odors. A pitcher-like spout stands five inches above the floor, creating a long waterfall. Other products can keep your pet's outdoor water bowl above freezing — hook the outlet to your temperature monitor and turn it on when it gets cold.

✔ **Let your pet out:** It's one thing to put a pet door into your house, but how do you keep other animals out? Smart pet doors today sense a magnetic key on your pet's collar and unlock to allow your pet to push through the flap.

✔ **Stop your dog from barking:** Is your neighbor's dog driving you crazy? Systems can detect dog barking and issue a humane and effective high-pitched tone that quiets noisy dogs without inflicting harm or pain. The tone doesn't cause pain to animals, but most dogs don't like it and will stop needless barking.

✔ **Stop those scratches on the doors:** Most dog or cat owners have a lot of scratched paint by the door, where Fido or Fifi wanted to be let out. Well, why can't they just page you like most normal pets? They can, with a wireless door chime. When your pet steps on the paw-shaped pad, it signals a wireless chime to the speaker unit.

✔ **Keep your pet in the yard:** Some electronic dog fences have a small low-voltage wire that you string under the ground along your yard's perimeter; others are wireless. A sensor on your pet's collar issues a warning tone when he or she starts straying off your property. Soon, you'll have computer chips in your pet's collar that can interface with the Global Positioning System (GPS) and a wireless phone network so that you can look on your computer and see where your pet is.

✔ **Keep your dog warm (or cold):** Make your doghouse a zone on your HVAC system and keep it automated with the rest of your house. Put a floor warmer in the doghouse, and in cold weather, turn up the heat on that puppy, literally!

You can find smart pet-device sections at Smarthome, Inc. (www.smarthome.com).

Pool, Anyone?

Pools are great to have, a pain to have, and a worry to have. Pools provide fun under the sun but have to be maintained. And if you have little kids around, a pool is a constant worry. A smart home can maximize your enjoyment and minimize your fears in the following ways:

- ✔ **Control your watery environment:** While a pool seems simple — it's just a hole in the ground (or a tank above ground) filled with water — it can get quite complex, particularly if you add a spa, a waterfall, house and garden lighting, and other such amenities. Vendors such as Jandy (www.jandy.com) offer home-automation kits that can help you control filter pumps, pool and spa heaters, and many more electrically operated features with the push of a button. The system also allows for handheld wireless remote-control access, telephone access, and PC access of all features driven by its system. It can also interface with any RS-232 "intelligent" home-automation system. (RS-232 is a communications protocol used by many computers and automation systems. See Chapter 20 for more information.)

- ✔ **Monitor water levels:** A low water level risks serious damage to your filter system and pump. Overfilling your pool wastes water and greatly reduces filter and skimmer effectiveness. A water-level controller maintains water at the preset level. You just attach a garden hose, adjust the float level, and you're ready to go. Check out www.poolkeeper.com for one that's easy to install.

- ✔ **Use in-pool movement alarms:** A range of devices can alert you if someone falls in the pool. These protect kids and pets alike. (Pets find it difficult to climb out of pools.) Make sure that the alarm solution you select can be used with a solar blanket on the pool. Check out www.poolguard.com for its Pool Guard PGRM-2.

- ✔ **Use gate alarms:** All pools should be fenced, but the weakest link in a fence is the gate. A gate alarm mounts next to any gate that gives easy access to your swimming pool. The gate alarm has a delay switch that allows an adult to pass through the gate without the alarm sounding.

- ✔ **Get some turtles:** If you have a child, especially one aged 1 to 4, you need a turtle for your pool: a Safety Turtle, that is, from Terrapin Communications (www.safetyturtle.com). Safety Turtle is a watchband-like water-sensitive device that transmits a special signal to its base station when the wearer comes into contact with water for a duration of time. Fencing and gate alarms aren't enough. Safety Turtle is not just for kids. Pet owners buy them for their precious furballs, and spouses buy them for their elderly in-laws (in Florida, more elderly people die in pool accidents than kids).

✔ **Think about automatic pool covers:** Automatic pool covers eliminate water evaporation, seal in heat, and reduce pool equipment use. In fact, a good cover can act as a giant passive solar collector, and in combination with its thermal qualities, can raise the pool water temperature 10 degrees or more in season. This in turn can mean up to a 70 percent reduction in heating costs, chemical bills, pool pump electrical bills, and pool water bills. And you can link your pool-cover-control mechanism to your home-automation system to make sure that your pool is covered when it's not in use. No more Saturday mornings cleaning the pool. Check out www.sunsystemsinc.com.

The great thing about a lot of the pool safety devices is that they can be integrated into your regular alarm and security system, including their monitoring and alert mechanisms. So if you're not at home and someone is in your pool, something can still be done about it. (Sorry, Pat, no more sneaking into the neighbor's pool!) Remember, though, that none of these safety products replaces the need for adult supervision of all people in the pool area.

To Infinity and Beyond!

In the previous sections of this chapter, we describe things you can do today, to some degree. In this section, we want you to imagine what you'll be able to do with a home network in the near future.

Connect your kitchen appliances and more

Being interconnected will make it possible to use common consumer devices to do seemingly odd tasks. Here are some examples:

✔ **Check your e-mail on your refrigerator:** New, thin, touch-screen, flat-screen computer monitors will fit nicely into your refrigerator door — which is mostly insulation anyway — without compromising much. Add the appropriate computer chip and LAN access to the innards, and you have a heavy computer that also serves ice. Now you'll have a place to keep your shopping lists, send and receive e-mails, and maintain all your phone numbers.

✔ **Surf the Web on your microwave:** We have no idea why you'd want to use this feature, but trial products are on the market that allow you to surf the Web from your microwave. Waiting three minutes for your lunch to warm up can be a pain, but that's probably not enough time to check a Web site. Still, occupy your lunch-warming time with closing stock quotes, appointment reminders, weather predictions, school closings, and so on. Personally, we'd go with the refrigerator.

A speech odyssey

HAL2000 software, from Home Automated Living Company (www.automatedliving.com), will allow you to operate TVs, DVD players, CD players, tape players, and other household components just by ordering them around. HAL2000 uses its own speech-to-text software to send commands to designated devices. You can turn on lights, announce who's on the phone all over the house, and check your e-mail. If the system doesn't understand you, it prompts you to be more specific, with questions such as, "Did you mean a tape from the VCR or a tape from your audio tape player? . . . Dave? . . . Dave? . . ."

✔ **Tie your sprinkler system to www.weather.com:** Never get caught watering your lawn in the rain again! By tying your sprinkler to the Internet, you'll be able to check the weather predictions and let your sprinkler system decide whether to water the lawn as scheduled. During periods of high temperatures, the system may decide to water more frequently. And if you're in a drought area, it can forgo a cycle by monitoring bans on watering lawns.

✔ **Keep your car tuned:** Most new cars have computer chips that track the vehicle's health. Imagine driving into your garage each night and having a remote sensor interrogate your automobile about its day — and interact with remote databases and troubleshooting systems at your car's manufacturing facility. This system will be able to track your oil change needs and automatically schedule an appointment with your dealership. It will also be able to download to your car's hard disk the latest maps for your area, your updated calendar, and revised phone contacts for your car's cell phone.

✔ **Talk to your TV:** New technology coming out of the voice recognition industry will turn your home into *Star Trek*'s USS Enterprise. If your smart home has a microphone in each room, you can say, "Computer, put the incoming message on the screen," just like Captain Picard. (By the way, in case you haven't figured it out yet, our lives revolve around *Star Trek* and Disney World!) For more information on this brave new technology, check out the sidebar titled "A speech odyssey."

✔ **Stay healthy:** Interconnecting your kitchen with computer resources in your home and on the Internet will give you great access to all sorts of nutritional information and online recipe sites. Imagine tracking your diet on a device in your kitchen, and asking for a suggested dinner based on what you ate last week and what you have in the pantry right now. You'll be able to converse with your virtual chef to refine the menu given your preferences for the evening.

Let your TV show you the Web

Because people without computers are keen on using their familiar television interface to surf the Internet, manufacturers have been scurrying to bring the Web to your TV screen. A smart home allows you to directly access the Web through your TV set. The current technology works almost like a toggle switch — you can either view the TV or surf the Internet, but not necessarily at the same time, except maybe by using picture-in-picture capability. (This is what Microsoft's MSN TV2, — what used to be called WebTV — does.)

What's coming down the pike is a wonderful combination of the two together, and the sky is truly the limit here. Here are some things you'll be able to do:

- ✓ **Click your favorite actor:** Ever watch a movie and say, "I know that actor from somewhere," and then for the rest of the movie try to figure out who the guy is? With these emerging TV/Internet technologies, you click the actor's image to access his or her resume, complete with prior roles. Want to go to that actor's fan site? Click an icon designed for that purpose. Want to send the actor an e-mail? Click another icon. When your TV and the Web are connected, they can intertwine shows and databases to create awesome opportunities.

- ✓ **Click your favorite product:** Imagine watching a 30-second commercial and wanting to find out more about the advertised product. With converged TV/Internet products, you'll be able to click the product and go to a Web site that lists the product's features and characteristics. Click another place and see reviews from leading publications such as *Consumer Reports.* Click an icon and see the lowest prices for that product. Like the new gadget James Bond is using in his film? Find out where to buy one by clicking it. The appearance of specific products on TV shows will change drastically, going well beyond the crass commercialism in *The Truman Show.*

- ✓ **Click Grandma:** Combine a small video camera and microphone with your TV monitor, and you create an instant videoconferencing opportunity. Using your smart home's data backbone, you'll be able to hop on the Internet and conference with others. Let Grandma share in your Christmas by enabling her to watch her grandchildren open their presents on the screen. Click your siblings, too, and have a family video-conference. What a great way to show everyone the new baby!

Make phone calls on your computer

You may not realize that your phone calls are really data calls. When you speak into your telephone, your local phone company most likely digitizes your call and sends it across its massive telephone network to either another phone locally or another local or long-distance carrier for completion. These telephone networks are carrying data — bits of your phone conversation.

So when people first started talking about carrying voice calls over data networks, many said, "What's new about that? Businesses have been doing that for a while." What *is* new is consumers having the capability to make calls from their computers.

The combination of the audio hardware found on almost all new PCs and broadband Internet connections allow you to easily make *VoIP* (Voice over Internet Protocol) phone calls from your computer using software such as Skype. In fact, you can make VoIP phone calls without even touching your PC by using a device called an *ATA* (analog telephone adapter).

With the capability to make calls from your computer and over the Internet, you can do the following:

- ✔ **Have a home PBX:** A PBX (private branch exchange) or switch, which most companies use to run their phone networks, is like a mini telephone-company switch that can transfer calls from one extension to another, provide voice mail, do call holding, and so on. By running your home phones on your data network instead of your phone network, you can provide each handset with sophisticated features that you may not otherwise be able to afford. Some of the newest services on the market enable firms to extend their PBX functionality to employees' homes through high-speed local-access connections. You could have one or more extensions at home that look and operate the same as at work, including allowing interextension dialing within the corporation.

- ✔ **Receive faxes on your TV:** Just like phone calls, fax transmissions are beginning to move to the Internet. You can buy equipment or services that translate faxed documents into digital Internet packets and send them over the Net. At the receiving end, you can choose to print the fax on a fax machine or receive the document as an e-mail attachment. When your TV becomes part of your home's Internet connection — and that will happen soon — you'll be able to preview and read your incoming faxes on your TV screen. (Later, you can print them over your home-computer network.)

- ✔ **Shop in Hong Kong:** Envision going to a booth at your local mall, having your body's dimensions scanned, and then using this information to shop anywhere in the world. No more too-short shirts! You'll be able to surf the Internet on your TV, find the outfits you want, choose the color and patterns, and then order a custom-fitted garment. You'll even be able to use your videoconferencing link or Internet telephony capability to talk with the tailors about your suit. In addition, many larger firms in the textile industry cut their garments using computer-driven lasers. Imagine having your scan feed directly into that!

Check up on your house over the Net

Although home-automation systems have been around for a long time, they're still in their infancy. Most of the systems are either old technology (the inexpensive X10 systems) or expensive, custom-built systems. Luckily, a bunch of vendors are starting to offer solutions based on new standards such as ZigBee and Z-Wave (see Chapters 19 and 20 for more information) that combine better performance and reliability with ease-of-use and installation.

We're starting to see home-control systems that integrate more fully into your data and telephone networks, enabling them to be controlled remotely. Traditionally, custom systems have a telephone interface that enables you to dial in and use the keypad (or even your voice in some instances) to issue commands to the system controller. The next logical step in this process is to provide a Web interface — and many are launching these services now.

Suppose that one of your home's PCs, using an always-on fast Net connection, also powers your home-control systems. This home-control software functions as a Web server to allow you to access your home-control system from your office desktop, an airport kiosk, or even your Web-enabled handheld PC. You simply bring up the URL of your home server, log in, and then navigate through the home-control Web page to turn on lights, turn up the heat, or even fire up the hot tub. Pretty cool, huh?

With the newest systems, you don't need to involve the PC. Your standalone home controller, like those sold by Control4, www.control4.com, can handle all your needs without a PC. For example, the Control4 home-control system connects to your broadband Internet connection and "talks" to Control4's Web servers. Without setting up your own in-home Web server, you can log into my.control4.com and (using a username and password to authenticate yourself) remotely control your system from any Web browser anywhere in the world.

Here are just a few of the tasks that this type of interface will be able to perform:

- ✔ **Control your appliances' usage:** More and more, companies will give you incentives to behave in certain ways. For instance, the power company may encourage you to run laundry at certain hours of the day. A smart home-automation system will be able to interact with the power company's pricing system to determine the best time of the day to do certain tasks, and then perform those tasks according to those schedules, if that's what you want. Power companies in some parts of the country already have different rate periods.

✓ **See through walls:** Your home-network security system will include a video monitor for the front door, allowing you to see who's there before you open the door. By further interconnecting your security system with Internet access, you can monitor your home remotely, from any Web interface. Suppose that you're at work but think that someone sent an important overnight package to your home office by accident. With this technology, you'll be able to call up your smart home's Web page and check out the video picture of your front stoop. If your hunch is correct, you can go home and get the package. You'll also be able to monitor your nanny from work, or make sure that the kids aren't throwing wild parties while you're away!

✓ **Turn up the heat:** With a good smart-home design, your telephone system will be interconnected with your heating and cooling systems, which will allow you to monitor and control those systems remotely. Going to go up to your smart vacation home for the weekend? With a remotely controlled home-automation system, you'll be able to call ahead and turn the heat on.

✓ **Check who's home alone:** Or have your system dial out to your own pager number when someone (maybe a burglar) enters the back door. With an interconnected system, almost anything is possible.

Chapter 4

Timelines and Budgets

. . . .

. . . .

*Y*our smart-home adventure starts in two places: in your head and in your wallet. You need to know where you're going and how much you're willing to spend to get there. In addition, you need to figure out how much of this project you're willing to do yourself. All sorts of consultants, systems integrators, contractors, and others can help ensure smart-home success. This chapter helps you figure out when to use these folks. You also find out about budgetary and timeline considerations.

New or Existing Home?

The most important issue when wiring your home is whether you have a new home or an existing one. We present all possible options in a home that you're wiring from scratch. But we also describe choices that you can pursue if a whole-home wiring solution isn't possible in all parts of your home.

Even if you have an existing home, wired solutions aren't necessarily out of the question. Contractors can snake cables through walls to install alarms, intercoms, phone systems, data networks, and automation systems. You may want to rely more heavily on wireless systems or ones that utilize existing wires. If you instead decide to run new wires, you should search for an experienced telephone or alarm installer who can find some creative ways to run and hide new wires without having to rip open walls.

What Do You Want from Your Home Network?

The first step in planning your home network is determining what you want it to do. Do you want a fully automated home, with lights that turn themselves on, drapes that open and shut on their own, and a remote-controlled HVAC (heating, ventilation, and air-conditioning) system? Do you want a high-speed computer network that lets you plug a PC or laptop into a jack anywhere in the house and get Internet access? Do you want a sophisticated communications system, with multiple telephone lines, video monitors at the doors, and intercoms throughout your home?

Going for broke (literally) from the beginning is neither necessary nor wise. However, it is wise to use any wiring or rewiring opportunities (such as a newly constructed home or one that you're ripping apart for remodeling) to get enough wires to enough places to enable your home network to grow with your needs, without the hassle and expense of doing the wiring all over again.

Whatever you decide to do, it's best to install a home network all at once in a well-thought-out fashion. Home networking in a haphazard way results in, well, what most ad hoc do-it-yourselfers' wiring projects look like — a mess.

So before you begin designing a network and wiring plan for your home, think through how you're going to use each room in the home. Do so with an eye toward the future. Suppose that you have a spare bedroom that needs only a phone jack and a cable TV outlet. That room may be your home office someday, in which case you'd need wiring for an extra phone as well as some computer networking capabilities. Or perhaps the room will turn into a nursery, so you'd want an intercom and maybe a video monitor. And when the kids get older, they may need a place to hook up a computer or plug in an entertainment system.

As you explore your many home-networking options, aim toward flexibility for the future.

Deciding How Much to Spend

Prewiring your entire home for every contingency may not be as expensive as you think. Several well-respected vendors offer all-in-one kits that put high-speed data communications, telephony, video, home entertainment, and (in some cases) security wiring in place with little or no thinking on your part. Check out Chapter 2 for more information on all-in-one cable solutions.

You can also apply the everything-everywhere solution and run high-speed data cables, coaxial video cables, and speaker cables to several jacks in every room of your home. Many homeowners follow this route.

Even though you'll be making choices about what you can do right now, don't forget about building a robust, futureproof wiring system into your home. In fact, running higher-quality, more capable wiring doesn't cost much more than running old-fashioned telephone and cable TV wires. And while you're at it, install conduits (mentioned in Chapter 2) to make running cables easier in the future.

 One of the great things about building a smart home is that many of the network's components — wiring panels, cable runs, keypads, switches, and so on — are already part of the home's structure, which means that you can usually finance this cost as part of your mortgage. This option helps you stretch out the upfront cost of installing these systems.

Going Over the Costs

The cost of a home network varies depending on many factors, such as the costs in your particular area and how fancy you get. We can, however, provide general information about how much you can expect to spend. We base our prices on a typical home: two floors, three bedrooms, two-and-a-half baths, and a partially finished basement. To cover a larger area, you need to add the cost of extra wiring runs and some extra endpoints.

Most of the cost of an audio- and video-distribution system is in the audio and video equipment itself rather than in the networking infrastructure and components. Audio and video equipment is usually housed in the home-media center. (Part II explains this equipment in detail.) Here are some general costs:

- ✔ **Home theater:** A home theater can cost you as little as $1000 if you go with a moderate-sized TV set and a home-theater-in-a-box surround-sound audio system. A really great home theater runs $7,000 to $20,000. Installation costs about 10 percent of your component parts.

- ✔ **Coaxial distribution panel:** Expect to spend about $300 to $400 for a coaxial distribution panel for your home network.

Other networks in your home involve the following costs:

- ✔ **Phone system:** A phone system costs $50 to $100 per outlet or from $500 to $1500 for a centralized whole-home phone system.

- ✔ **Data network:** Data networks are relatively inexpensive — less than $200 to buy and install the necessary central components and about $50 to $100 per cable run, including cable, connectors, faceplates, and so on.

✔ **Home-security system:** A home-security system averages about $1200 to install. You also pay about $25 a month for monitoring fees — about half of that if you use one of the Internet-based monitoring services we discuss in Chapter 18.

✔ **Home-automation system:** The cost of your home-automation system can vary widely. The cost to turn some lights on and off with a computer-controlled timer is much less than the cost to have androids serve breakfast in bed, for example. The average simple DIY home-automation project costs around $500 to $1000 (for example, to install a lighting-control system), and a fancier, centrally controlled whole-home system (with professional installation and configuration) starts off at around $5000.

Depending on what you need to do, you may be able to get away with paying less than these amounts. But we'd rather scare you with big numbers first — while showing you all the ways that you can step down in price and still have a great home network — than throw unrealistically low numbers your way and set the wrong expectations.

Whatever you do, don't start the process by saying, "I don't want to spend a lot of money on this project." Instead, approach the process with an open mind: Think about what features you'd like to have, share that information with some home-networking experts, and see what happens from there.

The Home Team

The people involved in your project vary according to what you're trying to accomplish. If you plan install a major home theater — complete with theater seats, a popcorn and candy stand, and screen curtains — you'll probably bring a home-theater consultant into the process. Most people don't want or need to go to that level.

The cast of characters for your home-networking project can include the following:

✔ **Architect:** This person helps you lay out the initial plans for your home and coordinate with other designers to get their respective visions on paper. Architects create the plans that guide all the activity in the house, but they need the contribution of your individual contractors. Many architects don't have the level of specialty necessary to finalize your wiring plans, but the architect's drawings are key to making sure, for example, that all your speakers are correctly placed in your home-entertainment theater.

✔ **Audio/video consultant:** Your audio/video (A/V) consultant helps you select the right mix of components for your sight and sound systems and then integrate all those components. Your A/V consultant makes sure that the appropriate wiring is run to support your installations and then installs the gear when you're ready. If you're installing a dedicated home theater, expect your A/V consultant to get involved with the architect early on, too, making recommendations for room sizes, building materials, and so on. The A/V consultant may also hand you off to a specialized home-theater consultant if the job is too complex for his or her comfort. (Home-theater consultants get into additional details such as soundproofing, seating, lighting, and the room's shape and construction).

✔ **Contractor/builder:** The general contractor/builder's role is to direct the other specialty contractors and make sure that they carry out the intent of the designers. Passing correct information from one contractor (such as the home-theater consultant) to the people doing the work (such as the cabinetmaker who builds the home-theater cabinetry) is crucial. The details are what count here, such as cutting out the right size cubbyhole for the kitchen media center.

✔ **Computer-systems contractor:** If you work at home or have complex computer-networking needs, bringing in a computer-systems contractor to network your computer hardware and interface it to the appropriate systems can be a great timesaver.

✔ **Electrical contractor:** The electrical contractor is a staple of any new home project. Because your smart home may require additional or different electrical wiring (for example, special configurations in your electrical panel to allow home automation over power lines), hiring an electrical contractor who is experienced with smart homes is a plus.

✔ **Heating/cooling contractor:** Having a smart home is not just about having a home-control system that turns fans on and off. A smart heating and cooling system has many nuances, such as different zones for maximum control and specialized controls for specific areas (such as that wine cellar you were thinking about). Your heating/cooling contractor can make sure that your system is energy efficient while meeting your requirements.

✔ **Home-systems integrator:** This person integrates all the different electronic systems in your house but may or may not do the actual installations; specialists for each subsystem may do part of the work. The integrator should be able to provide your architect with recommendations regarding where to put your centralized wiring closet or where to run the wires for specific applications. The home-systems integrator also works with the interior designer to address layout and appearance issues.

✔ **Interior designer:** This person is responsible for making sure that your home-network technology doesn't stick out like a sore thumb. Installing a state-of-the-art home-entertainment center in the living room is one thing — making it fit with the overall scheme of your home is another. The interior designer works with your consultants to ensure that what is visible is pleasing to the eye.

✔ **Kitchen designer:** This expert helps you figure out not only a sensible layout for your kitchen but also your options for integrating the latest technologies into your smart-home design. This designer should work closely with the home-systems integrator.

✔ **Lighting consultant:** Often an overlooked task on a to-do list, lighting design has an important effect on the ambiance of your home, so consider specialized lighting in key areas. A lighting consultant works early on with the home-systems integrator and the architect to define the lighting-control requirements and to select a system. The actual wiring, however, is typically handled by the electrical contractor or home-systems integrator — unless the lighting arrangement is complex, in which case a specialized lighting contractor may be called in.

✔ **Security consultant:** The security consultant and contractor design a system specifically for your home, and then install it. They make sure you have the right coverage to meet your security goals and ensure that the system interfaces with other subsystems, such as with telephone lines for calling out to the central station if a burglar trips a sensor.

Whew! Did we leave anyone out? Depending on the amount of money you want to spend, you may indeed have this many people making your smart home a reality. A more modest project has a more modest number of people stomping around your house. Also, many of the previously mentioned professionals — kitchen designers, for example — include their services when you purchase their equipment.

Make sure that you choose advisors who share your vision of an ideal smart home. The people you choose should have experience with smart, networked homes. Some contractors are conservative and don't want to overbuild. Others are liberal and plan for everything under the sun. Find your wired personality and match it with your contractors, and you'll have a winning combination.

You might have a hard time finding some of these contractors — it's not like the phone book has a section titled "Smart Homes" (at least not yet!). For the more traditional groups of professionals (such as architects), we tend to rely on word-of-mouth, recommendations from in-the-know friends, and a thorough review of the contractor's references. For contractors who will be installing your home's electronics and wiring infrastructure, we do these same things, as well as check their credentials. The Custom Electronics Design & Installation Association, or CEDIA, is one of the best places to start. This group (www.cedia.net) has a rigorous training and qualification program for people who do nothing but build and install smart-home systems for a living.

Starting Down the Smart-Home Path

Your first step in building your whole-home network is to visualize what you want. Then you need to sit down with your designers and consultants to refine your vision into a cost-effective reality. The following list is a rough timeline you can use as you're planning and building your wired home. Your timeline, however, may take half as long or twice as long:

- ✔ **Month 1:** Meet and interview various key consultants, and then hire your choices; visit demonstration rooms; visit libraries and bookstores for ideas and cappuccino. (By the way, you'll be doing great if you can keep this effort to only one month.)

- ✔ **Month 2:** If you're part of the 1 percent who can afford a custom-designed home, you're ready to sit down with your architect and start brainstorming the design. Plan to spend at least a month or two in this process. Then the architect or builder creates the plan with your specific needs in mind. Although it's early in the process, you may also want to choose an interior designer.

- ✔ **Month 3:** You make the final refinements to your plans. Typically, the architect draws up not only floor plans but also electrical wiring plans for key subsystems. Unfortunately, few architects will read this book before designing your system, so they may provide a standard plan. You need to find a home-networking specialist or work closely with the architect to describe the needs of each room and the system as a whole.

- ✔ **Month 4:** You request bids and select a builder; you finalize the budget and plans; you and the builder approve the detailed drawings of wiring schematics and special construction; and the builder applies for and receives permits. These things may take more than a month, but we're optimists.

- ✔ **Month 5:** The lot is cleared; the foundation is dug; the security team is on hand to survey the site and external installations; the pipes and wiring are installed under the foundation; and the foundation is poured.

- ✔ **Months 6–8:** The framing is finished; the windows and roof are installed; key consultants tour the site for revisions and planning; and plumbing and heating contractors install their wiring, piping, and conduit. (If your new house is big or the weather is bad, this phase could take longer than two months.)

✔ **Month 9:** Both before and after the electrician does the electrical work, various contractors install data, telephone, security, audio, video, and other special wiring. The insulation goes in.

✔ **Months 10–12:** Sheetrock and plaster are installed; interior wood and finishing work begins, including any special cabinetry; the A/V contractor installs any in-wall speakers and intercom systems; the telephone/data systems team installs the data/telephone systems; the security contractor installs endpoint devices and the control system; the electrical contractor and lighting designer install lighting and controls; the plumber installs fixtures; and the home-automation expert coordinates installation of the home-control system.

✔ **Month 13:** Final construction is performed on the interior of the house; subcontractors finish their installations; testing is performed; and systems are checked. You're probably closer to month 18 by now, and you've probably blown your budget. But the important part is to make it through alive and with your marriage intact.

Don't forget about the building inspector. The best-laid plans can succumb to a busy building inspector whose approval is often required to go to the next stage of your multistage project.

You do need to coordinate what kind of cables will be installed in any special conduits placed to make running wires easier. For instance, running electrical wiring in the same conduit as your telephone, data, or A/V wiring is a bad move because electrical lines create electromagnetic flux that ruins your data and video throughput, not to mention your phone calls. Installing electrical cables adjacent to other cables is surprisingly common in many new-home construction projects, so look out for it.

After all the rough-in work is complete (and wires are all over the place), the sheetrock and other wall coverings go up. Although some items, such as in-wall speakers, go in before all the finish work is complete, much of your gear goes in only after everything else is just about finished. You attach all your components to their connection points, and install the control panels.

After the rough-in work and wiring is finished but *before* the sheetrock goes up, use a video or digital camera to document what wires are running where (including where the empty conduits start and stop). Some day you might need to add a cable to a conduit, or fix a wire that a rodent ate through (yes, they do that; and yes, we're talking about rats; and yes, depending on where you live, you can get rats in your house, no matter how often you clean the kitchen and take out the trash).

Testing can be exhaustive, but you can never test too much before accepting a house from your collective of contractors. Make sure to hook equipment to all your outlets and test, test, test.

Part II

Making Your Home an Entertainment Center

The 5th Wave   By Rich Tennant

"It's a letter from the company that installed our in-ground sprinkler system. They're offering Internet access now."

In this part . . .

Face it: The television is a major focus of almost any home, worldwide. In our business, we've traveled all over the globe. We've seen tents in the desert with camels parked out back, dinner cooking over a fire, and a TV set inside. People like and want their video. Those enamored with audio feel just as strongly.

The key is building your home-entertainment system so that you can enjoy it everywhere you want to — not just in the confines of a particular room or a particular space. Your home-entertainment system should be in the whole home, omnipresent to the point of total flexibility.

In this part, we tell you how to create a home-entertainment backbone in your house. We discuss the major elements of a whole-home audio and video network and the advantages of connecting all multimedia elements together. We talk about the different inputs and outputs required and provide some tips and tricks for ensuring the success of your home-entertainment system. We also make sure you're up to speed on the latest developments in entertainment equipment and networking, such as HDTV and Internet-based content, and on the effect these innovations will have on your networking strategy and requirements.

Chapter 5

Breaking the Entertainment Bottleneck — Without Breaking the Bank

In This Chapter

▶ Making your home more fun

▶ Understanding tubes, screens, and thinner media

▶ Bringing the roof down (with sound)

Most homes contain a plethora of entertainment equipment — televisions, radios, CD players, stereo receivers, and more. (If you're like us, you also have an old-fashioned turntable sitting prominently on a shelf someplace.) People tend to think of home-entertainment gear as stuff that's used in a particular room — a stereo in the living room, televisions in the family room and bedroom, and maybe a radio in the kitchen.

The best home-entertainment system is a network that leverages your investments in expensive audio and video equipment and lets you enjoy it wherever you are in the home. You put the bulk of the equipment in a common media center (such as a home-theater room), and then set up a suitable network infrastructure (wired or wireless or something else) to distribute the audio and video. In this chapter, we discuss the components you need to set up a home-audio and -video network.

TV and Video Systems

This section looks at some of the radical changes that television is undergoing — and we're not talking about programming. Like most other devices before it, the television is in the midst of a leap from the analog to the digital world. Unlike many of those devices, however, TV is making the leap in a series of agonizingly slow steps. We discuss how this transition might affect your choices in the video world. We talk also about the various kinds of TVs you can buy.

The conversion from analog to digital and old-style TV to next-generation TV comes into play in many places:

- ✔ The encoding of the programming signal itself
- ✔ The transmission path that the signal takes in getting to your house
- ✔ The receiver — internal or external — that receives and decodes the signal for display

In the progression of standards and technical development, change is taking place along all three of these paths.

Analog still rules the roost — but not for long

The vast majority of television signals coming into homes are still analog. Analog TV signals reach homes through over-the-air broadcast TV, by traditional cable TV systems, and by satellite. (We discuss all the different ways TV signals get into your house later in the chapter.)

In North America, an analog television format known as NTSC (National Television Standards Committee) has been in place for decades — in fact, it hasn't been changed or updated since the advent of color television in the 1960s. Although this standard is capable of producing a surprisingly good picture under ideal circumstances, its analog nature makes it susceptible to various kinds of interference and signal degradation. Consequently, the picture can be downright awful by the time it gets to your television (which is why the TV world is slowly turning digital).

There's not much we need to tell you about analog TV — if you've turned on a television in the past fifty years, you've seen it.

Just as the NTSC standard is common in North America (and Japan), a couple of other standards — known as PAL and SECAM — are common in other parts of the world. Unless you have a special TV designed for the purpose, you can't watch PAL with an NTSC TV, and vice versa. This is one reason why you can't buy videotapes in many parts of the world and use them at home.

Digital is here!

The move from analog to digital is well afoot. Tens of millions of homes have some form of digital TV, but the conversion from analog to digital is still an evolving process. The key concept behind any kind of digital TV is that the audio and video programming is converted from an analog signal into a series of digital bits (a whole lot of ones and zeros that make up a video picture). The primary technology behind any kind of digital TV (at least in the United States and Canada — other countries have their own variant of digital TV) is something called MPEG.

Several video and audio compression and digitization standards are based on *MPEG* (Motion Picture Experts Group). Most are named by adding a number to the end of the word *MPEG*. The MPEG-2 standard is by far the most common in the video world, with MPEG-4 coming on strong.

The digital television that people receive today uses MPEG-2 to carry standard, analog NTSC TV signals digitally. This is an important fact to repeat: Much of what you see as "digital TV" is a standard analog TV signal, converted to digital. Digital over digital is our nirvana and is part of the HDTV world, as we discuss shortly.

When this digitized signal gets to your house (over a digital cable system or a DBS satellite system), a set-top box converts the signal back to analog NTSC TV, which your TV understands and can display. This digital signal coming into your house isn't inherently different than an analog one, but it usually looks and sounds better because the digital transmission path is cleaner and isn't susceptible to the interference that usually messes up analog signals.

Next-generation digital TV

Much of today's digital television isn't all it can be. In the late 1990s, the FCC (the controlling regulatory authority for broadcasters, cable companies, and telephone companies in the United States) brought together a big bunch of television industry folks and — after a long, painful, and contentious process — came up with a new generation of digital TV. This new system, which goes by the name *ATSC* (Advanced Television Standards Committee), had defined a bunch of new, higher-definition television standards.

Specifically, digital video signals (not analog ones) are transmitted using digital technologies and played on TVs set up to display these digital signals. It's digital all the way, baby, as sportscaster Dick Vitale would say. (Did we mention we're Duke Blue Devils fans, too!)

What's different about ATSC?

When we talk about new ATSC-based televisions, we're talking a whole new ballgame (or at least a whole new way to watch a ballgame). It takes only a glance to see the striking difference between older NTSC displays and the new ATSC ones.

In general terms, the clarity and crispness of a television's display is determined by the resolution, the scanning refresh rate, and the scanning method.

You may be familiar with the concept of *resolution* if you own a PC, because PC displays are usually rated in terms of their resolution, or more specifically, the number of *pixels* (individual points of light and color in the display) that you can see. For example, smaller home-PC displays are set to show 800 pixels across by 600 pixels vertically; larger displays are often set to show 1024 across by 768 vertically, or more.

Television manufacturers don't usually mention the number of pixels across the screen, but they do list the vertical number — the *lines of resolution,* or scan lines. Today's analog TV systems usually max out at 480 lines of resolution (and you don't even receive all 480 — a few lines carry other information such as closed captioning). ATSC systems (HDTV, in other words) can broadcast at 480, 720, on up to 1080 lines of resolution. When looking at two screens of the same size and quality, the more lines of resolution, the better the picture.

The other factor in determining the quality of a television or video signal is the *scanning method.* People generally talk about PC monitors and video systems in terms of their screen refresh rates — often using a number such as 75 hertz. This figure means that the picture on your PC's video screen is updated 75 times every second. When talking about televisions, people discuss the scanning method to illustrate the same principle.

TV puts an interesting twist on the scan line refresh rate, however. A TV with a *progressive scan display* refreshes *all* lines of resolution (480 or 720 or 1080) during a cycle. (TVs refresh at a rate of 60 cycles per second — for comparison, film movies do so 24 times a second.) Other TVs offer *interlaced scan display,* which means that they refresh half the screen — every other line — each cycle, so each line is refreshed only 30 times per second. Theoretically, a progressive scan system has a better picture than an interlaced one, but because both refresh the picture many times per second, the difference isn't immense.

These new higher-definition television standards are different than the digital TV discussed in the preceding section. To view them in all their glory (and we've seen enough of high-definition television to tell you that it is indeed glorious), you need to buy the newer, fancier, better, more expensive TV.

ATSC signals can be divided into different groups, depending on the resolution and the scanning method (as we discuss in the "What's different about ATSC?" sidebar). They are further divided into SDTV, or standard-definition television (signals that are about the same or a little bit better than NTSC), and HDTV, or high-definition television (which has truly spectacular, film-like picture quality). Within the ATSC standard are dozens of SDTV and HDTV variations, but you're most likely to see just four, as shown in Table 5-1.

Table 5-1		Common Digital TV Variants	
Name	*Lines of Resolution*	*Scanning Method*	*Quality*
480i	480	Interlaced	Standard definition (same as NTSC)
480p	480	Progressive	Standard definition
720p	720	Progressive	High definition
1080i	1080	Interlaced	High definition

To take advantage of all the benefits of digital TV, you'll eventually have to replace your televisions. Today's televisions don't have the internal circuitry to decode digital TV signals, and they generally don't have screens that can display high-definition ATSC pictures in all their glory. (And HDTV is the big deal in this story — we focus our discussion on HDTV rather than SDTV.)

Today's TVs aren't even the right shape; the *aspect ratio* — the ratio of screen width to height — of HDTV signals is wider than that of NTSC signals. NTSC is 4:3; HDTV is 16:9. Figure 5-1 shows the difference in aspect ratios — the HDTV screen has an aspect ratio like the elongated screens in movie theaters. (You may have already been exposed to this aspect ratio because many movie DVDs today allow for this sort of widescreen viewing as an option.)

HDTV-capable TV sets, which became available at the end of 1998, are more expensive than traditional sets. However, prices have come down significantly. When we wrote the first edition of this book, HDTVs were often more than $6000, but now you can get one for $750 or less.

What about 1080p?

If you are tuned into the HDTV world, you have no doubt heard a lot of talk about 1080p. This is the highest current resolution in the HDTV world — it's simply a progressive scan version of 1080i, drawing the entire 1920 x 1080 pixels in each frame, rather than half of them at a time.

Why don't we have 1080p in Table 5-1? Well, the simple answer is that 1080p is not going to be part of any broadcast (over-the-air, cable, or satellite) TV system anytime soon. Where you *will* find 1080p is in source devices that live in your home, such as Blu-ray and HD-DVD disc players and in gaming consoles such as Sony's PlayStation 3. So 1080p can and probably will have a place in your home. But it won't be coming in over your set-top box or other broadcast reception system.

Figure 5-1:
An HDTV
screen is
this much
wider than
an NTSC
screen.

4:3
Aspect ratio

NTSC TV

16:9
Aspect ratio

HDTV

Two types of digital HDTVs are available: HDTV-ready TVs and HDTVs. HDTV-ready televisions have only a standard NTSC receiver; they have no built-in digital television receiver. However, you can connect them to an external HDTV receiver and display high-definition programming. The second type, HDTV, has a built-in receiver (or at least comes with an HDTV receiver that you hook up externally), so there's nothing more to buy to receive over-the-air HDTV.

TIP

We think it's better to buy an HDTV-ready TV — you save a few hundred bucks, and then you can buy a receiver that works best with the system that provides HDTV (that is, an over-the-air antenna, digital cable, or satellite).

I want my HDTV!

Where are you going to get your HDTV programming? (And yes, we want our HDTV!) As we hinted, three possibilities are the same places where you get NTSC today: over-the-air broadcasters, cable TV systems, and satellite TV systems.

For broadcast TV, the FCC gave (for free) each broadcast TV station the requisite additional broadcast spectrum for a different channel over which they could broadcast in ATSC digital format. The deal was this: The TV stations had to completely transition to digital by 2009 (February 19th of that year to be precise — after the Super Bowl), and then give the FCC their old channel so it could be assigned for other uses. In the summer of 2002, the FCC, trying to push this process along, made a ruling that every TV sold in America must have a receiver that can get ATSC broadcasts by 2007. Keep in mind, this doesn't mean that these TVs will be able to display HDTV (for example, they may not have a high enough resolution, or they may not be able to display widescreen content properly), but they will be able to receive it and display it at lower resolutions and at a 4:3 aspect ratio. Eventually, when enough of these TVs are in people's homes, analog TV as we know it will go away, replaced by SDTV and HDTV.

So far, there have been no requirements for cable and satellite companies to offer ATSC signals, but each has begun offering a number of channels of HDTV to go along with their existing programming. In fact, the biggest competitive battle between cable and satellite TV providers these days revolves around the number (and quality) of HDTV channels they offer. You can expect to get 20 or more HDTV channels from either kind of provider, and both groups are making major upgrades to their networks to bring you hundreds of channels.

After the switch to digital TV is complete, you won't have to pitch your old TVs. Digital TV tuners, like those that the FCC is requiring in new TVs, will allow you to watch DTV programming on older TVs. Of course, the picture quality and resolution won't be as high as it would be with a new digital set, and you might not have a widescreen (16:9) aspect ratio.

TV types

For a long time, televisions have been pretty much identical, except for differences in their internal electronics and the quality of their construction. The advent of technologies from the computer world and the desire of many consumers to build home theaters that use large-screen TVs have dramatically altered this situation.

A fourth option

Cable, satellite, and broadcast are no longer the only games in town. *IPTV* (Internet Protocol TV) is the newest option, available to a small but significant (and growing) number of people. IPTV uses a combination of broadband connections to the home (such as DSL) and the Internet Protocol used for Web surfing, e-mail, and many phone calls (such as Vonage) to bring you cable and satellite-style TV over the Internet. The biggest proponents of IPTV are the phone companies, who are using the technology to compete with cable companies in the realm of what many call the triple play: high-speed Internet, voice services, and TV.

In the United States, AT&T has invested heavily in IPTV and is offering it over a very high-speed variant of DSL called, appropriately, VDSL — very high-speed digital subscriber line — and is offering an IPTV service in dozens of its markets. Verizon, the other big phone company in the United States, has its own system for TV services, called FiOS, which replaces DSL and copper phone lines entirely and offers services over lightning-fast fiber-optic cables to the home. FiOS actually *is not* an IPTV service (both use the same technology that cable companies use, only over fiber instead of coaxial cables), but we expect that Verizon too will switch to IPTV eventually.

It's likely that even cable TV providers will begin using some IPTV technology because it is more spectrally efficient, thus allowing them to offer more TV channels over the same cable. Many cable companies are already using some elements of IPTV for their video-on-demand services.

In the future, it's possible you'll hear less about IPTV (the technology) but see a lot of IPTV as many TV service providers move towards IPTV as one of their underlying technologies, while providing you a service that looks and feels just like their old-fashioned services.

We've already talked a bit about digital TVs and HDTV. Now we're going to talk about three different forms of TVs (direct-view, projection, and flat screen). None of these TV styles are inherently analog or digital — a specific model within each of these groups can be analog only or HDTV and digital compatible. Having said that, almost all projection and flat-panel TVs on the market today are HDTV-ready.

Tubes for all: Direct-view TVs

The traditional television — or a video display of any kind, for that matter — has always been the direct view, picture tube type. The screen you see is actually the front of a specially treated glass tube with an electron gun built into the back of the tube. This system works by shooting electrons through electronically controlled devices and onto the back of the picture tube's screen. When the electrons hit the specially treated glass, it lights up in different colors and intensities (depending on how the electrons are aimed) and creates your picture.

Tubes are a mature technology — having been on the market in large quantities for about 50 years — and they work pretty darn well. They do, however, have a few disadvantages:

✔ They're big (in depth) and heavy (ever try to move a 35" television?).

✔ The technology itself limits screen size (few direct-view televisions are larger than about 40" measured diagonally).

✔ Large picture tubes with electron guns sophisticated enough to handle HDTV's high resolutions are difficult to build (several makers have such models on the market, but they don't offer the full 720 or 1080 lines of resolution needed for real HDTV).

Tube TVs are essentially a dead-end technology. Most manufacturers have begun to shut down their picture tube factories and have moved to projection and flat-panel TVs instead. With a few exceptions, you'll find that tube TVs are available only in the smallest sizes and for the cheapest models (think 13" $75 tube TV for the guest room).

Projection TVs

After you move beyond pretty large big-screen TVs (35" or so) to huge oh-my-goodness big-screen TVs, the form of the television changes from direct-view to projection, or *PTV*. Projection TVs come in two main types, as shown in Figure 5-2:

✔ **Front-projection models:** These high-end models consist of a projector mounted on the ceiling and a separate screen. Like a movie projector, these models project the TV video onto the front of the screen.

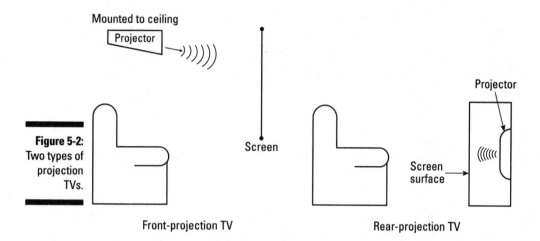

Figure 5-2:
Two types of projection TVs.

Mounted to ceiling

Projector

Screen

Projector

Screen surface

Front-projection TV

Rear-projection TV

✔ **Rear-projection models:** The screen and projection systems are in the same chassis in these all-in-one units. Like a direct-view TV, these models beam the TV image onto the back of a screen.

The cheapest rear-projection models cost between $1000 and $2000. High-quality front-projection models cost $3000 on up to $30,000 for the projector alone (not to mention the cost of the screen and professional installation, alignment, and focusing).

Traditionally, projection TVs used CRTs, or picture tubes, (like the ones used in old-fashioned tube TVs) to project the image on a screen. These systems are what you find in the cheapest rear-projection TVs on the market — and what people used to think of as a big-screen TV — but like tube TVs, CRT-based projectors are being slowly but surely phased out. While they offer a great picture, they are hard to set up (and keep properly aligned, focused, and calibrated), and they are big, heavy, and bulky.

The projector world has since moved on to *microprojector* systems, which use ultra-high-resolution chip-based picture engines instead of tubes. These microprojector systems are lighter, brighter, and significantly thinner (so they fit into your home, instead of you having to fit your home around them). They also offer excellent picture quality and don't require nearly as much tinkering to maintain picture quality.

Three main technologies are used for microprojection systems (for both front- and rear-projection TVs):

✔ **DLP:** An invention of Texas Instruments, DLP (www.dlp.com), or *digital light processor,* is a system that uses a chip containing millions of microscopic mirrors to reflect light onto the screen and make up a picture.

DLP TV systems have very high resolutions (most are now capable of 1080p), have a bright picture, and are excellent at color reproduction.

✔ **LCD:** LCD technology is familiar to most people due to the LCDs used for computer monitors, cell phone displays, and LCD flat-panel TVs (discussed in the next section). But LCD can also be used for a projection TV system, using three tiny (about 1" measured diagonally) LCDs through which a bright light is shined. Each of the LCDs handles a specific color (red, green, and blue), and the converged images make up a full-color image on the screen. LCD projection TVs are high resolution (HDTV). However, many are not capable of the full 1080p resolution and top out at 720p.

✔ **LCoS:** The newest technology for microprojection systems is called *liquid crystal on silicon* (LCoS). This technology, familiar to many through brand names such as Sony's SXRD, is a new variant of LCD technology that embeds the LCD crystals on a computer chip. The big functional difference is that LCoS systems *reflect* the light that makes up the picture instead of *transmitting* it through an LCD panel like LCD projection TV does. This provides a noticeably brighter picture. Like DLP, most LCoS projection systems are capable of 1080p resolutions.

When compared to the flat-panel TVs we discuss in the following section, projection TVs are a bit bulkier (at least the rear-projection units are), but they are cheaper and can offer a bigger picture. We think rear-projection systems offer the most bang for the buck for many users, while front-projection systems are the ultimate in big screen systems (think 100" diagonally).

Hang your TV on the wall: Flat-screen TVs

The hot item in the TV world today is the flat-screen TV. Similar to the screen of a notebook computer stretched to previously unimagined proportions, these new TVs use computer technologies such as LCD (liquid crystal diode) and plasma display systems to provide a large-screen television system that is usually only 4" or 5" deep. Hundreds of different models are on the market.

You can find flat-screen TVs at big home-electronics stores and warehouse clubs, as well as in more mainstream stores such as Wal-Mart and Target. The first models were super expensive, often costing $12,000 to $15,000. Since then there's been an explosion of manufacturers getting into the flat-panel TV game and prices have plummeted. Now you can easily find a 50" plasma HDTV for about $2000, only a few hundred dollars more than microprojection rear-projection TVs of the same size.

You can also find smaller and cheaper flat-panel TVs for those parts of your home that don't need (or can't fit) a big TV. The market is almost overrun with inexpensive 20" to 30" LCD TVs that can fit anywhere in your home — and often double as PC monitors to boot.

Making the plasma versus LCD decision

As folks shop for flat-panel TVs, many are confused about the choice between plasma and LCD, particularly as LCD TVs get bigger and bigger and begin to encroach into plasma territory. (It used to be easy: If you wanted 50" or more, you got plasma; smaller than 42", you got LCD.)

Well it *is* a difficult choice, but the good news is that you're choosing between two very good alternatives. Putting aside the pricing and size for a moment (though you should consider those too), let's look at the differences:

✔ Plasma TVs (and we're speaking generally here) have better color reproduction, better blacks, a wider viewing angle (meaning you can sit farther to the side and still see a good picture) and a smoother picture during rapidly moving scenes (such as in sports). On the downside, they tend to be heavier, run hotter, use more electricity, and are often limited to 720p resolutions (which isn't the end of the world, but more is always better when it comes to resolution).

✔ LCD TVs (again speaking generally) have higher resolutions, use less power and — most importantly to some folks — are not susceptible to *burn-in* (or image retention) when a static image (such as a video game) is on the screen for hours on end. Where LCD TVs fall down is in the viewing angle and in the *response time* (the measure of how quickly the picture changes on screen).

These lines get blurrier every day. For example, 1080p plasmas are now available, and most plasmas are pretty much immune to burn-in when used with just a modicum of care (for example, not leaving the stock ticker on for three days straight). And LCDs are being designed with wider viewing angles and faster response times to improve their viewing experience.

In the end, we still generally recommend plasma for really big flat panels (over 60") and LCD for the relatively smaller ones (37" and below). In between, we think the decision comes down to a TV-by-TV comparison rather than a technology-by-technology one.

The two technologies in the flat screen world are

✔ **Plasma:** These TVs use a special grid of electrodes that excite a gas into a plasma state, putting off light. Plasma TVs typically start off at 42" (though some smaller models are on the market), and the sweet spot for plasma begins at about 50". Most plasma TVs are limited to a 720p resolution, though the first 1080p plasmas are hitting the market as we write this.

✔ **LCD:** The same LCD technology used in projection TVs and computer monitors has hit the TV market with a vengeance, and hundreds of manufacturers are offering LCD flat-panel TVs of different sizes. For the most part, the sweet spot in the market for LCD is TVs smaller than 42", but several manufacturers have begun to offer LCD TVs that compete head-on with plasma in the 50" and above range. When comparing LCD to plasma, you will find that you pay a bit more for the same size screen, but you do get a full 1080p resolution.

If you're considering buying a flat screen, keep in mind that the same amount of money could buy a projection TV that's bigger and (potentially) has a better picture. However, nothing is cooler than hanging your TV on the wall.

Video source components

Video source components are the magic black boxes that let you record or watch movies, play games, watch the baby, or even surf the Web on your home's televisions. A huge number of video source components are on the market (and probably already in your home), including the following:

- ✔ VCR (videocassette recorders)
- ✔ PVR (personal video recorder) such TiVo or a PVR built into a cable or satellite set-top box, which uses a hard drive to record, store, and play back video

---

Serving up media

Over the past few years, the world of PCs and home-video and home-audio entertainment components have mixed in an exciting way. You can put a TV-tuner card in your PC and watch cable on it, or you can plug the PC into your TV and use its DVD player, online streaming video player, and MP3 jukebox to play back material on your audio/video network's big screen and good speakers. Perhaps the neatest development of all, however, is the rise of PC technology-based *media servers* that store videos, music, digital pictures, and other content on a hard drive and then connect to both your PCs and audio/video systems. With a media server, you can watch videos, listen to audio, and look at any digital pictures on *any* display devices or networked audio systems in your house.

PCs equipped with Media Center Edition software (Windows XP or Vista) are a great example of the current generation of media players, as are the multitude of MP3 audio jukebox devices that can store your CD collection on a computer hard drive. This initial generation of media servers sits next to your TV or audio amplifier and

plays back media over that local connection — much like a DVD player or CD player does today. Request (www.request.com) uses the TV as the interface to these media servers and allows remote servers to synchronize so that you never have to worry that your favorite song is on the other server. But like stand-alone players, media servers can be incorporated in your home-entertainment network so you can use them anywhere in the house.

Companies such as Apple Computer are also releasing media server devices, such as the newly announced Apple TV, which allows you to connect to your iTunes library on a Mac or PC to bring audio to your receiver and video to your TV over a networked connection. You can use the Apple TV to purchase and download movies from Apple's iTunes Store and play them back on your computer or on your TV whenever and wherever you want.

You can also build your own media server, using a fast PC with a big hard drive, the proper audio and video cards, and some specialized software. We talk about creating these PCs in Chapter 12.

PVRs are also often called *DVRs* (or digital video recorders)

✔ Laserdisc player (rare, but not quite gone yet)

✔ DVD (digital versatile disc or digital video disc) player — including the new high-definition variants, Blu-ray and HD-DVD

✔ In-home video devices such as a doorbell camera or a video baby monitor

✔ Video game machine

✔ PC (such as one outfitted with Windows XP or Vista Media Center Edition software) that can work as a PVR, an Internet content player, a DVD player, and more

Most folks tend to view these kinds of video source devices as dedicated, one-room components. If you want to watch a movie on the DVD player, for example, you go to the room that has the DVD player. In a properly networked home, however, you can connect your video source devices to your video network and use them from any TV in the house. (We show you how in Chapters 6 and 7!)

TV Connections from the Outside World

An important part of television is its capability to bring programming into your home from the world beyond. Like televisions themselves, these connections to the outside world are undergoing a series of major changes. New ways of receiving programming are becoming common, and established methods are revamping themselves for a digital world.

Broadcast TV

In spite of the proliferation of cable and satellite television and compact discs, old media such as broadcast television and radio are still alive and kicking. In addition, increasing consumer acceptance of DBS satellite television systems has resulted in a resurgence of demand for run-of-the-mill television antennas. Why? Unless you live in a big city, these systems might not carry programming from the big networks or local stations. If this scenario sounds familiar, you need to keep some level of cable television service or buy an antenna to watch local news or the local weather report.

Another factor behind the survival — and resurgence — of the antenna is the transition to HDTV and digital broadcasting. Most folks in the United States can now pick up several *free* over-the-air HDTV broadcasts and, with an HDTV with a built-in tuner, get HDTV for the cost of an antenna and some cabling.

Luckily, television antennas have improved too, so without spending too much money, you can avoid the nightmare of fine-tuning a set of rabbit ears on top of your television. The two general categories of television antenna are

- ✔ **Indoor antennas:** These antennas sit on or near your television.

- ✔ **Outdoor antennas:** These antennas mount on your roof or alongside your DBS satellite dish.

Whether your television antenna is outside or inside, you have to connect it to the TV. Most modern antennas use the same coaxial cable that cable television and DBS satellite systems use. (See Chapter 7 for strategies for wiring antennas into your video network.)

Choosing the right antenna for your location can be complex. Luckily, an online resource will do it for you. Just point your Web browser to www. antennaweb.org and click the button that says Choose an Antenna. The system asks you a few questions about your location and the type of home you have (for example, a single story versus multiple story) and then calculates the type of antenna you need to buy. As a bonus, the system tells you exactly which digital broadcasts are available in your area, and even gets down to the level of detail of telling you which way to point your antenna (if you need to use a directional antenna to pick up faraway signals). The Antenna Web system uses a color-coding scheme that matches the color codes on the boxes of the antennas in the stores (or online), so you can simply find the color (or colors) you need when shopping.

Cable TV

The prevalence of cable service nationwide makes it an important part of any home-networking strategy — for both you and future owners of your home. And with the range of services offered by cable companies, you can get a lot more than television (Internet access and even telephone service, for example).

The operation of a cable system is straightforward. A central office, or *head-end site* (similar to the central equipment office of the telephone company), receives television signals from various sources (mainly from satellite feeds as well as local over-the-air broadcasts). Cable companies then assign the signals to specific channels and distribute them over a combination of fiber-optic and coaxial cables (which, coincidentally, make up the final portion of the network that enters your home). The two types of cable TV systems are analog systems and digital systems. In most parts of the United States, analog systems are being phased out in favor of digital systems, but this transition will take years to complete.

When your cable system goes totally digital, you *will* need either a digital set-top box or a *digital cable-ready* TV (discussed in the upcoming "Digital cable" section) to receive TV stations in your home.

Analog cable

The channel system for cable is different than the one for over-the-air broadcast television. Therefore, the frequency of, say, Channel 20 on a cable system is likely different than the frequency of Channel 20 in a broadcast environment. What this difference means to a you as a homeowner is that you can't plug your cable TV feed into the back of any old television and expect it to work. Instead, you have two options:

- ✔ **Cable-ready television set or VCR:** You select a cable mode and then use the internal television tuner to decode and display the television signals. Most TVs made in the last few years are cable-ready, so all you have to do is plug the coaxial cable into the back of the TV and you're set (after you run through the setup routines to set the time, add the channels, and so forth).

  Note: Cable-ready TVs do have a few disadvantages. Most of these sets can receive only a limited number of channels. Second, these sets probably can't take advantage of special services from the cable company, such as digital cable, premium movie channels, and pay-per-view programs.

- ✔ **Set-top box (or converter):** These devices use a single broadcast channel (usually Channel 3 or 4) to feed the cable television signals to your television. With your television tuned to that single channel, you channel-surf through the set-top box. For digital cable services, which we discuss in a moment, you *must* use a set-top box or a special kind of cable-ready TV known as DCR, or digital cable ready.

Digital cable

Cable set-top services are becoming increasingly sophisticated. Most cable providers now offer a digital service, with two-way communications from the head end to the box and back again. The fancy set-top boxes used with these services have lots of extra built-in features, such as an onscreen program guide, reminder timers, VCR timers, and hard drives to store shows online for later viewing (PVR service, in other words). As an aside, this is an example of competition at work: When we wrote the first edition of this book, only DBS satellite systems offered this kind of neat TV functionality, but the cable companies responded to the threat and now match the DBS providers feature for feature.

Most digital television signals sent over digital cable systems (which aren't even all the channels you get — lower numbered channels are still sent in analog on most systems) are *not* ATSC, SDTV, or HDTV signals. They're just NTSC signals transmitted digitally using a system called QAM (quadrature amplitude modulation — say that fast three times!). Most cable companies are sending at least a few HDTV channels to their customers, but the majority of channels are still old-fashioned NTSC.

To tune into digital cable, you need one of the two following things:

- **A digital set-top box:** This is the modern-day equivalent of the cable converter, described in the previous section. Digital cable set-top boxes contain the QAM tuner that turns digital cable broadcasts into something your TV can display and the *conditional access* system that can unscramble premium channels. The digital set-top also includes an onscreen interface that lets you see a channel guide, program the PVR (if one is included), and select and view *Video on Demand* (VoD) programming.

- **A digital cable-ready (or DCR) TV:** A growing number of TVs, particularly HDTVs, include a QAM tuner that lets you plug directly into the cable TV feed to pick up analog and digital cable signals without a set-top box — including HDTV signals. A smaller subset of these TVs include a device known as the CableCARD (see the sidebar titled "What's the CableCARD all about?" for more on this), which handles the conditional access tasks so that you can view premium, scrambled channels without a set-top box.

What's the CableCARD all about?

The CableCARD system is a smart card that you can rent from your cable company and plug into a special slot on CableCARD-equipped TVs (and even other devices, such as TiVo PVRs or — in the near future — CableCARD-equipped PCs. The CableCARD lets you decode (unscramble) premium channels without a set-top box. It makes for a nice, neat installation, with just a single coaxial cable running from the wall into your TV.

Sounds great, huh? Well, there are problems. First, cable companies *prefer* to rent you a set-top box, so support for the CableCARD (although it is mandated by law) is weak. Second, and more importantly, the CableCARD is a one-way system that doesn't provide communications back to the cable company. So no onscreen program guide, no VoD, none of the fun new stuff that makes digital cable so attractive.

There is good news on this front, however. The FCC (Federal Communications Commission) has mandated that cable companies use the CableCARD system *within their own set-top boxes* by July 2007, so development of a two-way CableCARD system that supports onscreen guides and VoD is well under way. We think that CableCARD, as it exists today, is fine for the bedroom TV, but not so great for the main home-theater room. When the 2.0 (two-way) version becomes available, we think it will be an interesting alternative to a digital cable set-top box.

Satellite TV

Millions of homeowners are cutting the cord to cable TV and installing satellite TV receivers. Satellite TV, especially the new, small-dish varieties, can provide high-quality video programming — with more channels than all but a handful of cable systems — to homes just about anywhere in the world.

Direct broadcast satellite TV

If you look around your neighborhood, you've no doubt noticed a profusion of small (18" to be exact), white or gray satellite dishes popping up on housetops. These are receiving dishes for direct broadcast satellite (DBS) television.

Here's what you get when you choose DBS:

- **Channels galore:** Depending on which service and service level you buy, you can get hundreds of channels.

  HDTV channels are increasingly a big part of what DBS providers are offering.

- **Digital quality:** DBS systems use MPEG-2 to transmit channels digitally, reducing interference. The majority of these channels are NTSC, not ATSC. Also, as with digital cable, a few of the channels are in HDTV.

  Both of the big satellite TV providers — DISH network and DIRECTV — are moving towards a newer version of MPEG: MPEG-4. This will allow even more channels (including local channels and hundreds of HDTV channels) to become available on their systems. If you have an older satellite receiver and dish, however, you'll need to upgrade to pick up the new satellites broadcasting in MPEG-4

- **Audio channels:** Plug into your stereo or home theater for audio-only programming.

- **Easy-to-use graphical interfaces:** Easy-to-view menus, with telephone-line access to providers for pay-per-view programming.

- **Internet access:** With a slightly different dish, you can also have high-speed Internet access, as we discuss in Chapter 13.

As with everything, DBS has some downsides:

- **You might not get local programming:** In rural parts of the country, you still need a broadcast antenna or basic cable television service to view local channels and local news as well as broadcast (FOX, ABC, NBC, and CBS) programs.

✔ **You need a receiver:** The receiver acts like a digital cable converter box and converts the satellite's digital television signals to signals that your television can understand. If you have more than one television, you may want additional receivers for each TV because, like a cable converter box, the receiver puts out only one channel at a time. (We tell you how to share a single receiver with multiple TVs — but keep in mind that you'll be watching the same thing on each set.)

✔ **You need an available telephone line:** The receiver must be plugged into a telephone line to communicate with the DBS provider's headquarters for billing and service provisioning. This can be your normal phone line, because the system typically talks to headquarters in the middle of the night when most of us are asleep. Digital cable, however, talks back to the head end over the cable line, so it doesn't need that extra phone jack.

✔ **You need to be able to "see" the satellite:** You may have a hard time getting a satellite signal if you live in an area far away from the satellite's orbit. If you live in upstate Maine, for instance, you may have more problems getting an EchoStar signal than a DIRECTV signal because of the satellite's physical location. (In some cases, the dish has to be aimed so low towards the horizon that mountains and atmospheric clutter can get in the way.)

✔ **You have to install the system:** The system isn't hard to install, but something about getting up on the roof conjures up visions of back surgery. Of course, you can mount the dish on the side of your house or put it in the yard. One company even makes nifty fake rocks that cover the dish and keep your neighbors happy. And a growing number of companies will do the installation for free.

When we wrote the first edition of this book, DBS systems had a huge advantage over cable in terms of features and quality. As we mentioned earlier in this chapter, cable companies have reacted to this competitive threat, and now digital cable systems provide most of the same bells and whistles: digital transmission (of at least some channels), onscreen programming guides, music channels, and so on. We like both systems. Compare prices and features in your town before you decide. One new feature is video on demand, which lets you watch movies (for a fee) like you watch VCR tapes and DVDs — you can pause, rewind, and fast forward. This feature is more prevalent (for technical reasons) with digital cable than with DBS, but DBS providers are experimenting with built-in PVRs to allow a similar service on their networks.

Two competing DBS systems are currently on the market in the United States. Compare prices and services and choose the one you like best. As we write this, DIRECTV and EchoStar have agreed to a merger and are just awaiting regulatory approval. So don't be surprised if there's just one "choice" when you go shopping.

✔ **DIRECTV:** DIRECTV (www.directv.com) uses an 18" dish (bigger for some locations and for receiving all the new MPEG-4 broadcasts) and the digital MPEG system to send its audio and video signals. A variety of companies manufacture the widely available DIRECTV hardware — and a few TV manufacturers incorporate DIRECTV receivers into their high-end TVs.

✔ **EchoStar, or the DISH network:** EchoStar (www.dishnet.com) is similar to DIRECTV, using an 18" dish (or, like DIRECTV, bigger for local channels and MPEG-4) and digital MPEG encoding technology to transmit its video and audio. EchoStar sells their own receivers.

If you live in Canada, you're prohibited from getting DIRECTV or EchoStar service. These are legal prohibitions, not physical ones, because the satellite signals cover much of Canada. Bell Canada offers a similar system called ExpressVu (www.expressvu.com).

C Band

The grandfather of today's DBS satellite television systems is the C Band satellite system — those huge satellite dishes that used to sprout like monstrous mushrooms. At about seven feet across, the average C Band dish is expensive and difficult to place. Zoning restrictions keep C Band dishes out of many suburban areas, so you tend to see them only in rural areas. Still, in the early 1980s, having one of these dishes in your backyard meant that you could pick up channels from all over the world. Unfortunately, many of the channels that C Band systems once picked up for free are now encrypted, so you must subscribe to a service to receive them.

The advent of DBS and almost universal access to cable television has severely limited the growth of the consumer C Band marketplace. These days, most C Band users are either satellite hobbyists or businesses, such as hotels. Many television networks and cable systems also use C Band systems to distribute programming.

Satellites and your home

If you decide to go with a satellite dish, you may run into some resistance from homeowner's associations, neighborhood covenants, zoning laws, and the like. Don't take this lying down — the FCC ruled in 2001 that these laws can't be used to prevent you from installing a small dish (not a big C-band seven footer!). The only big exceptions are for safety (for example, you can't be too close to a power line) and for homes in historic districts. Otherwise, no one can keep you from using a dish if you want to. Know your rights. Look online at http://www.fcc.gov/mb/facts/otard.html for the long-winded bureaucratese text of this ruling.

C Band refers to the chunk of frequency spectrum allocated to these services. DBS satellite systems use the Ku band — though only hard-core satellite techie types call them Ku band systems.

Audio Systems

The other piece of the entertainment puzzle is an audio system — components that will play back your own music collection, radio, and the sound from movies, TV, and audio-only channels on cable and satellite systems. Today's audio systems are designed to reproduce audio signals in *high fidelity*. In other words, the equipment should recreate the music so that it sounds like it did in the studio or concert hall where your favorite recordings were made.

A high-fidelity sound system has several components:

- ✔ **Source component:** This component can be a CD player (or one of the new SACD or DVD audio players), a cassette deck, a radio tuner, a satellite tuner (such as an XM radio), an MP3 player or jukebox, or the audio portion of a video source such as a VCR, laser disc, or DVD. The source component produces a low-level audio signal — called a *line-level signal* — that's usually transmitted over an RCA cable.

- ✔ **Preamplifier or control amplifier:** This device amplifies (or increases the power of) the line-level signal and also serves as a switching device to allow you to select from different source components. The preamplifier also contains a volume control, which determines how much the signal is amplified. The control amplifier connects through another interconnect cable (or internal wiring if you're using an integrated amplifier) to the next stage in the sound reproduction process.

- ✔ **Power amplifier:** This unit adds more power to the audio signal — enough power to make your audio signal audible through the speakers. The preamplifier doesn't have enough power to drive your speakers. (Yes, we know it sounds silly to have two amplifiers, but that's just how it is.)

  Note: An *integrated amplifier* is a preamplifier and a power amplifier integrated into one component. Add a radio tuner to this box, and you have a *receiver*.

- ✔ **Loudspeakers:** Connected to the amplifier by speaker cables (what else?), the speakers use electromagnets to move sound drivers — the woofer and tweeter — back and forth. This movement, which corresponds with the audio signal coming from the amplifier, pushes the air in front of the drivers rhythmically, creating the sound waves that you hear. Loudspeakers can range from a full surround-sound five- or seven-speaker home-entertainment center to remote speakers in your kitchen or dining room to the intercom speakers throughout your house.

As audio systems expand from a single room to multiple rooms, a new breed of component has come onto the marketplace — the *multizone* system. Traditional audio systems have always been *single zone,* meaning that the control portion of the preamplifier — the switches that let you select which audio source you want to listen to — lets you select only one source at a time. This is fine for a stereo system that you're using in only one room (you can't really listen to more than one thing at once, right?), but this solution lacks flexibility for multiple rooms.

Newer, multizone systems have control sections that let you select more than one source component at once. You and your spouse can listen to a Dunne Roman CD in the living room and your kids can "emo" out to Fall Out Boy in the basement. As we mentioned, if you want to use a multizone system, you need additional amplifiers — one for each independent source that you want to play back at one time.

Intercom Systems

Unlike a stereo system, an intercom system isn't designed with the highest audio quality in mind. Its main function is to get your voice from point A to point B without weakening or incurring interference. Intercoms aren't cheap or unsophisticated; they just have a different mission.

Intercoms fall into two main categories:

✔ **Wireless systems:** These intercoms use radio *transceivers* (*trans*mitter and *re*c*eiver*) to carry voice signals from room to room. Just install a simple device on your desk, raise the antenna (and do the same with the other device), and you're ready to communicate. Variations on this theme include fixed wireless intercoms (which you can mount on the wall), portable baby monitors, and many cordless phones that use a speakerphone on the base station to create a simple, point-to-point intercom system.

✔ **Wired systems:** As the name implies, these intercoms are wired together and send your voice as an electrical audio signal between rooms. Wired intercom systems run the gamut from simple voice systems to advanced audio systems that can also carry radio and other audio signals. Figure 5-3 shows a typical wired intercom system. Some telephone systems have intercom systems; these are covered in more detail in Chapter 10.

Intercoms can be a useful feature (though phone networks can serve a similar function). Danny finds his intercom useful in his four-story house. The Fisher Price monitor that he and his wife used with the first set of twins has been replaced with a simple press of the Monitor button on the Nursery intercom unit. The babies' cries can now be heard all over the house. (Wait, is that good?)

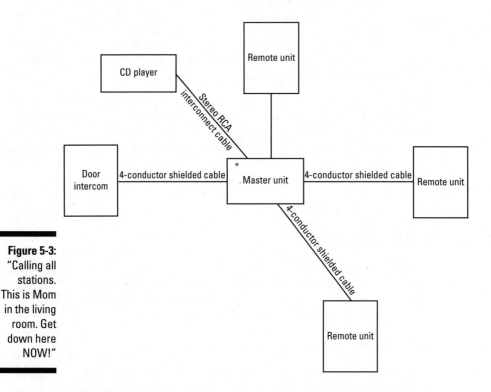

Figure 5-3: "Calling all stations. This is Mom in the living room. Get down here NOW!"

Most decent intercom systems have an *audio in* source option, too, whereby you can plug your home-entertainment system into your intercom system. By tying the two together, you save yourself money.

As you map your wiring runs, keep in mind that many intercom manufacturers void your warranty if you don't use their proprietary wiring systems. However, using their wiring is more expensive and goes against the idea of a uniform backbone over which all communications travel.

Chapter 6

Getting Video Where You Want It

*Y*ou can wire gobs of capabilities into a video network — a much greater variety of choices than is possible in most other networks we discuss (such as data networks or phone networks). That's the good news. The bad news is that we have to hold the number of pages in this book to less than that of the *Encyclopedia Britannica,* so we can't go into all the possible choices. On second thought, maybe that's good news, too, because rather than confusing you with a laundry list of all the different video possibilities and boring you with technical drivel on this super-video whatsit and that video-switching doodad, we concentrate on showing you how to wire the most common video network features. These features include the following:

✔ Coaxial video outlets in all rooms that may one day contain a television

✔ In-home video connections in rooms that may contain video sources, from VCRs to baby-monitor cameras

✔ Inputs for cable television and a broadcast TV antenna

✔ Provisions for adding a DBS satellite system to the network

✔ A central distribution node tying all this good stuff together

These devices, taken together, make up the video backbone in your smart home. The network we lay out for you uses *broadband RF video distribution* (whew!), which means most of your video is being distributed as "channels" of video that are picked up by TV tuners at various locations in your home. This type of distribution network takes care of the broadcast, cable, and satellite TV signals coming into your home and gets them to your TVs.

For in-home sources of video such as surveillance cameras or video sources that you want to share with other rooms such as DVD players, you can create your own TV stations that bring those signals from one point to another. The traditional approach for such in-home TV stations has the use of special devices called *video modulators,* which send the signals from video sources (such as VCRs or security cameras) through the wires in your walls and broadcast them on TV channels not used by your local or cable TV stations. Just tune to the right channel — like you tune to Channel 3 for your VCR — and you can watch these sources anywhere in your house. Unfortunately, for folks with digital cable or satellite systems, modulators don't always work reliably — or at all — because there simply aren't any empty channels available to use for your in-home sources. In Chapter 7 we talk about some systems that use wireless or CAT-5e/6 cabling (the cable used for computer networks) to get your video around the house.

In this chapter and the next, we take you through the process of wiring a home-video network backbone.

Distance Counts in Video Signals

You can get video signals from place to place in two basic ways: *baseband distribution* and *broadband distribution.* The difference between these two methods is in the amount of information that the cable carries. A baseband transmission carries only a single channel of video, so you generally use baseband cable for the connections between video components such as your DVD player and TV. Generally, baseband cables are short. Broadband (or *RF* — radio frequency) systems (such as coaxial cable used for antennas or cable TV), on the other hand, are designed to carry many video channels over greater distances.

Cabling between components (A/V interconnect cables)

Baseband video is the distribution of a single channel or program over a cable. The *Video Out* port on the back of VCRs, cable converters, satellite receivers, DVD and laserdisc players, and camcorders are baseband video signals, as are the *S-video* ports of the same devices (we discuss S-video in more detail shortly). In general, baseband video distribution is best suited for connections over a short distance, such as between components in the same room. Baseband video uses video patch cables to connect components in a system and requires audio patch cables to carry the corresponding audio signals — because you need both sets of cables, we refer to this set of cables as *A/V interconnect cables.*

Home systems commonly use three types of analog A/V interconnect video cables (which we list from least sophisticated to most sophisticated):

- ✔ **Composite video:** This connection system is on all video source devices. Composite video carries all components of an NTSC video signal over a single wire and connects devices using standard RCA or phono plugs — the same type of plugs used to connect stereo components such as CD players and amplifiers. See Figure 6-1. (For more on NTSC, the standard U.S. television system, see Chapter 5.)

- ✔ **S-video:** You find S-video on more sophisticated VCRs and on DVD players, DBS dishes, digital cable boxes, as well as on many camcorders. This method uses a single cable with multiple conductors to carry the brightness and color parts of a video signal separately, resulting in a better picture. See Figure 6-2.

- ✔ **Component video:** The majority of DVD players and most new televisions have component connections, usually in addition to composite and S-video connections. (You also find component video connections on some digital TV receivers — it's one of the most common ways of carrying HDTV signals to an HDTV.) Component video breaks down the video signal into three parts, each carried on a separate cable. This breakdown lets you avoid much of the internal circuitry in both your DVD player and your TV, so you get a better picture. At least that's what all of the videophiles we know tell us. You can see component video connectors in Figure 6-3.

Figure 6-1:
Composite video connector.

Figure 6-2:
S-video connector.

Figure 6-3:
Component
video
connectors.

When more than one of these options is available to you, always choose the most sophisticated. If your source and TV both have component video, use that. Most of these source devices also have an RF (antenna cable) output that works on Channel 3 or 4 of your TV, but you should consider this choice only as a last resort because the video quality will most likely be lower than one of the baseband connections.

In the digital video — HDTV — world, some *digital* video interconnects can replace the rat's nest of wires (up to nine of them) connecting digital TV receivers, DVD players, and other high-definition sources (such as the Sony Playstation 3 gaming console) to HDTV monitors.

Several competing efforts are underway to standardize connectors and incorporate a DRM (digital rights management — or copy protection) system. Following are the leading candidates in the fight for standardized digital interconnection of video equipment:

✔ **DVI, or Digital Video Interconnect:** This is a familiar connection to most PC owners, because DVI has been an option for connecting PCs to monitors for some time. In the TV world, a variant of DVI called DVD-D is included on many HDTVs and source devices (such as DVD players). DVI connections used in the TV world include a copy protection scheme called *HDCP* (High-Bandwidth Digital Content Protection), which is designed to keep users from making unauthorized copies of a program.

DVI is being slowly but surely phased out in new home-entertainment gear in favor of *HDMI*, discussed next.

✔ **HDMI, or High-Definition Multimedia Interface:** HDMI is, for all intents and purposes, a souped-up, supercharged replacement for DVI. HDMI is unique among *all* A/V interconnect technologies we discuss here because it carries both video *and* audio signals over a single cable. In addition, HDMI, unlike the other AV interconnects, can carry the highest quality HDTV signals (called *1080p*). Like DVI, HDMI includes the HDCP copy protection (or should we say, *prevention*) system. Figure 6-4 shows an HDMI connector.

✔ **FireWire, or IEEE 1394 (or one of many other brand names):** This is a more open, computer-like interface that isn't included on most TVs or video source devices, but a few manufacturers *do* use FireWire. It's most commonly found on PCs and Macs and on video cameras and is used to connect these devices to each other.

Figure 6-4:
The HDMI
cable and
connector is
your HDTV
choice.

Digital video connections such as HDMI are great — they offer both convenience and the utmost in picture quality. But digital video connections have some gotchas. That's because content owners — the TV and movie studios — want tight control over the *Digital Rights Management* (DRM) aspect of digital entertainment. Because you can make bit-for-bit perfect copies of digital material, they're pushing their own digital interconnect technologies that incorporate strong encryption and authentication techniques. These schemes tend to tie the material to a specific format and device, so they may keep you from using the media in a different way — such as playing it on your computer or recording it to watch in the bedroom or your vacation house.

Keep an eye on these standards as you shop for an HDTV. For most folks, HDMI is the connection of choice for HDTVs, but a few manufacturers are still pushing FireWire. Within the realm of HDMI, there are some variants — HDMI Version 1.3 is the latest version as we write in early 2007, and if you have the choice, it's the way to go.

Cabling the video-distribution network (broadband)

A broadband (or RF) video-distribution system combines many different video signals — and their corresponding audio signals — onto a single cable by *modulating* the signals onto different radio frequencies, or channels. In simplest terms, this process involves dividing the available bandwidth of a cable into equal parts (channels), and then placing the information representing the video program into one of these channels by varying the electrical signal in some standard way (this is the actual modulation). These frequency divisions correspond to the standard channels on your television, which has an internal tuner that demodulates the signal and displays it on the screen. Figure 6-5 shows how program signals are assigned by broadcasters or cable service providers to different frequencies (channels) and sent over the same cable.

Figure 6-5:
Modulating
multiple
channels
onto
different
radio
frequencies.

Broadcast and cable networks modulate multiple channels. (In the case of broadcast, the modulation doesn't use up bandwidth on a cable but rather divides the over-the-air radio frequency spectrum into smaller parts). Just about all video source devices include a broadband output — usually switchable between Channel 3 and Channel 4. An internal modulator converts the baseband video signal into a modulated video signal, and allows you to connect the source to older televisions that don't have baseband video inputs.

Coaxial Video Networks

Although you can create a video network without running cables (as described in Chapter 7), running cables for your network almost always increases performance, flexibility, and capacity. Wireless alternatives are usually more expensive than their cabled partners, and they do less. Bottom line: Anytime you can build a video network by running wires, we recommend that you do so.

The wired version of a video network is one that distributes video signals (separated into different channels) over coaxial cable to each television in your home. If you've had cable TV, you've had a network similar to what we describe, except that traditional cable TV networks have been paltry, one-way video networks in comparison to the two-way video-distribution system that we describe.

Cable-modem broadband services run on coaxial cable. Because they send data in two directions — as do the new digital cable set-top boxes — cable modems affect your coaxial video network design. We discuss the implications of these technologies as we go through building a network in Chapter 7.

Coaxial cable

Coaxial cable — usually called *coax* — is a metallic cable most often used for transmitting radio frequency (RF) signals such as broadband television video and radio signals. Coaxial cable has two conductors, or *axes*, that carry data. A layer of dielectric insulating material surrounds a single center conductor. The other conductor is a metal shield that goes around the dielectric (insulating) layer. The outermost layer of coax cable is an insulating jacket.

Coaxial cables are rated by their *impedance,* which is basically the AC version of electrical resistance. Different applications require different impedances. In the home, almost all systems that require coaxial cable use 75-ohm impedance coax, although some computer LAN systems (older ones, not commonly found in the home) use 50-ohm coax. (*Ohm* is the unit of measurement for impedance.) Table 6-1 lists the three main type of coaxial cable found in homes.

Table 6-1		Video Coaxial Cable Grades	
Coaxial Cable Type	*Cost*	*Use*	*Comments*
Unrated 75-ohm coax	Lowest	Older cable TV installations and aerial antenna-to-TV connections	This low grade of coaxial cable suffers from high resistance to the video signal and provides poor picture quality. Not recommended for video networks.
RG-59 coax	Medium	Cable TV and antenna-to-TV connections	This is the standard grade of coaxial cable found in most existing installations, suitable for standard cable TV and broadcast antenna use.
RG6 coax	Highest	Cable TV, DBS, and cable-modem connections	This is the highest grade of coaxial cable found in the home. It provides the best resistance from interference and the least amount of signal degradation. Required for DBS and cable-modem installations and recommended for all new installations.

You may encounter coaxial cables labeled RG6QS or RG6 Quad Shield, which means that the cable has four layers of additional shielding beneath the cable jacket. These layers provide additional protection from external interference. The difference between RG-59 and RG6QS is similar to the difference between CAT-3 and CAT-5e/6 UTP cables, which we discuss in Chapters 11 and 15. They look similar and do similar things, but the higher-rated cable is a bit more capable of carrying your signals cleanly — and for longer distances. The price difference is minimal, and we strongly recommend that you choose RG6QS for your coaxial cabling needs; the small extra cost ensures that your wiring can handle the future needs of your network. In fact, applications such as DBS require RG6QS and specifically tell you not to use RG-59.

Coax connectors

Like almost all the networking cable we cover, coaxial cables use standardized connectors. Residential applications use only one type of connector — the *F connector,* which is shown in Figure 6-6. If you have cable television, you're already familiar with this screw or push-on connector.

Figure 6-6: RG6 coaxial cable and F connectors.

RG6 coax without F connector

Female F connector

Male F connector

Like most connectors, F connectors come in male and female versions. In general, female connectors are on video equipment and wall outlets, and male connectors are used to attach the cables to these outlets.

Components

The cable and connectors are the permanent parts of your video-network infrastructure — the parts that you put in your walls and expect to keep there for 20 years or so. The other components that your video network needs, such as distribution panels and modulators, will probably be less permanent members of your household electronic family. Over time, your network needs may change and new technologies such as digital television will become available, precipitating changes in some of your network components. These changes will cost money (the price of progress?), but the main part of your investment — namely the materials and labor used in installing the coaxial cabling in your walls — will remain intact and useful.

Outlets

If you're like us, you don't want coaxial cables and F connectors dangling out of holes in the wall. Luckily, an assortment of coaxial cable in-wall outlets fit into standard electrical junction boxes and use standard faceplates. Dozens of companies manufacture these outlets, which come in many combinations and sizes. If your budget allows, we recommend running two RG6 cables to each room. The first coaxial cable allows you to receive video signals from an external source such as cable TV. The second lets you send out video signals — from devices such as DVD players or baby monitors — to the rest of the home. You might not want to run two cables to every spot in your home, but certain areas will require that you do.

A coaxial outlet for this cabling consists of two female F connectors, one above the other, in a compact, single-gang junction box. Single-gang means that the Dalton boys don't ride with Jesse James. Okay, *gang* simply refers to the size of the box and cover. For reference, a single-gang junction box is the same size as a typical two-receptacle electrical outlet or a single light switch. Many twin coaxial outlets have large faceplate openings and use a standard-sized faceplate called a Leviton Decora. (These are the same faceplates accompanying large light switches in many newer homes.)

As you design your home networks, you may find that you want to put several different kinds of outlets together on a wall — speaker connections for an audio network, a phone line or two, and your coaxial outlets, for example. Consider using a larger double- or triple-gang junction box and installing a multipurpose outlet that can terminate all these cables in one place. Most major outlet manufacturers make all sorts of combination outlets.

Low-voltage signals such as coaxial video networks don't get along with AC power lines. You should keep at least three feet between the two to avoid noise and interference. Never try to connect your coaxial lines and power lines in the same junction box — the result is a mess. If you're building a house, make sure that the electrical and communications cables are not through the same holes in the studs — some contractors do this, thinking that it's compact and tidier.

Distribution panel

The key component in your video network is the *distribution panel*. This device is the central node for your video network — all coaxial lines to the various rooms of your house begin here. A distribution panel has several functions:

- ✔ It accepts one or optimally more coaxial, broadband, or video signal input.

- ✔ It combines these input signals into a unified broadband output.

- ✔ It splits this output to feed *multiple video endpoints* (in other words, televisions).

- ✔ It amplifies the outgoing signals to make them stronger (because splitting the signal weakens it).

Figure 6-7 shows a typical video-distribution panel.

Figure 6-7: The distribution panel is the center of a video network.

Note: All cables are RG6 coax with F connectors.

When you're shopping for a video-distribution panel, look for the following:

- ✔ **Number of inputs:** Choose a unit that has at least two (and preferably more) inputs. Doing so allows you to take a local video source (such as a DVD player) and distribute its signals throughout your home, instead of to the nearest TV.

✔ **Number of outputs:** Each television that you want to connect to your video network needs its own output on the distribution panel. These panels are engineered to maintain the proper signal strength and quality when used in a "one television per outlet" way. If you try to cheat and use a coaxial splitter to connect an extra television to a single output, you're throwing away the design and engineering expertise that went into the panel, and you probably won't be happy with the results. Most panels have from 5 to 12 outputs, so you should be able to satisfy your home's needs without having to install a second panel.

Distribution panels are often described as 3 x 8 or 5 x 12. The first number is the number of inputs, the second is the number of outputs.

✔ **Amplification:** To maintain a signal that's strong enough to produce a good television picture, you need to amplify the signal. Most distribution panels have built-in amplifiers that take care of this for you. Sophisticated models have different levels of amplification so that some outputs are optimally amplified for shorter cable runs, and others are optimized for longer runs.

Why different levels of amplification? Because overamplifying a signal is almost as bad as underamplifying it. Panels that have different tiers of amplification typically have several outputs designated for short distances (0 to 50 feet, for example) and some for longer runs (perhaps for 50 to 150 feet). Models with several outputs (such as the 5-x-12 panel) may even have a middle tier of distance ranges.

If you're using a digital cable service, make sure you chose a bidirectional video-distribution panel. Many older-design distribution panels don't let signals flow back through them onto the cable network. Because digital cable set-top boxes communicate back to the cable network, you need to choose a distribution panel that will let them do this! You can also find distribution panels with a cable-modem bypass that lets you keep your cable modem out of the loop — further reducing the possibility of your distribution panel's amplifier causing interference and slowing down your Web surfing.

More than you ever wanted to know about modulators

After the RG6 cabling and multiple-input distribution panel are in place, you have the makings of a two-way, whole-home video network. Now you just need an easy way to select the source you want to watch. That's where modulators come in. A *modulator* translates a source's baseband video and audio signals into a standard TV RF channel — just like the ones that broadcast and cable companies send you. So that they don't interfere with existing channels, modulators must be *frequency agile*. In other words, instead of transmitting on only a single frequency, modulators must be capable of transmitting over a range of frequencies (or TV channels), so that you can adjust them to an open channel on your system.

Following is a typical scenario for modulator use. Suppose that you have a main VCR in the living room, a baby monitor in the nursery, and a PVR and a DBS satellite receiver in your home-theater room. You want to be able to view any of these signals on any TV in the house. No problem. You just need a modulator that can modulate four inputs onto different channels on your coaxial cable, so that they're available at each jack in the house. Perhaps Channel 87 is the baby monitor, Channel 89 is the VCR, Channel 91 is the PVR, and Channel 93 is the satellite receiver. When you want to watch one of these devices somewhere else in the house, you tune to the appropriate TV station. Simple!

You probably have several modulators already: in your VCR, in your DVD player, in your laserdisc player, or in your DSS receiver. However, these modulators give you only two choices — Channel 3 or 4. Their sole purpose is to provide a means of connecting these devices to televisions that lack separate, baseband A/V inputs. In most television networks, Channels 3 and 4 aren't unoccupied, so these modulators make use of an internal switch (the VCR/TV button on your VCR's remote) that disconnects the antenna or cable feed to the TV, preventing interference with existing channels.

Chances are that you won't be able to use these Channel 3 and 4 modulators for distributing video throughout the home because your coax will have existing cable or over-the-air channels. (The VCR/TV switch works for a TV connected directly to the device but doesn't work for the whole house.) Even in the unlikely event that you don't have existing channels on Channels 3 or 4, building a Channel 3/4 modulator into a source device won't do much for a whole-home network because you can add only one source device for the entire house. You can't modulate more than one device onto a single TV channel. And even if Channels 3 *and* 4 are unoccupied, modulators shouldn't be used on adjacent channels.

Think about the following when you're choosing a modulator:

- ✔ **Digital or analog:** Analog modulators are much cheaper than digital ones, but they usually aren't as flexible in the frequencies you can choose from, so you have to buy a modulator that is factory-set to the channel you have available. Analog models tend to drift off stations just like those old dial radios did, requiring frequent readjustment. Digital models, though more expensive, are more reliable and accurate; you basically set them once and forget them.

- ✔ **Single or multichannel:** You can buy modulators that translate a single video source onto a single television channel, or you can buy ones that translate up to four separate input sources onto four different output channels. A multichannel unit may better serve your needs for two reasons:

  - • A multichannel unit allows you to distribute the video signals from several collocated video sources (such as in a home-theater room) throughout your whole house.

- With a multichannel modulator, you eliminate the confusion and complexity of using coaxial splitters to increase the number of internal video inputs on your distribution panel.

✔ **Mono, stereo, or no audio:** Most modulators transmit the audio output of your source device as *monaural audio* — no stereo separation, no surround sound, just mono (the same thing out of both speakers). Even if they have two inputs (for left and right channel audio), they're probably mono. You can buy modulators that transmit *MTS* (the stereo system that TVs use), but they cost significantly more. If you're installing a modulator that will be carrying the video from a surveillance camera, you can save money by purchasing a modulator that has no sound input.

✔ **Shape and size:** Modulators don't come in a standard shape and size. You can choose from the following options:

  - **Black box:** These modulators don't look pretty, but they will fit in with the rest of the stuff on your A/V equipment shelf.

  - **Wall outlet size:** Much less obtrusive are modulators that fit in a standard wall outlet gang box. The same size as a light switch (or a coaxial outlet), these miracles of miniaturization make sense for places where you don't have a huge rack of video equipment in place.

  - **Distribution panels:** You can get modulators out of the room entirely by purchasing an all-in-one distribution panel that has a modulator or two built right into the same box. This option limits you because your source devices must be close to the distribution panel — that VCR on the third floor is out of luck!

✔ **Loop-through capability:** Many modulators offer something called an *A/V loop through*. Many source devices — except for some DBS receivers and DVD players — have only one set of baseband video and audio outputs. If you plug these into a modulator, you don't have any way to make a baseband A/V connection to the local TV — you have to use the source's built-in Channel 3/4 modulator instead. The loop through provides an extra set of baseband video and audio outputs on the back of the modulator so you can connect to the local TV directly using composite or S-video cables, instead of using the modulated signal routed back through the distribution panel.

When you're using a modulator system to create your own TV channels in your home, keep the following points in mind:

✔ **Install a signal amplifier between your antenna and the distribution panel or modulators:** When you create your own TV channel, you're doing pretty much the same thing in your house that cable companies and broadcasters do at their head-end offices and stations. If you're using an antenna feed to receive broadcast TV stations, you could end up sending your video out your antenna and over the airwaves (and into your neighbor's TV perhaps). The FCC doesn't like this idea, so it requires you to install a signal amplifier between your antenna and the distribution panel or modulators. Amplifiers are inherently one-way — signals don't pass back through them — and they help pick up those distant stations better. Bidirectional amplifiers let signals go both ways, but the ones going back upstream to the cable company are low-frequency signals that won't interfere with television channels.

✔ **Skip channels between modulated channels:** Most modulator manufac-turers recommend that you skip at least one channel between modu-lated channels to avoid interference.

✔ **Be aware of signal interference:** Channels that your TV can't pick up may still be strong enough to interfere with your internal channels — this is often the case in the higher UHF band for broadcast TV. The same can apply to cable TV — just because you don't subscribe to a particu-lar channel doesn't mean that its signal isn't taking up bandwidth space on your coax. If this problem occurs, adjust the modulator to a different channel.

✔ **Make sure you have free channel space:** Channel space isn't much of a problem if you use an antenna — even the most crowded urban areas have plenty of unused channels. However, cable service providers in many areas are beginning to saturate their available channels with pro-gramming. They're also using TV channels for other services, such as cable modems and audio services. So if you're planning on modulating several channels onto your network, do your homework and make sure you'll be able to find open channels. You can do this by physically look-ing at channels you think are unused on one of your televisions (making sure a scrambled signal isn't there) and by checking the complete listing of channels provided by your cable service provider.

Chapter 7

Wiring a Video Network

*I*n Chapters 5 and 6, we spend a fair amount of time talking about all the pieces and parts that fit into a video-distribution network. That's important stuff to know — but it doesn't do you much good if you don't have everything connected properly. So in this chapter, we tell you about the model to use in setting up your network. The technical term for this model is *topology* or *network architecture,* but don't be intimidated. These words just mean a way of thinking about your network so that you know what to connect where.

We tell you how to get the right cables in the walls (and how to buy the right infrastructure devices) to create a futureproof, two-way video network. Maybe you don't plan to install all the equipment that we describe in Chapters 5 and 6 right away. No problem. As long as you get your wires in place, the general network model that we describe in this chapter will serve you well as your needs change and grow in the future.

Don't feel like you have to wire a video network (or any network) yourself. If you're hesitant about drilling holes and running cables through your walls, do yourself a favor and hire a professional.

The discussion of video networks and especially that of modulators is probably the toughest in the book. You might need to reread some sections a few times. That's okay. We get confused here too. Stick with it, because video entertainment is the heart of your smart home.

Another warning to you — and again it's a warning about modulators. Many folks have digital cable or satellite TV systems as their main source of "outside the home" video programming. These systems make it very difficult, if not impossible, to use modulators as a technique for distributing "inside the home" video sources. If you have one of these systems as your TV source, we recommend that you look at other alternatives, such as video-over-CAT-5 cabling or wireless, for in-home distribution. We talk about these systems in the second half of this chapter.

Connecting Your Video Network

The fundamental building block of your video network is the coaxial cable. We recommend that you build your whole-home video network with two segments of RG6 coaxial cable connected to each video outlet that you install in your major rooms — one cable that brings video into the TV and one cable that allows you to distribute video source devices (such as VCRs) through the network. Specifically, you should have at each location:

- **An external video connection:** This connection carries video signals from your distribution panel to your television. Think of *external* as *outbound*.

- **An internal video connection:** This connection carries video signals from any source devices in the room back to the distribution panel, where they can be combined with your external video source (cable or broadcast TV) and sent back out on the outbound lines. Think of *internal* as *inbound*.

Note: We use the words *external* and *internal* in reference to the central hub of the video network, the video distribution panel. *External,* or *outbound,* means away from the video distribution panel, and *internal,* or *inbound,* means toward the video distribution panel.

Consider running four RG6 cables (two double outlets) to your home office and your media room or home-theater room. You might need the extra capacity or you might decide you want to rearrange the furniture. (It sure helps to have an identical set of outlets on the other side of the room when you switch the sofa and the TV to opposite walls.)

Running just one outbound coaxial cable allows you to receive signals in that room and may be sufficient for rooms in which you don't intend to send any video sources back through the network. However, it's hard to predict which rooms will fall into that category.

Figure 7-1 shows the layout of a typical, centrally connected, coaxial video network. In the next sections, we walk you through the network, from a single room back to the distribution panel.

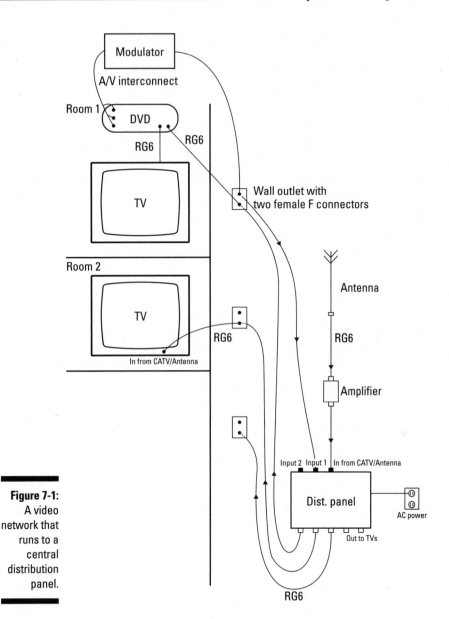

Figure 7-1:
A video
network that
runs to a
central
distribution
panel.

If you use digital cable and also want to use modulated sources, building a
video network can get complicated. Digital cable systems do some funky
things with their signals *and* use up a lot more of the frequency spectrum. So
you'll have a hard time even finding a free channel to modulate your source
devices onto. In the "Dealing with digital cable" sidebar, we talk about some
ways to get around this problem.

Dealing with digital cable

Digital cable is a great service. Tons of channels, a neat on-screen program guide, and more. Unfortunately, the sheer number of channels and the different channel structure used by digitally transmitted channels (typically, the lower channels are still transmitted in analog) make it hard to find empty slots in the bandwidth in which to insert your modulated programming. Even if you find an empty channel, there's no guarantee that it will stay open — cable providers constantly add channels and reshuffle their lineups. To make things more complicated, the channel numbers you see on your digital cable set-top box (for example, 200 for HBO) don't equate to the channel numbers you select on your modulator.

If you have digital cable and want to use a two-way, modulated video network, you can try the following:

✓ **Talk to your cable company:** Ask the installer or call the technical support line — see whether they'll identify some open channels for you.

✓ **Use a notch filter to block out a chunk of channels:** This isn't an elegant solution. *Notch filters* block multiple channels (often five to ten), not just one. So you might lose access to some channels you want. Notch

filters start at around $70 to $80, and the price goes up rapidly as the width of the notch (the number of channels being blocked) gets smaller because blocking fewer channels is more difficult.

✓ **Separate the digital cable signals onto a different RG6:** This scenario is similar to how satellite TV signals are incorporated into a video network (discussed in the "Special Needs of Satellite Systems" section). You'd need a third RG6 cable for locations using a digital cable set-top box. Instead of being connected to your distribution panel, these cables would be patched together in a physically separate network (using a splitter from the cable company or another distribution panel). Modulated video from in-house sources would then be distributed over the other two RG6 cables.

✓ **Skip the modulation and use a different network to distribute internal video sources:** We describe these systems at the end of the chapter (video over CAT-5e, wireless, and phone lines).

We think the last two approaches are the best ways to go. And using a good installer — someone who's familiar with your local cable company — can really pay off.

As we discuss in Chapter 6, digital cable set-top boxes *and* cable modems need to send data back upstream to your cable company. You might wonder if internal RG6 cables can carry this data — the answer is no. Cable modem and digital cable upstream data goes back up the *external* cable. The key here is to buy a video distribution panel that is labeled bidirectional and that allows data to pass back through the amplifier and onto the cable provider's network. Look for these words on the manual: *a 5 to 42 MHz return path.*

TIP

Where does HDTV fit in?

High-definition TV (HDTV). The mere words make us smile. Widescreen TV images with film quality. Is your video network going to be ready for it? Or for any of the new digital television (DTV) variants we discuss in Chapter 5?

In most cases, the answer is yes (aren't you glad?). DTV signals are compatible with the standard RF infrastructure (RG6 cabling) that carries today's NTSC signals. The only thing to keep in mind is that many over-the-air DTV broadcasts use higher frequencies and have larger variations in signal strengths than do regular broadcast and cable TV stations. So to handle HDTV, you must have a high-quality distribution panel and amplifiers. The major vendors of these systems — such as Channel Plus

(www.channelplus.com) or Leviton (www.leviton.com) — offer amplifiers and distribution panels that are HDTV capable, and they often clearly label them so (using an official DTV logo authorized by the ATSC — the group that sets the standards for DTV).

Modulators are a different story. They're designed to work with yesterday's NTSC analog TV standard. As new video source devices (such as digital VCRs or high-definition DVDs) are developed to record or display HDTV/DTV pictures, your existing modulators won't be able to do anything with those signals. In the long-term, you'll probably need to replace your modulators. By then, there will be modulators designed to deal with HDTV signals.

Filling your walls: Running the cables

When wiring a video-distribution network, the first task is to run two RG6 coaxial cables between the distribution panel and each area of the house where you want video outlets. You'll probably want to hire a professional cable installer to run this cable for you. For an attractive appearance, the cables should connect to wall-mounted female coaxial connectors, as described in Chapter 6.

TIP

To make connection and future system changes easier, label your RG6 cables. At a minimum, you need to know which room the cable is coming from and whether it's the internal or external line. (Nothing inherent about a cable makes it internal or external — it's just the logical use you apply to the cable.) We recommend that you buy RG6 cable in two colors (it usually comes in white or black); use one color for all internal runs and the other for all external runs.

Tying it together: Making connections at the distribution panel

If you do everything right when completing the steps in the preceding section, you should have a gob of cables running into a central point, which we call the *central wiring closet* (see Chapter 2 for more info on the wiring closet). Here's how to connect these wires to your distribution panel to complete your network:

1. **Connect each external RG6 coaxial cable to one of the distribution panel's external female connection interfaces.**

   If your distribution panel comes with multiple levels of amplification, take the time now to double-check the amplification levels. Each of your meticulously labeled cables should be connected to outputs with amplification levels that correspond to the distance of each cable run. (Check the manufacturer's recommendations — often each output has a recommended distance label right next to where the cable plugs in.)

2. **Connect each internal RG6 cable into one of the modulator inputs (sometimes labeled *local*) on your distribution panel.**

   You may find that you have more internal video cables in your wiring closet than you have inputs (remember that most panels have five or fewer inputs). If you don't have any video sources connected to a particular cable, you can leave it disconnected — but well labeled — until you need it.

   If you *still* don't have enough inputs on your panel, you can use a good quality splitter/combiner to connect two or more internal cables to a single panel input. If you choose this option, don't try to save a few bucks on a cheap splitter/combiner — the 99-cent specials from your local discount store are worth exactly what they cost (next to nothing). Spend $15 or $20 on a high-quality model from a manufacturer such as ChannelPlus (www.channelplus.com) or Channel Vision (www.channelvision.com).

3. **Connect the RG6 cable from your antenna or cable TV feed to the Antenna/CATV input on the distribution panel.**

   If you're using modulators and an antenna to pull in local broadcast stations, you need to install an amplifier between the antenna and the distribution panel — otherwise you can actually start broadcasting your internal video over your antenna and out to the world. You probably don't want to be doing this (for many reasons), and the FCC wants you doing this even less. Most manufacturers of distribution panels have such signal amplifiers for sale, as well — use the amplifier that they recommend for your specific distribution panel.

   You can't simply plug the output of your DSS satellite system into your distribution panel's Antenna/CATV input. Read the "Special Needs of Satellite Systems" section, later in this chapter, for information on this unfortunate phenomenon.

Most distribution panels (except those without built-in signal amplification) need electrical power to do their job. The majority use a small *wall wart* AC/DC power adapter like those used by cordless phones, modems, and tons of other small electrical appliances. Make sure you install a nice quad electrical outlet nearby — we always seem to be adding something in our wiring closets that needs power.

As we mentioned, if all this two-way video sounds like something that you'll never, ever want to get involved with, you *can* build a similar video-distribution network that forgoes the second RG6 cable to each outlet. Just follow the same basic architecture guidelines — all outlets individually wired with a length of RG6 cable running back to your central distribution node — and skip the second cable run. At the risk of being repetitive, we think this type of abbreviated network is a false economy, but it's a perfectly valid way of constructing a home-video network. If you set up your network this way, we strongly recommend that you at least run a second cable to the room containing your home theater or media center. Chances are that's where you have all the fun source devices, and a second cable there gives you the opportunity to share those sources throughout your home later.

Hooking up: Making connections in the TV rooms

With the cables run, it's time to connect the TVs and video source devices in each room to the network. Figure 7-2 shows typical *in-room* video connections.

Figure 7-2:
Plugging
video
equipment
together.

Assuming that you've finished making your cable runs between the rooms and the distribution panel, just follow these steps:

1. **Determine the video source devices (such as a VCR, DVD player, video-capable PC, or camcorder) that you want to distribute to other areas of the house, and connect them to a *modulator*, typically using an RCA or S-video cable.**

   Modulators allow you to broadcast a device's video signal around your house over an unused TV channel. We explain modulators as well as RCA and S-video cables in detail in Chapter 6.

   If you have several video source devices in the same room (such as your home-theater room with a PVR and a DVD player), you can use a multichannel modulator to broadcast multiple audio and video signals onto unused channels.

2. **Run a length of RG6 coaxial cable with male connectors on both ends from the output jack of your modulator to the *internal* female coaxial connector jack in the wall.**

   A coaxial wall jack is basically a faceplate with a female connector sticking out both sides. Remember that your point of reference for *internal* is inbound to the distribution panel. So when you're standing in the room with the TV, the internal jack runs *out* of the room toward the distribution panel. If you think about it too long, you'll get a headache.

3. **Connect another length of RG6 cable with male connectors between your TV or cable set-top box and the *external* connector on your coaxial outlet.**

   If you're using a VCR or PVR, it should be connected in-line between the wall outlet and the television or set-top box with an RG6 coaxial cable. Use another RG6 coaxial cable to connect the output of the VCR or PVR to the TV. You can also use RCA or S-video cables from the Audio and Video Out jacks of the VCR or PVR to the Audio and Video In jacks on the TV. Figure 7-3 shows the signal path for watching a VCR in another room.

   If your VCR or PVR is connected to a modulator that has a loop-through connection (see Chapter 6), you can use these outlets and RCA cables to connect your VCR to your TV.

4. **Perform Steps 1 through 3 for each room and pair of coaxial cables in your network. Lather, rinse, and repeat as desired.**

You now have a whole-home video network up and running! However, your work isn't finished. You still need to program each modulator to an unused channel. We're not going to give you step-by-step instructions on this task because each manufacturer's model is different. For the most part, though, digital modulators are easy to tune in — it's just a matter of pressing a program button a few times. Many models even have LCD or LED digital displays so that you can't mess up.

Figure 7-3:
Watching a
VCR or PVR
in another
room.

Summing Up

The information in this chapter is a lot to grasp in one big gulp, so we thought
we'd step back and give you a quick recap of what goes where in your whole-
house video network:

✔ In the wiring closet:

- RG6 coaxial cable feeds from your antenna, or cable company, or
  both

- A coaxial distribution panel to tie everything together (some vendors call these RF distribution panels)

- An amplifier (may be built into the distribution panel) to boost
  antenna signals and to keep modulated signals from being broadcast over your antenna (optional for cable TV)

✔ In each room:

- Two RG6 cables connected to the distribution panel (one to the in
  side of the panel, and one to the out side). Optionally, home offices
  and media rooms get four RG6 cables for extra flexibility.

- An additional RG6 cable for the satellite receiver (optional).

As long as you've installed a bidirectional distribution panel and an amplifier, you should be able to install a cable modem onto any of the external RG6 outlets in your house. An even better approach, however, is to get a distribution panel with a bypass for the cable modem (as we mention in Chapter 6). In this scenario, you just need to connect one of the RG6 cables running to your home office (or wherever the cable modem ends up in your house) to this bypass, instead of to one of the outputs of the distribution panel.

Special Needs of Satellite Systems

DSS (Digital Satellite System) small-dish satellite systems are a great way to receive TV programming, but they're sort of a pain to integrate into your video network. The frequencies that satellite systems use and the way that coaxial cables carry the signal are different than those for standard TV signals. You can't connect your satellite to your video distribution panel's connector and distribute it through your house. To integrate a satellite into your network, you have to be a bit devious. In this section, we tell you how.

We provide two methods of running your DSS satellite signal across your video network. The difference between these methods depends on whether or not you want a two-way network that can bring video back from various rooms.

Running a one-way satellite network

You may be thinking to yourself, "Heck, I've got this dish, so I don't need cable." And we have just the solution. You can build a video network for your DSS system that will carry the outputs from a DSS dish to multiple receivers throughout the home by using a multiswitch instead of a distribution panel. The downside to using a multiswitch is that the satellite network is one way. You still have to install a distribution panel if you want to share video sources across the network as we describe in the "Connecting Your Video Network" section, earlier in this chapter. If you want a two-way network with a satellite, check out the following section on a hybrid video network.

To run your satellite picture to different receivers around your home, you need to replace the distribution panel with a special device known as a *multiswitch,* or *voltage switch.* The multiswitch connects to both outputs of a dual LNB (low noise block) dish and provides coaxial connections for up to four separate receivers. You simply use RG6 coaxial cable to connect each LNB output to your multiswitch and then run individual lengths of RG6 to each receiver location.

Some DSS dishes include *integrated multiswitches,* so you don't need to buy anything extra. Just run RG6 cables from the back of the dish (where the multiswitch is located) down to the receiver locations.

In some locations, you can't get signals from the major broadcasts networks (such as Fox, NBC, CBS, or ABC) with a satellite. Nor can you get any local independent channels. You have to hook up an aerial antenna or get the basic package from your local cable company.

If you're interested in running an aerial TV antenna to pick up local stations, buy multiswitches that accept the output from a broadcast TV antenna and carry it over the same RG6 cables to your DSS receivers and televisions. These multiswitches include a device called a *diplexer* (check out the sidebar "What if I just want satellite and none of that fancy stuff?"), which lets you integrate both the satellite and local TV signals onto the same RG6 coaxial cable.

Creating a hybrid satellite/video network

The drawback to using a multiswitch as the hub of your video network (as we describe in the preceding section) is that it creates a one-way network — from the satellite dish to the TV. If you want to be able to watch in one room video that's sent from a device in another room (whether from a VCR, a DVD player, or a video camera in your baby's room), you need to use a separate distribution panel for the return signal (or use alternate technologies such as CAT-5e, wireless, or phone line systems — which we describe later in the chapter).

You have a couple of options if you want to get the best of both worlds in a hybrid two-way satellite/video network:

✔ **Build a separate video network for your satellite.** Build a video-distribution network for your DSS dish, with independent runs of coaxial RG6 cable from the dish, down through the attic (or from wherever the dish is mounted), and on to each location that will have a satellite receiver. With a multiswitch connected to the outputs of your satellite dish, you can connect up to four separate receivers to a dish. You can then build a video-distribution network using a distribution panel to handle the return signals and any signals you receive from cable or broadcast TV.

The benefit of this system is that it gives you the ability to watch up to four DSS channels on four TVs simultaneously, while still allowing you to, say, watch in your bedroom a tape playing in a VCR in the home-theater room. The drawback of this system is the added expense and complexity of building a separate network — more cable to run and more equipment to buy.

Although most people mount the multiswitch right at the dish, you might also consider mounting the multiswitch in your wiring closet (vendors such as Leviton and Siemon make rack-mounted versions you can install right next to your video-distribution panel). In this scenario, you'd just run two RG6 cables from the dish to the wiring closet (to connect the two satellite LNBs to the inputs of the multiswitch), and then add another RG6 out to each room that will have a satellite receiver. In fact, if you're not using a modulator in these rooms, you can take the second RG6 from that room (the internal one) and connect it to the multiswitch instead of the distribution panel — so you don't need a third RG6 for satellite in that room.

✔ **Treat your DSS receivers as source devices — just like VCRs or DVD players.** You still need separate RG6 cabling runs from the dish to the receivers, but you can then use modulators to send the output of these receivers to every television in the house. Just install receivers in your two favorite watching areas and modulate them onto different channels for viewing from other TVs in the house.

This solution has the benefit of adding only moderate cost (you have extra runs only to the receivers) and limited complexity. The drawback is that without using a multiswitch or voltage switch, you can watch only two DSS stations simultaneously (assuming you have a *dual-LNB satellite* that allows you to run two coaxial lines from your receiver. With a single-LNB receiver, you can watch only one station).

As we mention in Chapter 6, DSS systems can carry high-definition TV signals to your home. To view these signals (assuming you've subscribed to them), you have to jump through a few extra hoops. First, you need to have an HDTV-ready TV and an HDTV satellite receiver (or an HDTV with a built-in HDTV receiver). Second, in most cases you need an antenna with a *third* LNB (because the HDTV signals come in on a different satellite than normal programming). You might not need to run extra cables from the dish to your receivers, however, because some of these triple LNB dishes include a built-in multiswitch that combines all three LNB outlets onto single runs of coax. If the dish isn't so equipped, you may need to run an extra RG6 cable to the locations that have the HDTV receivers.

Making satellite connections

After running a satellite network, you should have a satellite input coaxial connector in each room. Depending on whether you opted for a hybrid system, you may or may not also have internal and external video jacks for sharing modulated source video devices.

To complete the installation, use a short RG6 patch cable to connect the satellite receiver to the jack on the wall. Doing so brings the satellite signal from the wall to the satellite receiver. After connecting the receiver to your television, you should see crystal-clear satellite television.

What if I just want satellite and none of that fancy stuff?

If you decide that you don't need or want a full-fledged, two-way video network and you're going to use only DSS and local channels in your video network, you need to become familiar with the diplexer. The *diplexer* looks just like the splitter/combiner but combines broadcast or analog cable TV signals with the output of a DSS dish on a single length of RG6 cabling.

You must use diplexers in pairs — one near your DSS dish where the antenna/cable feed is combined with the output of your LNB and another at the far end of your RG6 cabling, immediately before the cable plugs into your DSS receiver. The first diplexer combines the two cable feeds onto a single RG6 cable. The second splits this signal back into two separate signals — one

connects to your receiver's LNB input, and the other connects to the Antenna/CATV input on the back of the receiver.

If you feed two DSS receivers directly from a dual LNB dish (without using a multiswitch) and you want to add your local channels from cable or antenna, you need four diplexers. If you use a multiswitch to send the output of your dish to more than two receivers, you need to buy a multiswitch with a built-in diplexer and then use an additional diplexer at each receiver.

Even though diplexers and regular splitter/combiners look pretty much the same, they're two different devices. Don't try to save $20 by using any old splitter in your system: It won't work.

Here are a few more tips on DSS systems that are important to remember:

- ✔ **You need a phone line in every room that has a DSS receiver.** The DSS service provider uses this phone line to authenticate your box and provide pay-per-view movies, ACC basketball games, and the like. If your receivers aren't connected to phone lines, you won't be able to get pay-per-view or certain sports programming, and you'll have to pay a full subscription fee for each additional receiver in the house — instead of an extra $5 per receiver.

- ✔ **You can use a so-called *wireless phone jack* to run the phone line across your electrical cables.** They're not really wireless, because they use electrical cabling, but they save you from stringing a phone line across the room like a trip wire. (See Chapter 11 for more on these devices.)

- ✔ **You should install special *inline amplifiers* if the distance between the dish and a receiver is longer than 100 feet.** These amplifiers boost signal strength for long cable runs and are pretty cheap (between $25 and $100, depending on the level of amplification). They draw their power over the coaxial cable from the receiver, so they're easy to install — just cut the cable and connect the amplifier between the two cut ends of the cable.

✔ **You may want to install coaxial surge protectors on the RG6 runs from your dish.** Doing so prevents lightning strikes on your roof from destroying your DSS receivers. Be careful when you choose a surge protector, though, because the standard cable TV models available in most electronics stores don't pass the entire DSS signal. You need to buy special-purpose surge protectors that specifically support DSS. Some surge protector manufacturers (such as Panamax — www.panamax.com) sell surge protectors that do triple duty — protecting the RG6, the phone line, and the power cord connected to your receiver.

We don't tell you in this chapter how to remotely control all this video equipment from other rooms. We haven't forgotten; we have a long description of how to remotely control video (and audio) network components in Chapters 19 and 20.

And in This Corner, CAT-5e/6

The backbone of your video network — the primary electrical highway that carries TV and other video programming around your house — should be constructed using RG6 coaxial cable. Bottom line: It's just the best (and easiest, and most compatible) way of doing things. But sometimes you need to get video to and from places where RG6 doesn't go. And sometimes you just can't put any more video on the RG6 cable — for example, if you have a digital cable service that simply has no "room" for your in-home sources. A smart home has a great alternative already in the walls — the CAT-5e/6 cabling that's also used for phone networks, data networks, and more. (You could use either type — CAT-5e or CAT-6 — for the applications we discuss in this section.)

 CAT-5e/6 is great for distributing locally sourced video (from DVD players, PVRs, and the like) around the house, but it's not suited for carrying multi-channel incoming video from broadcast antennas, cable TV feeds, or satellite dishes. So don't mistake what we're about to discuss as an alternative to an RG6 network. Instead, it's a complementary network.

The key to using CAT-5e/6 to carry video lies in the electronic devices attached to the ends of the CAT-5e/6 network. These electronics make the CAT-5e/6 unusable for other services, such as telephones or data LANs. You can't just plug a video device into one of your phone jacks and expect it to work. It won't, and neither will the phones until you unplug the video electronics.

But if you read our discussion of a flexible CAT-5e/6 network in Chapter 2, you might have an inkling of what we're getting at. (If you don't, take a break from this discussion and take a quick peek.) To use CAT-5e/6 for video, you need to go into your wiring closet and separate (physically and electrically) the cable runs you want to use for video from your other networks. These cable runs then need to be cross-connected together on your main distribution panel (or on a separate panel set up for your video over CAT-5e/6 network) so that all locations on your CAT-5e/6 video network are wired together. Some manufacturers, such as Leviton, make a special hub for your wiring closet to connect together video over CAT-5e/6 systems.

After your CAT-5e/6 cables are connected together in your wiring panel, all you need to do to enable video over your CAT-5e/6 cables is to install some endpoint devices designed for the task. These devices can take a few forms:

- **Stand-alone sender and receiver units:** These are small boxes (smaller than many video components) that can sit on the rack next to the TV. The sender device sits in your media room (or wherever you want to share the video component) and connects to it like a modulator does — using the RCA composite or S-video connections on the back of the shared component. The sender is also connected by a CAT-5e/6 patch cable to the RJ-45 wall jack that you've dedicated to video. On the far end, you do the reverse — plug the receiver into the video-dedicated RJ-45 jack, and plug the composite or S-video outputs into your TV or home-theater receiver. The majority of these CAT-5e/6 video-distribution systems also carry stereo audio signals coming from your source device, so they can do double duty as a music distribution source.

- **Senders and receivers integrated into wall outlets:** These devices are functionally the same as the stand-alone units but are shrunk to wall outlets. The connection between the source components and the remote TVs stays the same, but instead of connecting an external box to an RJ-45 outlet, you replace your RJ-45 outlet with this device.

Note: In some systems, you'll see a bit of a mix-and-match approach, with a stand-alone sender and remote wall outlet receivers.

The stand-alone units are the most common and typically have better picture quality. Eventually, the outlet-sized units will catch up, but right now they're better for low-fidelity applications such as babycams.

The majority of the video-over-CAT-5e/6 systems we're discussing can carry only one video program at a time — they're basically like extensions of composite or S-video. You can't plug a DVD and a PVR, for example, into one of these devices and carry the signals to different TVs in the house simultaneously. Every TV receives the same signal with these systems, and you can't put two senders on a single CAT-5e/6. A few high-end, expensive systems, such as those made by Crestron (see Chapter 20), can be used as a multi-source video-transmission system.

Ack! Two warnings in a row — you must think that video-over-CAT-5e/6 is bad news. It's not, but we need to tell you one more thing. Some video-over-CAT-5e/6 solutions on the market are *point-to-point* solutions, meaning only one receiver can go along with the sender — you can send video from one spot to another but not to several others. If you want multiple receivers, make sure you buy a system that can handle that demand.

As we write this, video-over-CAT-5e/6 systems are still new and relatively expensive. We think that they'll become a better alternative to the distribution of in-home video sources than the more traditional modulator and RG6 approach — mainly because they'll be able to carry higher-quality video signals (such as component video or even HDMI) and fully digital audio signals. For example, ChannelPlus's SVC-10 system can carry S-video and Dolby Digital surround sound to a remote location over CAT-5e/6 (try that with a modulator!). And Gefen (www.gefen.com) has systems such as the HDMI•1000HDS, which can send HDMI high-definition video over CAT-5e/6 as far as 333 feet. As these systems mature and become capable of supporting higher-quality video and audio signals in a truly *multipoint* way (from one location to several others), they may make modulators obsolete.

Cut the Cord: Wireless Alternatives for Video Distribution

Phones and data networks aren't the only things in your home that can benefit from advances in wireless networking. A few products that use wireless technologies work well for your home-entertainment network if all you need to do is add a device (for example, one TV or one set of speakers) rather than take care of your entire whole-home-networking needs.

Wireless video-distribution systems accept the video and audio outputs of a video source — such as a VCR, DSS satellite receiver, or DVD player — and send them somewhere else in the home using an RF wireless link. These systems basically consist of two small units, each containing an antenna. The transmitter unit attaches to your video source through standard RCA-type audio and video connectors. The receiver unit usually offers both an RCA and an RF output to connect to the television on the far end. Figure 7-4 shows a wireless video-distribution network.

If you're looking into a wireless video system, here's what you should keep in mind:

✔ **What frequency spectrum does it use?** Some of these systems use the 900-MHz frequency band; others use the higher 2.4-GHz band. In general, 2.4-GHz systems perform better because higher-frequency RF signals run cleaner with less interference from other systems and pass through walls and ceilings better. Additionally, 2.4-GHz systems provide more available bandwidth to carry the video signals.

✔ **Does the system transmit audio in mono or stereo?** If your video source includes high-quality sound, you probably want to spend a bit more to get stereo audio.

✔ **Does the system carry IR (infrared) control signals?** Some do, and it sure is handy to be able to do things such as pause, rewind, or change channels while watching a program in the bedroom without having to walk to the living room. This feature is a must-have to us, unless you already have an IR control network built into your home — but if you have an IR network installed, we're pretty sure that you want to have a coaxial video-distribution network as well, so you won't be needing the wireless system.

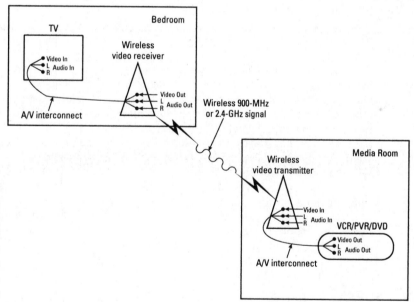

Figure 7-4:
Using
wireless
systems in a
video
network.

If you live in an older historic home, the type with tin ceilings, know that these reflect and block signals. Therefore, RF video transmitters may not give you the quality you'd like.

Coming soon: HDMI over the air

An alternative to CAT-5e systems for distributing high-definition video is on its way. Although no systems are commercially available as we write in early 2007, several vendors have announced *wireless HDMI* systems, which can take the HDMI output of a source device — a digital set-top box, an HDTV satellite receiver, a Blu-ray or HD-DVD player, and so on — and transmit it wirelessly across the room or across the house. These systems, at least the early ones that will be on the market in 2007, are point-to-point, so they're not designed to send a signal to every room in the house. Their primary application will be within a home theater or media room, getting HDTV signals to a flat-panel TV mounted on a wall somewhere in the room without requiring any wires to be installed in the walls. In the longer term, however, we expect more of a whole-home angle to these systems, with multi-point distribution (one source, multiple TVs) as a part of follow-on products.

An example of one of these systems is the WHDI (Wireless High-Definition Interface) system from Amimom (www.amimon.com). This system carries a single channel of HDMI (including its audio) up to 100 feet (or more), at resolutions of up to 1080i. Amimom and several other companies are working to build their receivers right into HDTVs, so all you would need to "cut the cord" would be a transmitter that connects to the HDMI output of your source devices. Pretty cool stuff; we can't wait to get our hands on it.

The folks at Ruckus Wireless (www.ruckuswireless.com) have a successful wireless distribution system that uses Wi-Fi wireless networking combined with some neat antenna tricks that "beam form" your wireless signal to maximize reach and speed to distribute HDTV over a wireless link. Their system is primarily available through TV service providers as part of a complete TV network of set-top boxes and wireless extenders. But consumers can buy a *MediaFlex* system for their own in-home video distribution for *IP video* sources (such as gaming systems and IP set-top boxes for Internet TV services and computers). The MediaFlex system isn't designed to work with traditional video sources (such as cable set-top boxes or DVD players), so it's really a solution for video sources coming from the Internet and your broadband connection. But it works well for those IP sources and can also be used as your home's primary Wi-Fi wireless computer network.

Use What You Already Have: Phone Line Alternatives for Video Distribution

Most of the action in developing home-networking systems that run on existing phone wires is in the data-networking field, but some companies are looking into ways to use phone lines for home-entertainment systems. Like the phone line data-networking systems we discuss in Chapter 16, these products utilize digital signal processing to carry entertainment signals on different frequencies than those used by the telephone service. This means they can be used simultaneously with telephone equipment connected to the network.

These systems use different frequencies than analog telephone systems use, but there's no guarantee that they use different frequencies than the phone line data-networking systems use. That means interference could be a major problem if you try to use both systems in your home, so we strongly recommend against it. Single-purpose wiring eliminates this kind of conflict, which is why we think it's the best way to go.

You won't find any phone line video-distribution systems available directly to you as a consumer. Like the Ruckus wireless system we describe in the section "Cut the Cord: Wireless Alternatives for Video Distribution," phone line systems are sold as part of a complete package by a TV service provider.

These systems use a technology called *HPNA* (Home Phoneline Networking Alliance) — specifically, the latest version of this technology called *HPNA 3.0*. HPNA 3.0 provides speeds up to 320 Mbps over regular phone wires, which is fast enough to carry several channels of HDTV at one time. You'll find HPNA integrated into digital set-top boxes for IPTV services from phone companies and other service providers. For example, if AT&T is your local phone company, you may be able to get TV services from them (as a replacement for cable or satellite TV). AT&T's set-top boxes use HPNA to send video signals from the main set-top box to satellite set-top boxes in other rooms — and even use this as part of a *multiroom DVR* service, which records programs on one set-top box but allows you to watch them on any other set-top box.

Chapter 8

Bringing You Music

. . . .

In This Chapter

▶ Getting the sound around (the house, that is)

▶ Zoning out

▶ Untangling cables and components

. . . .

*L*ike the video systems we discuss in the previous two chapters, home-audio systems are increasingly becoming *whole*-home-audio systems. Wiring your home to provide music everywhere and anywhere from a central set of source components is convenient and a money saver. What's more, it's a great way to tap into some of the music services available over the Internet. By focusing and centralizing, you make it easier to interface with anything.

When you start looking into a whole-home-audio system, you will find that you can take two main approaches: a wired system using speaker wires (or other kinds of wiring, as we discuss throughout this chapter) or a wireless system (typically using an 802.11 Wi-Fi system like the ones used for wireless computer networks). Many folks automatically think that the wireless systems, by virtue of being newfangled and high-tech, are the best way to go. We admit to being big fans of these systems, but we also remain strong proponents of going with wires when you can, simply because they're inexpensive and work reliably in just about any home (something that can't always be said about wireless).

This chapter looks at many of the cabling issues involved in creating a whole-home-audio network. In Chapter 9, we will dig into those wireless options we just mentioned.

Zoning Out: Single-Zone versus Multizone Systems

In a *single-zone audio system,* you have only one audio source, which you distribute across the network at any given time. You can turn various sets of speakers on or off, but you don't have the ability to listen to different audio sources in different parts of your house at the same time. A *multizone audio system,* on the other hand, allows one family member to listen to, say, a CD while another person listens to the audio channel of a VCR.

Single-zone systems have a few advantages:

- ✔ **Inexpensive:** A single zone needs the smallest number of components to get up and running, and the components themselves are the least expensive to purchase.

- ✔ **Easy to set up:** In the simplest case, a single-zone system can consist of a single source — such as a CD player or a PC — connected to one amplifier and then, through an *impedance-matching system,* to several sets of speakers. (We discuss impedance matching in the "Matching impedance" section, later in this chapter).

- ✔ **Upgradeable:** The hardest part about building an audio network is getting the right wires into the walls in the right places. Once you do that, you can easily switch from a single-zone system to a multizone system by simply upgrading a few components and swapping out a few connections.

Multizone systems provide the following benefits:

- ✔ **Multiple audio sources:** Multizone systems allow different members of your family to listen to different audio sources in different areas at the same time. For example, you can send the output from your iPod to one room and the output from your AM/FM radio tuner to another. This feature tends to increase domestic tranquility, just as our Founding Fathers recommended.

- ✔ **Video-network integration:** Multizone systems integrate better with your video-distribution system. The video-distribution network that we describe in Chapters 5 and 6 brings audio and video to each television in your house. With a multizoned audio network, however, you can take that one step further to send the stereo audio portion of any video program to a set of speakers near your remote TVs. This feature is appealing for two reasons: Stereo video modulators are pretty darn expensive, and separate speakers usually sound much better than those inside your TV.

Regardless of whether you choose to install a single-zone or multizone system, the basic wiring infrastructure is similar (see Chapter 9). So remember that you can start with something simple (single zone) and upgrade it to something more sophisticated (multizone) later.

The trouble with multichannel audio networks

The stereo audio standard, in which sound is separated into two channels (one for the left channel and one for the right), still dominates music production. With the advent of home theater, however, music can now be produced using multiple channels to drive a multitude of speakers. These new audio standards use speakers in front of you, behind you, and possibly alongside you to recreate the spatial dynamics of the concert hall in your home (at least that's how fancy magazines describe it). They can simulate a train passing by on the left, for example, by having sound come from the front speakers, then the left speakers, and finally the rear speakers, with fading at the end.

You can buy an audio system that supports home-theater standards, such as Dolby Digital or DTS, or the new SACD (Super Audio Compact Disc) and DVD-Audio systems, which use a multichannel system to create neat sound effects. Movie soundtracks, multichannel audio discs (still rare, but becoming more common), and a few TV shows come through speakers in front of you, behind you, and beside you. These multichannel systems also sometimes support subwoofers (which give you really deep bass sounds), floor-shaking transducers (devices that mount in the floor and literally shake it), a special-effects channel, and other wild-and-wooly add-ons.

For the average home (read that as a non-millionaire home), we recommend that you don't add multichannel capabilities to your whole-home-audio network, at least not right now. The wiring solutions we recommend here will enable you to add multichannel capabilities in the future. Although you can build an audio network that goes beyond the two-channel (stereo) limit today, the network quickly becomes extremely complicated and prohibitively expensive.

By all means, go ahead and set up a special multichannel amplifier, a surround-sound decoder, and surround-sound speakers, but do so in your home-theater or home-entertainment room. When you run your whole-home-audio network, stick with good old stereo.

Audio Connections (in the Short and Long Run)

The wires that connect the various parts of an audio system can be divided into two groups: the wires that run between components such as CD players and amplifiers, and the wires that connect amplifiers to speakers. (A third group of wires — those that connect control devices such as touchpad panels from Crestron (www.crestron.com) or Control4 (www.control4.com) — is covered in Chapter 20.)

We'll also talk in Chapter 20 about some great wireless systems (such as ZigBee and Z-Wave) that let you skip that extra set of wires (the control wires). Control systems are *definitely* an area where wireless is ready for primetime.

More about digital audio connections

Most digital audio devices — such as CD, SACD, and DVD players — let you carry a digital (rather than analog) signal between the component and the amplification system. To use such a function, you need a digital-to-analog converter built into the amplifier or receiver to convert the digital signal to an analog signal that can drive your speakers. (If your amplifier or receiver supports this function, you should see a Digital In jack on the back.) Digital audio connections are common — pretty much mandatory — in the home-theater realm, because these cables are required to carry surround-sound signals from a DVD player to a home-theater receiver.

Two main types of cables are used for this kind of connection: fiber-optic cables (called Toslink) and special coaxial cables with a standard RCA jack on each end (which one you use depends on what kind of connections your equipment manufacturer installed on its equipment — there's no single standard). At present, digital signal transmission is an uncommon method of distributing audio *throughout the home*, but we expect that to change as systems that can use CAT-5e/6 cabling for digital audio become prevalent. (See Chapter 9 for more information on these CAT-5e/6 systems, and how they can form an alternative to speaker wiring in your walls.)

Your audio system generally carries audio signals between components in one of two ways:

- ✔ **Line-level signals:** These are low-power electrical signals that contain an analog, electrical representation of the musical sound wave but not the electrical power to move your speaker diaphragms and create sound. Line-level signals are used by everything in an audio system up to the power amplifier — the CD player, the tape deck, the audio outputs of a VCR or DVD player, to name just a few. These are usually short-run connections between components.

  Digital equivalents of these line-level signals are used to connect digital audio sources such as CD players, DVD players, and gaming consoles to receivers and amplifiers. These are also typically used only for short-run, inside-the-room connections.

- ✔ **Speaker-level signals:** These are higher-powered signals that come out of your amplifier (or receiver, if you don't have separate components) and drive your speakers — that is, they cause the electromagnets in your speakers to move, creating the sound you hear. These are generally the long-haul connections that run through your walls and around your house.

For most people, running lengths of speaker wire from a central location (in pairs, for two-channel stereo audio) is the best way to build a whole-home-audio system. The wire is reliable, inexpensive, and easy to configure in a variety of different ways.

Making your music digital

In the old days — say back in the late 1990s when we all still rode horse-drawn buggies to work — there weren't many audio source devices to connect to your whole-home-audio network. You had CD players, cassette decks, radio tuners, and the audio coming out of video devices such as VCRs and DVD players. That was about it.

Computers, the Internet, and portable music players such as the iPod have turned the audio world upside down. These devices offer you a *convergence* of the computer and audio worlds. Computer-based audio files, such as MP3s (and WMV files for Windows-based systems and AAC files for Apple's iTunes and iPod-based systems), have taken the music world by storm — tens of millions of people use MP3 players as their primary means of storing and listening to music. You can take advantage of this in a whole-home-audio system in three ways. You can connect your computer — with its stored MP3 files,

streaming online music services, and network connection — to play music through your audio system. You can use your portable music player (such as an iPod or a Zune) as a source device that feeds your whole-home system (the best way to do this is with a *docking system* that lets you not only get the audio out of your portable player, but also send control signals in from remote locations. Or, if you're really serious about digital music, you can buy special-purpose devices such as Request's AudioRequest (www.request.com) or Escient's FireBall Digital Music Manager system (www.escient.com). These devices are a kind of *home media server*, as we discuss in Chapter 5. They use standard audio interconnects (RCA jacks) and connect to your whole-home-audio system just like a CD player does. We'll give you specific advice on how to integrate these systems into your whole-home-audio network in Chapter 9.

Although the simplest, cheapest, and most common way to carry long-haul connections is to use speaker wire connections, it's not the only way. A growing number of manufacturers are offering systems based on a technology called *A-BUS* (www.a-bus.com). This technology, developed by an Australian company called LeisureTech, uses standard CAT-5e/6 cables (which we discuss throughout the book, and first introduced way back in Chapter 2). A-BUS systems carry line-level audio signals from a receiver or centralized hub over CAT-5e/6 cabling to remote modules where you want to listen to music. The cool thing about A-BUS is that the CAT-5e/6 cabling also carries *control* signals and *power*. The modules have built-in amplifiers and also let you *input* your controls (such as volume and change track) — all over one single wire, with no need for a separate wired or wireless control system and no need for any electrical power at the remote location. Pretty cool. You can look on the A-BUS Web site for manufacturers. Several leading vendors, such as Leviton (www.leviton.com), Harman/Kardon (www.harmankardon.com), and Onkyo (www.onkyo.com) make A-BUS systems — Harman/Kardon and Onkyo even incorporate A-BUS right into their home-theater receiver systems. We talk about A-BUS and other CAT-5e/6 systems in Chapter 9.

Line level (for the short haul)

Cables called *line-level interconnects* carry *line-level signals,* the unamplified signals that move between audio components. Any cable with this type of jack is generically called an *RCA cable* (because RCA created it). Interconnect cables are usually shielded wires and typically come in *stereo pairs* (two separate wires bound in a left and right channel configuration).

The rise of multichannel audio in home theaters has led many manufacturers to create interconnects with an odd number of cables and connectors — five, for example, to connect the two front, two rear, and single center channels, or single cables to connect subwoofers to the receiver.

The number of choices you'll find in the interconnect marketplace can be bewildering. Go to a stereo store, and you'll find interconnects ranging from freebies thrown in with a stereo system to $1000-a-foot cables wired with precious metals — silver or gold or copper mined by old-world artisans somewhere in Bolivia (or so the typical advertising pitch goes). Whether or not these super-expensive cables make any difference is a matter of intense debate among audio aficionados — go check out one of the audio newsgroups on the Internet (such as `rec.audio.opinion`) if you want to see some people really slugging it out on the subject.

You probably get what you pay for with really cheap (or free) cables. You may want to seek out a knowledgeable and trustworthy expert if you haven't made up your mind on what to buy. At the same time, we recommend that you don't spend a week's wages on a cable — it will make the system sound better only because your mind forces you to *think* it does.

Speaker level (for the long haul)

The wires that connect your speakers to your amplifier are beefier than those that carry delicate line-level signals. Like interconnects, a huge range of speaker cable designs are available. In general, all cables consist of two conductors; each conductor is a solid wire or a bunch of smaller wires stranded together within a common jacket or insulator.

In a whole-home-audio system, you can run speaker wire in two places:

   ✔ **Through the walls:** You use special in-wall speaker cabling to connect your centrally located amplifier or amplifiers to remote outlets or in-wall speakers throughout your home. (We talk about what to look for when you choose in-wall cabling in just a moment.)

✔ **From the wall to the speaker (patch cabling):** This speaker wire connects your stand-alone speakers to speaker outlets installed in your walls. You can use the same cable you have in your walls if you'd like, or you can run down to the stereo shop and pick up some shorter lengths of precut and preconnectorized standard speaker cable for this job.

The only reason not to use the same wire that's in your walls is aesthetics, really. The wire in your walls is usually covered with lots of silk-screened writing and labeling that stands out like a sore thumb. You can buy speaker patch cables that are easier to hide than the in-wall stuff, and you can even paint some brands to match your walls.

Cables and Components

Like the other networks in your home, a home-audio network can be as simple or as complicated as you'd like. In this section, you find out about a few components that are common to just about every home-audio network.

Control systems

A *control system* is the switching device that allows you to select your audio sources, such as your CD, tuner, or iPod. The control system matches the audio source device that you want to listen to with the amplifier that powers your speakers. (We're not talking about the remote-control networks that allow you to control, say, your CD to your tuner from another room. For more information about remote-control networks, check out Chapter 20.)

The preamplifier or control amplifier installed in your audio system — or the one built into your integrated amplifier or receiver if you aren't using separate components — performs the source-switching function for a single-zone, single-amplifier system.

Single-zone control systems

If you're creating a single-zone distribution system but want to use multiple amplifiers, you face an obstacle. In general, audio source devices such as CD players have only one set of line-level outputs, so you can't just plug one device into two separate amplifiers. You can choose one of the following strategies to distribute your audio signal. Each uses a different piece of audio equipment:

✔ **Multiroom integrated amplifier:** This special amplifier accepts the stereo line-level input from a source device and amplifies *the same signal* into several pairs of stereo speaker outputs (these amplifiers usually feed up to four or six pairs of speakers).

Don't confuse a multiroom amplifier with *multichannel amplifiers* in surround-sound systems for home theaters. In a home theater, each speaker (the front, center, surround, and subwoofer) receives a different audio signal — for example, a five-channel amplifier has five separate line-level inputs from your surround-sound decoder. A multiroom integrated amplifier takes a single stereo pair of line-level inputs and internally sends this signal to more than one pair of amplifiers.

✔ **Signal-distribution amplifier:** This device takes the output of a source device, splits it into multiple outputs, and then amplifies these outputs to ensure that your signal is not degraded (if you split the signal without amplifying it, it would be too weak and would cause distortion that you would hear as a background noise or hiss). You can then connect these outputs to individual stereo amplifiers — one for each pair of speakers.

If you're just splitting the signal from an audio source device to a pair of amplifiers, you can save money by using a Y-splitter audio cable that splits a single pair of stereo audio signals into two pairs — one for each amplifier. You can buy these cables at Radio Shack and similar retailers. If you're trying to send a signal to more than two amplifiers at once, you're much better off with one of the solutions we just mentioned.

Multizone control systems

Multizone systems require special control systems that can take the output of several source devices and route these line-level signals to multiple amplifiers (one for each zone, remember). Two kinds of components can be the basis of a multizone audio system:

✔ A high-end preamplifier or receiver with built-in multizone capabilities (most of these systems are limited to two zones).

✔ Multizone control systems that can feed any of your audio source component's signals to a specific zone's amplifiers (these systems allow up to eight or more zones).

Do not attempt to put in a multizone system unless you have access to an audio geek. The documentation is awful, and the installation requires adept handling of a remote-control device.

Because of the increased costs, you may decide *not* to install a multizone audio system in your home right away. By following some of our guidelines throughout this book, however, we feel that you can indeed get a multizone treatment without breaking your bank account. No matter what decision you make, you should install the proper wiring infrastructure in your house ahead of time (and we tell you how in Chapter 9).

Mating your amplifiers and speakers

The basic job of an audio amplifier is to increase the power of an audio signal enough to let the speaker recreate sound. How loud those speakers get depends on two factors:

- ✔ **The power of the amplifier:** How many watts of head-banging power the amplifier pumps out.

- ✔ **The sensitivity of the speakers:** How many decibels of loudness the speaker produces when a given number of watts comes from the amplifier.

Amplifiers are one of the largest issues you confront when putting together a multiroom home-entertainment system, so be sure to put adequate time into researching your options. Don't make the mistake of assuming that you can just run speaker wire all over the house and then use your present amplifier. The salesperson at your local stereo store should be able to help you figure out all your amplifier needs. To get the best help from the stereo-store techie, we recommend that you draw a picture of the interior of your house and note where you want each device and speaker to go, along with accurate distances and likely conduit paths. This way, the salesperson can help you calculate your needs based on the equipment that store carries. Try a few stores, compare differences in approaches and pricing, and make a decision.

Impedance matters

When making the match between an amplifier and speakers, you need to take into account the speakers' impedance. *Impedance* is the force that the current coming from your amplifier pushes against. All you need to know about impedance is that if it dips too low, you may damage your amplifier! That's because lower-impedance speakers may cause an amplifier to overheat, which is never a good thing for a piece of electrical equipment.

The impedance rating of your speakers and your amplifier must match. Most speakers are rated at 8 ohms impedance, but some are rated at 4 ohms. Lower-impedance loudspeakers are more difficult for amplifiers to power. In fact, many inexpensive amplifiers are incapable of powering 4-ohm speakers and may overheat or just plain not work if you try to combine them.

Wiring more than one speaker to an individual amplifier channel greatly decreases the overall impedance that the speakers present to the amplifier. So even if you have an amp rated for 8-ohm impedance and speakers rated at 8 ohms as well, if you wire two speakers to the same output (in different rooms, for example), you effectively halve the impedance — to 4 ohms. Drat. Adding more speakers lowers the impedance even more. Double drat. Pretty soon you're going to damage your amplifier.

Matching impedance

Adding more than two sets of speakers to an amplifier may cause it to mal-function, because you lower the impedance that your amplifier is "seeing." If you're thinking about installing a multizone system, you can skip this part — multizone systems are designed with individual amplifiers for each set of speakers.

You can avoid this impedance problem in one of the following ways:

- **Use separate amplifiers for each extra pair of speakers:** If you use a separate amplifier for each set of speakers, you won't need to worry about impedance matching. (You still have to make sure that the rated impedance of your speakers matches that of your amplifiers.) You can blithely skip this section.

- **Use an impedance-matching device:** This device lets you connect multiple speakers to an individual amplifier channel without causing impedance problems, but it does decrease the amount of power that each speaker receives (and therefore the speaker's maximum loudness).

You may be tempted to hook several speakers up to one central unit, but overall, the more amplifier power you have, the better. If you can afford addi-tional amplifiers — they're relatively inexpensive — get them.

If you decide to go with a single amplifier for your home-audio network, you need to get some sort of impedance-matching device into your system. You have a couple of choices:

- **A central impedance-matching transformer system:** This device is a small box that accepts a single stereo pair of speaker wire connections and has several sets of speaker outlets. The internal transformer matches the impedance, so even if you have several pairs of speakers simultaneously connected to the amplifier, the amplifier functions cor-rectly. Many of these transformer boxes also double as speaker selector switches — on/off switches for your speakers — so you can control which speakers are playing music and which are blessedly silent.

- **An impedance-matching transformer built into an in-wall volume con-trol:** These volume controls, which you place in each room with speak-ers, perform the same function as a central matching transformer, plus they let you adjust the volume without using a remote control. Some of these devices even have built-in on/off switches, so you can disable the speakers in the room — a nice feature to have in a single-zone system when you don't want to be disturbed.

If your audio network will be limited — feeding only two rooms, for example — you can probably get away with not using an impedance-matching system. Just be sure to choose an amplifier or receiver that has two sets of speaker outlets, and make sure that it can handle the impedance load that your speakers put on it. After you get beyond two sets of speakers, though, we highly recommend that you install an impedance-matching system. Skipping this step is not worth the risk of damaging expensive equipment.

Speaker cable

The backbone of your home-audio network is the speaker cable you install in your walls. You can't just pick up any old speaker cable for this job — you need to use cabling designed for in-wall use. Look for the following when choosing cable:

- ✔ **Gauge:** The thickness of the conductors in your speaker wire is measured in units known as AWG (American Wire Gauge). AWG works on an inverse scale: lower numbers denote thicker cables. Most audio experts recommend that you choose a minimum of 16-gauge in-wall wiring (a recommendation with which we agree). Many people go with 14 or even 12 AWG wires — for most folks, 12 AWG is overkill except for runs that are exceptionally long (100 feet or longer); these heavy gauge cables are really thick, making them hard to pull through the walls.

- ✔ **UL listing:** Underwriter's Laboratories (UL) rate in-wall cables for safety and quality. Look for wires that are rated at least class two (UL CL2) or class three (UL CL3). The class rating is usually silk-screened on the wire jacket.

Always check with your electrician or local building inspector to confirm your town's cable rating requirement. Although a *national electrical code* lays out minimum standards for in-wall wiring, many municipalities have more stringent requirements. In fact, the array of such requirements is bewildering, and not meeting them could result in your local building or electrical inspector making you rip out your wiring and start over.

- ✔ **Extra features:** Some wire manufacturers design their speaker cables with features such as super-slippery cable jackets that slide through your wall more easily, length markers silk-screened on the jacket, and easy-to-remove insulation for terminating the wires — the kind of stuff that makes installers happy.

Audio connectors

Unlike video cables (and most of the other wires and cables we discuss in the book), speaker wires have no standard, one-size-fits-all family of connectors.

You can terminate speaker wires in many ways, leaving enough options to make the whole matter confusing. Following are the ways you can connect speaker wires:

- ✔ **Bare wire:** Many people choose not to get too fancy and just strip off the insulation and use the bare wire ends to terminate their speaker wires. We don't like this method because the exposed copper wiring tends to corrode. Also, having exposed wire ends increases your chances of accidentally short-circuiting the wires.

- ✔ **Pins:** Many manufacturers install (or sell for you to install) gold-plated pins that you can crimp or solder onto the ends of your wires, as shown in Figure 8-1. These pins make hookup much simpler, and they look neater, too (in case your neighbors are snooping around the back of your speakers). Hardcore audiophiles tend not to prefer this method of terminating speaker wires, but we think it's a good, reliable, and flexible choice.

- ✔ **Banana plugs:** No fruit is harmed in the manufacture of these speaker terminations — they're so named because these cylindrically shaped pins bend outward in the middle and roughly approximate the shape of a portly banana. Banana connectors come in both single and double varieties. In other words, you can have a single banana on both the positive and negative conductors of your speaker wire, or you can connect both wires to a double banana. The double bananas are spaced apart by a standardized distance, so they fit correctly into the banana connectors on your amplifier, speaker, or speaker outlet. We really like banana plugs because they're so easy to plug in and the outward bend in the middle of the plug ensures a nice, tight connection.

- ✔ **Spades:** Hard-core audiophiles (the people who live and breathe audio equipment and have a stack of dog-eared stereo magazines next to the bed) believe that these connectors offer the most secure, airtight connections. Spade connectors are U-shaped and fit over standard, screw-type binding posts — allowing you to get in there with a wrench or strong pair of fingers and tighten things down. We agree with the audio types — spades are the best connection method if your equipment has binding posts.

Figure 8-1:
From left to right, a pin connector, a banana plug, and a spade connector.

Any of the last three speaker wire terminations is better than using bare wire ends. Which one you choose will probably be driven by the kinds of connections available on your amplifiers and speakers.

You find the following connectors on typical amplifiers, speakers, and wall outlets:

- **Spring-loaded clips:** These are simple connectors with a spring-loaded clip that you push down to accept a thin, bare wire or pin connector. When you release the spring, it holds the wire or pin in place. You find these on most older audio systems and on less-expensive current models.

- **Banana-plug receptacles:** Some speakers and amplifiers accept only banana plugs. Be sure to check that your banana receptacles are designed to accept double bananas before you terminate your speaker wires. (Double bananas do have a standard, but some brands of audio equipment — mainly from Europe — are not built to this standard and require you to use two single bananas on your speaker wire.)

- **Five-way binding posts:** This speaker connector is the most flexible because it can accept single and double bananas, bare wire, pins, and spades. Five-way binding post connectors consist of a pair of metal posts with a couple of holes — one running parallel to the length of the posts to accept bananas and one running through the posts at a 90-degree angle to accept bare wires or pins. See Figure 8-2. Spade connectors simply slide over the posts, like a well-thrown horseshoe wrapping around a metal pole. Five-way binding posts also have plastic, screw-down caps on the posts, which you use to tighten the connection on bare wire, pins, or spades.

Figure 8-2:
Terminate your speaker wires like Arnold would.

Speaker outlets

A whole-home-audio system uses speaker wire connections to distribute music — that is to say, you run speaker wires through your walls to each room that's part of your network.

And now for something completely different

Traditional speaker wire systems are not the only way to get audio around your home, but for most people they're the best and easiest method. As computer networks and audio networks converge in more ways, however, it's possible to skip the traditional speaker wire network and get your music by alternate means. We describe in detail some alternatives for audio networks in Chapter 9, but thought we'd mention a few cool options right now.

✔ You can use CAT-5e/6 cabling (the same kind used for computer networks) to distribute line-level audio signals around the house. You'll need some special devices on the ends of these cables to make this work (described in Chapter 9), but these new devices are becoming cheaper by the day. Audio over CAT-5e/6 networks is still new and rare, but that will change as more people wire their homes with CAT-5e/6.

✔ You can converge (or combine) your audio and computer networks and use PCs and computer-based PC peripherals to store and play your music. You still need speakers and amplifiers to play the music, but you can use the CD player inside your PC to play CDs, or you can store your music as MP3 files on the PC (or on a special music server, such as an AudioRequest). Music can then be carried over your home's computer LAN to remote locations for playback. Computer-based audio systems also give you the option of getting your music from online music services offered by many broadband ISPs such as DIRECTV DSL and Road Runner.

Some of these computer-like audio systems are sophisticated. For example, Request's ARQ Zone system syncs with a central AudioRequest to provide multizone audio in your home. You can even sync these devices remotely.

If you don't want speaker wires dangling out of holes in your walls, you'll need finished outlets for ending runs of in-wall speaker cable. Like the video outlets we discuss in Chapter 6, these outlets are designed to fit into standard single-, double-, or triple-gang electrical junction boxes, and they come in all sorts of neat combinations. For example, you can buy a double-gang-sized outlet that contains two RG6 video-cable outlets and a pair of five-way speaker binding posts, which allows you to make your audio and video connections right next to each other. You'll find a host of speaker outlets in any good home-electronics store or catalog.

When you purchase speaker outlets, do yourself a favor and skip any that have those spring-loaded, clip-style connections and go right for the banana or five-way binding post types. The spring-loaded clips won't accept expensive speaker cables with the huge, gold-plated spade connectors. Besides, the clips are pretty flimsy.

In-wall speakers

When you're considering a whole-home-audio system, you need to know about a subcategory of speakers: those that can be flush mounted in your walls or ceiling. (See Chapter 5 for information on woofers and tweeters and that kind of stuff.)

In-wall speakers are appealing to many homeowners because they greatly increase the neatness of your installation, and give you that cool, custom look. Just imagine — no outlets, no exposed wires, no ungainly speakers to put on stands or bookshelves. Definitely a great way to go!

In-wall speakers, like conventional models, come in all sizes and shapes, but you should look for a few specifics:

- ✔ **Listen to them:** Unlike standard models, in-wall speakers require a commitment — namely a big hole in your wall. Always listen to your speakers in a reputable stereo store before you take the leap. You'll be glad you did.

- ✔ **Check the speaker size:** Make sure that whatever speakers you choose are going to fit in your walls without major modifications. Most of the common, rectangular wall models are designed to fit between standard stud spacing (16 inches), but all the same, go ahead and check your walls ahead of time.

- ✔ **Check the speaker depth:** You probably don't want your in-wall speakers sticking out a few inches. Again, most in-wall designs take into account the average depth of your wall, but double-check before you start cutting holes.

- ✔ **Think upward:** The walls aren't the only place to stick a speaker — ceilings are appropriate locations as well, especially in locations where your audio system serves primarily as background music. In those situations, you won't be quite as concerned about having some geometrically perfect speaker arrangement that allows you every nuance of the stereo music experience. If keeping your sound out of sight is a priority, you can even find round, in-ceiling speakers that look just like light fixtures.

- ✔ **Check out the speaker grill's design:** Many models have paintable grills, so you can make them match the walls around them — or make them stand out if you like that kind of design statement. Most speaker grills are innocuous (some even claim to be invisible when installed), and we won't fault you if looks are just as important as sound quality.

If you really want to hide your speakers, check out the speakers sold by Gekko (www.artgekko.com). These very thin speakers hang on the wall, like a picture. You can even outfit them with printed artwork!

Chapter 9

Running Audio Here, There, and Everywhere

*I*n Chapter 8, we describe the various pieces and parts that fit into a whole-home audio network. In this chapter, our goal is to tell you how to hook all these pieces together. As you probably guessed if you read Chapter 8 first, you do have to begin this process with a decision. Do you want to run a centrally powered (amplified) audio system that uses speaker wires to carry music to remote locations, or do you want to use a system that carries *unamplified* signals around the house (using CAT-5e cabling — the cables used in a computer LAN — or Wi-Fi wireless technology)?

That's a decision that we can't make for you, but we'll begin with a quick discussion of the pros and cons of each approach.

Then we'll get into speaker wire systems, with a description of the simplest whole-home audio network: a single-zone system that provides a single audio source simultaneously to each room. Then we move on to a brief description of more sophisticated, multizone audio systems, which let you listen to different audio programs in different parts of the house. Hot on the heels of this discussion is a description of those systems that distribute audio using CAT-5e/6 cabling. We don't stop there — we also discuss wireless alternatives to a home-audio network.

Making the Big Choice

As we said in the introduction, building a whole-home audio system requires you to make a few fundamental choices up front. The first and biggest choice to make is whether you want to go for a more traditional, centrally amplified audio system or one of the newer *distributed* systems. A centrally amplified audio network consists of a big multichannel amplifier in the middle (the virtual middle, it can be located anywhere in your home), and a series of speaker wires (and control wires, as we discuss in Chapter 20) running out to each room or location where you want sound.

The distributed systems, on the other hand, move the amplification to each location where you want to have speakers. Your sources may be in a central location (though they don't always have to be — some distributed systems let you plug in an audio source anywhere you want), but the amplifiers that run your speakers are located in the room with those speakers.

Tables 9-1 examines each of these systems for their pros and cons:

Table 9-1	Centrally Amplified versus Distributed Systems
Centrally Amplified	*Distributed*
Typically less complex	More complex electronics
Typically cheaper	Typically more expensive
Usually won't accept "remote" source devices	Often allows "remote" sources
Tried and true technology	Newer technology
More vendor choices, can mix and match	Fewer vendor choices, often locked into one vendor
More cables to run (in most cases) location)	Fewer cables to run (often only one per location)
Requires a separate control network	Control network is intrinsic
Always wired	Can include (or be entirely) wireless

We find that most people today (it's early 2007 as we are writing) still choose the centrally amplified (speaker wire) solution. It's a proven technology that almost all installers know how to handle easily. It does, however, have a bit less flexibility — for example, if you want to dock an iPod in the bedroom and play it on a whole-house system, that doesn't always work with a speaker wire solution. And while it is usually cheaper to go with speaker wires, once you start layering control networks and fancy multizone controllers on top of your speaker wires, you can easily spend more.

Our advice is to look at the capabilities and prices of the solutions out there — and in this chapter we'll name several companies that are leaders in these products — and do a comparison based on your own needs. Over time, advances in things such as *Class D Digital Amplification* (used in the remote amplifiers in distributed systems) and better wireless (like the emerging 802.11n standard we discuss in Chapter 16) will make distributed systems better and cheaper.

If you want to futureproof your home's audio system during new construction or during a remodel, we suggest that you do the following: to each location where you might want audio (and think hard, it might be *everywhere!*) run two lengths of CAT-5e/6 cabling (have them end up where you'd like to have a keypad or controller device) and a stereo pair of 16- or 14-gauge speaker wire. Bring them all back to a central location (your wiring closet or home theater/media room). And then you'll be able to hook them up and use them for either kind of system. Remember, cables are cheap, and it won't hurt to have too many.

This wiring advice is also useful when you consider that many manufacturers are developing systems that are a *hybrid* between centrally amplified and distributed systems. Some manufacturers (such as Niles Audio's ICS system, for example, at `www.nilesaudio.com`) use a central amplifier and then use CAT-5e/6 cabling for control and data purposes (like sending a list of songs on a music server to your touchscreen). You can also expect to see that CAT-5e/6 cable being used to feed remote audio sources (like that iPod dock in your bedroom) back into the central amplifier. And other manufacturers, like Control4 (`www.control4.com`) have *both* centrally amplified audio systems *and* CAT-5e/6 or Wi-Fi systems that can be mixed together and controlled as a single unified system.

Reaching for a Star

The speaker-wire audio network that we recommend is similar to the video network (and most of the other networks we talk about): a centrally distributed star configuration. All audio sources, amplification, and control systems are in one place, and speaker cables are distributed in a star fashion, with individual runs going to each speaker location. As is the case with your video network (but not with the other networks we describe), you probably want to use your home-theater room (or media room) as the central distribution point for your audio network. We describe the media room in Chapter 2.

The speaker wire audio network is different than the other networks in one major way — it's a one-way network. All audio source devices are located at the central distribution point. This type of network doesn't lend itself to a two-way architecture, in which remote source devices can send signals back to the central distribution point.

You can distribute an audio source located in a room other than your media room, but the process is difficult. Connect a long run of line-level component cable (the type of cable that typically connects components such a CD player and a receiver) from the remote audio source to your central amplifier control point. We don't address this option in our basic network architecture, so consult with a knowledgeable installer if you want to do this, or consider one of the distributed systems that will let you do this over CAT-5e/6 cabling.

If you're not using a CAT-5e/6 system, but want a remote audio source, the best way to distribute line-level audio signals over long distances is to use something called a *balanced line-level cable*. The pros use it in recording studios. The problem with trying to set up this kind of audio distribution on a consumer level is that only a small percentage of home-audio equipment is outfitted with these kinds of connectors (only the expensive stuff, for the most part). Many audio manufacturers have decided that these traditional balanced audio systems are not practical for the residential market, hence the alternative: using CAT-5e/6 UTP cabling to carry line-level signals around the house. We discuss this in detail in the "Catching up with CAT-5e/6" section, later in this chapter.

Single-Zone Simplicity

The simplest and most inexpensive way to move into whole-home audio is to build a *single-zone audio network,* which is a network that allows you to send an audio source to speakers in different rooms (although you can't listen to different audio sources in different rooms). We tell you about the functions of the individual components of such a network in Chapter 8; in this section, we tell you how to hook up this network.

Even simple, single-zone audio networks have a ton of variations. Your personal preferences, budget, and existing audio components play a big role in shaping your network. For example, you can choose between an all-in-one receiver and an integrated amp to handle the control and amplification roles, or you can use separate components. You can decide to use a single amplifier with impedance-matching devices, or you can set up separate amplifiers in your media room for each pair of speakers. You can choose in-wall speakers or conventional models.

Regardless of what you decide, the basic network architecture remains the same: pairs of speaker cables run in a star-wiring configuration from a central amplification point to each speaker location in the house.

Installing a single-zone, single-amplifier system

Here's a general layout for a single-zone, single-amplifier system:

1. **Using pairs of line-level audio interconnect cables, connect your source devices to the inputs of your preamplifier, or *control amplifier*.**

2. **Use a pair of RCA cables to connect your amplifier to your power amplifier.**

   If you're using a receiver (or an integrated amplifier) instead of separate components, you can skip this step. Instead, connect your audio source components directly to the receiver.

3. **Choose an impedance-matching system and do one of the following:**

   a. **If you're using multiple impedance-matching transformer/ volume controls in each room, connect the main speaker outputs from your amplifier or receiver to a *parallel connecting block* with a short length of speaker wire.**

   The parallel connecting block splits a single audio output into multiple audio outputs — like an audio cloning device.

   b. **If you're using a single impedance-matching/speaker-selector device that resides in the media room, connect the impedance-matching device to your amplifier's speaker output with a short length of speaker wire.**

   The impedance-matching/speaker-selector device both matches impedance and acts as a central selector for turning speakers on or off.

4. **Connect the speaker outputs of your connecting block (Step 3a) or speaker-selector device (Step 3b) to individual runs of speaker wire for distribution throughout the house.**

5. **Run pairs (left and right speaker) of speaker wire through your walls to the desired locations.**

6. **If you're going with multiple impedance-matching volume control units in each room, connect the speaker wires to the inputs of the wall-mounted, impedance-matching volume control.**

   The impedance-matching volume control units usually fit in a standard, single-gang junction box, which can be mounted just like a light switch in a convenient spot on the wall. (We explain junction-box sizes in Chapter 7.)

If you're using a central impedance-matching/speaker-selector switch instead, just blithely ignore this step and continue to Step 7.

7. **Terminate your speaker-wire runs (or a shorter run of speaker wire leading from the impedance-matching volume control's outputs, if you went that route) in one of two places:**

   a. **If you decide to use external, stand-alone speakers in this room, connect the ends of your speaker wires to a speaker-connector wall plate.**

      We prefer the kind with banana jacks or five-way binding posts.

   b. **If you're installing in-wall speakers, connect the ends of the speaker wires to each speaker's inputs.**

8. **For each set of speakers in your home, repeat Steps 4 through 7.**

   A wiring layout for a single-zone audio system is shown in Figure 9-1.

Figure 9-1:
A typical single-zone audio network.

Put on your favorite CD, pour your favorite beverage, and sit back for a listening break.

You may decide to start small, with speakers in only a few rooms. That's a fine way of setting up this kind of network, but go ahead and install runs of speaker cabling to other rooms now — while you have the walls open — in case you want to expand your audio network later. You can put a blank cover on the outlet box so that you don't have wires hanging out of your walls.

Phase matters

When you're working with speaker wires, you need to keep in mind the concept of phase. All speaker-level inputs and outputs are color-coded, usually with a red and black connector. It's important to make sure that you maintain consistency when you connect speaker wires, so that both speakers in a stereo pair have their wires connected to the amplifier in the same way. If you cross a pair of wires (red to red and black to black on one speaker, but red to black and black to red on the other speaker, for example), you won't blow up anything or start a nuclear meltdown at your local power plant. You will, however, have degraded sound, with decreased bass and a totally messed up stereo image.

Most speaker wires are well marked, with different colors of wire in the pair or with markings on one of the conductors. If you really can't tell or remember what's connected to what, use a test CD that puts your system through its paces to make sure you've hooked it up correctly. Pat has one for *Stereophile* magazine (www. stereophile.com) that features "Ralph the barking dog," who woofs from both speakers in and out of phase so that you can hear the difference.

Implementing a single-zone, multi-amplifier system

A single-zone, multi-amplifier system uses separate amplifiers in the media room for each set of speakers in the audio network. This network eliminates the need for an impedance-matching system and provides more power to each set of speakers.

The process for installing a single-zone, multi-amplifier network is similar to the one we delineated in the preceding section. The two main differences are

- ✔ You don't need the impedance-matching system because each speaker is powered by its own amplifier.

- ✔ You need to split the audio signals from your source components — a single stereo pair of outputs — to several pairs of amplifier channels. Doing so can be a bit of a sticking point. You have three options:

  - If you're installing speakers in only two locations, you can probably use a Y-connector cable, which takes a single pair of line-level outputs and splits the signal into two pairs of connectors.

  - You can buy a *distribution amplifier* that accepts the line-level input and provides multiple pairs of outputs (sort of an audio cloning device). This device also amplifies the signal (which gets weaker as it's reproduced) so that each power amplifier has the signal strength it needs.

- You can buy an integrated amplifier specifically designed for a multi-room system. This amp internally splits your source device signals amongst its amplifier channels. Companies like Niles Audio and Russound (www.russound.com) are the big manufacturers of these devices.

Mega-Multizoning

The basic steps for installing a multizone audio system (which is capable of sending different music sources to different rooms in your house simultaneously) in your home are similar to those needed to install a single-zone system. At least they are in a high-level overview.

As long as you get the right wires in the wall, you can change from a single-zone system to a multizone system later, by changing the components of your audio system and how some wires are connected in your media room.

The devil is in the details when you start setting up one of these systems, especially when you set up the control system. (We talk about how to remotely control audio systems in Chapter 20.) Figuring out the routing of the audio signals isn't too difficult, but equipment variations keep us from giving many details.

How do your audio and video systems work together?

How your audio and video systems complement each other is a confusing subject, no doubt. After all, your video network (by the very nature of the programming it carries) also distributes audio signals around the house. So why have two networks?

The coaxial network that carries TV signals around your home isn't suited to carrying the audio signals from other sources such as CD players, and the audio network is similarly unable to carry video signals. In the future,

when all audio and video signals that run between components are fully digital, you'll probably be able to use a single network to carry both. For now, if you want both audio and video, you need two networks.

If you're using CAT-5e/6 to carry your audio (as we discuss later in the chapter), you may find that the system you choose can carry both the audio *and* video signals over a single cable. This isn't the case with all systems, but some systems will do this for you.

Multizone audio systems can become nightmarishly complicated. Not only does the setup depend on marrying components from different manufacturers that may have strange quirks and weird setup routines, but also, when you get to *controlling* the zone audio with your remote control, it gets deadly. The goal is to be able to accomplish certain things regardless of which zone you're in (such as select and play a CD) but to accomplish other things *only* in your current zone (such as turn up the volume or select the VCR audio as the input source). Whether you can do something from all zones or only the current zone depends on how you hook up the wires from the control network and how you set up the multizone amplifier. Believe us, getting all this stuff to work seamlessly is a major hassle that increases as you add zones.

Many home-audio servers — the devices that store your music on a hard disk drive — are being upgraded to allow multizone audio over a computer network. Because these devices (available now from Request and Escient) are basically computers, they include built-in Web servers that let you stream music around your house — just like music Web sites do. With these systems, you'll be able to stream different music programs to different parts of your home over your computer network.

If you're going to jump right into multizone audio and you're not a gearhead, let a professional installer do the job.

Following is the basic layout of a multizone system:

1. Use standard RCA cables to connect your source devices to the multizone controller.

   The multizone controller contains all the electronics to switch each incoming source to different amps and zones.

2. If the controller doesn't have built-in amplification, use interconnect cables to connect the controller's outputs (one stereo pair per zone) to a multichannel amplifier.

3. Connect the amplifier outputs to pairs of speaker wire (one pair per zone).

4. Run the speaker wires through your walls to each speaker outlet or in-wall speaker location, as shown in Figure 9-2.

It sounds simple, doesn't it? And it is, from our 40,000-foot perch here. But getting the pieces together and working in sync can be a bit of a pain. That's why we recommend professional help (otherwise, you may end up seeking professional help of another sort).

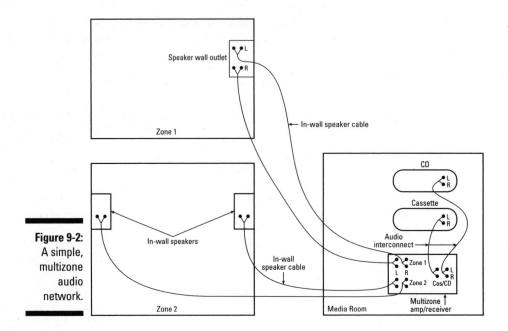

Figure 9-2:
A simple,
multizone
audio
network.

Other Ways to Send Audio

As we stated in the introduction to this chapter, a speaker-wire-based audio system isn't your only choice for a whole-home audio network. A bunch of vendors have begun selling systems that use CAT-5e/6 cabling or wireless systems like Wi-Fi as an alternative. Such systems tend to be a more expensive than the tried-and-true speaker wire, mainly because of the cost of the intelligent electronics involved and the expense of building independent amplifier systems for each remote location, but that costs comes with some benefits. Namely:

✔ These systems are more flexible. You can easily use a drop of CAT-5e/6 cable and add audio to any room. Wireless systems don't even need that — just a power outlet.

✔ These systems can be customized to the room. If you're installing a distributed system in a big room, you can choose a bigger amplifier and bigger speakers, or if its someplace that's not so big, you can choose a smaller system.

✔ You don't need a separate control system (with separate wires or cables) like you do for a speaker wire system. All the music, control commands, and even data about the music (*metadata*) can be carried over a single CAT-5e/6 cable or over the wireless link.

CATching up with CAT-5e/6 systems

As you skip around this book and look at the various networks we describe, you might note a recurring theme: CAT-5e (and its companion CAT-6, which is just a slightly upgraded version of the same thing) cabling is versatile stuff. CAT-5e/6 not only is the standard cabling for computer LANs and phone networks but can also be used to carry an increasing amount of other data around the house. In Chapter 7, for example, we talk about using CAT-5e/6 cabling to transport video signals around the home, and in Chapter 20, we discuss using this cable for carrying remote control signals (IR signals). There's almost nothing (networking-wise, at least) that you can't do with CAT-5e/6.

Audio is no exception. Line-level audio signals can be successfully carried over CAT-5e/6 cables in your walls using systems from a variety of manufacturers. These systems range from inexpensive ones that convert the left and right line-level outputs of an audio device into a balanced signal to full-fledged, expensive audio (and video!) distribution systems that provide true multizone audio over CAT-5e/6.

When you use CAT-5e/6 to carry audio, you can't use those same wires for your computer LAN or phone network. It's an either-or situation, and you need to use a separate network of CAT-5e/6 cables for each leg of the audio network. You *might* be able to use the same CAT-5e/6 cables to carry both audio and video signals — it depends on which CAT-5e/6 audio system vendor you use.

Yep, two warnings in a row. No, don't go run and hide. CAT-5e/6 audio systems are still relatively new to the market, and many of the companies that sell them use proprietary technologies. It's best to stick to one brand — don't try to mix and match.

A few of the most common ways of sending audio over CAT-5e/6 are discussed in the following sections.

Balun-ce your life

A *balun* is named for its function in the network — it converts a signal back and forth from *balanced* cable systems (such as CAT-5e/6 cables) and *unbalanced* cable systems (such as audio RCA cables). As we discussed, a balanced line-level signal is capable of going a long distance — up to 1000 feet in some cases. A balun isn't much to look at. It's not a big fancy box with shiny lights. Instead, it's just a little passive device (meaning it doesn't need any external power) about the size of a deck of cards, with receptacles on both sides (an RJ-45 on one side and two or more RCA jacks on the other).

Baluns are deployed in pairs, so you're not going to build a whole-home audio network with them. They fit into your network when you just want to get audio from one place to another (a point-to-point network).

One balun is associated with the source device (such as a CD player or the Audio Out ports of a receiver) and connects, through an RCA patch cable, to the left and right Audio Out channels. This balun is then plugged into the CAT-5e/6 cable using a CAT-5e/6 patch cable. At the other end of the network — down another leg of your home's CAT-5e/6 that you've dedicated to audio — the process is reversed. The second balun plugs into the RJ-45 outlet on your wall (again using a patch cable), and then plugs into the left and right Audio In jacks of the remote amplifier or receiver that you're feeding the signal to.

We're talking about transporting line-level signals, not speaker-level signals. You can't just plug the output of the remote balun into a pair of speakers and expect music. There is one exception to this: If you have powered loudspeakers (that is, with built-in amplifiers), you don't need an intermediate amp or receiver.

Audio baluns use one pair of the conductors in a CAT-5e/6 cable for each of the left and right stereo audio channels. Remember that typical CAT-5e/6 cables have eight conductors — so you have four left. Some balun manufacturers, such as MuxLab (www.muxlab.com) and Intelix (www.intelix.com) build baluns that use these four extra wires to carry composite or S-video signals (see Chapter 6 if you've missed what these are), so you can carry audio and video over the same CAT-5e/6. This is a great solution if you just need to share a source device such as a DVD player in one remote location — because DVD players also play CDs, you can carry video, audio, or both easily and cheaply using a couple of spare lengths of CAT-5e/6 in your walls. (This is an example of why we've said — probably a million times — that it's a great idea to put plenty of CAT-5e/6 in your walls, even in places where you don't think you'll use it for computers or phones. It will seem like a ridiculous amount of cable, but you'll use it.)

Getting on the A-BUS

Baluns are a great (and cheap — you can pick up a pair for just over $100) way to use CAT-5e/6 to move audio around your home, but they aren't going to cut it if you have a multiroom, multizone system in mind. Systems based on the A-BUS standard (which we mention in Chapter 8), however, will do the trick for you.

A-BUS (www.a-bus.com) is a CAT-5e/6 distributed audio system supported by more than a dozen vendors (there's a list on the A-BUS Web site). The cool thing about A-BUS is that each location requires only a single CAT-5e/6 to bring all the audio, power (for the amplifiers and keypads/controllers), and control signals you need. So you won't need to worry about running big heavy speaker wires and extra cables for the control system.

A-BUS systems range from single-input, single-zone systems (that take a single audio source and pipe it to multiple locations) to more complex multi-input, multizone systems. Because all of these systems use a single CAT-5e/6 cable, you can start off simple and upgrade by just changing out or adding components. Nice and simple, just the way we like it.

To make an A-BUS system, you need the following components (in addition to the runs of CAT-5e/6 cabling):

- An audio source (or sources) at the central point of the network.

- Speakers at each location where you want sound. (The speakers can be conventional or in-wall.)

- A *hub*, which is the central control and input point for your A-BUS system. The hub distributes your analog audio input(s) over the CAT-5e/6 cables. The hub requires AC power (which it then distributes to the rest of the network using CAT-5e/6).

- *Power modules*, which are the endpoints of your A-BUS system, providing control and amplification for your speakers. They're single-gang boxes, so they fit into your wall in the same space taken up by a single light switch.

To make it all work, you simply connect the CAT-5e/6 cables, plug in your source device, and connect your speakers to the power modules. One neat feature of the A-BUS power modules is their ability to connect to a local audio source, so you can use the same speakers and amplifier for both your whole-home system and a local audio device.

Vendors of A-BUS products include Russound and Leviton (www.leviton. com), as a part of their Leviton Architectural Edition powered by JBL system, which includes a range of components and speakers. You can also find A-BUS built into home-theater receivers by Onkyo (www.onkyo.com), in their high-end Integra line, and by Harman/Kardon (www.harmankardon.com) — the Harman/Kardon receiver is sold as part of the Leviton system.

Going with proprietary solutions

Although a number of vendors are using A-BUS, it's not the only game in town when it comes to whole-home audio over CAT-5e/6. Several vendors have created their own systems, using different methods towards the same aim — audio over CAT-5e/6. A few examples follow:

- **Control4:** Control4 (www.control4.com) is best known for its home automation and control systems, but the company also makes a range of inexpensive audio and video-networking products. Control4 makes traditional speaker wire-distributed whole-home audio systems, but they also have a neat series of Speaker Point products that use CAT-5e/6 to bring audio to remote locations. The Control4 Ethernet Speaker Point connects back to their Media Controller device over CAT-5e/6 and includes a built-in 50 watt per channel stereo amplifier. There's even a Wi-Fi speaker point for rooms where you've run out of CAT-5e/6 cable.

✔ **The ZON system:** ZON Audio (www.zonaudio.com) is a manufacturer with a sole focus on CAT-5e/6 audio distribution. The ZON platform is perhaps the most distributed of all the currently available CAT-5e/6 music systems. At the hub of the system is the ZON ZR-98 router, which can accept inputs from up to eight ZIM-4 input modules. These input modules can be anywhere in your home (as long as there's CAT-5e/6), and they can accept an analog stereo audio input, a digital coaxial input, *and* a digital optical (Toslink) input. They also have an IR output so you can run an IR cable to the front of the gear you're controlling. The last piece of the puzzle is the ZAC-60 audio controller/amplifier, which have a neat *jog* controller (think iPod and you'll understand it).

Two cool things about the ZON follow:

- You can put anything, anywhere. You don't have to have all your sources in one location. Just run a CAT-5e/6 cable and put an input module in any room of the house that has audio source devices — and those sources can then be controlled and listened to from any remote location with a ZAC-60.

- It's all digital. All the audio carried over the ZON system is high-quality (24-bit) digital audio, so you can preserve the quality of your audio sources even over long distances.

Wireless systems

Now all these speaker wire and CAT-5e/6 systems are great if you have the walls open and can run the cables. But what if you can't (or don't want to!) tear open the walls? Well, like many other systems in the home, wires are no longer required for whole-home audio. That's right: You can go wireless!

Wi-Fi? Why not?

We suspect that you're probably at least passingly familiar with Wi-Fi, the wireless technology embedded in more than 95% of the laptops sold today (and used for a myriad of devices including PCs, printers, cell phones, game consoles, PDAs, and, well, you name it). If you're not, run on over to Chapter 16 and give yourself a primer!

Wi-Fi is the centerpiece of a new generation of whole-home audio systems that dispense with in-wall cables and simply beam your music around the house over the airwaves.

These Wi-Fi systems are, so far — and we think this will change — designed to handle digital music files stored on a hard disk drive. They're *not* currently designed to take a whole bunch of different audio inputs (such as CD players and AM/FM tuners) and distribute them. But if you're part of the iPod generation (like a few tens of millions of people), this isn't going to be a major issue for you. We suspect that over time, Wi-Fi systems will expand to be more like wired systems, with multiple inputs for a range of sources. But as more and more people rip their CDs to hard drives or acquire their music online, this limitation won't be much of a limitation after all.

All Wi-Fi music systems we know of also include Ethernet ports that can plug into a whole-home computer LAN (described in Chapters 14 and 15). This is handy if you run into a situation where a room is out of Wi-Fi range. The key thing to remember here is that these devices can plug right into the Ethernet network you use for your computers — they don't need to be on a separate CAT-5e/6 cable like the systems we discussed in the preceding section.

The Sonos Music System

The Sonos Music System (www.sonos.com) is probably the most famous whole-home Wi-Fi music system. The Sonos system uses the 802.11g Wi-Fi system with a special "Sonos super secret sauce" that makes each Sonos device act as a *mesh* network which repeats the signal from other Sonos devices to improve wireless coverage. Sonos plays music stored on PCs and can also connect to hundreds of Internet radio stations and to many of the leading Internet subscription music services, such as Rhapsody (www.rhapsody.com) and Yahoo! Music. There are two main components to the Sonos system:

✔ The Zone Player: This is the guts of the system, and includes the computer hardware to make it all run, the wireless radio transceiver, and the audio hardware. Sonos has two models: the ZP100 ($499), which includes a 50 watt per channel stereo amplifier (so you just need to plug in a pair of speakers), and the ZP80 ($349), which doesn't (so it works with an existing amplifier and speaker system).

✔ The Sonos Controller: This is a wireless handheld controller that lets you control the system (like most controllers do) and "see" your music. The controller (which costs $399) has a color LCD display and a jog wheel (we're detecting an iPod-like theme here in this chapter) that lets you quickly browse through your music, set up playlists, and more.

✔ We lied. You need a third component, but it doesn't come from Sonos. You need a PC or a Mac to plug into one of the Zone Players. The computer holds your digitized music — Sonos just distributes it for you. Your music can be in the common MP3, AAC (iTunes), or WMV (Windows Media) formats, as well as in some more exotic formats such as Ogg Vorbis or FLAC. The Sonos system will even play downloaded music from several online music stores.

Unfortunately, iTunes Store downloads are not supported, but any other music you have in iTunes (that you've ripped yourself) *is* supported.

Figure 9-3 shows the Sonos system.

Figure 9-3:
The Sonos system fills your whole home with Wi-Fi'd audio.

Yamaha's MusicCAST

Another leading Wi-Fi whole-home music solution comes from Yamaha — the big Japanese company that makes everything from motorcycles to pianos. The Yamaha MusicCAST systems (you can find it at www.yamaha.com) is a hard-drive-based Wi-Fi system that can store and distribute all your digital music.

The center of a MusicCAST system is the $2000 MCX-2000 digital music server. This device includes a CD drive (which can read your CDs to rip music to the hard drive and also burn CD-R/RW discs that you can take with you), a 160 GB hard drive (which can store 2000 hours of music when recorded at 160 Kbps), and all the wireless and computer hardware to make the system work. You can place the MCX-2000 in your home theater or media room, and then plug it directly into your home-theater receiver for local listening and also use it to feed music around your home using the 802.11g Wi-Fi standard.

Making the iPod the center of your audio network

A lot of people keep all their music on an iPod. Pat has three iPods in his house, and only two people old enough to listen to one, and don't even ask about Danny's house, with four tweener/teen kids. Apple and its partners have made a lot of money selling a range of iPod accessories, ranging from car adapters to boom boxes, so it's no surprise that some enterprising companies have begun to build systems that make the iPod the center of a whole-home audio network.

A new company called EOS Wireless (www.eoswireless.com) had developed an iPod wireless system (called the EOS) that provides a cheap and easy way of making a whole-home iPod network. The EOS system uses a proprietary radio technology (which operates in the same 2.4 GHz frequency band as Wi-Fi but doesn't interfere) to transmit your iPod's audio up to 150 feet from the base station. There are two components: the base station ($200), which includes an iPod dock and an auxiliary input for other audio sources, and the remote satellite speaker unit ($150) which receives the audio beamed out from the base station and plays it back using stereo speaker drivers and a subwoofer. You can connect up to four remote satellites to the base station, and any iPod except the tiny Shuffle and the first-generation model is supported.

Another way of integrating an iPod to your whole-home audio system (whether it be a speaker wire, CAT-5e/6, or Wi-Fi system) is to use an *iPod Dock* connected to the main audio system. Many audio receivers (from companies such as Denon, Onkyo, Yamaha and Harman/Kardon) offer accessory iPod docks that plug into the back of the receiver. Connect the dock, drop your iPod into the docking station and — voila! — you have complete access to, and control of, your iPod from any spot in the house that can control the receiver. This is a cheap and easy way of iPod integration, because the docks usually cost less than $150 (on top of the price of the receiver, of course).

Finally, a few manufacturers are making *in-wall* iPod docks. An example of this is the iPort (http://www.iportmusic.com/). The iPort installs in a standard electrical box and lets you simply dock the iPod in the wall and play it back on local or remote speakers. The iPort uses a CAT-5e/6 cable to carry music, control signals, power, and metadata (song information) to remote amplifiers, speakers, and control systems. You can use the system for a single room (connecting to an audio system) or, with a longer run of CAT-5e/6, connect back to a whole-home audio system.

For remote locations, Yamaha offers several options, including the $600 MCX-A10 MusicCAST client. This device includes the Wi-Fi receiver, a remote control, an LCD display, and a built-in stereo amplifier that you can hook up to your own speakers. For locations with a wired Ethernet computer LAN connection, you can choose Yamaha's $600 MCX-C15P in-wall client/controller/amplifier. This device fits in a standard double-gang box in your wall (the same size as a double light switch) and includes the MusicCAST client, a remote control, an LCD display, and an amplifier that can power two speakers.

Keeping it simple with wireless media adapters

As you may have noticed, whole-home Wi-Fi audio systems aren't cheap. You can expect to pay $1500 or more to get a multiroom system set up with a Sonos or MusicCAST system. Perhaps your budget is a bit more limited, or your needs are less complex (maybe you only need to bring your music to one other location).

A cheap way of extending audio — in particular, computer-based audio — is to use a *digital media adapter,* or DMA. These devices are Wi-Fi-based networking devices that distribute digital audio from a PC or music server to a remote location in your home. (Like the whole-home Wi-Fi systems, digital media adapters also include Ethernet for CAT-5e/6 data networks.)

Note the word *media* in the name, and not *music.* Most DMAs will also transmit pictures and, in many cases, video from your computer network to your entertainment systems. For the most part, they don't work all that well for TV-quality video, but that will change as Wi-Fi improves.

DMAs are *adapters,* not *players.* They convert digital music to a signal that can be played by a receiver/amplifier and speakers, but have neither themselves. So you'll connect the DMA to the audio inputs of a local audio system to actually hear music.

Pretty much every manufacturer of home wireless-networking gear (Linksys, D-Link, NETGEAR, Buffalo, and Belkin, for example) has at least one DMA. A few companies specialize in DMAs, and we think they do the best job of building these devices:

- Roku Labs (www.rokulabs.com): The SoundBridge (there are two models, at $200 and $400) is a tubular-shaped, stylish metal-and-black plastic DMA with a big and super-bright fluorescent display. The display on the top model is a whopping 12 inches across, making it easy to read across the room. The SoundBridge models support Mac and Windows computers and can play back WMV, AAC, and MP3 audio files. They also support Internet radio stations, and you can install more than one unit in your home (up to ten, in fact).

- Slim Devices (www.slimdevices.com): If you ask any high-end audio nut what the best DMA is, you'll hear one answer consistently: SlimDevices. They have two models:

  • The $300 Squeezebox is the entry-level model (though entry-level is a relative term here). It supports 802.11g Wi-Fi networks and can play back a dizzying array of digital music file types, including all lossless formats (which audiophiles prefer). Like the SoundBridge, the Squeezebox has a nice big fluorescent display that's easy to read from a distance.

- The $2000 Transporter is the high-end model. And by high-end, we really mean high end. For your two grand, the Transporter gives you the kinds of internal electronics and circuitry you get in the fanciest audio equipment, with special designs to reduce things such as *jitter* (timing errors in digital audio) that give you that last degree of audio purity.

Speaking out with wireless speakers

The cheapest way to extend audio from one room to another is to use a simple RF wireless system. These come in two main flavors:

- ✔ **Wireless speaker systems** connect to the line-level outputs of a source device or preamplifier and send the signal over a 900-MHz or 2.4-GHz channel to a pair of self-amplified stereo speakers.

- ✔ **Wireless line-level distribution systems** hook up to your source components in the same fashion but send their signal to a receiver that hooks into your own amplifier and speakers on the far end.

One major potential difficulty with this sort of wireless system is that it uses a line-level input — and most source devices have only one. So you may run into trouble hooking up a CD player, for example, to both a receiver (or amp) for local listening and to one of these devices for remote listening. Luckily, many of these units also accept the output of your receiver or amp's headphone jack, so you can avoid this problem if you have a headphone jack available. (Alternately, you can use a simple Y-splitter audio cable, which has one set of stereo RCA plugs on one end and two on the other.) Prices for these wireless systems range from about $75 to $200. Major manufacturers include

- ✔ Sony (www.sony.com)
- ✔ Acoustic Research (www.araccessories.com)
- ✔ RCA (www.rca.com)
- ✔ Audiovox/Terk (www.audiovox.com)

The advent of Wi-Fi-based audio systems and DMAs has made this category of product somewhat obsolete. For the most part, you can still find wireless speakers, but wireless line-level distribution systems are being phased out.

Part III
Now We're Communicating!

"It was a compromise. I gave in on the home LAN connection, but I drew the line at the 2-way video feed."

In this part . . .

The key to a great home-phone system is the flexibility to have many different types of endpoints hanging out of a good, solid base infrastructure. By the pool, you may want waterproof phones; in the office, a good conference capability; in the kitchen, a cordless option. You may also need to be able to transfer calls, talk within the home on an intercom, use caller ID, and more, wherever you are in your smart home.

In this part, we tell you how to create a telephony backbone in your house. We discuss the major elements of a whole-home telephone network and describe the advantages of connecting all the telephone pieces and parts. We also tell you about some cool wireless-phone systems that have all the functionality of wired phones but require only a limited amount of telephone wiring in the walls. Finally, we talk about the different communications equipment and services available — including the latest and greatest services that use the Internet and broadband connections for phone calls.

Chapter 10

Planning a Phone System

· ·

· ·

*M*ost people take their telephone service for granted. Plug your phone into the wall jack, pay your monthly bill to your area's telephone monopoly, and, as Donnie Brasco might say, fuggitaboudit. As life becomes increasingly wired, however, you may want to do things that require a more sophisticated phone system than the trusty AT&T model you bought back in the '70s when you switched over to Touch-Tone. For example, you may want to send faxes, transfer calls within your home, or use your phone system as an intercom.

Not only are our telephone needs more complicated than in the past, but we're also beginning to face a plethora of choices in how we get phone service delivered to our homes. Thanks to deregulation by Congress and the Federal Communications Commission, a whole host of companies — some familiar, some not — are offering competitive local phone services to residential customers. Many of these companies are offering phone service over your broadband Internet connection — providing cheap (or even free) calls around the world. As if this were not enough, more and more people are using their cell phone as their home phone — finding that having both a local line and a cell phone line is redundant.

Your phone network in your home is important not only because you can place your voice calls over these lines but also because you may need your phone network for your alarm system, your Internet access, to access pay-per-view on your satellite TV service, and to do many other smart-home tasks. A phone line is a critical backbone element to your smart home.

In this chapter, we tell you about all the various pieces that make up a phone network and give you some advice in making choices for your phone networking needs.

Selecting Equipment for Your Phone Network

When you're considering any home-network system, one of the big questions you need to ask yourself is, what will plug into it? After all, why build a highway if it doesn't go anywhere?

You may be surprised at the number of choices you have about what you can plug into your home-phone network — much more than just phones. We don't even consider computer modems and network appliances here, just standard telephony equipment that lets you talk and otherwise communicate with the outside world.

Plug and play the old-fashioned way

The most common category of telephone equipment in a home network is analog, POTS-compatible (POTS is a telephone industry term meaning *Plain Old Telephone Service*) devices. Often called wireline phones because they are corded, these devices plug into your network of wall jacks, using standard a modular phone plug (called an *RJ-11 connector,* which we describe in Chapter 11) or the four-prong plugs or hardwired environments (meaning they're wired directly into the wall) in old homes.

Note: The RJ-11 connector family has several variations based on the number of telephone lines wired to an individual jack. For simplicity's sake, we use the term *RJ-11* generically to describe the one-, two-, and three-line versions of these connectors.

The most basic and common analog telephone device is the standard corded telephone. This is the trusty old telephone we've known and loved for decades and decades. Little has changed in corded phones for quite some time, although many features have been added over the years — such as hold and speed-dialer buttons, speakers for hands-free talking, and liquid crystal display (LCD) screens.

Besides cool new features, the biggest difference among various corded telephones is their capacity to connect to multiple phone lines. Although most telephones are still single-line phones, a growing number can be simultaneously connected to two or three telephone lines at the same time. As more people install multiple phone lines for home offices, teen lines, and other uses, multiple-line telephones are becoming increasingly common — and necessary.

Features, features, and more features

The basic design and functionality of corded telephones hasn't changed much over the years. With the exception of the transition from pulse to touch-tone dialing 15 or 20 years ago, the way corded telephones work has remained remarkably constant for generations.

What has changed is the number of features in low-cost consumer telephones — a result of the decreasing cost (and increasing power) of computer chips. For example, you can now buy telephones that include

- ✔ **Speed dialing:** This feature allows you do press one button to dial a preprogrammed number that you call often.

- ✔ **Voice-activated dialing:** This feature allows you to talk to your phone to have it dial (for example, "Call Holly at work"). Some of the more advanced models allow you to interface between the phone and the PC so that you can access your PC contact databases, such as Microsoft Outlook.

- ✔ **LCD displays:** These displays tell you the number you called and how long you've been on the call.

- ✔ **Built-in phone directories:** These directories can store hundreds of names and numbers and display them on an LCD screen.

- ✔ **Speakerphones:** These phones, which let you talk hands-free, come in two types: *half-duplex* models, which let you either talk or listen (but not both) at one time, and more sophisticated *full-duplex* models that let you do both at once. Full-duplex phones are immeasurably better, in our opinion, because you can carry on a hands-free conversation naturally, without choppiness or lost words. Few are half duplex today

(only the cheapest models). Speakerphones are typically part of the base station of a phone but can be found in more expensive cordless phone units as well.

- ✔ **Voice mail:** You hear a lot of different terms for the answering machine capability of a telephone, such as digital answering machine, tapeless answering machine, or voice mail. For the most part, that's semantics. Many phones offer an inherent function that allows you to have one or more voice mail boxes in which you can store inbound messages. These can be checked remotely, as well as from your house.

- ✔ **Conference calling:** Three-way, four-way, and even five-way calling is available on phones so that you can conference different parties. If you're doing this through your system, however, remember that you need to have a telephone line for each party you want to conference — if you want to conference two other people for a three-way conference, you need two telephone lines. Later in the chapter, we talk about conference services, which avoid this telephone line expense.

- ✔ **Caller ID displays:** This feature shows you the phone number and, in some cases, the name of the person who is calling you. Caller ID requires both the hardware on your end — either built into the phone or a stand-alone display unit — and a subscription to caller ID service from your local telephone company. Some caller ID services also include (for a bit more money every month) call waiting caller ID, which tells you who is calling when you're already on the phone with a different person.

If your telephone needs run to several lines, you may want to consider a telephone system that gives you more control over your lines and enables you to do things such as transfer calls between phones within your home. To take advantage of these features, you need something beyond a standard phone. Later in the chapter (in the "Fancy phone systems" section), we go into more detail about the key telephone system unit (KSU) and sophisticated KSU-less multiline phone systems.

Cordless phones

Wireline phones are great, but sometimes you just don't want to get up from the couch to answer the phone. So it should be no surprise that cordless phones are now found in nearly 90 percent of all homes in the United States. These phones consist of two main components:

- ✔ **A base station**, consisting of a battery charger and a radio transceiver, which plugs into an RJ-11 phone jack just like a wireline phone

- ✔ **The cordless handset** that communicates with the base station and carries your phone conversation over radio waves

You can choose from seven main types of cordless phones (which, like wireline phones, are available in both single- and multiple-line versions):

- ✔ **46- and 49-MHz phones:** These are the traditional cordless phones that have been widely available for many years. They send your phone signals over 46- and 49-MHz radio channels in an analog form. These phones are the cheapest available and generally have the shortest range.

- ✔ **900-MHz analog phones:** These cordless phones are similar to 46- and 49-MHz phones, except they use a higher-frequency radio channel to carry your phone signals. These higher-frequency radio waves have a longer range and are a little less susceptible to interference. Because these phones are analog, they're susceptible to being monitored by radio scanners.

- ✔ **900-MHz digital phones:** A step up in price from the analog models, these phones convert your phone signal into a digital format before sending it over the airwaves. These digital signals are less likely to suffer from interference and signal degradation, so you should end up with a clearer phone conversation with less static and noise.

- ✔ **900-MHz digital spread-spectrum phones:** The most sophisticated — and expensive — cordless phones, these models take the digital radio signal and send it over a large number of different radio frequencies in rapid succession. This *frequency hopping* decreases the likelihood that you pick up unwanted radio signals — such as your neighbor's cordless

telephone — and also increases security (because it's much more difficult for someone with a radio scanner to tune into very much of your
conversation as you switch frequencies).

✔ **2.4-GHz digital spread-spectrum phones:** The 2.4-GHz frequency is less
crowded than the 900-MHz spectrum, so you're likely to get less interference, but it is used by many Wi-Fi wireless computer networks.

✔ **5.8-GHz digital spread-spectrum phones:** The newest product entries
are in this spectrum, which up to now had been used largely for commercial wireless broadband applications.

✔ **DECT phones:** DECT (Digital Enhanced Cordless Telecommunications) is a
European digital cordless phone standard that was approved for use in the
U.S in late 2006. DECT uses frequencies in the 1.9-GHz frequency range.

You read all sorts of claims about distance comparisons between 900-MHz,
2.4-GHz, and 5.8-GHz phones. We'd love to give you a hard-and-fast rule about
which is best, but it depends on the phone and the implementation. Many
factors — not just the frequency spectrum that the handset uses — go into
your ability to hear well when you're 150 feet from your base station.

In ads and on Web sites, you'll see references to *expandable* cordless phones.
These systems are expandable because you can add more handsets to the
system without buying extra base stations (traditional cordless phones have a
limit of one handset per base station). You need to plug only the one base station into an RJ-11 or RJ-45 phone jack. The additional handsets require only a
battery charger station — which plugs into your electrical power lines — so
you don't need a separate phone jack for each additional phone. You can generally add up to twelve handsets on a given system, but some allow for as few
as four, so check the feature listing.

Expandable cordless phone systems can dramatically change the way you use
phones in your house. Before, when you wanted a cordless phone in a particular spot, you needed a power outlet and a phone outlet. Now you're free to
place these phones where there's just power. This means you have the freedom
to locate your cordless phones anywhere in the kitchen, for instance. Of
course, it's that many more phones to lose in the couch too! We like expandable cordless phone systems that have pager or intercom functions, so that
we can ping the phones and find them.

An example of these multiline, multistation cordless phones comes from
Panasonic (www.panasonic.com). We've been using their cordless systems
for years. The KX-TG4500B 4-Line Multi-Handset Cordless Phone System uses
5.8-GHz frequency hopping spread spectrum (FHSS) transmission to offer
four lines and up to eight extensions. The core of the system is a corded base
station, and there's one handset and charger. Out of the box, you get private

voice-mail boxes, intercom, auto attendant, conferencing, and most of the usual features such as hold, transfer, and caller ID. The Panasonic system is about $500 for the main unit and $100 per handset — a great price if you've ever shopped for a system as packed as this one. Other vendors of similar systems include VTECH (www.vtechphones), Siemens (www.siemens.com), and Philips (www.philips.com).

Soon you'll start seeing multimode wireless phones. The handsets of these phones have both cordless phone and cellular (or PCS) phone circuitry built in. When you're within range of your home base station, phone calls are carried over your standard telephone lines or over the Internet. If you take the handset outside your home, the phone automatically switches to its cellular mode, and phone calls are carried over the cellular phone network. Some manufacturers are starting to ship multimode Wi-Fi wireless and cellular phones, to allow you to make calls over your home's wireless data infrastructure.

A growing number of cordless phones have headset jacks on their handsets, so you can walk around without having to hold the phone to your ear. Most of these phones also have belt clips so you can clip the phone on and have both hands free. Cordless phones are designed to use headsets with 2.5mm plugs and won't accept headsets with modular plugs, which are commonly used with office phones. Some of the more advanced headsets are phones unto themselves with clip-on dial pads and remote handset lifters that take your desktop phone off the hook so you can dial — from several rooms away. Check out www.hellodirect.com and www.plantronics.com for more on headsets.

And for people who like the convenience of a cordless phone but the solid look and feel of a traditional handset station, some manufacturers offer cordless desk phones (with wired handsets). These look like a typical business phone, with an antenna to sync up with other cordless phones.

Although we love cordless phones and use them constantly, you need to be aware of a couple of drawbacks associated with them:

- **Quality:** No matter how expensive — and no matter what the ads may try to tell you — the quality of your phone signal on a cordless phone isn't as good as a wireline phone.

- **Security:** Your phone conversation is less secure and confidential on a cordless phone than it is on a wireline telephone. Although digital phones — especially spread-spectrum models — do offer increased security, any phone conversation that you have on a wireless system is susceptible to interception by unscrupulous folks with radio scanners. Some cordless phone manufacturers offer phones with an encrypted mode to lessen this hazard.

Fancy phone systems

We travel a lot internationally, and it's amazing the places we'll go to and see three or four phones on someone's desk, because the person needs three or four different phone lines. We saw seven in one office in Africa.

Lucky for us, we live in a country where technology has developed to meet the needs of the multiline user. A broad range of options is available for someone who wants to be able to have more of a phone *system* in the house. Generally, you will find phones that can handle one, two, three, four, or more lines today. A four-line phone system is great for many homes because you can allocate two lines to the business/home office (you need two for conferencing, we suggest), one for personal use, and one vacant for your future (or present) teen phone line.

Much of the functionality for multiline phone systems was developed as part of key phone systems for corporate applications. A *key system* generally consists of a central unit, called the *key system unit,* or KSU, that handles the intelligence of the phone system and coordinates access to the outbound telephone lines connected to it.

Because they deal with both analog and digital phone capabilities, the key systems being produced for home and small offices these days are often called *hybrid phone systems*. The term *hybrid* is also used to describe systems that have both wired and wireless capabilities.

With a key or hybrid phone system, you can

- Make a call on a free line while other lines are in use
- Transfer calls from one extension to another
- Connect several lines for a conference call
- Use your phones as an intercom system, paging between rooms or using the phones' speaker systems for hands-free intercom use
- Dedicate a specific extension for all fax or modem calls and let the key system automatically route incoming calls
- Pipe in music for people who are on hold (we find that old Spike Jones hits are conversation starters)

If you wanted to install a telephone network in your house in the past, you had to install a KSU-based business phone system in the home, complete with 25-pair wiring and bulky handsets.

Well no more. Installing a telephone network in your home can be as simple as plugging in an AC adapter and plugging a telephone cord into a central unit. The rest can be wireless. Throughout most of the book, we pitch wired as the far preferred mode of networking. However, the benefits of wireless phone networking are so immense that it has distinct advantages that should be seriously considered. If it weren't for the problems inherent with signal fade as you go throughout the house, we'd say always do wireless. If you have a larger home, lots of concrete and brick walls, or just a lot of interference in the neighborhood, wireline options (or systems that are hybrids of wireless and wireline) are still your best bet.

Key phone systems fall into two major categories:

- **Multiline key telephone system units (KSU/hybrid phone systems):** These systems are based on a central control unit (the KSU), which performs all transferring, paging, and other functions. Each telephone extension is wired (or connected wirelessly) to the KSU.

- **Multiline KSU-less phone systems:** In a KSU-less system, the intelligence of the central control unit is built into the extension phones themselves. There is no central unit — just independent, intelligent phones that communicate with each other rather than with a separate control device.

In practice, consumer applications — four telephone lines or less — have moved to a largely KSU-less environment. If there is a KSU, you probably don't notice it much because it's embedded in the master base station phone. If you need a more high-powered phone system at home — because you have many more rooms or need more inbound lines — you'll probably be better off with a centrally driven KSU/hybrid system.

KSU phone systems

A KSU or hybrid telephone system consists of a central control unit (the KSU) and a series of extension phones that the central control system controls. Your incoming telephone company phone lines connect to the KSU, which in turn connects to each individual extension phone by a single phone line or wireless connection. Every phone connected to the KSU system has access to all the external phone lines — usually by simply pressing a line button on the phone, such as Line 1 or Line 2.

A KSU system has both advantages and disadvantages. The advantages include the following:

- **The greatest capacity:** Most residential KSU or hybrid phone systems can handle 3 or 4 *CO* (central office — the lines coming into your home) lines out of the box, and most systems can be expanded to handle as many as 8 lines.

✔ **More extensions:** KSU or hybrid systems can often connect 16 or more extension phones — so if you have a large house with many rooms, you don't have to worry about limitations on the number of phones you install. You can see the benefit for businesses that grow from a few employees to hundreds.

✔ **More features:** Although KSU and KSU-less systems share many features (such as call transfer, paging, and intercom), typical KSU systems let you add additional features such as automatic routing of fax calls to the correct extension, sophisticated hold functions (such as foisting your musical tastes on people you put on hold), doorbell monitors and openers, and even high-capacity multiple-mailbox voice-mail systems.

The disadvantages to a KSU system include the following:

✔ **A higher price tag:** Base-model KSU systems start near $600, and the price can skyrocket as you add lines, extensions, and additional features.

✔ **More complicated installation:** Although KSU-less systems are more or less plug and play, a KSU system requires a more involved installation and setup procedure (but it's still pretty easy).

✔ **Special phone equipment:** Some KSU systems require you to buy a special key telephone for each extension, which can be an expensive proposition. A few systems even have specific requirements regarding the kind of telephone wiring you need to connect extensions to the central unit. Even systems that let you use "regular" phones will not provide the full range of features for these phones — you'll need to use special phones designed to be part of the system to access the full range of features.

An example of a hybrid phone system that's popular in the residential market is Panasonic's KX-TA824 systems (www.panasonic.com, price is determined by dealers). The base model supports 3 CO lines and 8 extensions in the home and can be expanded to as many as 8 CO lines and 24 extensions. The KX-TA824 supports features such as room-to-room intercom, a room monitor (so you can keep an "ear" on the kids), call conferencing, PC programming of the system (including offsite programming through a built-in modem, so your dealer can configure the system for your remotely), and background music support. The KX-TA824 supports CO-based voice mail (the voice mail service provided by your phone provider, in other words) or can be configured as an in-house voice mail system with an optional card. You can even configure the system with a card that lets you talk to folks at the front door from any location in the house and remotely unlock the door (sort of like buzzing someone in a high-rise apartment).

There are a lot of manufacturers of fancy and capable KSU and hybrid phone systems with a focus on business use. We mention this Panasonic model (there's also the KX-TAW824, which includes built-in cordless phone support) because Panasonic is just about the only game in town at the sub-$1000 consumer price point.

KSU/hybrid systems and the KSU-less phone systems we discuss in the following section use different frequencies than those used by POTS phone services to send calls between extensions in the home. This trick enables them to use a single phone line for both phone calls and intercom calls. Unfortunately, these different (higher) frequencies are also used by DSL high-speed Internet services. Most DSL installations use *microfilter* devices to isolate these higher frequencies from your phones (if they didn't, you'd hear high-pitched squawking sounds like the ones you hear when a fax machine is connecting). The DSL microfilters will therefore block your intercom features. In Chapter 11, we discuss some ways to get around this issue if you're using a KSU/hybrid unit or a KSU-less phone system.

KSU-less phone systems

A KSU system requires a rather large, upfront expenditure, but a KSU-less phone system provides many of the same features for less money. KSU-less systems, which are usually designed for three or four phone lines, connect to a standard RJ-11 or RJ-45 phone jack that you already use for your stand-alone phone systems and a nearby electrical outlet. Cordless KSU-less systems just plug into any nearby electrical outlet. They differ from standard phones in their internal intelligence. Built into each of these phones is an electronic brain that performs many of the same functions that are found in a central KSU system.

Choosing a KSU-less phone system over a KSU/hybrid system offers some advantages, including the following:

✔ **The price tag is initially lower:** These systems usually cost from $100 to $200 per phone.

✔ **You can start off small:** All you need to get started are two KSU-less phones — you can add more as needed.

✔ **Installation is simpler:** Basically, all you need to do is plug the phone into one or more RJ-11 wall jacks, and you're up and running. Some systems require that you set some small switches to assign an extension number to each phone.

✔ **Wiring requirements are less stringent:** KSU-less phone systems work in just about any kind of telephone wiring architecture, unlike KSU/hybrid systems, which can require a specific wiring topology. We explain all about topologies, architectures, and other important-sounding words dealing with phone systems in Chapter 11.

KSU-less systems have their share of disadvantages as well, including the following:

✔ **Less system capacity:** Most KSU-less systems don't handle more than four phone lines and more than twelve extensions. If your needs go beyond these limits, you should opt for a full-fledged KSU system.

✔ **Fewer features:** Compared to KSU systems, KSU-less systems typically have fewer features. Additionally, although most KSU systems are modular (meaning that you can add additional functionality to the system by plugging in cards to the KSU), KSU-less systems have all the functionality in the handsets, so you have to replace all of them to upgrade.

As we mentioned at the beginning of this section, we think the multi-extension, multiline cordless and corded KSU-less (whew!) systems are exactly what most homes need and are the most flexible. Be prepared to go wired and KSU if your performance or feature requirements dictate.

Panasonic (www.panasonic.com) and AT&T (telephones.att.com) offer a range of systems for single-line and multiline KSU and KSU-less systems, as do more business-oriented (and expensive) companies such as Nortel (www.nortel.com).

Fax machines

Although traditionally an office device, fax (facsimile) machines are becoming increasingly common in the home. Fax machines scan printed material and transmit the scanned data over a standard phone line to a remote fax machine, which then prints the material on the far end. Fax machines fall into two main types:

✔ **Thermal paper fax:** Increasingly hard to find, these models use long rolls of thermal paper to print incoming faxes. The quality of the incoming fax is low, the paper tends to curl up, and the image deteriorates over time. However, these machines are fine for occasional use.

✔ **Plain paper fax:** Most fax machines these days print incoming faxes on plain paper, using a mechanism similar to that found in an inkjet or laser computer printer. These models offer significantly higher print quality and your faxes don't end up in a tightly wound scroll on your desk. We recommend that you splurge for the plain paper fax machine.

Many fax manufacturers — and computer printer makers, as well — combine fax machines, printers, telephones, and even copiers into a single all-in-one home-office machine, sometimes referred to as a *multifunctional device* (MFD). These devices can be handy and are usually less expensive than buying all the components separately (and they take up less desk space in your home office). The latest ones sport telephone base stations, so you can get a 900-MHz or 2.4-GHz cordless phone system as well. Whew, that's like a whole telephone closet in one package!

Multifunction devices usually provide lower-quality output than separately purchased components. Generally, getting a great deal of functionality into one box at a reasonable price dictates compromises in the quality of the components.

Color multifunction machines can be expensive for ordinary black-and-white faxing. Look for machines that have separate color and black ink cartridges, so that you don't have to replace your expensive color cartridges when you print only black-and-white faxes all the time.

If you operate a home office, you may want a dedicated number that rings to your fax machine. Should you get a fax machine if you don't receive many fax messages? For the most part, a fax machine is just a scanner and a printer — and your computer setup probably has both of those — you might try a free service such as eFax.com (`www.efax.com`), which gives you your own telephone number for receiving faxes — and forwards any inbound fax you receive to your e-mail. From your e-mail, you can print the fax on your printer. This saves you from having to dedicate a local phone line (which can be expensive) to your fax machine. For outbound faxes, you can use your scanner to scan the document into your computer, and then either send that as an e-mail attachment or sign up for the for-fee eFax Plus, which accepts your e-mail (with attachment) and sends that as a fax message anywhere in the world.

Answering machines

Remember *The Rockford Files*? The title sequence of that show featured the lead character's answering machine taking an incoming call — a rare event back then (in the 1970s) when answering machines were huge, ungainly, and expensive. The computer revolution has touched on these devices in the intervening decades, and now answering machines are compact, inexpensive, and — as you no doubt already know — everywhere.

The least expensive answering machines you can find are those based on the same technology found in that old Rockford machine. A cassette tape — or in most cases, a smaller microcassette tape — records your outgoing greeting message and incoming messages. A bit clunky, but these machines usually work pretty well and typically cost next to nothing.

Newer answering machines use digital technology to record your voice and that of incoming callers as digital data stored on a computer memory chip. These tapeless answering machines have a higher voice quality and — because they don't have a tape or moving parts to wear out — aren't as susceptible to catastrophic mechanical failures.

The most expensive digital answering machines often behave like voice-mail systems found in businesses, offering features such as multiple mailboxes (so incoming messages can be directed to specific individuals in the household), multiple-line capabilities, and remote operation (which allows you to check your messages when you're away from home).

Many answering machines are not stand-alone devices. Instead, they often include a corded or cordless phone as part of the same device or are part of a multifunction printer/copier/scanner/fax device.

Although answering machines have become increasingly sophisticated and capable, we've become proponents of the voice-mail services offered by most local telephone companies. These services offer you an answering machine in the telephone network, where that answering machine is really a giant computer that many subscribers share. You typically find out that you have a message when you pick up your phone and hear a stutter dial tone; small light attachments also blink when you have a message. These services have become inexpensive and convenient. Before you spend a bundle on a fancy digital answering machine, we recommend that you explore the voice-mail service available in your area and see how the features and price stack up. Note a difference between the telephone company voice-mail services and your own device — if your phone line is busy, the answering machine can't pick up. Because we blab a lot on the phone, we use the telephone company's service.

If you have multiple phone lines in your house, you need to think about how you integrate these lines with your answering system. If you want to have one answering device for two lines, you'll need to get a two-line answering machine or tell the telephone company that "Line 1 rolls over to Line 2, on busy/no answer." (That is, if Line 1 is busy or there is no answer, send the call to Line 2, where the answering device will pick up if no one answers that line as well).

If you also have a cell phone that has voice mail, consider sending all calls from your home phone line on busy/no answer to your cell phone voice-mail system. That way, you won't have to check multiple voice-mail boxes all the time.

External ringers/lights

If you've ever hung around an auto repair shop (Pat likes to do that — don't ask why because he couldn't possibly explain), you may have noticed that when the phone rings in the main office, bells and whistles seem to sound everywhere. Those are external ringers — stand-alone devices that alert you to incoming calls when you're not near the phone.

You don't need to be an automotive technician to appreciate one of these devices. You may just have a big, noisy house (if you read our bios, you know that Danny has four preteen/teenaged children!) or spend time in the backyard far from the phone. Many hearing-impaired telephone users have attached to their telephone networks special visual indicators that light up when the phone rings. Such external indicators are inexpensive and easy to install; just plug them into an RJ-11 jack and — in some cases — AC power. You can find external ringers that let you choose what the ring sounds like, ringers that ring differently for different phone lines, and even ringers that give you a silent, visual indication of a telephone call.

TDD devices

A *TDD*, or Telecommunications Device for the Deaf, is a text device that enables hearing-impaired folks to communicate over telephone lines. Consisting of a display screen and a keyboard, it works like a computer chat system — without the computer.

Many telephone companies offer a service that lets non-TDD users connect with folks who are on a TDD. In these cases, an operator from the phone company gets in the middle of the conversation and types to the person with the TDD and speaks to the one without.

Choosing a Fixed Phone Service

In the old days, you had no choice when it came to ordering phone service for your home. If you wanted phone service, you had to go to the phone company, and you took the service that the company had to offer. In this section, we talk about the growing number of phone options to consider — both in terms of which company you buy service from and what kind of service you receive.

Changes in regulations in the United States are allowing other companies to go after your local phone business — everyone from cable television companies to mobile operators. Despite the entry of these new competitors, however, the majority of homes in the United States still receive phone service from the traditional local monopoly.

You can get landline (that is, non-wireless) phone service into your home in two primary ways:

- ✔ **Analog telephone service:** Usually called *POTS* (for *Plain Old Telephone Service* — no, we didn't make that up). This is the service we all know and love.

✔ **VoIP (often called digital) phone service:** VoIP (*Voice over IP*) phone services are carried over a broadband connection (such as DSL or cable modem) and use the Internet Protocol (IP, hence the name) to carry your voice just as Web pages, e-mail, and instant messages are carried).

Just about everyone these days has a mobile phone — which we discuss in the "Cutting the Cord: Going Mobile" section. A growing number of people are indeed "cutting the cord" and using their mobile phones as their primary home phone — skipping the entire landline network. Although wireless service can be a replacement for the single phone line to your home for your voice calls, it may not be a replacement for your smart home's phone network backbone. You may still need phone lines running in your house, and you are going to need access to a phone network for various things, such as your DIRECTV or DISH Network dish calling in the movies you've purchased or your alarm system calling in to say "HELPPPPPP!" As with all technologies, cellular services have a role to play in a smart home, but it's not *the* role. Eventually, we believe that many of these services will run over your always-on broadband Internet connection, instead of over a standard phone line. But even in that case we think it makes sense to have at least one regular phone line as a backup — and for emergency services such as 911. Analog phone service is cheap, and although we may complain about the phone companies sometimes, they do an amazing job at making their phone lines reliable and available.

POTS

The common denominator in telephone services is the analog voice connection (provided over copper wires) known as POTS. When you call the telephone company and ask the service folks to install a telephone line to your home, you usually get a POTS line. In this section, we briefly describe how the telephone network connects to your home.

With POTS service, an analog, copper phone line connects your house to the telephone network. The local *telco* (telephone company) has a huge network of local central offices — each serving individual towns or even neighborhoods, as shown in Figure 10-1. These central offices contain digital switches (usually) that connect phone calls onto the public telephone network. A call travels through the PSTN (Public Switched Telephone Network, the telephone network we're all connected to) to another telephone somewhere.

The gauge and the number of wires running to your house varies from telco to telco and installation to installation (depending on when your phone service was first set up). Generally, you find what's called a *quad wire,* consisting of two separate pairs of copper wire in a single sheath. POTS telephone service requires only a single pair of wires, so most people find that they already have adequate wiring for two phone lines connected to their homes.

Figure 10-1:
The traditional telephone network.

The telephone companies are working with manufacturers to find the right combination of technologies to make mass deployment of fiber-optic lines to the home economically viable. Many towns and new subdivisions are being outfitted with fiber optics in a series of ongoing and expanding fiber deployments (we discuss these in Chapter 13. Fiber optics will carry voice traffic for sure, but the promise of being able to carry substantially more video and data traffic is attractive to the telcos.

Connecting in new ways

Traditional telephone service and cellular phones have traditionally been the only real options when it comes to getting telephone service. That's changed over the past few years as companies that have had nothing to do with local telephone service have taken advantage of FCC deregulation and the explosion of broadband Internet services and entered the local telephone marketplace.

The cable squawk box

Coming soon (if it's not already there!) is local telephone competition from your cable company — and you're going to like this. The cable industry calls it the triple play: voice, data, and video in one cost-effective package. You'll get local and long-distance phone service, cable-modem Internet service, and cable TV over the local cable system.

When this service becomes available in your neighborhood, you won't have to worry about figuring out how to plug your telephones into the cable outlet. Instead, cable telephony systems will typically include a small device called a *splitter*. This small black box will be installed right at the point where your cable connection enters the home and will separate the telephone signals from the rest of the cable signals (television, audio, and cable modem). The telephone signals will then be connected to your home's standard telephone wiring (in place of the connection you now have with the local telephone company), and the rest of the cable signals will be carried over your home's cable network. Figure 10-2 shows such an arrangement.

Videoconferencing: I get the picture

The ability to see the person to whom you are speaking has been a topic of discussion since the phone was invented. AT&T tantalized and teased folks with its launch of its Picturephone at the 1964 World's Fair in New York, but the limited availability (three cities) and expense ($16 to $27 for the first three minutes) made sure that the service never went anywhere. AT&T tried again to launch a consumer videoconferencing product in 1992 with the ill-fated Videophone, which cost $1500 and offered only slow frame rates and jerky pictures.

Videoconferencing has been common in the business world for years and has required digital lines. Luckily, most people don't need business-class videoconferencing — their needs are much more restrained. Consumer-grade products are classified into a few areas:

✔ **Stand-alone analog devices:** These are phones with video capabilities that use your regular phone lines to deliver video signals in addition to the voice signals traveling over the same line. For example, Vialta (www.vialta.com) has a Beamer product line.

✔ **TV-mounted broadband devices:** These devices use your broadband connection and connect a camera mounted on top of a television to send pictures to someone else's television. For example, D-Link's (www.d-link.com) DVC-1000 broadband video

phone uses a small set-top camera/conferencing unit to videoconference to another DVC-1000 using regular phone lines.

✔ **Stand-alone broadband devices:** You can also find video phones that use your broadband connection but don't rely on your TV. Instead, these devices are fully integrated video phones, with their own built-in cameras and screens. An example of this type of device is D-Link's DVC-2000 i2eye broadband video phone.

✔ **PC-connected devices:** These devices enable you to use the power of your computer and its network connections to send video pictures to other similar devices elsewhere. We talk more about PC-based videoconferencing options in Chapter 12.

You generally find that only one kind can communicate with another of its kind. In other words, you won't find a TV-connected device that can communicate with a PC-connected device. They are usually paired offerings, where you need the same capability on each end.

As the PC and entertainment center become more linked, and as displays for TVs become more like computer displays, consumer videoconferencing over the Internet and your broadband connections will likely become commonplace.

Figure 10-2:
A voice-
over-cable
network.

Cable companies offer cable telephony in two ways:

- ✔ **Circuit-switched:** This is essentially POTS using a different wire. Circuit-switched cable telephony service looks and feels just like POTS because, for all intents and purposes, it's POTS using some different equipment on both ends of the call to facilitate the use of the cable system. Although millions of people are using this, all new build-outs of cable telephony are switching to VoIP, discussed next.

- ✔ **VoIP:** This service, as we discuss earlier in detail in the following section, uses the broadband cable-modem connection to carry voice calls as data using Internet protocols.

There's no functional difference to the user between circuit-switched and VoIP cable telephony — the big difference is within the cable company's own network, where VoIP saves them money. Regardless of which technology your cable company uses, you'll have a similar experience and the diagram shown in Figure 10-2 will still apply.

In late 2006, there were nearly five million customers of cable telephony in the U.S. This number is expected to grow tremendously in the future and drive down prices for local phone service. What's important to you is that the home-phone network you build today will still work if you shift your service to the cable company.

Several cable companies (such as Time Warner and Comcast) have teamed up with Sprint to offer a *quadruple play* service that adds mobile voice and data services to the cable triple play. The primary advantage of such a service is simply lower prices and a single bill for all your services, but over time we expect to see service enhancements that take advantage of all four services — things like integrated voice mail between your landline and mobile phone or the ability to transfer video between your cable DVR, your broadband connected PCs, and your mobile phone or smartphone/PDA. Pursuing a similar strategy are the big phone companies, especially Verizon and AT&T (the two biggest), who each own their own mobile phone networks (the two biggest: Cingular — soon to be called AT&T Wireless — and Verizon Wireless).

Voice over IP

People have gone crazy over *voice-over IP* (as in *Internet Protocol,* the language of the Net). Your home's data network runs on IP. The Internet runs on IP. The traditional, voice telephone network does not. However, the telephone companies are in the process of migrating a lot of their traffic to IP, in the belief that it's a more efficient way to transport your calls.

As a result, a lot of focus is being placed on the IP-ization of telephone calls. And that's leading to voice-over IP (VoIP) services, which pick up your calls originating from IP devices and deliver them to other IP devices or to regular phones anywhere in the world.

Voice-over IP services use your Internet connection to place and receive phone calls. This was the domain of hobbyists for a long time (heck, we even wrote our first *For Dummies* book on the topic more than a decade ago); they used a PC, special software, microphones, and headsets to make calls. Voice-over IP has become a little more mainstream as more user-friendly devices, such as phones and video phones that can connect over IP, have come on the market.

In the voice-over-IP scenario, your Internet access provider (that is, your cable, DSL, or dial-up access provider) carries your telephone calls as bits and bytes of IP data traffic through your Internet connection. That means you can make calls through your PC, home-phone network, or even through the set-top box on your TV. The VoIP providers will install a voice-over-IP gateway that will allow your calls to be carried from the Internet to regular phones on the POTS telephone network.

Understanding VoIP services

The initial reason most people gravitate towards VoIP service is because it costs less (often a whole lot less) than traditional phone services. You can expect to pay no more than $25 a month for a full-featured VoIP service with unlimited nationwide calling, voice mail, call waiting, and all the goodies.

International calls are also typically much cheaper than they are with traditional phone services.

But other reasons to like VoIP are the features that you can't get from regular POTS services — mainly you get *control*. What that means is that you can access your VoIP service through a Web page and take charge of your phones. You can activate call blocking, call forwarding, do not disturb modes, and so on — all on a Web site. In many cases you can customize those features (for example, certain calling numbers go right to your phone but others go right to voice mail). You can also use the Web to create phonebooks (for one-touch dialing), view your call logs (without waiting for the bill to come at the end of the month), or even use a "locate me" service, which automatically tries a number of phones (your mobile, your office, your parents, whatever you choose) and transfers incoming calls to you when you're not home.

Two main types of VoIP service are available (at least as we categorize them — there's some overlap):

✔ **Landline replacement services:** These services, from companies such as Vonage (`www.vonage.com`), SunRocket (`www.sunrocket.com`), Lingo (`www.lingo.com`), and Packet8 (`www.packet8.com`), are designed to replace your existing landline and even use your existing phone number but carry all your calls over your broadband Internet connection.

We'd categorize the cable company VoIP offerings among this group, as well as offerings from the phone companies themselves (!), such as AT&T's CallVantage service (`http://www.usa.att.com/callvantage`).

✔ **Supplementary, PC-based VoIP services:** These services are primarily marketed for use with a computer, rather than a regular phone, as the tool for making and receiving calls and are usually free for computer-to-computer calls. Examples of this type of VoIP service include Skype (`www.skype.com`) and Gizmo (`www.gizmoproject.com`). These services are built around an assumption that you use a landline (or cell phone) for a number of your calls — particularly local calls — and that the VoIP service will be primarily used for long-distance (or international) calls.

The biggest difference between landline replacement and the PC-based VoIP services is that the landline replacement services are designed to meet E-911 requirements. That means if you dial 911 from a Vonage or Lingo phone service, your call will be directed to your local 911 operator and information about you (such as your address and name) will appear on their screens. Services such as Vonage and Gizmo can make phone calls just like Vonage and Lingo, but they don't meet any 911 requirements and shouldn't be relied on in such circumstances.

Converging fixed and mobile

The next big trend in VoIP is called *fixed mobile convergence (FMC)*, or *unlicensed mobile access (UMA)*. FMC is a service that uses your mobile phone handset as both a mobile phone and a Wi-Fi VoIP phone. With such a service, you use your mobile carrier for phone calls when you're away from home but switch to VoIP carried over your broadband Internet connection when you get within range of your Wi-Fi access point.

For FMC to operate in your home, you need to work with your cellular service provider, who will provide you with a Wi-Fi-enabled handset and a Wi-Fi access point (if you don't have one). The intelligence for this system lies within your phone (and the service provider's network) — essentially your phone will look for the strongest signal and connect to it. FMC systems seamlessly *roam* between Wi-Fi and cellular — so you can leave the house while talking on a

Wi-Fi call and not lose your connection as the call is transitioned to the mobile network.

The best thing about FMC is that it saves money — for both the user (calls on your Wi-Fi network are usually free or subject to a small monthly fee and don't count against your plan minutes) and the mobile service provider (they reduce traffic on their cell towers and save money by not having to build as many). You also get better coverage at home, because you're connecting to a nearby Wi-Fi access point, and not to a distant cell tower.

The first example of an FMC service in the U.S. comes from T-Mobile (www.t-mobile.com), who launched a pilot service called Hot Spot @ Home in Seattle. For more information on this service, check out www.theonlyphone youneed.com/.

For 911 to work on a VoIP service, you need to configure your phone equipment. We can't tell you how because the process differs by provider, but essentially, you use a PC to access your VoIP phone equipment and provide information that will let the VoIP service provider properly route your 911 calls. Don't forget this step if you're getting rid of all of your POTS services. Also remember that VoIP systems, unlike POTS systems, tend to stop working when your power goes out. If you're going VoIP only, we recommend that you either maintain a basic service landline or connect your VoIP phone equipment *and* your broadband modem to a *UPS* (uninterruptible power supply).

Understanding VoIP phones and hardware

You can't just plug any regular phone into "the Internet" and make VoIP calls; you need to have some sort of hardware that converts your voice (or the signals coming out of an analog phone) into VoIP signals. You have three options:

   ✔ **A VoIP phone adapter:** This device, often called an *analog telephone adapter* (ATA), is designed to sit between your POTS phone and your Internet connection. All of your calls are routed through this device, which converts POTS to VoIP. VoIP phone adapters are often incorporated in a home-networking router (we discuss these in Chapter 14) and may even include a Wi-Fi access point (Chapter 16). Although you can buy a phone adapter from a number of retailers (basically anywhere you can buy home-networking gear), most folks get them directly from their VoIP service provider — we prefer the latter approach because it ensures that the phone adapter is properly configured for your service. Phone adapters are most often used with landline replacement VoIP services but are available for most VoIP services.

✔ **A VoIP phone:** Another category of VoIP devices are *VoIP phones*. These devices look just like regular phones, but instead of connecting to your home's phone wiring and network, they connect to your computer network or LAN (see Chapters 14, 15, and 16). Essentially, the components of an ATA are built right into the VoIP phone. You can find both wired and wireless VoIP phones. The wired phones look just like office desk phones, but instead of plugging into a phone network with an RJ-45 jack, they plug into your Ethernet network with an RJ-45 plug. The wireless phones connect to your home's Wi-Fi wireless network.

You can often take a Wi-Fi wireless VoIP phone with you when you travel, and use a public Wi-Fi hot spot (or the Wi-Fi in your hotel room) to make calls. The cool thing about this is that these calls will be coming from your home phone number, and you'll be able to receive incoming calls to that number as well, as long as you're connected to the Wi-Fi network and the Internet.

✔ **A PC as a phone:** Many VoIP services can use your PC (laptop or desktop, Mac or Windows) as the VoIP adapter, using special software called *softphone* software. The PC-based VoIP services are obviously softphones, but you can often get softphone software from your landline replacement VoIP service provider as well (for example, Vonage offers such a service) for use while you're on the road. The key to using your PC as a phone is to get a good headset (preferably a USB-based headset with noise cancellation, like those offered by Plantronics, www.plantronics.com); this will provide the best voice quality — using the speakers and microphone built into your computer usually sounds awful.

Keep in mind that using a PC as a phone isn't a whole-home solution, but it is a good way of integrating VoIP as a supplement to your traditional landline service. Many folks make use of services like Skype for their low international dialing costs but keep using traditional phone services for the rest of their phone needs.

If you don't like wearing a geeky-looking headset when you're making calls, buy a USB *handset* for your PC and softphone — the handset looks like a traditional corded phone handset. Even USB-powered speakerphones are available.

Cutting the Cord: Going Mobile

After television and radio broadcasts, cellular phones are probably the most common wireless communications systems found in people's homes (and cars, and purses, and shirt pockets).

In North America, all sorts of cellular systems are in use by the various cellular providers. A few of these are analog; most are now digital. Analog wireless systems are susceptible to interference and distortion, and they make it easier for unscrupulous individuals to eavesdrop on your conversation. Their biggest flaw, however, is that they use the limited bandwidth allocated to cellular systems by the FCC inefficiently. This inefficiency limits the number of calls the systems can handle at any one time and makes services more expensive than digital systems (meaning you pay more).

By 2003, 85 percent of Americans were using digital signals and most carriers were changing plans to encourage customers to convert from analog to digital, so it's doubtful you'll want an analog phone. (Most analog phones are emergency phones sitting in people's glove compartments.) The FCC has ruled that cellular providers can get rid of their analog signals by February of 2008.

The Cellular Telecommunications & Internet Association (CTIA) Web site (www.ctia.org) has a lot of great information for consumers who want to know more about how the cellular industry works. Here's what happens when a call is made: Your message is transmitted by low-energy radio signals to the nearest antenna site, which connects with the local phone network. From there, your call is delivered by the normal phone network to the office or home you dialed or by radio signals to another wireless phone.

Wireless technology uses individual radio frequencies over and over again by dividing a service area into separate geographic zones called *cells* — hence the name *cellular*. Cells can be as small as an individual building (such as an airport or arena) or as big as 20 miles across, or any size in between. Each cell is equipped with its own radio transmitter/receiver antenna. (If you have poor service, and you recall that a bunch of people in your neighborhood fought the construction of a new tower in your area, now you know why you can't complete a call. No tower, no signal.)

When a customer using a cellular phone approaches the boundary of one cell, the wireless network senses that the signal is becoming weak and automatically hands off the call to the antenna in the next cell into which the caller is traveling.

Wireless technologies are not all the same

Not all cell phones are alike, and understanding the technology behind the offerings is a good start to choosing the right service. The CTIA (go to the "Wireless 101" section of the CTIA Web site) represents a wide range of cell phone companies and equipment vendors in the United States. They offer some good background on the technologies and have a great consumer FAQ (frequently asked questions) document that explains the ins and outs of mobile phones better than we ever could. Check it out at `http://www.ctia.org/wireless_resources/index.cfm/AID/205/`.

When subscribers travel beyond their home geographical area, they can still make wireless calls. The wireless carrier in the area where they are traveling provides the service. This is called *roaming*. The terms *home area* and *roaming area* designate these boundaries, which are important because different rates are usually assigned to calling in each area.

Each cellular antenna is linked to a wireless carrier's own *mobile switching center* (MSC) — the wireless industry's equivalent of the telco central office — which connects your wireless call to the local wired telephone network.

Too many cell plans, cell phones, and different approaches to the technologies particular to your specific operating area are available to adequately cover all your options here. And the topic is beyond the scope of this book, because these phones are mostly about your phone calling outside your smart home; though we do provide some tips in this chapter and in Chapter 11 about how to extend your wireless signal throughout the home using Wi-Fi. See the sidebar titled "Converging fixed and mobile" in this chapter, and see the information on using cellular signal boosters in Chapter 11.

That having been said, here are some thoughts about buying cell service:

- ✔ **Think about how you'll use the phone:** For the most part, you buy a cell phone that's compatible with your usage area. If you travel a lot locally, the carrier that has the best coverage area and best pricing for you locally is likely your best answer. If you travel a lot, check out roaming fees for where you travel or some of the national calling plans.

- ✔ **Think about hands-free use at home, not just in your car:** You can get desktop chargers for your cell phone that are also speakerphones, enabling you to have hands-free discussions in your home office, just like with a regular phone. Most manufacturers have some sort of charging station with this option.

Stand by for docking

Tired of carrying your cell phone from room to room? Are you missing calls because your cell phone was turned off? Wish you could use a more comfortable handset with your wireless service? Wish you could use your cell phone as a second line in your home, for your office, or for your kids? Want to take advantage of the great free nights and weekends calling plans?

For those who want to use their cell phone as their primary connection to the world — and have their home network connected to that line, just as if it were the landline — a number of cellular docking stations are available to bridge the two domains. Some docking stations look like chargers; others look like full-fledged phones. But the setup is the same: You plug your phone into the docking station, run a regular telephone cord from the docking unit to a telephone jack on the wall, and plug in the AC adapter. Any phone plugged into your telephone wiring can receive and make calls using the cell phone service, through the docking station. When a call comes in, the unit rings your stationary analog phones with a special pattern so you know that the call is of cellular origin.

An upside of this approach is that many of the stations have an external antenna hookup, so if your signal reception is marginal at home, you can attach a Yagi antenna (a kind of super-sensitive antenna) and boost the signal. We talk more about cell phone signal boosters in Chapter 11. A downside is that if your power goes out, you have what remains of your battery power until you lose your phone service. But the docking station doubles as a recharging unit, so you'll probably have at least a full charge.

An interesting example of a cell phone docking station is PhoneLabs' Dock-N-Talk ($160), which incorporates a universal cell phone dock with a cordless phone system. You can even buy a Bluetooth module to use your phone's Bluetooth connection instead of physically docking it to the cordless phone base station. Pretty cool stuff, check it out at www.phonelabs.com.

 ✔ **Think about family plans:** If you have multiple phones in your household, call your provider and ask about family plans, where you can share a single bulk amount of minutes across the phones. This allows you to get some phones for your kids without having to worry about paying hefty fees every month to keep the phones active.

 ✔ **Think about getting your kids a prepaid phone account:** With a prepaid phone, you buy a certain amount of minutes and the phone stops making calls after that allotted amount (until you replenish the phone by buying more cell time). In this way, you can give your kids enough minutes to call home and ask for help but not enough to yak with friends.

Above all, accept the fact that your phone is something that is provider specific. That is, with some notable exceptions, your phone is likely tuned and specifically featured by your provider; if you switch providers, you'll have to change your phone number and your phone (including all the expensive accessories you bought, which is a pain). So as the knight guarding the Grail in *Indiana Jones and the Last Crusade* says, "You must choose . . . but choose wisely."

VoIP on your mobile phone

VoIP companies such as Skype are starting to create softphone software that runs on smartphones and PDAs (such as Palm Treos and Windows Mobile phones). With this software you'll be able to use your phone and its 3G data connection (see Chapter 13 for more on 3G) to place and receive VoIP phone calls. With such a system, you can make calls anywhere in the world at low rates (a few cents per minute) instead of paying the typical sky-high mobile phone service provider rates. All you need is an account with Skype and a data plan on your mobile phone (we'd go for an unlimited data plan if we were using this). We expect to see more VoIP providers offer such services, and you may even see the cell phone companies offering this. (VoIP is more efficient with bandwidth, so it can save them money as well.)

The good news is that most wireless providers will give you a month or so to try out the service on a money-back guarantee. If you don't like it, cancel the service.

Chapter 11

Making the Phone Connection

In This Chapter
▶ Choosing the right cables
▶ Hitching your wagon to a star
▶ Finding out that distribution can be fun
▶ Using "no new wires" approaches

As we tell you in Chapter 10, a ton of stuff fits into a home-phone network. A plethora of phone devices and a multiplicity of lines can add up to a big headache if you don't outfit your house properly for phone service. This chapter tells you how to avoid such headaches, as well as other headaches that may come up if you have your house wired and connected wirelessly in ways that don't allow you to take advantage of tomorrow's technologies. For example, although the cables that telephone companies run throughout your house are fine for most of today's uses, tomorrow you may be talking over a data networks such as the Internet. By running data-grade cabling to all your telephone and data outlets, you can futureproof your home.

With futureproofing your phone system firmly in mind, we tell you what kind of wiring to buy for your phone network and then discuss how to lay out your network. We concentrate primarily on how to create a phone network that relies on wires, which is the way that most people's phone systems work. But we talk also about some good whole-home wireless options that are widely available and not much more expensive than wired systems. We describe some of these options toward the end of the chapter.

What to Run Where

A good way to start planning a phone network is to make a list of places where you may need phone outlets. The phone network we describe here has the capacity to support up to four lines at each outlet station; you should be able to handle several devices at each outlet without any capacity problems.

There's a nuance we need to explain: the difference between the number of physical wires you run to each outlet box and the number of jacks at the outlet box that you enable. For instance, you could run a single four-pair cable to an outlet that has four modular jacks, and one pair would go to each jack. This would give you four telephone lines. However, as we state in Chapter 2, those lines would not be well futureproofed for data and other applications because Ethernet computer networks require eight conductors to work fully. So our recommendation is that wherever you have a jack, you should run a full CAT-5e/6 UTP telephone cable to that jack; a four-jack outlet would have four lines running to it. Sounds excessive? Well, in the years since we wrote the first edition of this book, almost everyone in the industry has gone towards that recommendation. In this chapter, we tell you how you can use something less than one line per jack, because some of you will simply want to make do with what's in the walls already or need to keep budgets under control. But remember that we recommend one line per jack.

Now back to the planning. You need to determine each room's minimum phone communications requirements:

- ✔ **Living room:** Depending on your home layout and your plans regarding an entertainment center and home theater, your living room can be simple or complex. We recommend that you put a single telephone outlet next to your favorite seat and another multiline outlet where you plan to have your television entertainment area.

- ✔ **Dining room:** A single outlet should suffice in your dining room. However, if you work at home, your dining room may double as your conference room. In that case, think about adding both phone and data access to this room. If you intend to use the dining-room table as the place to put your gear, consider a floor mount in the middle of the room (but recognize that to do so you have to cut a hole in your floor covering, which can be rough on Oriental rugs).

- ✔ **Family room:** Again, your phone requirements here depend on where your main entertainment equipment resides. Because these rooms can be big, we usually recommend that you put one outlet on each of two facing walls. Otherwise, you may have to run 20-foot-long patch cables — which, trust us, kids and dogs have a knack for getting wrapped up in — to your telephone across the room.

- ✔ **Kitchen:** Most people spend a good deal of time in the kitchen, so at least one outlet is in order here. Many people base their answering machine or cordless phone in this room, so make sure that your phone outlet is also near a power outlet. Try to create a nook for your phone and related equipment — you don't want to spill honey on that stuff.

- ✔ **Bedrooms:** Plan for at least one multiline outlet in each bedroom. Your master bedroom may require an additional outlet on the wall opposite your bed for your cable, DSL, or satellite set-top box access. Any bedroom that you may eventually convert to a home office may also require a second outlet.

✔ **Home theater:** A phone jack behind your A/V component shelves gives your DSS receiver or PVR the capability to show you the movies you want to see (DSS receivers need a phone line to order pay-per-view movies, and PVRs need the phone to download programming information). You may also want to include a phone jack near the seating area if you plan to have a regular telephone in this room.

✔ **Home office:** Your home office is probably a communications hub, most likely using all your phone lines. We recommend that you install at least two multiline jacks on opposite walls to give you a bit of flexibility. If you have an assistant, you may need to add extra jacks in this room.

Don't just think about one home office per house; you might need two. They might be at separate ends of the house (which we recommend for marital reasons), or they might be in the same room, to share devices such as a printer, fax machine, and photocopier. The same is true of kids' computers. They need a space where they can concentrate to do their homework and to play. Consider a computer room, where they each have their own spot and you get the advantages of having a lot of gear in one place.

✔ **Other places:** Don't overlook other parts of your home when you're planning phone outlets. We recommend that you include phones in the garage, the bathroom, the basement, and the exercise room. *Note:* If you want your phone system to double as an intercom, you need to run outlets to the places you'd like to intercom as well.

Throughout this book, we show you home-network functionality in every room. Much of this functionality depends on the telephone. Don't short-change yourself for a few dollars, counting on wireless options down the road. A wired infrastructure has many advantages. Almost any habitable room should have phone access.

Building the architecture

In Chapter 2, we mention that your phone network will include CAT-5e or CAT-6 cabling, RJ-45 connectors, patch panels, patch cables, and more. Now it's time to discuss how it all fits together — the architecture of it all. Think Greek!

In the past, if you wanted two lines at an outlet, you took two pair from the same wire and created two two-conductor RJ-11 outlets. If you wanted three lines, you might have a three- or four-pair line, or two two-pair lines, and split them off that way. We're not recommending that. If you're building a house, we recommend one full CAT-5e/CAT-6 line per jack. (If you have two jacks at a faceplate, two lines are running there.) This is so you can have a full RJ-45 CAT-5e/CAT-6 data-capable line at each outlet. This gives you maximum flexibility in the future and melds the phone network and the data network — at the physical level. If you have existing wiring, read on and we'll make do with what you have.

The *architecture* of a network refers to the logical model on which it's based. If you've ever seen one of those AT&T commercials where they show the company's switching network as red lines connecting big red dots and showing telephone calls boogying across those lines and dots, you've seen a model.

The not-so-good daisy chain

If you have an older home or are building a new one and let the electrician or telephone company wire your home for phones without any specific instructions, chances are you have a daisy-chained telephone network.

In this type of network model, a telephone cable (typically a quad cable — four conductors, capable of supporting two telephone lines) is connected to the telephone company's NID (network interface device). This cable runs throughout the home, from jack to jack, until it reaches the final, most-distant jack.

Phone companies and electricians often choose this method because it's easy and cheap. Unfortunately, many problems come with a daisy-chain system, such as the following:

- ✔ You lose your connection when more people pick up the line to take part in a conversation.

- ✔ You're limited to having the same outside line on each jack in the house — you won't be able to reconfigure a jack to connect to an extra phone line that you might purchase from the phone company.

Don't wire your telephone network in a daisy-chain configuration if you're starting from scratch. The star architecture that we describe in the following section is much more flexible and capable than the daisy-chain architecture.

Reach for a star

In the *star architecture,* each jack runs to a wiring hub that acts as a central connection point. If you draw this system on paper, it looks like a star (or maybe a wagon wheel with the spokes connecting at the hub).

The star architecture provides many advantages over the daisy-chain architecture we describe in the preceding section. Here are a few advantages:

- ✔ **Reliability:** If you use a daisy-chain architecture, any physical or electrical problems in your phone cable affect all the phones farther along on that cabling system. In a star network, only the phones at the end of the individual affected cable are out of order.

- ✔ **Greater capacity:** Daisy-chained telephone networks are useful for only the number of lines that start out from the wiring hub, whereas a star network lets you handle as many lines as each home run carries.

✔ **Flexibility:** In a daisy-chained network, each telephone jack station is stuck with whatever phone lines its cable is connected to back at the NID. In a star network, all the cables go back to a central point, which you can patch to different incoming lines with a minimum of fuss. If you decide to convert a spare bedroom into a home office, for example, you simply reconfigure your connections — to connect those remote phone jacks to your incoming fax line, for example — at the network's hub.

Starting from the telephone company's incoming service feed, you build a typical star-wired telephone network as follows:

1. **The telephone company installs an incoming line or lines (called a *feed*) from the local central office (or a remote unit such as a digital loop carrier, or DLC).**

   Depending on a host of factors — when your telephone company's connection was installed, which company did it, how many lines you have — the telephone cable may consist of two, three, or four pairs of copper wire. The wire may or may not be twisted (most older installations aren't). For the most part, many recent telephone-company installations use four-pair, UTP cable. The telephone company connects the incoming feed to the NID outside your home.

   If you're using an alternative phone system (such as a cable telephony solution from your cable service provider, or a VoIP solution from a company such as Vonage), your *demarcation point* (where the phone provider's network ends and yours begins) will probably move from the NID on the side of your home to a separate, broadband-connected device within your home. So in those cases, we ask you to mentally substitute cable telephony *gateway* or VoIP *telephony adapter* for *NID* here.

2. **Connect a UTP cable from the consumer side of the NID to the patch panel in your home's wiring center.**

   This line is the central feed between the outside world and your home-phone network. Attach each conductor wire within the line to the patch panel. (For information about choosing a location for your home's wiring center, beam yourself to Chapter 2.)

3. **Connect a UTP cable onto the terminal block.**

   This cable — commonly known as a *drop* — provides telephone service to an individual phone outlet.

   If you're planning to use RJ-11 jacks (not our recommended RJ-45, shame, shame) and four-pair UTP cabling, and your phone network is starting off with less than four lines used at a particular jack, no problem. You can leave some of the pairs of wires in your UTP cabling unterminated to start off. Just make sure that you label your cables so that you know which room each drop serves. Leave the unused cables coiled up out of the way at each end (in other words, behind your future wall outlet and near the patch panel). And in the future, if you add additional lines, you can simply connect additional feed and drop lines to the patch panel (and to your modular outlets at the endpoints of your network). Quick and easy reconfiguring is one of the biggest advantages of a star-wired phone network that uses four-pair cables.

4. **Run a UTP drop cable from your wiring center through the walls to a modular outlet in a room where you want to use a phone device.**

   Again, the entire cable should be allocated to its own RJ-45 jack. If you're going to use RJ-11 jacks, you have a fair amount of flexibility. You can connect your UTP cabling to two separate two-line outlets, four one-line outlets, or some combination thereof. The kind of phones and phone equipment you'll be connecting to the outlets drives your cable choice.

5. **Connect *end devices* — all the neat stuff we discuss in Chapter 10, such as phones, faxes, and modems — to the wall outlets by using simple telephone patch cables.**

6. **Repeat Steps 3 – 5 for each outlet in your phone network.**

Figure 11-1 shows the finished product — a star-wired telephone network.

Figure 11-1:
The star of
our phone
show.

Hybrid networks

If you discover the need for an additional outlet someplace in your home that you didn't wire with a star run, you can use a modified version of the daisy-chained wiring scheme. Running a daisy chain from a new outlet from the nearest star outlet is easy and acceptable when necessary.

Ideally, you should avoid this kind of hybrid network, but adding an outlet or two to a star network by daisy chaining won't mess things up. Remember, however, that these new outlets lose the flexibility of runs back to a central point. They have to be connected to the same phone lines as the star-wired outlet they're connected to, so you can't use them for different phone lines. Some great alternatives using wireless and electrical technologies are available, as we discuss later in this chapter and in Chapter 16.

Plugging into a KSU

The phone network described in the preceding section gets you up and running. It gives you multiline phone service available throughout the home, which is worth a good deal all on its own. However, you may decide that you want more. For example, you may want to transfer calls from one phone to another or use your phone as an intercom. You may even want to have some music available when you put that telemarketer on hold (ahhhh, sweet revenge). In that case, you need a KSU, or *key telephone system unit* (often also called a *hybrid phone system* — we discuss these in Chapter 10), to control your phone lines.

The KSU serves as your phone system's intelligence. The phone lines plug into the KSU, which is usually located in the same place as your punchdown block (discussed in Chapter 2). The in-home drops (the star-wired phone cables connected to each of your home's phone outlets) connect into the other side of the KSU, which allows the KSU to conference calls together, transfer calls, and ring any extension at any time.

The marketplace offers a huge variety of key systems, each with its own wiring and equipment requirements. Because the vast majority of these systems require exactly what you already have installed — a star-network architecture and UTP cabling — integrating a KSU into your phone network is simple. In shopping for key systems, you hear terms such as 6 x 16 (pronounced "six by sixteen"), which means that the system supports up to 6 lines and 16 extensions off those lines.

Here are a few things to keep in mind:

- ✓ **The central control unit — the KSU — installs in your wiring center between the incoming service feeds and the patch panel.** Incoming feeds use modular RJ-11 jacks to connect to the system's input side, and then additional patch cables connect the individual extension outputs to your service drops for each room.

- ✓ **Most KSU systems require just a single pair of UTP wiring to each extension, though a scant few require two or even three pairs.** Those requiring two or three pairs are either heavy-duty systems or are providing extra services, such as ISDN capabilities, to the extensions. You can cover all your bases by installing four-pair UTP at the outset.

> ✔ **Many KSUs have additional inputs and outputs.** The additional inputs and outputs are designed for things such as door phones, music inputs, and even a printer interface for printing *call detail reports,* which itemize phone numbers and times that calls are made from each extension.

Using KSU-less phone systems

In Chapter 10, we discuss *KSU-less phone systems* — sophisticated, multiline telephones that have a degree of networking intelligence built into each phone (as opposed to putting all the control functionality into a central unit). KSU-less phone systems have a price advantage over KSUs. However, the handsets themselves can be expensive, and if you're planning to install several KSU-less phones in your home, dropping the money on a KSU system up front may be financially advantageous. You have to shop around.

KSU-less phone systems aren't nearly as picky about network architecture as a KSU system. Most KSU systems require the star-wiring configuration we describe earlier in this chapter, but many KSU-less systems work in either a star or a daisy-chained wiring architecture. So you can utilize your existing phone wiring and still get many of the intercom, call transfer, and conference call features that KSUs provide.

Connecting Alternatively

You also have non-wireline options for distributing phone service throughout your home. These methods don't give you the same ultimate capacity as a wireline phone network (they're limited to three or four lines at most), but you can get much of the same functionality with some of these alternatives.

For wireless phones to work, you have to have some kind of phone connection into your house, even if it's a 1937 Ma Bell wiring job.

Taking the wireless route

The simplest way to expand an existing phone network is to use wireless phones and phone systems. You most likely have a cordless phone of some sort, so you're already using this technology in a limited way.

Conventional cordless phones (typically available in one- and two-line models) expand your network by adding a degree of mobility to your telephone devices. What they don't do, however, is offer more sophisticated call-control features such as call transfer and an intercom (except between the handset and the base station). They also don't provide connectivity for other telephony devices such as fax machines and analog modems. All they do is give you another telephone handset, sans cord. Some new cordless phone systems, however, let you do much more.

Multiline, multistation cordless phone systems

An easy way to extend (or build) your home phone network without worrying too much about wiring is to go cordless using a multiline and/or multistation cordless phone system. These systems differ from conventional cordless phones in that they use a single base station (plugged into a single phone outlet — or several outlets for the multiline models) and then use wireless technologies to reach handsets throughout the home. With these systems, your phone network can be as simple or as complex as you want it to be without the need for CAT-5e/6 cables running into every room of the house (save those cables for other purposes such as data networks and entertainment networks).

Remember that cordless phones require power to operate. If the lights go out, so do your phones. It's a good practice to keep at least one old-fashioned analog wired phone connected somewhere in your house for emergencies.

What's neat about many of these systems is that you can intermix corded and cordless units, including accessories such as door intercoms. You can buy regular phone sets, with an antenna on them, so you can carry them to the conference room for lunch (no more transferred calls). And wireless conferencing systems can fit into your network as well. Homeowners today are lucky to have such choices.

Going with cordless VoIP

Cordless systems are also becoming the most popular way to add VoIP services such as Skype or Vonage to your home's telephone network. Because many folks don't entirely cut the cord with their phone company, but rather use VoIP as a supplement (mainly for long-distance calling), they find it makes sense to use a dedicated cordless system for VoIP while maintaining the rest of the conventional phone network.

There are two approaches to getting cordless VoIP in your home:

✔ If your VoIP service includes a *telephony adapter* (discussed in Chapter 10), which has one or more standard POTS outlets, you can simply plug any cordless phone right into the adapter. For a simple cordless connection, any old cordless phone would do; for a whole-home system, you probably want to choose one of the multistation models described in the preceding section.

✔ Use dedicated VoIP phones that connect directly to your PC or that connect via Ethernet or Wi-Fi to your home's data network and broadband connection. All VoIP-to-analog conversion is handled in the phone, so you dial them like a regular phone (or use a built-in address) book, and the phone becomes a *client* on your network and does the work of making and receiving calls.

An interesting example of the second type of cordless VoIP system comes from the folks at Philips Electronics (`www.philips.com`). The VOIP3211G/37 Internet DECT Phone with Skype Control (phew, that's a long name!) is both a standard cordless POTS phone *and* a Skype phone, all in one sleek unit. Plug the base station into any phone outlet and also into the back of your PC (using the supplied USB cord), and you're set to go. You can look up your Skype contact list on the phone's screen, place SkypeOut calls (to regular phone numbers), or simply use your landline to make local calls. All for only $89. What we like about this phone is that it uses the new-to-the-U.S. DECT protocol for its cordless connection. *DECT* is a European standard for cordless phones that was approved for use in America in late 2006, and we've found that DECT phones have significantly greater range and better sound quality than most traditional cordless phone systems.

Adding a jack on the cheap, without wires

If you have only basic telephone needs and don't want to spend a pile of money, you may not want to go for an all-out phone system or expensive wireless solution. Suppose you need only a phone jack for your DSS receiver, and you don't have one anywhere near the TV location? Or perhaps you need a telephone in that unfinished attic that's now becoming a finished attic?

In that case, you may want to try one of the wireless phone jacks available from Radio Shack (`www.radioshack.com`). These devices use your home's power lines to carry phone signals — they're not really wireless; they leverage your existing wiring. The most basic configuration consists of a pair of small devices. The master unit plugs into an existing single-line phone jack and also into an AC outlet. The extension unit plugs into any of your home's AC outlets and has a standard RJ-11 receptacle for connecting a phone device. You can buy these remote units separately and add more extension units if you need extra outlets. A pair runs about $69.

These jacks aren't the end-all in sophistication — they handle only one line, and they won't work on modems faster than 14.4 Kbps — but they do allow you to plug in a DSS dish or add a phone or fax in some location that you never anticipated.

Part IV

Livin' Off the Fat of the LAN

In this part . . .

A home-data network used to be a rarity. Today, you may have a second, third, or fourth computer at home, and the fights over the printer, the scanner, or more likely, the high-speed Internet access link may be causing you some grief. A home-data network is no longer a luxury; it's a necessity, if only to bring peace to the household.

Putting together a home network is getting easier and easier, particularly with the ubiquity of wireless networks and networks that use your existing electrical or telephone wiring. With proper planning, you can pretty much access your home-data network from anywhere in the house.

In this part, we show you how to create a data backbone in your home. We discuss all the major elements of a whole-home data network and how this data network interfaces with your home-telephone and audio/video networks — the three have a lot in common, as more and more of our phone calls and entertainment content move onto the broadband Internet connection. We also tell you about the different types of data-networking equipment and services available and provide some advice for ensuring the success of your home-data network.

Chapter 12

A Cornucopia of Computers

*T*hree quarters of homes in North America have a PC, and that number is going nowhere but up. A growing number have more than one — and many have three or more! Computers become cheaper and more powerful by the minute, and every year you find new ways of using your computer.

Home offices, Web surfing, e-mail, videoconferencing, computer banking — you name it, and people are doing it on their PCs right now. Even more importantly, they're doing it over a network, connecting to the Internet using (in most cases) a broadband connection over fiber-optic cables, phone wires (DSL), or cable TV systems (cable modems) — even wireless. Broadband makes up about three quarters of Internet connections in the U.S. (and that number too is growing). More importantly, broadband connections are perfect for sharing amongst multiple computers and other devices in the home.

In this chapter, we tell you about the equipment that fits into a home-computer network — everything from PCs to printers to peripherals. We also discuss some devices that aren't PCs but fit into a computer network and make use of your home's Internet connection — devices such as telephone systems and gaming consoles.

An important note upfront: You probably have a vision of a computer as a particular type of device — you know, that tan-colored box with a big monitor and keyboard and all those wires. You need to throw that constrained vision of a computer out the window. Although we do describe that form of computer, we also talk about how the computer is becoming distributed throughout the home and how many, many devices can (or will soon) connect to your computer network. So knowing the pieces is important, and that's where we'll start.

Another important note: You're putting together a computer network in your house for two reasons. The first is for the things you know you want to connect, such as connecting your PCs to each other. The second is for all the things you don't know you want to connect but which require a computer network to work. This includes all the home-entertainment devices and other home-automation devices that need to send messages all over the house and all over the Internet. If you're part of the 25 percent of people in the U.S. who don't yet have a PC at home, don't skip this section because you think you might never need a computer network. You will — we guarantee it — even if you never purchase a computer.

Considering Computers of All Kinds

If you have at least one PC in your home, it makes sense to think about your computer networking needs as part of your total home-networking needs. Your present network may consist of only a modem that connects your PC to the outside world or perhaps a simple A/B switch that lets two computers share a single printer. But the plummeting cost of PCs, combined with the increasing speed of Internet connection methods and greater use of the PC in a whole-home environment, makes it worthwhile to install a more sophisticated home-computer network.

In the environment of an office or a school, computers are routinely networked to take full advantage of their capabilities, and we think the possibilities are numerous enough to justify your thinking that way at home.

Choosing traditional PCs

We use the term *traditional PC* to differentiate the types of PCs most families have from some of the emerging forms that computers are starting to take (such as Web-enabled TVs). We're definitely not disparaging your Core 2 Duo 3 GigaHertz new PC with the killer 3-D graphics card as an obsolete clunker (even though by the time you read this it might be).

When we talk about PCs (whether they be desktop or laptop models), we're basically talking about one of two things:

✔ **Windows-based PCs:** These PCs have Intel CPUs (or similar CPUs from companies such as AMD) and use a Microsoft Windows operating system (OS). Some people call these *Wintel* machines — people like us, for example.

✔ **Macintoshes:** These are Apple computers that run the Mac OS.

More advanced readers may be using other types of computers — such as a Linux-based computer — but if you're advanced enough to survive in the Linux environment, you don't need us to explain what a PC is. Actually, Linux has become a lot more user friendly over the years, with systems such as Ubuntu (www.ubuntu.com) using graphical user interfaces and familiar software (such as Mozilla's Firefox Web browser). Unfortunately there are just too many variants of Linux for us to get into it here. You can assume that anything we discuss concerning Windows and Mac will apply to Linux too, but you must also assume that you might need to do a bit of tweaking or deal with certain hardware and software incompatibilities that you probably won't run into on a commercial operating system.

For the most part, both Wintel and Macintosh computers fit into a home network the same way — other than a few minor differences in the connectors for peripherals. Which kind of PC you use is a matter of preference (we both have one or more of each in our homes).

Looking at laptops, desktops, and more

You need to consider the physical form of the computers you will be adding to your home network. For instance, you can choose between the following types of computers:

- **Desktop computer:** Traditionally, desktop computers were full-sized — and full-featured — computers that were portable only in the sense that a strong person could move them across the room without needing a quick dose of oxygen. The advent of small desktop PCs such as the Mac Mini have changed that equation, but desktops are still designed to sit on a desk, not on your lap. Desktops aren't as mobile as laptops, but dollar for dollar, they are more powerful, have larger displays, and can be more easily expanded and upgraded than laptop computers.

- **Media-center or home-theater PCs:** A number of vendors have begun offering desktop-style PCs with a twist — media-center or home-theater PCs are designed to look (and operate) more like a bit of consumer electronics gear (such as a DVD player or DVR). These PCs can reside in your home theater or media room, fit right on the rack with your other gear, and use your TV as a primary display.

- **Laptop computer:** Laptops can be taken with you from room to room or town to town. The first generations of laptop computers were inferior to desktops in just about every way — except, of course, in terms of portability — but current models have enough power and functionality to do just about everything the average user needs. However, they cost a bit more than an equivalent desktop computer. Most laptops have docking station options that allow you to plug your laptop into a system that has a large monitor and regular-sized keyboard attached to it. This makes it easy to have desktop-style computing with the option of portability.

Which of these computers you choose for your home network is a personal decision based on your own computing needs, but it's important to make sure that the system you choose has the capability to connect to your home network. In Chapters 15 and 16, we tell you about the various kinds of home LANs that you can install in your home, but regardless of which network type you choose, your PCs will require some sort of network interface card, or NIC. A *NIC* is the physical interface between your PC's internal systems and the outside network.

For desktop computers, the NIC — if it doesn't come preinstalled in the computer — generally fits into one of the internal *PCI* (personal computer interface) card slots in the PC. (The ones that look like they take a fat credit card.) Other slots in your computer can also accept NIC cards, but we prefer to use PCI NICs because they're a heck of a lot easier to set up. Laptop and palmtop computer NICs are often built in but can also use an expansion device known as a *PC Card*. Any PC built within the past three or four years has these expansion slots built right in — the only real concern is whether you have one free to install the NIC.

NICs are required for both wired (Ethernet) and wireless (Wi-Fi or Bluetooth) networks, as we discuss in Chapters 13 and 14.

The tablet computer — don't wander your home without it

The increasing integration of computer parts, the greater availability of wireless connectivity, and the desire to roam the home have all conspired to create a new class of computers with a touch-sensitive screen that lets users interface with the computer with a pen-like device, just as they would write on a tablet of paper with a real pen. This class of device is called, not surprisingly, a *tablet* computer. Some of these devices are tablet-only (meaning there's no keyboard); others are laptop computers that can be switched (usually by folding the screen out and hiding the keyboard) to tablet mode when the mood strikes.

Tablet computers (which mainly operate using the Windows operating system) use *handwriting recognition* and *capture* technologies, so you can simply write on the screen with the pen and operate the computer. So if you like to cuddle with an e-book next to the fire, consult your e-recipe book in the kitchen, or work on your e-mail in bed, you might want to check out tablet computers. To date, most tablet computers have been focused on the business market, where they're often used for specialized purposes in a business.

Serving up files with a home server

In the computer-networking world (and we're talking at a high conceptual level here — there are layers of nuance that we don't want to confuse ourselves or you with), computers can be broken down into two categories: servers and clients. For the most part, the computers you work with on a day-to-day basis are clients, at least in the networking sense. You use clients to connect to networks such as the Internet or a work network.

Servers are on the other end of that connection. When you get your e-mail, you connect to an e-mail server somewhere. When you read a Web page, you get the HTML files that make up that page from a Web server somewhere. Servers tend to be computers that share their data with many other computers. Until recently, most servers were outside the home, and you connected to them through an ISP.

That's changed with the introduction of home server devices that offer the same sort of functionality that big companies get with their own server systems. With a home server, you can do things such as the following:

✔ Back up all your other computers to one central location

✔ Have a central storage point for music, movies, and photos that you want to access on your TV, audio system, or other computers

✔ Have a centralized printer server that allows any PC in the home to print without a local printer

✔ Remotely access your files while you're away from home using your broadband Internet connection

Several approaches are leading the way in the home server market, including the following:

✔ **NAS:** At their simplest, NAS (network attached storage) devices are like the external hard disk drives that so many folks use to back up their PCs or store files that take up too much room on the internal hard drive. The difference is that whereas external hard drives are dumb devices connected locally to one computer (using USB cables, typically), NAS devices are full-fledged computers (usually running a specialized version of Linux) that connect to your network so that any computer in the home can access them. NAS devices offer a lot of benefits over an external hard drive, including the following:

   • More storage space: Most NAS systems have room for two or more hard drives, so you can expand them as your needs grow

- **Redundancy:** Most NAS systems can use *RAID* (redundant array of inexpensive drives), which distributes your data amongst the drives in the NAS itself. With RAID, you can survive a hard disk drive failure (which are more common than you might think). If a drive fails, your data is safe — just replace the failed drive and go. Note that using RAID decreases your total capacity because the data you save on the NAS devices is physically stored on more than one place on the drive. We don't think this is a huge problem because hard disk drives are getting bigger and cheaper at an incredible rate.

- **Remote access:** Part of the Linux software in most NAS drives is a remote access feature that lets you use a Web interface to connect into your drive while you're away from home. Forget a file while you're on the road? No problem. Just fire up your Web browser and go get it!

- **Additional features:** Many NAS devices include things such as print servers, automated backup software systems, and ports for connections to external hard drives (to back up your backup!). Sometimes it's all about the features.

Figure 12-1 shows a NAS device from Buffalo Technologies (www. buffalotech.com), one of the leading vendors in this area.

✓ **Microsoft's forthcoming Windows Home Server:** This one isn't widely available yet, but at the Consumer Electronics show in January of 2007, Bill Gates announced the new Windows Home Server software and hardware system. Microsoft won't be building the servers themselves (they've partnered with folks such as HP, www.hp.com, with their forthcoming MediaSmart Server). A home server built using Microsoft's Windows Home Server system will in many ways be similar to a NAS device but will have user-friendly Windows software and be tightly integrated into the Windows Vista environment. As we write this, all the details are not in, but expect these devices to have lots of storage, support for remote access, and support for print servers, automated backup, and external drives — all wrapped up in a way that makes nice with your Windows Vista PCs.

✓ **Media Center servers:** The Media Center PCs we mentioned in the preceding section are themselves essentially home servers with a focus on (you guessed it) media files. PCs running the Windows XP or Vista version of Microsoft's Media Center Edition software are designed to be a central storage spot for music files, downloaded videos, digital photos, and even recorded television programming. Using other Windows computers or extender devices (such as Microsoft's Xbox 360 gaming console), you can access this media over your home network.

Some folks (those we categorize as being *technically adept* — a.k.a. geeks) build their own NAS servers. You might want to do so yourself if you have an old desktop PC that has room for at least a couple of hard disk drives. Mix together the PC, a fast networking NIC, some big hard drives, and a software system such as FreeNAS (www.freenas.org, a Linux-based NAS software package). Note that this isn't for the faint-of-heart or for first-time Linux users, because things can get complicated when you start trying to throw RAID controllers and the like into the mix. For us, a NAS device such as one of the Buffalo Technologies TeraStation Live models does the trick.

Figure 12-1:
Buffalo
Technology
brings the
NAS to your
house.

PDAs, PDQ: Interfacing with Handheld Computers

PDAs (personal digital assistants) are a step down in computing power from traditional PCs but a step up in portability. These devices range in functionality from simple electronic address books to powerful handheld computers that can send e-mail, browse the Web, and do basic word processing and spreadsheet tasks. You see business people in airports with these little devices, looking up phone numbers or checking calendars.

Now that's handy — a PDA remote control

With a combination of IR, Bluetooth, and perhaps even Wi-Fi networking connections and an operating system capable of operating third-party software, the PDA has all the components needed to do double duty as a remote control in your home. At the simplest level, you can use the IR port on your PDA (along with software such as PDAWin.com's TV remote controller software, `http://www.pdawin.com/tvremote.html`) to create a universal remote control for your TV and home theater.

If you want to get more sophisticated, you're in luck. If you have a handheld PDA running the Windows Pocket PC or Windows Mobile operating system (and equipped with Wi-Fi), you'll find that many home-automation controller systems include software that lets you control just about everything in your home using a graphical interface on the PDA. Read Chapters 19 and 20 for more on this.

PDAs come in two broad categories:

- *Smartphones*, from companies such as Palm, Motorola, Nokia, and HTC. These PDAs are the whole package in one small container — cell phone and PDA/handheld computer functionality is wrapped into one device. For the most part, you buy smartphones directly from a cell phone provider such as AT&T, Sprint, or Verizon.

- Pure PDAs, without the cell phone component. These PDAs are available from companies such as Palm, as well as PC manufacturers such as Dell and HP.

Within each of these two groups, the functionality of PDAs differs greatly, but they are all capable of networking by connecting either directly to your PC to exchange data or through a network connection to other data networks such as the Internet. Many have an infrared (IR) device that allows you to print to a printer (or update internal databases) by aiming the device at a printer (or computer) — nifty, huh? Figure 12-2 shows how a PDA can network with a PC using infrared networking.

Figure 12-2:
Transferring data with light!

PC
IrDA port
Handheld computer
IR (infrared) interface between PC and handheld computer

Most infrared equipment uses a common industry standard for networking called IrDA (which stands for Infrared Data Association, the group that created the standard).

Beyond infrared networking (and cable connections such as USB), most PDAs now include Bluetooth or Wi-Fi (or both) wireless networking capabilities. (We talk about Bluetooth and Wi-Fi in Chapter 16.) With a Bluetooth connection, you can connect to your Bluetooth-equipped PC to synchronize data on the PDA/smartphone, and in many cases use this connection to piggyback on the Internet connection of another device (such as a networked PC or an Internet-enabled cell phone) for Web browsing and e-mail.

PDAs and smartphones equipped with a Wi-Fi NIC are even more capable and can be full clients on your home network, sharing your broadband Internet connection and connecting to other resources on your network. You can also, of course, use the Wi-Fi connection outside your home, connecting to Wi-Fi networks at your office, hotels, and public Wi-Fi access points (called *hotspots*).

Finally, don't forget that smartphones have a cellular radio system built right in, so you can use them to connect to the mobile network anywhere you have coverage. Most current smartphones include *3G* cellular radios for connecting to mobile network at speeds nearly as fast as most home broadband Internet connections.

Why Wi-Fi and Bluetooth are better than IR

When it comes to making connections with your PDA, wireless is where it's at. Although IR connections are wireless too, we're talking about radio-based (not visual-light-based) networks — such as Wi-Fi and Bluetooth. We describe these two networking standards in detail in Chapter 16, but for now we'll tell you why they're so cool compared to IR.

IR has a limited range (just a few feet at most) and must be within the direct line of sight of the target device you're beaming data to and from. RF signals, on the other hand, can pass through walls, doors, people, dogs, and everything, and they can go a lot farther too — so you can sit on the living room couch with your PDA and "talk" to your PC in the bedroom. In the case of Wi-Fi (the more powerful of these two wireless systems), you can find public access points in schools, airports, hotels, and coffee shops, so you can connect your PDA to the Internet even when you're far from home and a phone line.

In the past, PDAs were a localized device, slaved to a particular PC through a docking cradle and connection cable. With wireless networking included in many new PDAs, however, this connection is now more whole home, so PDAs can be updated anywhere in the home where they can log onto the network through its radio or infrared frequencies.

Monitors

Computer monitors are constantly evolving. It's one area where people tend to want the latest and greatest because it's what they look at all the time. We talk in Chapter 5 about the changes in TV displays, and it's not surprising that the same changes have been flowing through to computers as well. Unless you're shopping at the very bottom end of the market, all computers you find today will likely have flat-screen PC monitors, like the flat-screen TVs. It's just a matter of increasing volume driving production efficiencies, resulting in lower prices. And now the prices are low enough that you can have monitors in the headrests of cars, under the cabinets in the kitchen, and hanging on the wall in your home office.

Some key terms that you'll hear discussed in computer publications follow:

✔ **CRT:** Like the conventional direct view televisions described in Chapter 5, CRT monitors are based on *cathode ray tubes* — the traditional picture tube found in televisions since the 1940s. Although CRTs are bulky, they are cheap to make, can be very large (for a bit more money), and can have excellent picture quality. For most people, CRT isn't even a choice any more (flat screens are preferred), but surprisingly, for the really high-end monitor market (the type used by visual artists and photography professionals), CRT is still preferred for its more accurate color reproduction.

✔ **LCD:** We bet that you're already familiar with LCD screens — they're standard in every laptop or PDA on the market. LCDs used to be expensive to manufacture, but since the mid-1990s the technology has improved immensely, and dozens of LCD factories have been built around the world. As a result, LCD prices have dropped a ton, and most PC vendors now offer LCD screens as standard with their new PCs. The advantages of LCDs are many, but we think the biggest one is that they're much more space efficient than clunky old CRT monitors, so they can fit in a lot more places in your home. The biggest downside to LCD monitors is that the larger ones (starting at about 22 inches, measured diagonally) are expensive.

✔ **Plasma:** Also discussed in Chapter 5, plasma screens are the most common technology used for big, flat-panel, hang-on-the-wall TVs. Plasma screens aren't used much as PC monitors, mainly because LCD screens are cheaper and tend to have a better picture in the sizes typically used for PC applications. But like every other new computer-related technology, plasma displays are experiencing improved quality and reduced price. You find plasma as a PC monitor (in the home — in the commercial world they're common for big displays at airports and hotels) in a home-theater PC environment.

Just about any HDTV, whether it be a plasma, an LCD, or a projection system, can be hooked up to a PC. Many are explicitly designed for such uses, featuring connections such as VGA (the standard PC monitor connection), and the HDMI connection found on almost all HDTVs today can be easily adapted to connect to the DVI output found on many PCs. (See Chapter 6 for more on these connections.)

✔ **Touchscreen:** This type of monitor can be constructed based on CRT, plasma, or LCD displays. Electrical sensors are built into the face of a touchscreen monitor, enabling a user to simply point and touch with his or her finger to perform actions on the computer — instead of using a mouse or other pointing device. Touchscreens aren't as flexible as traditional pointing devices but can be useful in applications in which you want to use a more limited set of functions with your computer — such as controlling lights, TVs, or AC settings.

Keyboards

There have been a lot of funky attempts to reinvent the keyboard over the years, and nothing has caught the fancy of the mass market. (The only thing Danny has added to his keyboard is a big red panic button).

However, we did want to make three comments about keyboards. First, you can buy remote keyboards that have an infrared connection to a set-top box or other device. We think that RF, not infrared, is the way to go for these connections because infrared communications can be slow and unreliable if you type fast or move around a lot. To us, no better devices are available for keyboards and computer mice than those made by Logitech (www.logitech.com). As Bluetooth technology becomes more widespread, we believe it will become the most prevalent way of connecting wireless keyboards. Indeed, Bluetooth is popular today, but many wireless keyboard systems use their own proprietary radio connections, which can't be re-used for other wireless peripherals like Bluetooth can be. (We mention Bluetooth earlier in this chapter and discuss it in more detail in Chapter 16.)

Second, if you have kids, you might be tempted to buy a kid's keyboard. All sorts are available with large buttons and color coding, designed for very young kids. We advise against these because kids learn really fast, and they should learn on a real keyboard. Danny tried a lot of these kiddie keyboards on his kids, and in a week junked them all for regular keyboards. (His four-year-olds were beating him at *Ages of Empire* in no time flat.)

And finally, keyboard functionality will be used more and more around the house, so the interfaces might change from application to application. In some instances, you'll need a waterproof keyboard (so you can type in the hot tub, on the boat, while washing the dog, and so on). In other instances, you might find that you're using a remote control as your keyboard interface. And in yet other examples, such as with refrigerators, touchscreen is the way to go. If you find that your keyboard just doesn't look right with a particular application or use, go hunting around for other options.

Eeek, There's a Mouse on My Desk

Mice share much of the same development attention as keyboards, with a range of options on the market. We think no one should have a wired mouse, having used Logitech wireless mice since they were invented. And there are different styles of wireless mice — for example, a simple, three-button, hand-held wireless mouse for office presentation applications is great in the exercise room of your house, where you might have a remote monitor for Web surfing while you walk or ride the fat away.

If you've never used an optical mouse — the kind that use a small light and sensor instead of a moving mouse ball — you haven't really lived. (Even better are the mice that use lasers as their light source, because they pick up even more minute movements than conventional optical mice.) We think that the difference in functionality is amazing, and you never have to clean out the gunk that builds up inside your mouse. We've had some mice-cleaning gizmos over the years, and boy, were we glad to be able to finally throw those away (and usually we like gizmos). On the other hand, if your desk is as messy as ours, the old roller mouse is great because it works on top of the mess!

The neatest innovation in the mouse world revolves around mice that don't need to be sitting on a desk to work. The *air mouse* uses gyroscopes or other related technologies to track your motions in free space. These mice (the primary manufacturer is a company called Gyration, www.gyration.com) can be simply held in your hand and moved, and your motions are reflected on the screen. And they're not limited to left/right and up/down motions like a conventional mouse; they detect your motions in three dimensions. Pretty neat stuff. These air mice are especially handy for controlling a home-theater PC (when you don't have a desk in front of you to mouse upon), or for doing presentations (it's nice to be able to flip through your PowerPoint slides just by flicking your wrist).

Plugging in Printers and Such

Although a computer, monitor, keyboard, and mouse are all that you need to get up and running, no computer fulfills its potential without being hooked up to all sorts of neat peripheral devices — and indeed to other computers.

The number of things you can plug into a computer is almost limitless these days. Here are a few examples:

- **Printers** for getting your text and pictures on paper. New printers for your color photographs are surprisingly inexpensive — although beware the costs of ink refills!

- **Scanners** for getting text and pictures onto your hard drive and into e-mails. There are scanners for business cards and photographs as well as all-purpose scanners. We love the scanners from Visioneer (www.visioneer.com).

- **Modems**, including analog telephone, ISDN, xDSL, wireless, and cable modems — all of which we explain in Chapter 13.

- **Digital still cameras** that can capture still pictures and save them to your hard drive.

Using a PC as a video phone

As we discuss in Chapter 10, the video phone has been almost the Holy Grail of the telephone industry — something they've been searching for a way to do for nearly 40 years. The two big issues with telephone-based video phones are that the phones themselves are expensive, and the analog telephone lines that the majority of phones are connected to are too slow to carry a decent video signal. But while stand-alone video phones remain rare, videoconferencing on the PC has become almost commonplace. The PC has a few big advantages over a telephone system when it comes to videoconferencing:

- The CPU and video card of the PC can be leveraged to do the video signal processing — in modern computers, these devices are so powerful that you don't need a lot of pricey add-ons to handle video. This functionality, by the way, is one of the things that makes video telephones so expensive.

- Fast peripheral connection methods, such as USB and FireWire, can handle the signals from video cameras at full speed, so there's no longer a need for a special card inside the computer to attach a camera.

- Video cameras for PCs have become inexpensive. USB Web cams can cost as little as $40 and are available just about anywhere you buy PC accessories.

- Most importantly, PCs tend to be connected to high-speed broadband networks such as DSL or cable modems. These broadband connections, unlike analog telephone lines, have enough bandwidth to carry color video at frame rates fast enough to make the video look like video, instead of just a slideshow of still images.

Videoconferencing programs for the PC aren't just cheap — oftentimes they're free. Instant messaging programs such as AOL Instant Messenger, Yahoo! Messenger, and Apple's iChat include videoconferencing capabilities. So buy a cheap camera and get videoconferencing. If you have kids, one great use for these video phone programs is to use them to connect to the grandparents. Why wait until the next holiday for the kids to say "Hi!" face-to-face?

✔ **Digital video cameras** that let you videoconference or record movies to
your hard drive.

You can also use PC Web cams for security and monitoring — something
we discuss in Chapter 18.

✔ **Telephone management devices** that display, for example, caller ID
information on your screen or even open your contact management software and tell you exactly who is calling.

✔ **Docking stations** for a range of portable devices, including cell phones,
cordless phones, PDAs, and wireless headsets.

You can connect peripherals to a computer in two ways:

✔ **Connect peripherals directly to a single computer using that computer's parallel, serial, SCSI, Universal Serial Bus (USB), FireWire,
infrared, Bluetooth, or other port.** These peripheral devices are called
locally connected. If you want to know more about setting up your PC,
check out *PCs For Dummies,* 11th Edition, by Dan Gookin (published by
Wiley Publishing, Inc.).

✔ **Connect peripherals to a computer local area network (LAN) so that
you can share the peripherals among several computers.** This type of
peripheral is often called a *LAN-capable* or *networkable* peripheral. Many
devices today sport a wireless connection to the network, making them
LAN capable.

Many computer peripherals have either local connections or network connections (usually the LAN-capable type costs a bit more). Some peripherals,
such as many laser printers, may come equipped with both types of connections. In an ideal world, you'd probably want to choose only peripherals that
are networkable, but this standard isn't always practical.

Keep in mind that many devices that connect to a single computer may still
be used remotely by other computers on that network. For example, an inkjet
printer that isn't configured to plug directly into the LAN may be accessible
to other computers on the network if the computer that it *is* plugged into is
properly configured as a print server.

Now, this description is a little techie, and the purpose of this book is not to
teach a lesson in computer hardware. Some great *For Dummies* books do that
perfectly. But the message is this: In buying hardware or trying to make use
of hand-me-downs, you need to consider whether the equipment itself is networkable. Your local hardware dealer can help you determine that. So can
that neighbor kid who knows everything. In other chapters, we talk about
many more issues that you need to know about, so don't try to decipher
everything now.

Beyond the PC — Next-Generation Computers

The pieces and parts that make up a PC get smaller, faster, and cheaper every year. They also get used in more and more places — so you find, for example, computer hard drives in PVRs and MP3 players and computer graphics chips and processors in video game machines. Dozens of items in your home have most of the functionality of a personal computer — but few tie all that functionality together in a way that allows you to move seamlessly among them to read e-mail or surf the Web.

We think this is probably okay — PCs are very good at what they do, and PC-like devices are good at what they do. So we probably wouldn't want to throw out our PC in favor of a TV set-top box that we can use to surf the Web. Having said that, sometimes we might want to do PC stuff on our TVs or elsewhere in the home. Following are some good example of times when PC on the TV makes sense to us:

- ✔ **PC-powered TV:** In Chapter 7, we talk about PVR functionality and how a PC with a video connection can drive your viewing habits. Indeed, with PC remote controls that work from your living room, your dumb TV can do a lot more.

- ✔ **Context-based TV Web browsing:** This mouthful of terms refers to the times when you see something on TV (in an advertisement or during one of those PBS documentaries that we're nerdy enough to watch) and think, "Wouldn't it be nice to click a button on my remote control to display a Web page related to whatever's on the screen of my TV show?"

- ✔ **Quick checks of your messages:** Eventually, *unified messaging* will hit the market (it's been promised by telephone companies for years). UM (that's the insider's acronym) puts all your disparate voice-mail, e-mail, and fax accounts into one *uber* in-box that you can access from anywhere. The long-term vision is that you'll be able to read text conversions of your voice mail on a screen or listen to a computer read your e-mail to you on your phone. Why run back into the home office to check e-mail when you're sitting in front of the TV screen?

- ✔ **T-commerce:** The *T* stands for television. With the proper computer-like set-top box plugged into your TV, you can do online shopping or order a pizza from your comfy chair in front of the tube. Several telephone and cable companies in the United States and Canada let you do this today.

The common thread to these devices is that they take advantage of the computer power already built into set-top boxes and gaming machines, and eliminate the need for one of the most expensive parts of any computer — the display screen — by using your TV screen.

As technology makes small, LCD, flat-panel screens less expensive, we expect to see some next-generation computers that *do* have their own screens. A fridge with a computer screen is available today, but it costs about five times as much as a regular fridge.

Analog TVs aren't well suited for Web surfing or e-mail reading — the screens aren't sharp enough to display text clearly. But the advent of digital television (discussed in Chapter 5) is having a big effect on the integration of TVs and PCs as well. As higher-resolution digital TVs become more commonplace, the capability to do PC tasks on a TV increases. In fact, many HDTV-capable TVs are more like huge computer monitors than regular TVs, with the higher resolution and picture quality you expect from something that can display tiny letters on the screen in a readable form.

Game consoles on the Net!

The most popular alternative computing devices for the TV are gaming consoles — stand-alone gaming machines from Sony, Microsoft, and Nintendo. When you include both the hardware to play the games on and the software — the games themselves — the gaming industry is larger overall than the Hollywood movie industry! Gaming is not only big business; it's also big technology. Current generations of gaming consoles are basically high-end graphics computers, with lots of RAM, hard drives, fast CPUs, and killer graphics chips that may very well put your PC to shame.

The primary purpose of gaming consoles is — you guessed it — playing video games. But because these boxes are really high-powered, special-purpose computers, there's more to them than just gaming. Sony (with their PlayStation 2 and newer Playstation 3), Microsoft (with the Xbox and Xbox 360), and Nintendo (with the Wii console), have all created gaming boxes that are capable of storing and playing music files, storing files on their hard drives, and even surfing the Web.

The newest consoles (the Wii, PS3, and Xbox 360) include Web browsers for connecting to the Internet, and the PS3 and Xbox 360 can easily connect to your home network to find media on your PCs. Sony has even shipped a Linux-based kit (designed more for software developers than regular people) for the Playstation 2 console that lets the programmatically inclined do all sorts of neat PC stuff such as Web browsing on that older platform — so far, this hasn't arrived for the PS3, but here's hoping.

These Web and media browsing capabilities are cool, but they're not all you can do with a networked game console. The real reason for putting networking capabilities inside gaming consoles is to allow owners to use them for multi-player, online gaming. All of the current gaming consoles from Sony, Nintendo and Microsoft include Ethernet (and optionally, Wi-Fi) capabilities for connecting to your home network. Using these Ethernet connections, you'll be able to connect your game consoles to your home network, so you can play multiplayer games with other consoles in the house or use your Internet connection to play against others around the world. Imagine having that car race against someone 5000 miles away! First one to Monte Carlo wins!

Web-enabled TV — is it for me?

Another far less popular alternative computing device is the Microsoft MSN TV 2 Internet & Media Player (the descendent of the WebTV box that made a big splash a few years ago) — a small, proprietary Net computer that attaches to your television screen. Although it isn't designed to replace a full-fledged computer, the MSN TV 2 is a useful tool that allows you to do some neat stuff, such as

- ✔ Surf the Web
- ✔ Send and receive e-mail
- ✔ Access media such as digital music and photographs
- ✔ Print e-mail or Web pages
- ✔ Simultaneously view Web pages and TV programs using a picture-in-picture (PIP) system
- ✔ Access TV program listings and automatically program your VCR

If you don't need to do traditional PC tasks such as word processing, Web-enabled TV is an inexpensive and easy-to-use alternative to a PC. The low price of the MSN TV 2 (less than $200 for the top-of-the-line model) makes it affordable enough for the living room even if you have a PC in the house (so the kids can stay online but off your PC while you're trying to work at home, for example).

MSN TV 2 is not the only option for using a TV as an Internet terminal. Other options include the following:

- ✔ **Gaming consoles,** with built-in Web browsers. The Xbox 360, Playstation 3, and Wii all include some sort of Web browsing functionality. The Wii even lets you use its neat Wiimote to browse news and other Web content by just waving the remote.
- ✔ **Cable TV (and in a few regions, DSL) set-top boxes** that have enough computer power for surfing the Web and sending e-mail and can convert digital television signals to a format your TV can display.

For several years, the big set-top box vendors, such as Scientific Atlanta and Motorola, have been shipping devices that already contain enough power to perform PC functions. They've seen that the future is in supporting a seamless marriage of PCs and TVs. Most service providers (who control the software and functionality of the set-top box) haven't launched services that take advantage of all this horsepower yet. They will . . . don't ask us when, but they will.

Chapter 13

All Roads Lead to the Net

*M*ost people think about the Internet in terms of the neat (and not-so-neat) things it allows them to do, such as send and receive e-mail, surf Web pages, and watch video clips on YouTube.com. If you think of the Internet in this way, give yourself a gold star, because this way of thinking allows you to get the most out of your time on the Internet.

Before you do all this cool stuff on the Internet, however, you have to get connected to it. In this chapter, we tell you about the pros and cons of the many ways you can make that connection.

A World of IP Devices

Today, devices that communicate on the Internet — or on private networks using IP (Internet Protocol, the common language "spoken" by all devices on the Internet) — are basically all the same thing: computers. Personal computers, microcomputers, handheld computers, network computers, mainframe computers, and any other type of computer that you can think of (except, of course, that old Radio Shack TRS-80 that you now use as a doorstop). In fact, hundreds of millions (maybe billions) of computers in the world are somehow, sometimes connected to the Internet. And many more will be connected in the future.

Here are a few ways that the Internet may now (or soon) be a bigger part in your daily life:

✔ Telephone companies and Internet service providers are realizing that using the Internet is a much more efficient (and inexpensive) way to carry voice telephone traffic than the old-fashioned circuit-switched method. There are phone services explicitly marketed as Internet phone, such as Vonage (www.vonage.com) and Skype (www.skype.com), but the Internet is also being used to route regular phone calls too.

✔ Musicians and record labels are finding that using the Net is a great way to get music sent to people around the world. Online music stores such as Apple's iTunes Store have sold *billions* of songs over the Internet and are now branching out into TV shows and movies. All you need to jump into the world of online music (and video) is a fast Internet connection and a PC or Mac.

✔ Thousands of companies, big and small, are finding that *electronic commerce* (e-commerce) — using the Net to buy and sell stuff — is much cheaper and more convenient than traditional methods. You've probably already used Amazon.com or checked your bank balance online, and in the future you'll be able to do a lot more than this online.

✔ Manufacturers of home-automation and -control systems (which we discuss in Chapters 20 through 22) are turning to the Internet to allow users to remotely monitor and control all sorts of systems in their homes. Want to see the front door camera? Log into your home's Web site. Turn on the lights and fire up the spa before you get home? Turn to the Internet.

✔ Appliance and electronics manufacturers have decided that using the Internet is a great way to let future generations of smart products talk to each other and to service centers. Imagine a dishwasher that knows when it needs maintenance and can automatically notify the manufacturer — and even tell the technician which parts to bring for the service call.

All the wonders of the Internet and devices that speak its IP language aren't going to do you a darn bit of good if you're not connected. Getting connected to the Net is — in our opinion — as important as getting telephone service into your home and is probably a higher priority for most of us than stuff such as television. (TV watching has never been the same since *Seinfeld* went off the air.)

Traditionally, access to the Net was provided the old-fashioned way — through an analog telephone modem. Some folks are still stuck with this option, but it's going away quickly as faster and better *broadband* Internet services become mainstream. If you're on the Internet for anything more than the most basic purposes, you should go for a broadband connection — broadband isn't much more expensive than dial-up these days, it's hundreds of times faster, and it has the benefit of being always on (so you're always connected). If you're building a smart home, we think broadband is *mandatory*.

Analog Modems

We hope that you're lucky enough to live someplace where you can get a broadband Internet connection and service. If not, the primary connection between your computer — or computer network — and other computers (like all those millions of computers on the Internet) is most likely an analog modem. On a personal note, we both have high-speed connections — Pat has both a cable modem and a DSL modem in his house (he likes the belt-and-suspenders approach), and Danny has a cable modem in his house in Connecticut — so we tend to gloat and say "nyah, nyah" to our friends who are still using analog modems.

Okay, we'll cease and desist the gloating and get back to analog modems. These devices get their name from their function — which is to modulate and demodulate the digital data coming to and from your computer into analog signals that can be carried over the standard analog telephone system.

Figure 13-1 shows the route that information takes between an analog modem and the Internet. Your phone line goes to the telephone company's central office and then to your ISP, which has a group of modems that answer several phone lines. From there, you can use some of the bandwidth of your local ISP's connection.

Figure 13-1:
How an analog modem connects to the Internet.

Analog modems come in different speeds, but the following two are what you'll run into while modem shopping:

> ✔ **V.92 56-Kbps modems:** The latest and greatest technology, V.92 is the standard modem technology that you can buy today. V.92 is the name of the international standard that allows these modems to talk to each other, regardless of who sells them. The *56-Kbps* name is a slight misnomer, because FCC regulations force manufacturers to make these modems operate at a slightly lower ultimate speed (about 53 Kbps). V.92 modems have a few benefits that the older V.90 models lack:
>
> > • **Internet call waiting:** This feature works with your phone company's call waiting feature and lets you suspend your Internet connection when the phone rings. When you hang up, things pick up where they were, without you having to redial your ISP.

- **Quick connect:** The way the modem connects to your ISP (called the *handshake*) is improved because the modem remembers how it worked the last time you dialed up — so you can connect up to 50 percent faster.

- **V.PCM:** Yet another super-secret industry code name, V.PCM gives you a faster upstream speed (up to 43 Kbps).

Because modem technology is in many ways a dead end, many Internet service providers have never upgraded to V.92 modems in their part of the network, so the *upstream* part of your connection (from your home to the Internet) won't reach the maximum speed of 53 Kbps. V.92 modems are backwards-compatible with V.90. Therefore, if your ISP still uses V.90, things will work, but the special features are enabled only if the modem on the other end of your connection is also V.92. Unfortunately, few ISPs have adopted V.92.

✔ **V.90 56-Kbps modems:** These modems are the most common and are standard equipment in just about any computer these days. V.90 modems reach their maximum speed only in one direction — the downstream flow from your Internet service provider (ISP) to you. The upstream speed — from your computer to the Internet — is limited to 33.6 Kbps, the same as standard 33.6-Kbps modems.

Besides speed, modems can also be differentiated by their *form factor* — what they look like and how they connect to your PC. Analog modems come in three basic forms:

✔ **External modems:** These are freestanding devices that connect to your computer's modem serial port (often called the *COM* port) or USB port.

✔ **Internal modems:** These devices plug into an internal slot inside your PC. It used to be common for all new PCs to have a built-in modem, but the rise of broadband has relegated modems to second fiddle status, and a growing number of new PCs no longer include an analog modem.

✔ **PC Card modems:** Roughly credit-card-sized, these modems (which adhere to the PC Card, or PCMCIA — personal computer modular card interface adapter — standard) slide into the corresponding PC Card slot found on most notebook computers and some handheld computer devices.

You may also encounter modems that expand upon the basic computer-to-computer data communications function and add extra features. For example, many modems also contain circuitry that enables them — with some corresponding software on your PC — to act as fax machines. With a fax modem, you can send just about any document on your PC's hard drive to remote fax machines, and you can receive incoming fax messages, which you can view on your screen or print.

Other additional features often found on analog modems include the following:

- ✔ **Speakerphone:** A few modems come with speakerphone software that lets you use your PC (with microphone and speakers) as a hands-free phone.

- ✔ **Voice mail:** Using your PC's hard drive to store messages, modems with voice-mail software can handle any calls that come in when you're away (or just don't feel like answering the phone).

As good as analog modems have become — we remember the days of 2400-baud modems, which were agonizingly slow — we think that today's broadband Internet access technologies are so much better that we'd never go back to dial-up. We won't try to sell you on the upgrade based on the Web surfing and file downloading benefits (as good as they are), but rather on this point: Broadband technologies are always on, not dialed up. When you connect not just your computer but an entire house full of devices, all of which can potentially connect to the Internet, a constant and persistent connection makes all the difference. In fact, as we mention earlier in the chapter, it's almost downright required.

DSL

Digital subscriber line, or DSL, is the phone company's broadband method of sending data over existing copper telephone lines. Several DSL technologies have been widely developed, which is why we sometimes refer to DSL technologies as *xDSL,* with the *x* representing a range of other letters, such as *A* for *asymmetrical*. In this section we describe the most common types of xDSL available today — there are also HDSL and SDSL variants of xDSL which are not commonly offered as residential services — phone companies use them to provide T1 data circuits to businesses.

Digital subscriber lines — ADSL in particular — were developed as a way for telephone companies to compete with cable television providers — the high downstream speed is capable of carrying lots of digital television programming. In fact, in the mid-1990s, most major telephone companies had large divisions and joint ventures in place to jump into the cable TV market. This plan never worked out, though — the trials of such services weren't such great successes that cable TV seemed like a profitable direction for these companies to move in.

But then the Internet became popular, and there was finally a new need for providing this kind of bandwidth to the home. (Times have surely changed, however, as most DSL providers are moving rapidly *back into* the TV business — see the sidebar titled "Going V-ery fast with VDSL" for more on this).

DSL modems use the same single copper-wire pair that POTS (Plain Old Telephone Service — in other words, regular phone service) does, but their sophisticated digital signal processors (DSPs) can make use of a lot more of the frequency spectrum, giving them greater bandwidth capabilities. The frequencies that DSL devices use are generally much higher than those used for carrying POTS phone calls, so there's no interference between the two. You can literally pick up the phone in the middle of a DSL connection and make a phone call without a problem.

When we wrote an earlier edition of this book, we spent a considerable amount of time discussing something called ISDN (or integrated services digital network). ISDN is a phone company technology that allows — among other things @ phone lines and special ISDN modems to connect to the Internet at about 128 Kbps. ISDN is still out there in some places (especially outside the U.S.), but for the most part it's been superseded by DSL and other forms of broadband connectivity. That's because ISDN isn't fast enough for future (or even current) high-speed Internet connection requirements.

Table 13-1 shows some of the many flavors of DSL. Note that *downstream speed* is the speed at which data is sent to you from your service provider, and *upstream speed* measures the data heading back the other way.

Table 13-1	Types of DSL Technology	
DSL Technology	*Downstream Speed*	*Upstream Speed*
ADSL	Up to 8 Mbps	Up to 1.5 Mbps
ADSL 2/2+	Up to 28 Mbps	Up to 3.5 Mbps
VDSL	Up to 52 Mbps	Up to 12 Mbps
VDSL 2	Up to 100 Mbps	Up to 100 Mbps

Different service providers offer DSL services using just about all of the technologies shown in Table 13-1, but for the residential market, ADSL and ADSL 2/2+ is by far the most common technology. Keep in mind that the table lists the maximum speeds. When you get ADSL service, it will probably be a bit slower, but it's so far above analog modems that the difference doesn't matter.

Services driven by ADSL technology have the disadvantage of being *asymmetric,* which means that the upstream and downstream speeds are different. The problem with asymmetric bandwidth is that some symmetric applications that send large quantities of data both ways, such as videoconferencing (you want to see them as much as they see you!), can't take advantage of the maximum speeds available. If you have 1.5 Mbps downstream but only 64 Kbps upstream, symmetric applications run at 64 Kbps down and 64 Kbps up.

Going V-ery fast with VDSL

One of the DSL variants in Table 13-1 probably stood out as being the one you'd want in your smart home. VDSL, or very high speed DSL, is like a super tricked-out, twin-turbo V8 compared to ADSL's economical 4-cylinder speeds. VDSL (and its faster variant, VDSL2) is fast enough to let phone companies do all sorts of neat services, including multiple channels of TV, HDTV, voice, and high-speed Internet, all on the same phone line. The downside is that VDSL is very short range (about 6000 feet max) compared to ADSL (18,000 feet; some variants go even farther). So VDSL works well only if you put the VDSL equipment (called a DSLAM) right out in the neighborhood, near the houses. Putting all the equipment near the house is a great thing for performance, but not necessarily a great thing for phone companies trying to

trim expenses. VDSL is also completely different than ADSL, so phone companies who want to deploy it would need to abandon their investment in ADSL (and they've spent billions).

VDSL isn't a new technology (it's been around since the late 1990s), but it's still relatively rare. That's changing, however, as big phone companies decide they absolutely *must* offer TV services to compete with their cable competitors. In the United States, the biggest phone company, AT&T, has begun rolling out something called *Project Lightspeed*, which is bringing VDSL2 to millions of customers, along with a full IPTV service (see Chapter 5 for more on IPTV). So if you are an AT&T local phone customer, keep your eyes peeled for this service — the brand name for it is *U-verse*.

Fortunately, most applications for the Internet are asymmetric — your request to view a page is very small, typically just the address of the page on the Web, but the page downloaded is usually packed with data. Most home users are incredibly happy with even 356-Kbps upstream speeds (about eight times faster than analog modems), and the majority of home users tend to utilize much more downstream bandwidth anyway (for things such as Web browsing and file downloading).

Regardless of which DSL variant your service provider offers, the interface is similar. The DSL service enters your home through a standard copper telephone line that carries your POTS traffic. To extract the high-speed DSL data, you need a DSL modem. Generally, you'll find two variants of these:

✔ **External DSL modem:** This device looks and acts just like a souped-up version of the analog modem that you're probably familiar with, but it doesn't plug into the modem serial port (the COM port) on the back of your computer. Those modem serial ports are just too darned slow to handle the kind of speed that xDSL gives you. Instead, a DSL modem typically has an Ethernet (10/100BaseT) connection running to your computer and an Ethernet network interface card (NIC) inside your computer. Some modems also use a USB (universal serial bus) connector to hook up to your computer or have both Ethernet and USB.

✔ **Internal DSL modem:** Just like an internal analog modem, this one plugs into a slot inside your PC — an ISA or PCI bus slot for desktop computers or a PC card for laptops. Because these internal buses are much faster than the serial port that connects standard modems, you don't need an Ethernet interface.

If your provider gives you a choice, choose a DSL modem with an Ethernet interface. The other kind of DSL modem is great if you're looking to hook up a single computer but makes it more difficult to connect to your home network (because almost all networking equipment connects using the Ethernet standard). You shouldn't have a hard time convincing your DSL provider to do this for you because Ethernet modems are the most common.

If you want to get DSL, you need to choose a provider. Unfortunately, the number of companies offering DSL has been greatly reduced over the past few years due to some prominent failures in the telecommunications market. Two types of companies can offer DSL: incumbent telephone companies (your local telco) and competitive telephone companies, who lease lines and facilities from the incumbent. During the Internet boom years of the late 1990s, dozens of companies entered the competitive telephone company market and began offering DSL services — too many, in fact. Because of the intense competition (among other factors), a lot of these companies ended up going out of business. Today, residential DSL service is offered primarily by the incumbent telco and usually one of the remaining large competitive providers:

✔ Verizon: Serves the northeastern U.S. and a few markets elsewhere in the U.S. — areas where GTE used to be the phone company (www.verizon.com).

✔ BellSouth: Serves the southeastern U.S. (www.bellsouth.com). In early 2007, BellSouth merged with AT&T and eventually their name will be changed to AT&T.

✔ AT&T: Serves much of the central and southwestern U.S. (www.sbc.com).

✔ Qwest: Serves the northwestern and mountain region of the U.S. (www.qwest.com).

✔ Covad: The last remaining big competitive provider, serves nationwide (www.covad.com).

When you choose a DSL provider — such as Covad or your local telco — you usually have a choice of which ISP you want to use. The DSL provider gives you the connection, and the ISP provides Internet services such as e-mail, Web site hosting, and music services. Most DSL providers offer their own ISP service, but you can also choose from both local ISPs (in most cases) and big national ISPs. Some of the bigger ISPs who focus on DSL services include the following:

- ✔ EarthLink (www.earthlink.net)
- ✔ Speakeasy (www.speakeasy.net)
- ✔ AOL (www.aol.com)

Which to choose? We recommend that you look at the options and prices and find the ISP that offers the services that best fit your needs. This isn't earth-shattering advice, but each of these ISPs has their own specialties and services. We like to choose ISPs that explicitly support home networks. Many will often provide you with networking hardware, extra e-mail boxes (one for everyone in the house) and other neat Internet features such as fixed IP addresses (helpful if you want to use applications such as videoconferencing) and firewall services (to keep the bad guys out of your computer).

When it comes to planning your home network, DSL services will play a major role down the road for the telcos and therefore should have a major influence on your planning. DSL services will bring a lot of bandwidth into your home, bandwidth that is likely to be shared by a lot of applications. If your spouse is watching TV in the living room, you are working in your office in the basement, and the kids are playing online games in their rooms, you all may be using the same DSL link.

Filtering out noise

We mentioned that DSL — particularly the ADSL technology used in residential DSL — uses different frequencies on the phone lines than your voice telephone service does. Unfortunately, electronic systems don't always work so neatly in the real world, so even though your phone (on the lower frequencies) and your ADSL modem (on the higher frequencies) are not supposed to interfere with each other, a little bit of overlap can occur.

Early DSL modem installations used a device called a POTS splitter to keep your voice and the DSL modem on different segments of phone wiring in your house. This brute-force approach of keeping things separate solved the interference problem but came with a price: A phone technician had to come to your house to install this splitter, which took time and cost money, and only one phone outlet in the house could accept your DSL modem.

The current solution is more elegant. When a DSL modem is installed, you simply plug some small filters into your wall outlets — between the phone and the outlet. These filters (known as low-pass filters because they let only the lower frequencies pass through) correct any interference problems and let you plug the DSL modem into any phone outlet in the house. They also let you do the installation yourself, which saves you both time and money.

Getting your IP fixed

When you connect to a broadband service provider, your computer or home networking router (if you're using one) is assigned an IP address. You can think of the IP address as the Internet equivalent to your home's street address — it's a universally understood address that lets other computers find yours, just as a street address lets other people find your house. Most broadband service providers (and all dial-up Internet providers) give you a *dynamic* IP address that changes on a regular basis. This is fine for regular Web browsing and e-mailing and the like but just won't do for applications such as videoconferencing or hosting a Web server on your own computer. For these kinds of applications, you need an IP address that *never* changes — a *fixed* IP address. Most broadband providers will give you one for an extra $10 or $15 a month; a few, such as Speakeasy, include a fixed IP address in the base price. Think you'll never videoconference

or have your own Web site, so you don't need this? Think again — many applications require or would benefit from a fixed IP address, such as a home-automation system that has a built-in Web interface so you can adjust things remotely through a Web browser.

If you can't get a fixed IP address (or if your provider charges too much for such a service), you can utilize a *dynamic DNS* service. These services (many of which are free — just search Google for *dynamic DNS* to see dozens of them) let you create a *host name* for your Internet connection's IP address. The service then maps your changing IP address to a fixed hostname (which would look something like `yourhost-name.dyndns.org` if you were using DynDNS's service — `www.dyndns.com`). A fixed IP address is a more foolproof solution, but dynamic DNS services work really well, and you can't beat the price!

One of the neat things about DSL is that you're always connected to the network, 24 hours a day. If you leave your computer on the entire time, all sorts of things are possible. For instance, you can receive automatic software downloads while you're asleep. Or you can receive phone calls on your PC through Internet telephony. Or you can have all the major newspapers downloaded to your PC for when you wake up. A DSL line turns a historically reactive relationship with the telecommunications networks into an active one.

If you want to find out even more about DSL, check out Broadband Reports (`www.broadbandreports.com`).

Lighting the Way with Fiber

When it comes to fast Internet connections, the copper wires that phone companies use have some serious shortcomings. It takes a lot of engineering wizardry to send 20 or 50 or 100 Mbps of data down the same set of wires that get maxed out at 56 Kbps with an analog modem (to put that in perspective, 56 Kbps is .056 Mbps). While the folks who design DSL systems keep improving the breed, each new improvement is a bit harder to implement than the one before it. And although the speeds of today's fastest DSL systems seem pretty high, they run into a couple of problems:

✔ In the real world, speeds to a home (your home, perhaps) are a lot less than the maximum speed. Vagaries in the condition of phone wiring and distances between the DSL modem and the *DSLAM* (where DSL connections are terminated and concentrated onto faster network connections) can bring the real world speeds down by 50 percent or more from the theoretical maximums.

✔ Even if the maximums were reached, they might not be enough in the longer term. As phone companies begin to throw Internet service, IP phone services, *and* IPTV over the same wire, the bandwidth gets used up pretty darn fast. HDTV is the biggest concern here, because an HDTV channel can use up to 20 Mbps of bandwidth all by itself. In a world where HDTVs cost less than $500 and homes have an average of more than three TVs, it's easy to see how even a 50 Mbps connection could get overwhelmed.

Therefore, many phone companies are at least exploring the use of *fiber-optic* systems, which use light waves, instead of electrical signals, to bring mind-bogglingly fast Internet and TV connections to homes. Two main types of fiber connections are used to connect homes and businesses to the Internet:

✔ **Active system:** In these networks, an individual fiber-optic cable links the home and the telephone company central office (or side-of-the road equipment pedestal). This approach offers the most speed, but it is expensive to implement and is mainly used for very-high-speed and very expensive connections to businesses.

✔ **Passive system:** In a passive system (which is what is commonly found in the residential word), a fiber connection is passively split (hence the name — it means that the light waves are split off without the use of electronics) between a number of homes (typically 16 to 32 homes per connection). Each home gets an individual fiber-optic cable connection, but this connection is shared back at the central office among 16 or 32 homes. These passive networks are usually called *PONs* (passive optical networks).

PON connections are a lot cheaper to implement because expensive components can be divided among multiple homes. That said, the biggest expense in deploying a fiber network to someone's house is running the fiber-optic cabling. It costs $1000 or so to send out a team of folks to dig trenches and run and bury the cables that lead up to the side of a home. Multiply this expense by the tens of millions of homes that each big telephone company serves and you see that this starts to become an expensive proposition.

Luckily for (some of) us, some phone companies realize that fiber is the future. Well, they all realize that fiber is the future, and most of the *core* of their networks (the parts that run between central offices and from remotely located gear to the central offices) is already fiber. Not every phone company has yet been convinced that spending tens of billions of dollars on bringing fiber to the "last mile" (to the home, in other words) is worth it. But some have.

In particular, in the United States, Verizon (the second largest phone company) is in the midst of a multiyear, tens of billions of dollar project called *FiOS*. FiOS brings a complete telecommunications and television service to the home using a PON system. With FiOS, users can get a full standard and high-definition cable TV type of package (with all the bells and whistles such as video on demand), multiple lines of phone service, and a super high-speed Internet service. FiOS customers can get services as fast as 50 Mbps (on the downstream side) for not much more than they would pay for DSL services that max out at 5 or 6 Mbps.

By the way, in case you are interested, FiOS stands for fiber optic service or is an Irish word meaning *knowledge*. Our Irish is a bit rusty (okay, nonexistent) so we can't verify that, but Verizon has used both definitions!

To learn more about FiOS, and to see if you can get it (you lucky dog you!), go to www.verizonfios.com.

Phone companies in Europe and Asia (particularly in Japan and Korea) are also jumping on the fiber bandwagon, as are smaller groups. For example, some towns and cities in the United States are building their own fiber networks. And many big developers are including fiber as part of the amenities when they build new communities — part of the package includes not just the house and the community swimming pool but also high-speed Internet!

Cable Modems

Cable television providers are in a frenzy to provide additional services beyond television. Foremost among these services, for most cable companies, is cable-modem Internet access. A cable modem is basically a very fast modem that connects to the cable company. It can transmit at up to 30 Mbps and connect to your computer through an Ethernet connection. Like the DSL modems we talk about in the preceding section, cable modems are usually rented as part of the service. Monthly service is typically priced in the $40 or so range.

Why are cable modems so hot?

Cable companies are well positioned to offer cable modems, the leading-edge Internet service, for several reasons:

✔ **They get it.** By this we mean that the cable industry, as a whole, has committed itself to broadband and has invested both money and brainpower (through an industry group called CableLabs, which helps develop standards for cable systems and which approves equipment to be interoperable within cable networks) to creating full-service broadband networks. Cable providers want to give you every data service you'd ever need (with the possible exception of mobile wireless services), and they've spent billions creating an infrastructure to do so.

✔ **They already have a high-speed network.** Most cable television networks consist of super-high-capacity fiber-optic cable running from the central offices to local distribution points and — even more importantly — coaxial cable running from these distribution points to your home. Coaxial cable can carry a lot of data — a heck of a lot more, in most cases, than the copper wiring that connects telephone companies to your home.

✔ **They have an important booster.** That booster is Microsoft, which has invested billions of dollars into the industry in an effort to move things along. In addition to Microsoft itself, Paul Allen, one of the co-founders of Microsoft, has spent a few billion dollars of his own nest egg to buy some cable companies and turn them into providers of Net access and other advanced services.

Although many independent cable television companies are going it alone and working to offer their own versions of cable-modem services, big nationwide cable companies (often called MSOs, or multiservice operators) predominate. The biggest ones include the following:

✔ Comcast: www.comcast.com.

✔ Cox Communications: www.cox.com.

✔ Charter Communications: www.chartercom.com.

✔ Road Runner: Time-Warner, one of the largest cable television providers, as well as one of the biggest content producers in the world (movies, television, music, magazines, books, you name it), merged with AOL (the world's biggest ISP) in the 1990s. The combined company, AOL Time-Warner, runs its cable-modem operations under the Road Runner brand. Moving forward, many Time-Warner cable areas will also allow you to use AOL as your ISP, so you'll have a choice of Road Runner or AOL (and usually another, unaffiliated ISP such as Earthlink). You can find out whether Road Runner is available in your area at www.rr.com or check for AOL broadband at www.aol.com.

If you live in Canada, cable-modem service is available from the following big providers:

- Rogers: www.rogers.com.
- Shaw: www.shaw.ca.
- Videotron: www.videotron.com/portail_en/index.htm. This is the English version of the page, but they have a French one as well because they're based in Montreal.

Most of the time, the company that provides your cable television service and your cable modem is also the company that provides your ISP service. In other words, if Cox is your cable company, you'll get your cable modem from them, and your e-mail address will be something like smarthomesfordummiesreader@cox.net. As something called *open access* becomes more common, however, the cable world is becoming a bit more like the DSL world. With open access, other ISPs, such as Earthlink or AOL, are allowed to sell services to cable-modem customers. If you have open access, you'll still get your cable TV service from your MSO, and your cable modem will be connected to them as well, but you'll get all your Internet services from someone else. This is happening across the country, but it's most likely to be found wherever AOL Time-Warner owns the local cable company — that's because the FTC (Federal Trade Commission) required AOL Time-Warner to open up their cable systems to other ISPs as a condition of the merger.

Regardless of your service provider or ISP, cable modems fit into one of two categories:

- **Telco-return modem:** This type of modem is used in less sophisticated cable systems and is generally much less desirable. The one-way modem receives data at high speeds over your cable system's coaxial cable, but any upstream (outgoing) data uses a standard analog telephone modem — so you send data as slowly as you would with a conventional analog modem (plus you tie up your telephone line whenever you're online). These modems are okay for e-mail and surfing Web sites, but their asymmetric nature makes them less than perfect for all the neat new things you can do on the Net, such as videoconferencing, Internet telephony, and online gaming. Luckily, telco-return cable modems are gradually disappearing as cable providers complete the updates of their systems to full two-way networks.

Telephone-return cable-modem services are going the way of the dodo bird and becoming extinct. We mention them simply because a few places are still stuck with this option.

✔ **Two-way modem:** This is the modem you hope your service provider uses (and the big ones, such as Cox, AT&T and Road Runner, typically do). Two-way modems both send and receive data over the coaxial cable and typically offer high speed both ways (although the reception is often still faster than the upstream data rate — the upstream is usually limited to about 500 Kbps, and the downstream ranges between 2 and 10 Mbps).

A few cable modems are internal devices (which plug into an ISA or PCI bus slot in your PC), but most that we've seen are external, stand-alone boxes. The cable system's coaxial cable connects to the modem, and the modem connects to your computer (or your computer LAN) through a standard Ethernet 10BaseT connection (which we talk about in more detail in Chapter 15). If you don't have an Ethernet card in your PC already, don't worry — the cards are cheap, and many cable-modem service providers give you one as part of the service package. In Figure 13-2, you can see how a cable modem connects to the Internet.

Cable-modem networks are usually (not always, but most of the time) built using a standard called *DOCSIS* (Data Over Cable Service Interface Specification — say that ten times fast). Developed by the folks at CableLabs, DOCSIS is a standard that tells cable-modem equipment manufacturers how to make their gear and how to make it *interoperable*. This means DOCSIS gear from vendor A should work with gear from vendor B.

Because of DOCSIS, you can buy a cable modem off the shelf at Fry's or Circuit City and bring it home to plug it in yourself. In the DSL world, you still need to get the DSL modem from your phone company or ISP.

Figure 13-2:
How a cable modem connects a home LAN to the Internet.

More than one version of DOCSIS is available, as the technology matures and improves:

✔ DOCSIS 1.0, the first version, allowed speeds of up to 38 Mbps downstream and 10 Mbps upstream (remember that this is shared among several users, so no one home will see this speed).

✔ DOCSIS 2.0, the current version, keeps the same downstream maximum but bumps the upstream to 30 Mbps.

✔ DOCSIS 3.0, the "coming soon" version, can use multiple channels (cable modem systems essentially "steal" a TV channel to provide Internet access) and can reach speeds of up to 160 Mbps downstream and 120 Mbps upstream.

The connection speed that you as an individual user get depends on which variant of DOCSIS your cable company uses (most use 2.0 today), how the cable company has architected their network (how many users share the same bandwidth), and even what service level you've chosen.

When DOCSIS 3.0 comes out, the cable companies should be able to at least match the speeds offered by the fastest DSLs and will be in the ballpark of some of the fiber systems.

One big advantage for the cable modem folks is that the Internet bandwidth provided by the DOCSIS cable-modem systems isn't used to carry TV signals. The same wires are used, but TV stations are on different channels. So where a 50-Mbps VDSL connection would cordon off 35 Mbps or so for TV, a 50-Mbps cable connection would be (theoretically at least) able to offer all that bandwidth for Internet service.

Beaming Internet in from Satellites

If you live out in the hinterlands and can't get DSL or cable (not to mention fiber-optic service), you might think that you're stuck with dial-up analog modem service. Nothing can be further from the truth! Look to the skies and you'll see your option — satellite Internet service.

With satellite Internet service, your data is beamed down to you from on high, from one or a series of earth-orbiting satellite systems that connect back to the Internet through ground stations. While the data *to* your home comes over the satellite connection, you may have two options for how data gets sent from your computer to the Internet:

✔ **You can buy *one-way* service:** In this scenario, a standard analog modem sends data back upstream (onto the Internet). This limits your upstream speed to the same 33 Kbps as a dial-up ISP account.

✔ **You can buy *two-way* service:** With two-way service, which requires a different antenna and receiver (one with a built-in radio transmitter), you can use the satellite to send data in both directions. Because of FCC regulations, if you get two-way service, a professional must install and aim your dish.

The trend in the satellite Internet industry is towards the two-way model, and if you're shopping for satellite Internet access, we definitely recommend that you choose such a system.

As we mentioned, for some people, satellite Internet access is the only game in town. And it's great for your otherwise off-the-grid cabin in the mountains, or if you're a rancher ten miles from the telephone company's central office. If you have a choice to go with DSL or cable instead, however, we think you should. Here's why:

✔ **Relatively low speeds (bandwidth):** Satellite Internet just plain isn't as fast as DSL or cable modem, with most systems topping out at about 1.5 Mbps downstream speed, and 200 Mbps upstream. The one-way systems max out at a speed of only 33.6 Kbps upstream, which is the same speed as a dial-up modem (which is what they use). These speeds aren't awful (except for the one-way upstream), but you pay $60 a month or more for them, whereas the cheapest DSL service plans (at about the same speed) are less than $20 in most locations.

✔ **High latency:** Latency is the measure of delay in a signal — the time it takes to get, for example, from a Web server on the Internet to your computer. Because of the sheer distances involved in sending radio signals up to a satellite and back down (and some other factors as well), satellite systems have higher latency than DSL or cable. This isn't a big deal for Web pages or e-mail, but it can be a big deal if you're videoconferencing or audioconferencing over the Net, making phone calls, or playing multiplayer online games.

✔ **You might not be able share your Internet connection (right now):** Early satellite Internet systems were designed to be connected directly to one computer only — so no network (and no smart home networking!). Most systems shipping today *can* support a network, but make sure you read the fine print before you shell out the cash.

✔ **You can't install it yourself:** Because the two-way system has a satellite transmitter, all sorts of regulations and FCC rules are involved in satellite Internet and you aren't allowed to install it yourself. (Folks would be pretty mad if you bumped off their American Idol signal with a misdirected satellite feed!) Installers cost money, which leads to our next problem with satellite Internet.

✔ **It'll cost you:** The hardware to get a satellite Internet system up and running costs hundreds of dollars. And unlike the cable and DSL world, the price isn't usually subsidized as much by the provider (so you pay up front). Shop around between services and see whether anyone is offering free dishes or receivers or both — you'll have to sign on to a longer-term contract, but the savings may be worth it to you. Also, as we mentioned, the monthly service fee is higher than competing DSL and cable-modem plans. Over time, as competition grows, we hope we see some price cuts!

Despite these disadvantages, satellite Internet has one big advantage over most competing high-speed Internet access systems. You can use it just about anywhere in North America, something that can't be said about cable modems or DSL. satellite Internet providers offering similar services in Europe and in Japan.

Most of the satellite Internet companies offer a mobile version of their service and hardware that can mount on your RV or boat. So you can take your Internet with you, even when you're out of range of cell phone providers. This isn't a smart home application, per se, but we think it's pretty cool.

You can find several providers of satellite Internet service. In the U.S., the big three are as follows:

✔ **HughesNet:** We describe the DIRECTV TV network in Chapter 5. Hughes Electronics, the company that built the DIRECTV system, has also developed a satellite Internet access system called HughesNet (http://go.gethughesnet.com, formerly called DirecWAY). HughesNet is a two-way system, capable of speeds of up to 1.5 Mbps down and 200 Kbps up, with three service plans offering varying speeds and features.

✔ **StarBand:** StarBand is a newer provider to the U.S. residential market (although the company's been around since 2000). StarBand (www.starband.com) offers two two-way Internet service plans — a PRO service that doesn't support networks in your home and a more expensive ULTIMATE that does.

✔ **WildBlue:** WildBlue is another new competitor to HughesNet, offering three service plans in the U.S. All are two-way and all support home networks. Speeds range up to 1.5 Mbps downstream and 256 Kbps upstream.

We should note that while we've been a bit hard on the satellite Internet services, we do know people who have them and love them. It's all a factor of where you are and what your options are. If we had to choose between dial-up and satellite, it would take us all of about two seconds to come down on the side of satellite.

Figure 13-3 shows a one-way satellite connection that uses a regular modem to send data out to the Internet. The two-way connection looks pretty much the same, except that data returns to the Internet through the satellite link.

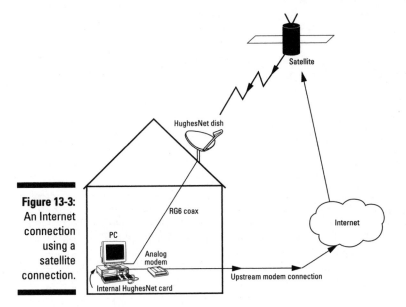

Figure 13-3: An Internet connection using a satellite connection.

Connecting Wirelessly

While the telephone and cable television companies slowly develop and build network connections to bring data into your home at high speeds, a host of companies are working on ways to do the same thing without wires.

Traditionally, most of us equate wireless with portable — and indeed many wireless service companies are emphasizing this benefit of using wireless technologies. Increasingly, however, service providers are looking toward wireless technologies as a way to quickly and cheaply provide data and telephone services to a fixed location — such as your house. New advances in wireless technology are rapidly bringing down the costs of the network equipment, such as transmitters and receivers, and setting up a wireless service is usually quick. Instead of digging trenches or putting up utility poles and running wires, wireless providers need only put up an antenna and then provide one for each customer.

Understanding mesh networks

If you're looking into wireless broadband networks, you may hear the term *mesh networks.* Mesh networks are based on smaller, lower-powered antenna/radio systems that don't necessarily have to talk back to the master base station. In a mesh network, traffic is bounced from antenna to antenna within the network footprint. So your traffic might bounce off three other peoples' antennas before it gets to the base station and sent off to the Internet over a wired connection (such as a fiber-optic line). Similarly, your antenna might not only pick up and receive your Internet traffic but also relay someone else's traffic. The big advantage of mesh networks is that they tend to use more inexpensive components, so the service provider can build up the network gradually as new customers sign up, instead of investing a big chunk of money up front.

Mesh networks can be built using specialized, proprietary radio systems. That's usually not the most cost-effective way of doing mesh, however. The more common approach is to use Wi-Fi as the radio technology for a mesh network, and then add some specialized hardware and software that creates the "mesh." Several companies focusing on the metro Wi-Fi are using or investigating mesh technologies.

Only a few wireless Internet services are available to residential customers today — in the early 2000s, the first generation of wireless companies went into Chapter 11 and out of business in an industry-wide flameout about as spectacular as any we've seen. That doesn't mean that wireless to the home is dead (and, by the way, we know you sharp readers picked up on the fact that the satellite Internet systems discussed in the preceding section are wireless, but we're using the term here to refer to *terrestrial* wireless systems, not space-based systems). Although a lot of wireless startups went broke during the first generation of wireless mania, the big guys (such as your local phone company or big nationwide telecommunications companies such as Sprint and AT&T) are testing their next-generation wireless services and will be launching them in the future, so check their Web sites if your other options are limited.

You can find a list of wireless ISPs at Robert Hoskin's Broadband Wireless Exchange Web site: http://www.bbwexchange.com/.

Wireless service providers can offer service to residential customers in a few ways:

> ✔ **Fixed and portable NLOS (non-line-of-sight):** These solutions (and we use the plural because there are many different ways to skin this particular cat) use a series of base-station radio/antenna towers that can transmit and receive data communications out to homes and businesses in their cell (like a cell for a mobile phone system). Fixed systems refer to those that require an antenna that is mounted (usually on the roof) and then aimed to get the best transmission possible. Portable systems are

designed with antennas that aim themselves, so you can perform the installation without the need of a professional radio engineer to align and aim antennas. As long as you're within the cell, you can take your system from work to home to a new house when you move across town, without needing a new professional installation.

✔ **WiMAX:** The biggest hype (and promise) in broadband wireless services comes from a technology called WiMAX. WiMAX (the name stands for Worldwide Interoperability for Microwave Access) is not just one technology — it's actually a group of NLOS wireless systems that can be fixed, portable, or mobile (like a cell phone). The two main variants of WiMAX are

- **802.16d:** This is the fixed version of WiMAX, designed for installations where the user doesn't get up and move. It's an older version of WiMAX, and most wireless service providers are waiting for the newer version (which we discuss in the next bullet). A few companies, such as the DSL company Covad and the ISP EarthLink, are offering 802.16d-based services now.

- **802.16e:** Also known as Mobile WiMAX, this is big news in the wireless world. 802.16e can be used as a fixed or portable system but can also be used as a truly mobile service (for example, you can connect in a moving car or train). Most of the big players are making their wireless plans around 802.16e — Sprint, for example, will be migrating their high-speed Internet services to this technology in the next few years.

WiMAX can potentially offer speeds as fast as DSL or cable modems and at prices that aren't too far from what the wired guys offer. And because it's wireless, a home has a better chance of being "on the network," without waiting for a physical upgrade to wiring and central offices.

✔ **Metro Wi-Fi networks:** These short-range networks make use of the 802.11, or Wi-Fi, wireless local networking technology that you might be familiar with in your own home or office network. (We talk about this technology in Chapter 16.) Although Wi-Fi was designed for short-range transmissions (300 feet or less), it can be modified to go greater distances. Most service providers offering Wi-Fi networks are *not* using it to send data to and from people's homes. Instead, they're using it to provide broadband services in hot spots such as hotel lobbies, airports, and cafes for people toting laptops or PDAs with Wi-Fi capabilities. However, a few service providers are examining Wi-Fi with an eye towards providing broadband to homes, particularly where homes are close to each other (and may therefore be within range). The biggest disadvantage of Wi-Fi in this scenario is the extremely short range we mentioned. The biggest advantage is the fact that Wi-Fi gear is extremely inexpensive, and millions of people already have it in their homes and computers. Big cities such as San Francisco and Philadelphia are in the midst of deploying citywide metro Wi-Fi networks as a public service and alternative to wired solutions — other cities such as Long Beach, California, already have these networks up and running.

✔ **3G mobile services:** Mobile phone providers have launched data services across the world. Many current services are still 2.5 G (the *G* stands for *generation,* and these services are an interim step after 2G — 2G being the transition to digital voice services for cell phones). 2.5G services offer speeds up to about 40 Kbps, roughly equivalent to analog modem speeds, but newer 3G systems can be as fast as 1 to 2 Mbps. For the most part, 3G systems remain the province of mobile users — mainly business users — because they'll probably cost significantly more than other broadband solutions. But with unlimited usage plans coming down to about $50 a month for some wireless carriers, we are beginning to see some users cut the cord and move all their telecommunications to the mobile network. See the sidebar titled "Getting 3G into your home" for information on how to make a 3G connection part of a whole-home network.

The bottom line on wireless Internet connections to the home is that the technology is here, the service providers are testing it, some of us can get it, and we'll *all* probably see it soon. The biggest roadblock is whether wired solutions such as cable modems and DSL will reach enough homes to alleviate the need for wireless solutions. We don't think that will happen because too many people in rural areas of the U.S. and Canada are out of cost-effective reach of wired networks. So we expect to see wireless offerings hit the market in a real way in the near future.

Getting 3G into your home

Although 3G mobile data services such as EV-DO (offered on CDMA networks such as Verizon Wireless and Sprint) and HSPDA (offered on GSM networks such as Cingular/AT&T and T-Mobile) are primarily for on-the-go users, they can work as a broadband source for a home network. We think DSL and cable modems are a better value for most folks (and offer higher speeds), but 3G may be an option for homes that aren't reached by standard wired broadband services.

For a single computer, a 3G connection requires nothing more than an *air card,* which is a NIC for 3G networks that fits into a PCMCIA port on a laptop computer. For a network, however, something more is needed: a *3G router.* These devices work just like regular broadband routers (discussed in Chapters 15 and 16), providing the smarts that direct data to and from the Internet and the computers in your home. Most 3G routers include both Ethernet and wireless (Wi-Fi) connections, so that you can connect just about any PC in your home to the router. Among the companies offering 3G routers are Linksys (www.linksys.com), Kyocera (www.kyocera.com), Junxion (www.junxion.com), and D-Link (www.dlink.com).

By the way, although you may not want to use one of these routers as your primary source of Internet connectivity, you may want to consider buying one as a backup. If you have an air card for use in your laptop on the road, a 3G router will let you quickly reuse that air card for the whole home during DSL or cable outages.

Power Companies

We know what you're thinking right now. "Power companies? What the heck do they have to do with the Internet, besides maybe having a Web site that tells me what to do when I have a gas leak?" (Incidentally, when you have a gas leak, run like heck.) Well, believe it or not, utility companies are trying to figure out how to get on the Internet bandwagon.

Just like telephone companies with DSL technologies, cable television companies with cable modems, and wireless companies with some of the new services they're planning to offer, utility companies want to offer you high-speed Internet access to go along with their traditional services.

Why are power companies a good candidate to jump into a business they don't have any experience in? They have a few things in their favor:

- **An existing communications backbone:** You'd probably be surprised at the complex and sophisticated communications network these companies already have — hundreds of miles of fiber-optic cable, copper wire, and wireless systems are already in place and online for the internal use of these companies. The smarter ones thought ahead and laid down extra capacity while building out their own networks, so they have much of the infrastructure in place and ready to go.

- **Rights of way:** If you were to try to build your own communications network, one of the biggest problems you'd run into is getting the *rights of way* to lay your fibers and cable across literally hundreds of miles of private and public property. Even wireless providers run into this problem when they try to put up antennas (the neighbors like having the phones but hate seeing all those working parts). The power companies already have these rights of way for their electrical lines.

- **Ubiquity:** Think it's rare to find a home without a cable television connection or at least a telephone line? It is, but it's even rarer to find one that's not connected to electrical power. You'd have to go far into the backwoods to find one, and even then, chances are good that those households don't have power because they don't want it — back-to-nature types, you know.

Power companies can provide high-bandwidth communications services to you in two ways:

- They can use their rights of way to run new wiring to your home from their network. This option isn't necessarily cheap, depending on how far their network access point is from your home.

- They can devise ways to use the existing electrical power line to also carry broadband data and communications signals into the home. If they can do this — and some big power companies and communications equipment vendors say they can — all they have to do is install some sort of box in your home that splits the data out from the power. The data is then sent off to your telephones, computers, and whatever else needs it in your home network. This is a neat idea, and something that you may be seeing in the not-so-distant future.

Note: The first deployments of this technology are happening outside the U.S. because of differences in how the electrical-power distribution networks are designed. Basically, the first systems being tested use a converter box at each transformer in the power network to connect the fiber-optic backbone to the power line. Compared to Europe and Asia, the U.S. has fewer customers served by each individual transformer in the network, which means that many more of these (expensive) converters would be needed. At the present pricing levels, this state-of-the-art, experimental equipment is too expensive to install here. We do think, however, that the almost inevitable increases in computer chip power and corresponding decreases in prices will soon make this idea an economically viable solution in the U.S. as well. If you live in Germany, you can buy broadband over power lines today!

We want to point out a recurring theme here. Many different companies have sophisticated, high-speed communications networks (cable, telephone, and power utilities) in place right now but none have a widespread, high-speed, two-way means of connecting your home to these networks. Although it would be nice if they would all get out their backhoes and work crews to upgrade this last-mile connection, the procedure is expensive. So most of the companies are looking at ways to reuse their existing connections in new and bandwidth-rich ways.

Chapter 14

Designing a Data LAN

• •

• •

*I*n a simple form, a home-computer network can consist of a single computer connected by modem to the Internet or to another external network (such as your office's network). A network can also be two stand-alone PCs that share a printer with a simple A/B switchbox. We strongly encourage you to think beyond these examples, though.

As the number (and type) of computers in your home increases and the price continues to decrease, consider installing (or at least preparing your home's wiring for) a full-fledged computer *local area network (LAN)* to allow your computers to quickly share access to the same resources. A home LAN provides a high-speed data connection among all the computers in your home, allowing them to do things such as share files, share networked peripherals (for example, a printer), and even play networked games. Multiple computers can more easily share high-speed Internet access devices, such as DSL or cable modems, over a home-computer LAN. Home media servers, which we discuss in Chapter 5, also fit into your computer LAN because they provide content not only to TVs and audio systems but also to computers throughout your house.

In this chapter, we discuss the basics of computer LANs and some of the ways to set up a LAN in your home. We also talk about some of the difficulties you may encounter when you try to connect several networked computers to your Internet account at the same time.

Flipping the Wired or Wireless Coin

The first step in choosing a LAN technology for your home is to decide whether you should go with a wired or wireless solution. If you've perused other sections of this book, you know that we spend most of our time talking about wired solutions. Data networks, however, have experienced an explosion of no-new-wires networking systems (the immensely popular Wi-Fi networking products).

Here's our take on the issue: If you're building a new home or undertaking a major remodeling of an older home and if the walls are open, by all means install the wired alternative. Yes, you may (and probably will) want to add a wireless network to your home. Having the wired infrastructure in place in your walls actually makes it easier to add a whole-home wireless network because you can add wireless *access points* in multiple spots within your home, closer to where you need your wireless signals.

Although we think that putting the right kinds of wires and cables into the right part of your home is the best solution to creating flexible and future-proofed home-networking solutions, we do live in the real world. And in the real world, you may not be able to get the necessary cabling systems installed in your home for a number of reasons, including the following:

✔ You rent your home.

✔ You live in a condominium and can't easily access shared spaces in walls, attics, and basements.

✔ You live in a historic home and have to run any changes past the planning commission.

✔ Your home has design problems that keep you from easily running cables, such as no crawl space, basement, or attic in which to hide wires.

Whatever the reason, you may not be able to squeeze those fat CAT-5e/6 and coaxial lines through the walls in your home. Luckily, you have some options: You can use wireless systems to do the job, or you can use the phone and electric power wires already in your walls (often called no-new-wires solutions). We discuss these alternatives in Chapter 16.

Wireless and no-new-wires systems are great, but they do have some disadvantages when compared to a wired infrastructure:

✔ **You'll get lower speeds without wires:** Although wired LANs can run at 100 or even 1000 Mbps, the fastest wireless alternatives max out at well below 50 Mbps. This isn't a big deal if you're talking about sharing a 1- or 2-Mbps Internet connection, but it is when you start thinking about sending large video or other media files between computers in your home.

✔ **You'll probably pay a bit more.** Prices of wireless LAN equipment for the home have dropped like dot.com stock prices over the past few years, but they're still higher than those of wired LAN equipment.

✔ **You'll have to contemplate which industry standard to use.** Although the early competition between standards in wireless LANs is over, a new wireless standard (called 802.11n) is on its way to market. As we write, this new standard isn't complete, but vendors are offering systems ahead of the final standard. What this means is that you can end up buying pre-n wireless gear now, and face the possibility it won't work with the final standard when it hits the streets in late 2007. We talk about this issue in detail in Chapter 16.

✔ **You may not like the way the wireless options work.** In optimal conditions, wireless systems work great, but things such as long distances (if you have a big house), thick walls, and metal objects can cause problems. Danny, for instance, has a house that was built in the late 1800s, with 18-inch stone walls. He loves his wireless LAN, but unfortunately it doesn't work very well upstairs.

We hope we don't sound down on wireless LANs — because we're not. We think they're just about the greatest thing since sliced bread. Being able to take your laptop to the bed, or the sofa, or the back patio without any tethers is an almost life-changing experience. You'd be in for a big fight if you tried to take our wireless LANs away from us. But we've seen many situations where a wired LAN connection can be better. In practice, if you have the opportunity to wire your house, we think you'll probably want both a wired and a wireless LAN — they coexist nicely.

The effect that choosing all wireless options — phone, data, audio, video, and so on — has on your home is unclear. However, we can tell you that many wireless technologies compete for the same spectrum in your home. For example, many cordless phone systems use the same 2.4-GHz frequency band that most wireless LANs use, and they can cause interference. Because these are _unlicensed_ frequencies, no authority controls all the devices transmitting on the frequency — so no one is ensuring that phones and wireless LANs and wireless video transmitters don't run into each other on the airwaves. And even if you are in control of your airwave use, there's nothing saying that your neighbor is as well.

Running Cables Here, There, and Everywhere

In Chapter 15, we spend a bit of time discussing the various methods that you can use to create LAN connections throughout your house. In this section, we want you to think about where you may want to place these network connections in your home.

Bedrooms

You may not consider bedrooms as prime locations for computer LAN outlets, but you probably should. With a bedroom outlet, you can work from your bed by plugging a laptop into the network, for example. You may also want a network outlet near the bedroom TV that allows you to connect future generations of Web-enabled TVs or similar products to your LAN for some TV-based Web surfing.

Also, the latest versions of PVRs (like the latest TiVo models) are able to synchronize over high-speed Internet connections and share data between different locations in the home, so you'll want to have a data connection nearby.

The master bedroom isn't the only place to consider providing LAN connection points. Your kids are probably hogging time on your PC, but with PC prices plummeting, getting the kids their own computers and connecting them to a home network makes a lot of sense.

You should also think long term here: Today's nursery is tomorrow's teenager's room, and someday maybe a home office. Or your guest room may be hosting one of your computer-geek relatives, who just can't leave home without his or her laptop. Having those rooms LAN-ready just makes sense.

Living room

Computers in the living room? Probably not in most homes, especially if you limit your concept of computers to PCs (although Pat is trying hard to convince his wife that they need a new 20-inch flat-screen iMac next to the living-room sofa). New devices are coming to market, however, that require LAN connections *and* fit into the living room. Leading the way are today's network-able gaming consoles and PVRs (discussed in Chapter 5). But also think about screen phones or set-top boxes that let you read e-mail or shop on e-commerce Web sites. Eventually, you'll probably want to access this stuff from your recliner.

Home office

You obviously want to have a LAN connection in your home office. However, we suggest that you think of your home office not in terms of whether or not to include LAN connection points but in terms of how many and where. Consider providing at least two or three network outlets in your home office — enough to support two computers and a networkable printer.

More and more devices are network-enabled, and the concept of a monitor, printer, computer, and keyboard all in the same place is rapidly going by the wayside. Danny has extended an extra keyboard, wireless mouse, and monitor to his treadmill and can now read the *New York Times* every morning and clear his e-mail before work — using the same computer that's on his desk in the home office down the hallway — while losing weight. (Pat needs to do the same.)

What's great about Ethernet hubs is that you can cascade them throughout your house if you run out of ports on your central hub. Suppose that you're using all your ports to run to different rooms, but your kids want four Ethernet ports in their room instead of the two you provided. No problem: Connect your Ethernet's uplink port to the wall outlet, and the other ports are available for that room's networking — and everyone can still communicate with everyone else on the home LAN.

Home theater or media center

You should consider including your home theater in your LAN plans for a couple of reasons. First, you'll probably have a Media Adapter, TiVo or some other Internet-enabled media server in your home theater, or you may want to have some sort of Web-enabled TV set-top box (such as Microsoft's MSN TV2) so that you can take a break from movies and surf the Web on your widescreen tube. You may even want to install a media center PC in your home theater to surf the Web, to keep track of your movie inventory, or even to feed streaming media (such as YouTube videos) from the Web to your audio or video systems.

Right now, broadband Internet service from DSL or cable TV companies reaches your house through a modem (and you'll probably install that modem in your home office or wiring closet). Some providers, particularly cable companies (but also some DSL providers who are looking to offer television services over DSL), are bringing to market set-top boxes that incorporate the broadband modem. If this is the case, you'll definitely want to have a network connection behind the TV so that you can share this Internet connection with the rest of your network.

Toiletly serious business

In Japan — where people evidently take certain elements of the bathroom a bit more seriously than Americans do — high-tech toilets are all the rage. Besides heated seats and other luxury items, these toilets have . . . er . . . facilities that perform medical evaluations of the . . . umm . . . contents of the toilet. Look at Jasmin by TOTO USA, Inc. (www.totousa.com), which has an optional warm seat feature and built-in catalyzed-disk fan that freshens the air (activated by sitting down). Also, by pressing a button on the LCD remote control, which looks like a Nintendo control pad, you are "bathed in a gentle, aerated, warm water stream with massaging action." Ohhhh-kay. We wouldn't be surprised to see this kind of thing become more common. The next step is a Net-connected toilet that can give reports to your healthcare provider (yes — really). Frankly, if these catch on in the U.S., we have no clue how you'd network. We'll leave that to the fourth edition of this book.

Kitchen

We think that having some sort of Net-connected computer device, whether a full-fledged PC or something scaled down (such as the Internet refrigerator or Internet microwave), is going to be a great way to do a whole host of kitchen tasks. Imagine accessing your network's recipe database CD-ROM from an inexpensive PC on your kitchen counter, placing your grocery order online while standing next to your empty fridge, or quickly ordering your favorite pizza when you don't feel like cooking. (Although some of the online grocery startups such as WebVan have shut their doors, many brick-and-mortar grocery chains such as Safeway, www.safeway.com, still do online grocery ordering and delivery in limited areas).

Some day, your kitchen appliances will use IP to send information about themselves to repair facilities and possibly to your home-automation system. (Warning! The freezer is malfunctioning!) In fact, if you want to spend about $6000 for a refrigerator, a few companies will sell you one with a PC and flat-panel display built in. Right now, most of these appliances use an Ethernet connection, but we think that they'll ultimately use the power line to communicate — there's just not enough kitchens with extra Ethernet jacks behind the fridge these days, and no matter how many people read this book, that isn't going to change any time soon. We still think it's a good idea to get at least one Ethernet outlet in the kitchen, just to be on the safe side.

Other places

Where else in the home should you extend your data network? Well, personally speaking, we're proponents of including data cabling in just about every room in the house. We're not going to give you any specific recommendations for network connections in other places in your home. Instead, we challenge you to spend a bit of time thinking about the long-term uses of each part of your home. For example, do you hope to one day finish your attic or basement? If so, you may as well get the wire there ahead of time.

Some of the wireless or no-new-wires (telephone or electrical) networking solutions that we discuss in Chapter 16 can also be good ways of extending a network to unexpected places. These products allow you to interface with an existing wired network and get the connection to places that you just never anticipated during your planning process (places such as the garage, where soon-to-arrive cars will dock into a home port to update their files and do their diagnostic workout).

Migrating Your Computer Flock to the Net

Coming up with a general design of your home-computer LAN is the first big step forward on this long march to networked nirvana. A home LAN helps you get all your computers onto the Internet and certainly makes your computing life easier and more fun.

Unfortunately, most consumer Internet accounts allow a single computer to attach to the Net. In other words, when you log on to your analog modem, DSL, cable modem, or other high-speed network Internet account, your computer and modem communicate with your ISP's server and are assigned a single IP address. (The *IP address* is how the Internet knows what information you've asked for and received — sort of like your mailing address for data.) A single IP address works fine when the modem is connected to a single computer. When you're trying to serve several computers at the same time with that Internet connection, however, you need some way to separate those different requests so that the data doesn't get jumbled. To solve this problem, you can choose a *router*, which is a hardware solution, or a proxy server, which is a software solution.

Many DSL and cable modem accounts give you only a single IP address for the base price but will provide your other computers with their own IP addresses for a monthly fee (usually about $3 to $5 per month per additional computer). If you choose this option, you need just a regular Ethernet hub — not one of the home-networking routers or proxy servers we're about to discuss. Each approach has pros and cons — the primary benefit of paying your service provider to do this for you is that you don't have to lift a finger to make it work, but the costs can add up if you have lots of computers and computer-like devices on your network. In the end, however, we think you'll want to add a router to the network.

Understanding home-network routers

If you were to go into the dark recesses of your office's telecommunications and data center, you'd probably find several weird-looking devices mounted on racks and shelves. One of these devices is most likely a router.

A *router* is the piece of equipment that consolidates all Internet traffic coming in and out of your office's LAN and sends it to the appropriate computers in the public network. The router performs this bit of Net magic by creating its own *subnet* (or private IP network) within the office and assigning private IP addresses to each computer connected to the router. The router is assigned a public IP address (one that other computers on the Internet can send data to and from) when it connects to the Internet, and then it figures out which packets of data go to which computer in the subnet.

Setting up a router for a large network is a complicated procedure — another one of those reasons why IT workers in your office make such good salaries. Luckily, routers designed for small home networks are relatively easy to configure.

These *home-network routers* or *residential gateways* act as the interface between your modem or broadband connection to your ISP and the rest of your home LAN, receiving all incoming Internet data and sending it to the correct machine on your network without your intervention. The first time you set up your router (or when you change the configuration of your network by adding or removing computers), you'll have to use some network management software to get things organized, but most of these routers have easy-to-understand, wizard-style programs (accessible through your Web browser) to lead you through this process. Figure 14-1 shows how you would set up a home-network router.

The technology that makes your home router work is called NAT (network address translation). NAT *translates* between the private IP addresses of the computers on your network and the public IP address that they all share, and is smart enough to make sure everything ends up in the right place.

Many home-network routers use your Internet browser as the software to configure the system. The configuration software is written as *HyperText Markup Language* (HTML) files — the language of Web pages. To set things up, you simply open your Web browser software, type the Web address of your router (it's usually a number, something like 192.168.1.1), and open these files. Fill in a few blanks, answer a few questions, and click a few buttons, and your router is ready to go.

Figure 14-1: Using a router to share a modem across the network.

Home-network routers range in price depending on what kind of modem is included (if one is included at all) and how many computers they can work with. The majority of home-network routers on the market today work with only cable or DSL broadband connections — they have an Ethernet interface to hook into the DSL or cable modem, and no way to connect to an analog modem. So, if you're still stuck on dial-up, you'll have to shop around a bit to find a model that works for you. (A few models are available with a built-in analog modem, but they're getting scarce.) Other features that influence the price of a home-network router include the following:

✔ **Firewalls:** Although NAT itself provides some network security functions, many home-network routers also contain sophisticated firewalls, which keep hackers out of your computer.

✔ **Wireless LAN support:** The wireless networks we talk about in Chapter 16 are often supported by home-network routers — many have built-in wireless access point functionality, so you can support both your wired and unwired computers from a single device.

✔ **Other home-networking support:** Besides the wireless systems just mentioned, many home-networking gateways also include support for connecting PCs to your network using existing telephone lines or even electrical power lines. We talk about these systems in Chapter 16 as well.

✔ **Support for VPN:** Many business use VPNs (virtual private networks) to allow their employees to securely connect their computers from remote locations back into the corporate network. Not all home-network routers will let you connect in this way. (VPNs have special protocols that not all routers will pass through to the Internet.)

The cheapest home-network routers start at about $50 (these boxes were at least $200 just five or six years ago). The major vendors of home-network routers and router/modem combos include the following:

✔ Belkin (www.belkin.com)

✔ Buffalo (www.buffalotech.com)

✔ D-Link (www.dlink.com)

✔ Hawking (www.hawking.com)

✔ Linksys (www.linksys.com)

✔ NETGEAR (www.netgear.com)

✔ SMC (www.smc.com)

Although you can buy your own home-network router directly from the manufacturer or from online and other retailers, you may also have the option of getting one directly from your Internet service provider. DSL providers such as BellSouth, AT&T, EarthLink, and Verizon will provide you with a home-network router — usually for a monthly fee. Although you might end up paying more for such a solution over time than just buying the router yourself, you do have the advantage of having someone to support you if you run into any problems.

Some broadband companies don't like the idea of a customer being able to hook up multiple computers to your broadband connection without paying more to do so — so they frown on customer-owned home-network routers. We haven't heard of any providers prohibiting their customers from doing so (it would be hard for them to even know that you're using a router, technically speaking), but some folks in these companies are looking into ways to keep you from using home-networking routers that you haven't rented from your ISP (for a nice big monthly fee).

Using your PC to route packets

Routers are the hardware-based way of sharing an Internet connection. Given their low price, we think they're also the best way. But they're not the only way. The software-based alternative is to install or use a *proxy server* program on one of your networked PCs. This program performs pretty much the same function as a router — that is, it distributes Internet data packets from a single connection to multiple PCs on a network.

We don't recommend that you take the proxy server approach. Home-network routers are so cheap and effective that setting up a proxy server is more work than it's worth. If the $50 for a home router is more than you want to spend, scour eBay or Craig's List (www.craigslist.com) for a used router.

In this scenario, you designate one of the PCs in your network (the one with the modem connected to it, generally) as the proxy server for the rest of the network. This proxy server PC collects all incoming and outgoing Internet traffic; the proxy server software then determines which networked computer the data is intended for and sends it on its way. Figure 14-2 shows a typical proxy server setup for an Internet connection other than through an analog modem. (This configuration requires two NICs in the proxy server.)

Figure 14-2:
Sharing an
Internet
connection
through
proxy server
software.

Proxy server software is usually easy to set up, and the programs themselves are inexpensive — free, if you're using a modern Windows or Mac operating system.

If you have a Windows computer with Windows 98, Second Edition, or a later operating system, you can set up a proxy server without additional software by using the Internet Connection Sharing (ICS) control panel built into the OS. For Windows XP and Vista, this functionality is built into the Network Setup Wizard (in the Network Connections Control Panel). Mac users with OS X also have this functionality built right in to the OS.

You can also find inexpensive third-party software to operate as a proxy server, which some folks choose for a greater number of features. The most popular proxy server software for Windows users is made by a company called WinGate (www.wingate.com). For Mac users, a program called IPNetRouter is probably the most popular choice (www.sustworks.com).

To use a PC or Mac as a proxy server, you must choose a computer that has *two NICs*. One NIC connects to the Internet connection, and the other connects to your LAN. For a wired network, you'd need two Ethernet NICs in your computer; for a wireless network, you'd need one Ethernet NIC for the Internet connection and a wireless one for the LAN. Many computers have both an Ethernet and a wireless NIC, but very few come standard with two Ethernet NICs.

Routing and bridging with data networks is a complicated topic, and we've just touched on it here. As you get into your data-networking plans, check out *Home Networking For Dummies,* 4th Edition, by Kathy Ivens (published by Wiley Publishing, Inc.) — it will help you figure out the next level of detail on this topic.

Chapter 15

Choosing the Parts for a Wired Data LAN

*C*hances are good that you have more than one computer in your home. If you don't, we suspect that you soon will. You also probably have several, perhaps even many, devices that can be networked with your computers for doing things such as printing, storing files, making phone calls, listening to music, and watching video. To make the most of all of these devices, you need a home-computer network — a local area network, or LAN. And to make use of these devices *anywhere* in your home, you need a *whole-home LAN*.

In this chapter, we tell you about the equipment and wires in a wired LAN and how to have it installed in your house.

Even if you think that you're going to rely primarily on a wireless network (which we discuss in the Chapter 16), you should still at least skim this chapter. Wireless is great and we recommend that everyone include at least some wireless in their computer network, but having a wired backbone in your home makes your whole network more flexible and better performing.

Building CAT-5e/6 LANs

The backbone of a computer network — regardless of the types of computers connected to it or the types of network software used to make it work — consists of the physical wiring and components that connect everything. The most common type of wired computer LAN uses a special type of copper cabling, CAT-5e or CAT-6 UTP (unshielded twisted pair).

We discuss the differences between CAT-5e and CAT-6 cabling in Chapter 2. CAT-6 cabling is capable of higher data rates than CAT-5e, but both are capable of handling up to and including Gigabit Ethernet (1000BaseT), which is as fast a network as should be needed for a good number of years in the home. Yep, saying that out loud is almost a guarantee that something will pop up. (Remember when Bill Gates said a PC wouldn't need more than 64K of memory?) But realistically, most home networking gear is only 100BaseT, and 1000BaseT can handle even multiple channels of high-definition video (which is the biggest bandwidth hog in the home). In Chapter 2 we help you decide whether to choose CAT-5e or CAT-6. For the purposes of this chapter, they are identical, and are treated as such.

Nearly all LAN technologies share a few basic building blocks:

- **Cables:** Cables usually provide the connection between networked devices. But in some cases, the physical connection doesn't take place via wires — many emerging LAN technologies make use of wireless communications techniques to get data around your home (discussed in Chapter 16).

- **Network interface cards (NICs):** You must install NICs (pronounced like the New York basketball team) — in each device that connects to the network. The NIC bridges the gap between the cables (or wireless devices) and the individual computers or other networked devices. NICs generally work with only one kind of network, such as an Ethernet NIC for Ethernet-based networks. Most computers today are shipped with Ethernet NICs already installed.

- **A network protocol — such as Ethernet:** *Ethernet* is a hardware specification that controls access to the network, allows individual devices on the network to find and identify each other, and determines when each device can transmit and receive data. The key thing about Ethernet is that each Ethernet system adheres to a set of protocol standards that enables various devices from different manufacturers to communicate.

Ethernet is the most common LAN for the home or small office (or in big business for that matter). The total bandwidth and the type of cable the network uses define different variations of Ethernet. For example, 100BaseT — the most common variation — transmits data at speeds up to 100 Mbps and uses UTP copper wires as its physical media.

Scores of Ethernet variations are available, but you need to consider only the following:

- **10Base2:** 10 Mbps over coaxial cable (this network is just about extinct, so we mention it only in case you run across it in an existing installation)

- **10BaseT:** 10 Mbps over twisted-pair cable

- **100BaseT:** 100 Mbps over twisted-pair cable — often called Fast Ethernet

The shortest Ethernet primer in computerdom

Ethernet in its traditional form is a shared network. All computers and other connected, networked devices share the 10 (or 100 or 1000) Mbps of bandwidth available on the network. Ethernet uses a protocol called *CSMA/CD (Carrier-Sense Multiple Access with Collision Detection)* to divide access to the network. Basically, CSMA/CD means that all devices on the network listen for a free moment on the network before sending data. When the coast is clear, the data goes out. If two devices happen to choose the same moment to send data, a collision occurs. The devices then each wait a random amount of time before resending their data.

Newer versions of Ethernet hardware systems are *switched*. These Ethernet networks use a sophisticated device — the switch, of course — to direct data throughout the network. Instead of sharing 10 or 100 Mbps, each device has that amount of bandwidth dedicated to it at all times. The switch basically keeps each segment of the Ethernet network separate from the others — directing data between the devices that are talking and keeping data off the wires running to other devices, instead of sending the data to every device. This process can reduce the number of collisions and make the overall network faster as more and more devices are connected to it.

✔ **1000BaseT:** 1000 Mbps over twisted-pair cable — often called Gigabit Ethernet, or Gig-E

The first number in each of these names stands for the bandwidth of the system in megabits per second, so 10Base2 is a 10-Mbps connection. The last number or letter tells you the kind of cable that it goes over; for example, *T* means twisted pair.

Like the other networks we describe in this book, local area networks support different architectures. LANs are particularly flexible, however, in allowing you to mix and match architectures as you grow.

The two basic choices for how you model your LAN are the bus architecture and the star architecture (sometimes called *home run* because each cable runs back to a central home). If you've read other chapters in this book, you already know that we prefer the star architecture, hands down. In fact, we don't believe the bus architecture is really worth talking about, so we just concentrate on the star.

Twisted-pair Ethernet LANs (such as 10BaseT or 100BaseT) use a network architecture called a star. In a *star configuration,* all hardware connects to a central device called a *hub* or a *switch.* The hub transmits the data from each incoming cable to every other cable that attaches to the hub — and, therefore, to each device that attaches to the far end of those cables.

Hubs and switches do basically the same thing. They are the central point to which each run of CAT-5e/6 UTP cabling connects back to, and they allow data to flow down different legs of the network to get from device to device. The difference is that a switch uses internal intelligence to figure out which legs of the network the data needs to flow over, but a hub just sends the data (usually called *packets*) down every leg of the network simultaneously. If only two computers are talking to each other, the difference between these approaches isn't significant. But as more devices start to talk to each other, a switch can make things much faster. Because switch prices have dropped immensely, we recommend that you install a switch rather than a hub in the center of your network.

We show a network built using a star architecture in Figure 15-1.

Figure 15-1:
A typical 100BaseT network with a network printer.

Need to add another device to the network? Just run another length of network cabling and connect it to the hub. Someone drive a nail through one of your network cables? Your whole network doesn't go down — just the affected segment.

Star architecture is a key concept in home networking because you can use it for all sorts of networks, such as a telephone system or a video-distribution system. In these systems, as in Ethernet and other LANs, the star topology greatly increases the flexibility, reliability, and expandability of a network.

Your star network can be expanded easily by hooking up a hub at one of the endpoints you've wired into your network. So if you have a single Ethernet outlet in a bedroom and need to connect two or three devices to it, you can just plug a hub into the outlet, and then connect those devices to the hub. All computers connected to this remote hub will be able to "see" the rest of your network — just as if they were connected to one of your Ethernet jacks.

Cables and Connectors

If you're getting ready to create a new data network (or telephone network, for that matter) in your home, you'll have to make sure that your baseline cabling for this is CAT-5e/6 wiring, as we discussed in Chapter 2. For data, you need CAT-5e/6, period.

Of course, cables don't do you much good when they're just a bunch of bare wires hanging out of the wall — you need something to connect them to your networked equipment. Luckily, this problem has an easy solution. Like telephone networks, computer LANs utilize a common connector, the RJ-45. The standard jack and plug for all UTP computer LANs, RJ-45 connectors look exactly like the familiar (old-fashioned) telephone jacks called RJ-11s, which we discuss in Chapter 2, only bigger (wider). RJ-45 connectors are designed to terminate all four pairs of wire found in typical CAT-5e/6 UTP cables.

CAT-5e/6 cabling is designed for high-speed, high-performance networks. Therefore, if you use CAT-5e, the entire system — the plugs, jacks, patch panels, and connectors, in addition to the cable — must be CAT-5e rated. The same is true for CAT-6; everything must be CAT-6 rated. A LAN is only as good as its weakest link, so if any one piece of the puzzle is rated less than CAT-5e/6, the entire LAN will be as well.

The network components

Besides the cables and connectors, a few other pieces are necessary to install a smart-home LAN. This equipment is pretty universal, whether you're installing an inexpensive one-room 100-Mbps Ethernet network or a sophisticated Gigabit Ethernet network throughout the home. The key is to use CAT-5e/6 components throughout the network. That way, even if you start off with just a 10BaseT Ethernet system, your wiring is in place to upgrade by simply replacing a few components — no ripping down walls and starting over from scratch for you!

The 1000BaseT, or Gigabit Ethernet, system is being deployed in corporate office networks. It's still expensive, relative to 10BaseT and 100BaseT networks, and most folks don't *need* Gigabit Ethernet. Some day, however, you may want Gigabit Ethernet in the home — mainly because it's fast enough to let you use your computer LAN to carry things such as HDTV signals. As long as you have a star-wired CAT-5e/6 network, you'll be ready for Gigabit Ethernet when you need it. Just upgrade your NICs and your switch or router, and you'll be there!

Punch it down!

Your home LAN's *central node* — the place from which all your cabling runs start — begins with a device called a *patch panel* or a *punchdown block* mounted in your central wiring closet. If you read Chapter 2, where we discuss wiring, and Chapter 10 on telephone networks, you're already familiar with this device. A data network uses a punchdown block that is just about identical to the one your telephone uses. The one major exception is that the punchdown block needs to be CAT-5e/6 rated to allow high-speed data transmissions. You don't need this level of cable and component quality for telephone service — but it's a good idea to use this for all your UTP wiring infrastructure because it lets you easily repurpose cables (for example, turn a phone jack into an Ethernet jack by just reconnecting it in the wiring closet).

Switches and hubs and routers for everyone

The key component in an Ethernet network is an *Ethernet hub* or *switch,* the device that ensures that data gets from point A to point B in the network. A hub or switch (we'll just talk about switches from here on out, because they're the superior way to go and don't cost much more) is a small electronic box with a number of RJ-45 connectors (called *ports*) across the front. Inside the switch is a circuit board that electrically connects all these RJ-45 connectors to each other in the proper way — *the proper way* means that the wire carrying outgoing data from one computer connects to the wires that carry incoming data to all other computers that are part of the switch. We know all this information can be confusing, but don't let it stress you out. Honestly, you don't need to spend much time thinking about how hubs and switches work. They're simply one of those magical boxes that allow your computers to talk to each other.

The *uplink port* (also sometimes called a *WAN port*), which is a special RJ-45 port, is another feature of a typical switch. Unlike the other ports, the uplink port doesn't cross the incoming and outgoing data signals. Instead, it sends them straight through (incoming to incoming, outgoing to outgoing). This capability becomes useful if, for example, you want to connect two hubs or if you have an Internet connection device, such as a cable modem, that you want to connect to all computers in the network. In these cases, you use the uplink port instead of a standard port.

It's just about impossible to find a hub, switch, or router without an uplink port, but if you ever do run into one, you can use a special kind of CAT-5e/6 patch cable, called a *crossover* cable, to connect your network to your broadband connection. A crossover cable *crosses over* the transmit and receive conductors in the CAT-5e/6 cable so that data flows the right way between your modem and your LAN. By the way, the regular cables used to connect computers in the LAN are sometimes referred to as *straight through cables*.

Some Ethernet switches and hubs don't have a dedicated uplink port. Instead, they have a switch (a button, in other words) next to one of the regular ports that lets you configure the port to act as an uplink port.

You might be thinking, "Well, where do home-network routers fit in?" Great question. Most home routers have built-in Ethernet switches. So you might not need to buy a router *and* a switch. Just go shopping for a home-network router (from companies such as NETGEAR, Linksys, or D-link), and you'll be set. (For more on home routers, see Chapter 14.) Keep in mind that most home routers have a four-port switch. You might end up connecting Ethernet devices in more than four rooms. If this is the case for you, you'll want a separate switch that you'll connect to one of the LAN ports on your router.

Like ice cream, switches (and routers and hubs for that matter) come in many flavors — the one you purchase is a matter of taste. Be sure to look for the following, though:

- **Number of ports:** Be sure to buy a switch that has enough ports to connect all the computers and networkable devices (such as printers and cable modems) that you plan on installing in your home LAN.

- **Speed:** 100 Mbps (100BaseT) is still the standard Ethernet installation for most residential applications, but you may want to move up to the faster 1000BaseT. There's still a big price difference between 100BaseT and 1000BaseT switches, so you should look at your requirements closely as you make this decision.

Both 100BaseT and 1000BaseT use the same wiring infrastructure, so you can start off with one and upgrade to the other just by changing the switch and putting new network interface cards (NICs) in your PCs. A growing number of computers have 1000BaseT Gigabit Ethernet NICs built in, but 100BaseT is still the standard.

- **Router integration:** As we mentioned, many switches designed for the home are part of an overall home router device. This can be handy (less boxes to install), but most of these router/switch devices are limited to four ports, which means you'd need an external switch anyway!

Most of the integrated router/switch devices available for the home also include wireless (Wi-Fi) networking functionality as well. See Chapter 16 for more on this.

✔ **Price:** Take a quick trip to any computer superstore or browse through any computer equipment catalog, and you'll find an amazing range of prices for switches that are equivalent in speed and number of ports. The last time we went shopping for a small, four-port, 10/100BaseT switch/router, we discovered that the big name companies offered them for about $50, while Gigabit versions were about double that. Doing a little online detective work at a site such as shopper.cnet.com can help.

NICs galore

All the cables in the world won't do your computer a bit of good if it doesn't have the right hardware that lets it "talk" on your LAN. The network interface card, or NIC, performs that job.

NICs come in different forms to fit the varying kinds of internal buses in today's (and yesterday's) PCs and Macs. The most common internal bus found in new desktop computers is the PCI (or peripheral component interconnect) bus. Some older computers also use the ISA (industry standard architecture) bus, but this standard is becoming less common. You can find NICs for both architectures, but PCI is more common. If you have a choice of using either, choose PCI.

PCI and ISA are the card slots visible at the back of your computer. You insert these cards by popping the cover off your computer and sliding a card into an empty PCI slot inside, leaving the RJ-45 jack part sticking out the back of the computer. Although the PCI bus theoretically offers faster data throughput, for the NIC cards used in a home LAN there's really no difference. We recommend that you utilize whichever slot you have available — just be sure to check what's free inside your computer before you buy one (or go to your local computer superstore, have one installed, and ask a lot of questions).

For laptop computers, the most common bus for NIC cards is the *CardBus* (also called the PCMCIA) slot. CardBus, the little credit-card-sized slot on the side of most laptops, is functionally a specialized (miniaturized) PCI bus. Many laptop computers come with only one (or even no) CardBus slots, so the Ethernet NIC is usually *embedded* on the motherboard of the laptop — in which case you already have a NIC and don't need to do anything with it.

A new standard called ExpressCard is beginning to appear in the laptop world. ExpressCards look a bit like CardBus cards, but they're not inter-changeable. We're not going to worry too much about ExpressCard here because if you have an ExpressCard laptop, it's almost assuredly equipped with embedded Ethernet.

You may also run across *external* NIC cards, which connect to your computer through a USB cable and one of your computer's USB 2.0 ports. We don't see these too often, but they can come in handy in the unlikely event that your PC has no built-in Ethernet and also has no open PCI or CardBus slots.

NICs offer different interfaces to the LAN — in other words, they have differ-ent connectors on the back for different kinds of LAN cabling. If you're follow-ing our advice, and we hope that you do, you should choose a NIC with an RJ-45 jack.

Finally, NICs are designed to connect computers to different kinds of net-works. For example, some connect to 10BaseT Ethernet networks, some to 100BaseT Ethernet, and others to 1000BaseT networks. Almost all NICs on the market today will work with slower variants of Ethernet. So, for example, if you buy a NIC (or a new PC with a built-in NIC) for Gigabit Ethernet, it will work fine on 10BaseT and 100BaseT networks as well. This functionality (where the card adapts to the network switch it is attached to) is called *autosensing*. It's hard to find a NIC that's *not* autosensing these day, but you should check. You are definitely better off with an autosensing NIC.

We recommend that you install NICs that supports at least 100BaseT net-working. Or if the price (about $30) fits your budget, install Gigabit Ethernet NICs. They are autosensing, work with whatever network you install, and allow you to upgrade your network in the future without having to buy a bunch of new NICs.

Most PCs are now being sold with NICs preinstalled from the factory — a great thing, in our opinion. For example, as we wrote this, even the least expensive Dell desktop PC ($350) included a built-in 10/100BaseT autosensing NIC. If you're in the market for a new computer, get one with a built-in NIC and avoid the hassle of installation.

With cables and connectors, patch panels, NICs, and hubs, you're 90 percent of the way towards putting together a home LAN. The final key to the puzzle is another set of CAT-5e/6 cables called *patch cables.* Patch cables fill the gap between wall outlets and computers; they also connect the patch panel to your Ethernet switch or home-network router.

Just like all the other components in your network, your patch cables should be rated CAT-5e/6. Most are, but some of the cheaper ones are rated CAT-3 or even unrated. You don't want these — they're a false economy that may keep your network from reaching its maximum speed or working reliably.

Software to put it all together

The one additional component to making a LAN work — probably the most difficult one for many people — is configuring all the network protocols and software on each of your home's PCs. This used to be the domain of hard-core networking experts, but it has become less onerous with each successive release of Windows and Mac OS software.

Our focus in this book is to get you the infrastructure you need to have a home LAN — we simply don't have the room to talk about binding protocols and configuring networking software. If you're not comfortable with doing this on your own, check out *Networking For Dummies,* 8th Edition, by Doug Lowe or *Home Networking For Dummies,* 4th Edition, by Kathy Ivens (both published by Wiley Publishing, Inc.).

Visualizing How a Data LAN Works

In the star architecture, each *LAN station* — the outlet into which you can connect a computer to the LAN — is served by its own length of UTP cable radiating out from a central node, like the spokes on a wagon wheel. Probably the best way to visualize this kind of LAN network is to follow your data from a PC back to the central node of the LAN and back over the network to its final destination:

1. The computer uses its networking software to send a chunk of data from a program to your NIC.

2. The NIC converts the data into the proper format for the network (Ethernet, for example) and sends it as an electrical signal over the patch cable.

3. The patch cable carries this data signal between the NIC and the nearest RJ-45 connector installed in a wall outlet.

4. The RJ-45 connector attaches to one end of a length of CAT-5e/6 UTP cabling, which carries the data signal back through your walls to the central node of your LAN (in the basement, garage, or utility room — wherever you choose to house it).

5. The UTP cable terminates where it's punched down into the patch panel, which carries your data signal across its internal wiring to another RJ-45 connector.

6. Another patch cable carries the data signal from the back of the patch panel to the Ethernet switch or home-network router.

7. The switch takes your outgoing data signal and sends it on a U-turn trip back through the patch panel and over a different CAT-5e/6 to its final destination on your network (another computer, a printer, or elsewhere).

The devices that communicate over your Ethernet LAN don't have to be computers. Many peripheral devices such as printers have Ethernet ports, as do things that might have nothing to do with your PC — such as a video gaming console. If you want to use your Xbox 360 with Microsoft's online gaming service, you can use Ethernet to connect it to your broadband Internet connection.

Working with your Internet connection

The scenario we just went through describes how data is shared between computers across your LAN. But that leaves out what is, for many folks, the most important thing: getting data to and from the Internet. That's where the home-network router that we've talked about so much fits in. A router's main purpose (besides switching local LAN traffic) is to send data between your Internet connection and the computers and devices on your LAN.

A switch is a device that connects multiple PCs on a LAN. A router connects the computers on a LAN to a wide area network (such as the Internet). Most home routers that we discuss have a built-in switch but not all switches are also routers.

Conceptually, transferring data through a router is really just like Steps 1 through 7 in the preceding section. The difference is this: In the scenario in that section, the local LAN traffic makes a U-turn and is sent back to another computer in your home. When you're using your network for Internet access, the Internet traffic goes through the router and gets sent to your cable or DSL modem and off to the Internet (and vice versa for the data that you receive from your Internet connection).

This leads to a key question: Where should you put the broadband modem? In pre-networking days, you just stuck it on your desk, right next to the computer. After all, that computer was the only thing using it, so why put it far away? But now that we're all networking our computers, there's no obvious place to put the broadband modem. Most people narrow it down to two options:

- ✔ Put the broadband modem in the wiring closet, next to the router and the CAT-5e/6 patch panel. This is a nice, neat, easy solution, with everything in one place. Your cable or DSL lines come into the home here, so you'll have something to hook the broadband modem to.

- ✔ Put the broadband modem in your home office (or wherever you keep your primary computer). In this scenario, you need two CAT-5e/6 cables — one to connect the output of the broadband modem back down to the router or switch in the wiring closet and another that connects the output of the router or switch to the computer in the room.

We like to use the second solution. Running that second CAT-5e/6 cable up to the home office is simple (we recommend extra CAT-5e/6 cables to the home office anyway), and it gives you a chance to keep an eye on your broadband modem. These modems are notoriously unpredictable, and sometimes you just need to pull the plug and restart them to get them working properly. You'll also be able to quickly check the status lights on the modem to make sure everything is hunky dory.

Integrating with no-new-wires networks

In Chapter 16, we describe several networking technologies that don't use CAT-5e/6 UTP cabling. Instead, they use wireless, power line, and phone line technologies to hook computers together. Even if you have a *wired* CAT-5e/6 network in place, you still might find these networks useful — particularly wireless LANs that let you roam around the house with your laptop or handheld computer without plugging into anything.

Combining these networks with your wired LAN is simple. Wireless LANs are the easiest of all — wireless LAN access points (the hubs of a wireless network) in almost all cases have an RJ-45 Ethernet connection, which is designed to be connected to a wired LAN. So just find a good place to put your access point (we give you some tips in Chapter 16), plug it into the nearest wired LAN outlet (and into the wall power outlet too), and you're set. And in many cases, the wireless access point is built right into your router, so there's nothing to connect at all!

You'll need to do a little bit of software setup. This varies from access point to access point, but there's one tip we want to give you. Most access points can act as DHCP servers as well — assigning IP addresses to computers. If you're using a router on your wired LAN and are using a separate access point (one that's not built into the router), the router is already set up to do assign IP addresses, and letting the access point also assign them to your PCs will mess up your network. Instead, you should set up your access point in what's usually called *bridging mode*. This lets the router do its job — the access point just transparently connects, or bridges, between the wired and wireless sections of the network.

Infrared — using light instead of wires

Infrared networking — using light waves instead of radio waves — is already a part of many computer networks. A relatively mature standard known as IrDA (Infrared Device Association) is in place. IrDA devices are commonly found in three main sets of equipment:

✔ **Printers:** Using an IrDA interface, you can beam print jobs from one or several computers to your printer without cables. You find IrDA interfaces mainly on high-end laser printers — the inkjet models that most people have in their homes don't have this capability yet. Remember, though, that a printer with an IrDA interface doesn't do you any good unless your PC has one as well.

✔ **Notebook computers:** Many laptops have a built-in IrDA interface to facilitate printing and to make for easy data synchronization with your desktop PC.

✔ **Handheld computer devices:** You also find IrDA interfaces on many handheld PDA (personal digital assistant) computers, mainly for synchronizing data with your desktop computer.

Depending on its implementation, infrared networking can be efficient and speedy — with data throughput rates reaching several megabits per second in some cases.

Infrared does have a major downfall, however, that makes it unsuitable for a whole-home network: Infrared signals are line-of-sight only. In other words, an infrared signal won't penetrate some of those pesky things you often find in the home — such as doors, walls, and giant-screen televisions. So although infrared is useful in a single room, it won't get you very far beyond that. In Chapter 16, we talk about a bunch of solutions that can give you whole-home networking without using CAT-5e/6 wires. IrDA is more of an adjunct to a home network for connecting peripheral devices and syncing things — not a replacement.

One more thing: IrDA is a computer protocol used for computer communications. IrDA is not typically used for noncomputer purposes, such as remote controls for stereos and TVs. Although these remote controls also use infrared signals, they're an entirely different critter.

For networks that run over power lines or phone lines, there typically isn't a central network hub such as the access point of a wireless LAN. What you will find, however, are Ethernet-to-power-line or Ethernet-to-phone-line *bridges* (there's that term again!). You'll use two (or more) of these bridges in your network. One bridge connects to an Ethernet outlet somewhere in the house (or directly to the switch or router in the wiring closet) and then plugs into a phone or power outlet. On the far end (where your remote devices are located), you use another bridge in the reverse fashion — the bridge plugs into a phone or power outlet (to pick up the data sent by the first bridge) and then connects to the Ethernet port of the device that you want to connect to the network.

Phone-line and power-line bridges are a great way to extend your Ethernet network to places where you just didn't think to put CAT-5e/6 cables. For example, if you don't have CAT-5e/6 next to your gaming console, but you want to connect that console to your LAN and to the Internet, use a pair of bridges and you're all set. We've been using some of these bridges from NET-GEAR in our homes, and they work great.

Chapter 16

Alternatives to a Wired Data LAN

In This Chapter

▶ Choosing A, B, or G

▶ Moving to N

▶ Letting your computers talk on the phone

▶ Plugging into power lines

▶ Mixing and matching

*W*e think that a wired computer network — using CAT-5e or CAT-6 cabling in the walls — is the best way to set up a home-computer network. Wired networks are faster, more reliable, and more secure. Having said that, we absolutely LOVE our wireless networks. Just try to take them away from us — just try. . . .

We think that the no-new-wires computer LAN technologies have come a long way in the past few years. They can fit into your smart home in one of two ways. First, if you can't get into the walls to run CAT-5e/6 cabling and your house isn't huge, you can build a satisfactory data network with no-new-wires technologies. Second, even if you have a wired LAN infrastructure in your walls, you'll probably find a reason to use one of these no-new-wires networks. You might want to add a wireless network so that you can use your laptop untethered, or you may find a spot where you don't have CAT-5e/6 but need network connectivity (such as behind your new Internet fridge).

In this chapter, we tell you about the three leading technologies for no-new-wires computer networks: wireless (this is by far the most popular and useful of the three), phone line (using your existing telephone wiring), and power line (using your existing electrical wiring). Most people choose to go wireless, but there are good reasons to consider all three, and you may run into situations where you'll use more than one of these technologies in your home.

In Chapter 15 we talk about building the wired infrastructure in your home for a computer LAN. We're strong proponents of having wires when you can, but we think just about anybody can benefit from a wireless LAN as well. Luckily the two technologies (wired and wireless) work together pretty much seamlessly. So even if you've installed a whole-home wired LAN, you should at least consider adding some wireless on top of that infrastructure. The mobility and flexibility that wireless gives you is worth the minimal expenditure.

Cut the Cord!

Probably the most exciting development that we've seen in the home-networking field over the past few years has been the emergence of wireless computer networks. Wireless networks have such a high coolness factor that many other networking technologies have taken the back seat in people's minds — despite some limitations to the technology. We can understand this because we too have been caught up in the wireless LAN mania.

When compared to wired Ethernet LANs, wireless networks have relatively limited bandwidth, are subject to interference from other electrical devices in the home (such as cordless phones and microwave ovens), and have some security issues (wireless signals will go right through your walls and into your driveway, street, or neighbor's living room, so you need to *encrypt* your data if you want to keep it private). We think the best way to use wireless is to incorporate it into your wired network — using your wired LAN for things that don't move (such as the desktop PC) and adding a wireless LAN for portable devices such as laptops and PDAs.

Understanding the standards

As is the case for many new and emerging technologies, various companies, industry groups, and international standards bodies are involved in the wireless LAN industry. If you shop for a wireless LAN, you'll run into competing standards.

Standards are vitally important to networking. For example, the various standards for wired Ethernet networks allow equipment from different vendors to work together right out of the box, with no special tweaking or esoteric settings to configure. The same is true in wireless LANs — equipment conforming to a specific standard should work seamlessly with other equipment that also conforms to the standard, regardless of the manufacturer. In fact, many standards bodies sponsor interoperability bake-offs on a quarterly basis to ensure that this is the case.

The problem with wireless networks is that multiple standards are available. For the most part, interoperability between different devices within a standard can be taken for granted, but deciding on a particular standard can be difficult, especially if you haven't spent a lot of time researching wireless networking technologies. An even bigger issue is that the newest of these standards (called *802.11n*) is still under development but many vendors aren't waiting for the standard to be finalized before they begin selling 802.11n gear. In this section, we talk in depth about the standards and how they might affect your decisions.

All the systems we're about to discuss fall under the general category of *Wi-Fi*, which is the industry term for wireless networks tested for interoperability between and among vendors using the *IEEE 802.11* standards for wireless networking equipment. A given piece of gear is Wi-Fi certified by the Wi-Fi Alliance (www.wifialliance.com/), which is an industry group formed to develop standards and test gear to assure its interoperability. If you buy Wi-Fi certified wireless networking gear (and you shouldn't buy anything that's *not* Wi-Fi certified!), you can be assured that it will work with other Wi-Fi certified gear *using the same 802.11 standard* regardless of which company made it.

As you begin your Wi-Fi journey, you might find gear using the following 802.11 standards available (or soon to be available) in your favorite brick-and-mortar or online store:

✔ **802.11b:** This was the first widely available LAN technology on the market. Tens of millions of 802.11b devices were sold in the first half of this decade, and many millions of them are still in use — a few vendors still ship 802.11b equipment, but for the most part 802.11b gear is no longer manufactured. Here's the technical detail we know you're waiting for: 802.11b uses the 2.4-GHz radio spectrum (we discuss the radio spectrum in Chapter 11) and can deliver a maximum of 11 Mbps of shared bandwidth to the devices in your home that are connected to the wireless network.

✔ **802.11a:** In a textbook example of the weirdness of standards naming, 802.11a is a newer technology than 802.11b. 802.11a uses a higher-frequency chunk of the radio spectrum than 802.11b (5 GHz instead of 2.4 GHz). The big advantage of 802.11a is that this higher-frequency spectrum is much less crowded with phones, microwaves, and other wireless LAN systems, so it can work better in an environment where 802.11b or g face too much interference. With a maximum speed of 54 Mbps, 802.11a is potentially much faster than 802.11b. Because 802.11a uses a different frequency (and has other differences in the way the signal is encoded and sent out over the radio) than 802.11b, the two are *not* compatible. That means if you want to move to 802.11a, you have to junk your 802.11b gear (or use it elsewhere in your network).

Because 802.11a isn't all that popular (compared to 802.11g, discussed next), most 802.11a gear is *dual-mode* 802.11a and 802.11g in the same device. This gives the user the flexibility to connect to the more common 802.11g (or even 802.11b) networks and still take advantage of 802.11a where appropriate.

✔ **802.11g:** 802.11g is *the most commonly used Wi-Fi standard* and uses the same 2.4-GHz frequency spectrum as 802.11b. 802.11g is backwardly compatible with 802.11b, meaning it will work with any 802.11b system on the market, dropping to the lower 802.11b speeds when interworking with those devices. 802.11g gear won't work with 802.11a systems. So what's the big deal? When 802.11g systems work with each other, instead of with an 802.11b system, they're more than twice as fast, with a maximum bandwidth of 54 Mbps (the same as 802.11a).

Most Wi-Fi gear on the market today, both the networking hardware itself and the network interface cards (NICs) built into new computers and laptops, will use the 802.11g standard.

✔ **802.11n:** 802.11g is the *current* Wi-Fi standard, and 802.11n is the *next* standard. The 802.11n standard is (in early 2007) considered to be a *draft standard*. This means that everybody in the industry has pretty much agreed on the technical specifications for 802.11n, but they've not quite dotted all the *i*'s and crossed all the *t*'s. 802.11n can use either the 2.4-GHz or 5-GHz frequency spectrum and improves upon 802.11g and 802.11a by using a technology called *MIMO* (multiple inputs, multiple outputs). MIMO technology allows the use of multiple receiving and transmitting antennas to improve both throughput (speed) and range. As we mention earlier in this section, many vendors are currently selling what they are calling pre-802.11n gear, which conforms to the draft standard but which may not completely meet all of the final standard's technical specifications. (Because they've not been finalized, no one knows exactly what they will be.) 802.11n provides a big jump in performance (speeds of over 100 Mbps) and will be backward compatible with 802.11b, a, and g (although at lower speeds than 100 Mbps). See the section titled "Is it time for N?" for more on 802.11n.

Got all that straight? Ready for your wireless LAN pop quiz? Don't worry. We won't do that to you. But what we will do is give you the handy little Table 16-1 to summarize what we just talked about.

A word about Wi-Fi speeds

The speeds listed in Table 16-1 are the *theoretical* maximum speeds of a given Wi-Fi technology. Real world speeds differ significantly from these maximums due to a number of factors including interference from other radio systems and distance from the base station. (Wi-Fi speeds drop off at longer distances.)

Also significant is something known as *overhead*. The theoretical maximum rates measure the number of bits of data that can pass over the network per second. These bits are not all *usable* bits that represent the data or voice signals or video you are carrying over your wireless network. Instead, some of these bits are part of the 802.11 signaling protocols. (That is, some of the data going across the wireless link is used by the wireless system itself to make the connection, encrypt the data, and direct traffic.)

Other overhead is related to the networking protocols you are using, such as Ethernet and TCP-IP (the Internet protocol), both of which use some of your data throughput for their own signaling.

When you subtract the overhead, the true *effective bandwidth* of a Wi-Fi system is about half (or less) than the theoretical maximum. So today's common 802.11g systems, which theoretically pass data at a speed of 54 Mbps, actually give you a usable bandwidth of about 22 Mbps. For most purposes this isn't a big deal (22 Mbps is faster than almost all broadband Internet connections, for example), but for applications such as high-definition video, which can use 22 Mbps all by itself, you start understanding the need for faster Wi-Fi systems such as 802.11n.

Table 16-1		Wireless LAN Technologies		
Technology	*Frequency*	*Speed*	*Compatibility*	*Availability*
802.11b	2.4 GHz	11 Mbps	802.11g	Now (being phased out)
802.11a	5 GHz	54 Mbps	none	Now
802.11g	2.4 GHz	22 Mbps	802.11b (at 11 Mbps)	Now
802.11n (draft standard)	2.4 GHz and/ or 5 GHz	100+ Mbps	802.11b/a/g	Draft gear now; final standard late 2007

Right now, 802.11g is by far the most available and widely used wireless LAN standard. It's also the cheapest (about $50 for an *access point* or *router,* plus typically less than $20 per computer — and it's built into almost every new laptop and many desktop PCs as well). Many offices have Wi-Fi networks, and thousands of hotels, airports, cafes, and other public spaces have Wi-Fi networks in place where you can get online wirelessly, and 802.11g will get you on to any of them.

Products that are Wi-Fi certified have a logo on the box saying as much. This testing and certification process means that these devices not only meet certain technical requirements but also can connect to Wi-Fi products from other vendors (using the same 802.11 standard). For example, an 802.11g product will have a logo like the one shown in Figure 16-1, saying "Wi-Fi Certified b g" (both b and g are listed, because all 802.11g gear is backward compatible on b networks). If the logo is not on the box, don't be surprised if the product doesn't work in a mixed-vendor network. You can find a list of certified products on the following Wi-Fi Web page:

```
certifications.wi-fi.org/wbcs_certified_products.php
```

Right now, there are *no* Wi-Fi certified 802.11n products. There *are* pre-n products that are Wi-Fi certified, but that certification is for the 802.11g functionality within the pre-n products, not for the 802.11n functionality. The Wi-Fi Alliance hasn't started a certification process for 802.11n yet, so you will have no true guarantee that a pre-n product you buy will work with every other 802.11n product in the future.

Is it time for N?

802.11n has been cooking in the labs for years. We've had pre-n gear in our home networks for over two years (it works great, by the way), and as we inch towards the finalization of the standard, more and more manufacturers are beginning to slap the *n* label on their new gear. So that leads to the question: Does it make sense to buy 802.11n gear now? Our answer is qualified because it depends on your willingness to take a risk. The 802.11n *draft* standard is very complete and is widely accepted (during the last vote on the draft standard, about 98 percent of the voters — representatives of the networking and semiconductor industries — approved the standard as is). Because of this high degree of support, we suspect that there won't be a lot of change in the 802.11n standard when it is (finally!) finalized.

And manufacturers seem to agree. For example, Dell and Apple have been shipping laptop computers with 802.11n-ready network adapters since mid-2006. And networking vendors themselves, as mentioned, have been doing so for more than a year.

There's a *but* here though. The IEEE standards mean a lot, but when it comes down to working through the minutia of interoperability (where a network adapter from vendor A works with an access point from vendors B through Z), sometimes some hidden gotchas don't get worked out until the testing process is well underway. This is why the Wi-Fi Alliance isn't certifying 802.11n gear yet.

So what to do? Well if you can wait (perhaps you have some old 802.11g gear laying around), wait. If you can't wait or don't want to wait, look for a vendor who offers an *upgradeability* guarantee. Many vendors will provide this ("buy my pre-n gear now, and we'll give you a software upgrade to make it 802.11n certified or your money back"), and it reduces your risk.

And if you're a risk taker (like us)? Go for it. 802.11n routers and access points are relatively cheap ($150 max, in most cases), and they *are* certified for 802.11g network connections. Stick with one vendor if at all possible — and if you can't, do some research online and stick with one *chip vendor*. Only a few companies make the 802.11n chips inside the gear, and if all your gear has the same chip, it should work well regardless of vendor.

Back to base (ics)

Regardless of the underlying wireless protocol or technology, wireless LANs share a few common elements, the most important of which is the base station or *access point*. If you think of your wireless network in the same way that you think of the wired LANs we discuss in Chapter 15 — in terms of having a hub and spokes — the access point is the hub of your wireless network. A wireless access point is usually a stand-alone, purpose-built device, but there you can implement a wireless hub for your network in several ways:

✓ **Buy a wireless-only base station (an *access point,* or *AP*):** These devices, which you can buy from a host of vendors (NETGEAR, Linksys, Apple, and D-Link are just a few), connect through a wired Ethernet connection to your home LAN or directly into your router, broadband DSL, or cable modem. The access point distributes Internet or local network traffic among all the wireless endpoints on the network (PCs, laptops, PDAs, Wi-Fi phones, and more).

✓ **Buy a base station and home router combo device:** Many of the home routers we discuss in Chapters 13 and 15 are available with built-in wireless base stations. Because they have both wireless and wired outputs (usually a multiport Ethernet switch), you can connect these devices directly to your broadband modem and use them as the central hub for your entire LAN, connecting both wired and wireless computers.

✓ **Use a computer as a base station:** With some operating systems (Mac OS X and Windows XP and Vista), you can replace the hardware base station with a dedicated PC. In this scenario, a broadband modem is connected to an Ethernet port on the base station computer, and then the computer is set up to share the Internet connection over an installed wireless network card. (This is really just a wireless version of the Internet-sharing proxy server concept we discuss in Chapter 14.)

Out of these three options, we think that the hardware-based approaches (first and second) make the most sense, unless you have a dedicated home server with wireless-LAN functionality bundled in. You'd have to try really hard to spend more than $200 for a wireless access point or router, and we've seen them advertised for well below $40. Using a computer as the base station means that you'll need to have that computer running all the time — and you'll probably take a performance hit if you use that PC for other things.

In the NIC of time

Just as computers need network interface cards (NICs) to connect to a wired LAN, they need wireless NICs to connect to a wireless LAN. Wireless NICs, or wireless LAN cards (as they're often called), either plug into a slot in your computer or sit next to it on the desktop and plug into a USB connector on your computer. Four main types of NICs are on the market:

- ✔ **PC Card NICs:** These are probably the most common — because they're designed for mobile computers, and mobile computers are the most likely candidates for a wireless network. The PC Card is about the size of a thick credit card, with a small antenna module on the end, and fits into the PC Card (sometimes called *CardBus*) slot of a laptop or handheld computer.

  The PC Card is slowly being replaced by the PCI Express Mini Card, which is a faster and smaller system that a few laptop vendors have begun supporting (for example, Apple includes only a Mini Card slot on its high-end MacBook Pro laptops).

- ✔ **PCI Card NICs:** For desktop computers that don't have a PC Card, there are wireless LAN cards that fit into an internal PCI slot (the same slots used for many wired Ethernet NICs or for video cards). If you use a PCI Card NIC, you still need an external antenna (which will come in the package), so everything won't be all neat and hidden inside your PC.

- ✔ **USB external NIC:** A better alternative for desktop computers is an external NIC that connects through a USB port. Virtually every computer made since 1999 has USB ports, and the external NIC requires no real installation — just plug it in and load the software driver.

- ✔ **Built-in (embedded) wireless NIC:** In the laptop and PDA world, built-in Wi-Fi NICs are increasingly common. There's nothing for you to do here — just turn on the computer and connect to the network. Because the NIC is built in, you can keep your PC Card slots free for other peripherals.

What fits into a Wi-Fi network?

Although we focus on computers in this chapter, they are far from the only devices that can fit into a Wi-Fi wireless network. In fact, Wi-Fi capabilities are being built into all sorts of devices, greatly increasing the usefulness of your wireless network and allowing you to incorporate your wireless network into other networks in your home (such as your audio/video network or phone networks). Among the devices you can find Wi-Fi in are the following:

✔ **Gaming consoles:** All current gaming consoles we discuss in Chapter 5 — Nintendo's Wii, Microsoft's Xbox 360, and Sony's PlayStation 3 — can connect to your wireless network (using embedded Wi-Fi or inexpensive Wi-Fi adapters that connect to a USB port on the console). Using these Wi-Fi connections, you can download pictures or music to your console, play videos, surf the Web and — most fun of all — participate in online head-to-head or multiplayer games.

✔ **Digital media adapters:** These devices (discussed in Chapter 9), provide a bridge between your PCs and your audio/video networks and systems and allow you to listen to digital music, watch videos, and display digital photos stored on your computer anywhere in the home.

✔ **VoIP and Skype phones:** Wi-Fi phones (discussed in Chapter 11) provide a portable connection to VoIP services (such as Vonage or Skype), so you can call regular phones anywhere in the world over your broadband Internet connection.

✔ **PC peripherals:** A growing number of PC peripheral devices such as printers, scanners, and network storage devices (all discussed in Chapter 12) include embedded Wi-Fi network adapters so you can access them from anywhere in your home — and you can *put* them anywhere in your home, rather than having them located next to your computer. Pat, for example, uses a wireless printer that he can hide in a closet, rather than have it take up valuable shelf space in his overcrowded home office.

You can even add Wi-Fi to any Ethernet-enabled device by buying a *Wi-Fi Ethernet bridge.* This simple device has a Wi-Fi radio and an Ethernet port. When you plug it into a power source and your Ethernet-equipped device, it acts as a Wi-Fi client on the network; any data flowing into and out of the bridge is translated from Wi-Fi to Ethernet (or vice versa). Most Wi-Fi manufacturers (such as Linksys, D-Link, Belkin, and NETGEAR) sell these bridges; they're sometimes called gaming bridges because the most common use is for connecting gaming consoles that don't have Wi-Fi (such as the previous generation of Xbox and PlayStation).

Battening down the hatches

The biggest advantage of wireless networks — the fact that you can connect to the network just about anywhere in range of the base station (up to 300 feet) — is also the biggest disadvantage. Because the signal is carried over the air, on radio waves, anyone else within range can pick up your network's signals too. It's sort of like putting an extra RJ-45 jack for your wired LAN out on the sidewalk in front of your house — you're no longer in control of who can access it. So securing a wireless network takes a bit more work. To make matters worse, if you've spent any time reading computer industry publications, you may have heard about the weaknesses in wireless-network security systems. The bottom line is this: If someone is dedicated and motivated enough, they can get onto your wireless LAN. The flip side of this coin, however, is that the chances of someone targeting your LAN and breaking in are slim. They need to be within a reasonable distance to be able to receive the radio signal, and then they need to have the skills, equipment, and interest to break in. Not too likely, we think.

That doesn't mean that you should leave your wireless LAN wide open for any and all comers — unless you want to (we talk about some reasons why people do this in the "Opening up to your neighbors" sidebar). You can take the following steps to secure a wireless LAN. Note that these steps vary from system to system, so we give only general instructions:

- ✔ **At a bare minimum, turn on WEP:** WEP (wired equivalent privacy) is the security system built into all Wi-Fi systems. It *encrypts* all data flowing between the access points and computers on the network. This encryption basically uses a mathematical function to make the data flowing across the network look like a bunch of random numbers to someone who doesn't have authenticated access to the network. We say WEP is a minimum step because the WEP protocol itself is easy to crack. Anyone can download software from the Internet, listen in on a wireless network, and use the software to figure out the WEP key. After they have the key, they're able to log right into your network and intercept all of your data.

- ✔ **For true security, use WPA:** The folks at the Wi-Fi Alliance were well aware of the shortcomings of WEP and developed (along with the folks at the IEEE who develop the 802.11 standards) a new generation of Wi-Fi security called *WPA* (Wi-Fi protected access). WPA offers a much improved mechanism for encrypting data; although no system is foolproof, WPA is pretty darn close. There are multiple variants of WPA, including some designed for business networks (called *WPA Enterprise*). If your equipment supports *WPA2* (the newest version, with the strongest encryption system), you should use it. It *will* keep your network safe.

- ✔ **Use a decent password:** This is probably the number one complaint we hear from IT folks running corporate networks. People use easy-to-remember passwords because it's a pain remembering an obscure one. But if it's easy for you to remember, it's easy for someone else to guess. Use alphanumeric combinations (numbers and letters together).

Many wireless access points ship with all these security settings turned off by default. If you want to be secure, turn them on.

Opening up to your neighbors

We're not talking about group therapy or wild hot tub parties. Wireless networks can carry through walls, across yards, and potentially around the neighborhood. Although wireless LANs were designed from the start for in-building use, the technology can be used in outdoors settings. For example, most college campuses are now wired with dozens or hundreds of wireless access points so that students, staff, and professors can access the Internet from just about anywhere on campus. At UC San Diego, where Pat's wife works, freshmen are outfitted with wireless PDAs and can schedule classes, send e-mails and instant messages, and even find their friends at the student center (using a locator program written by a student). Many folks are adapting this concept and setting up community wireless LANs.

Some creators of these community LANs have taken the openness of the Internet to heart and have opened up their access points to any and all takers. There's even an Internet subculture with Web sites and chalk markings on sidewalks identifying these open access points. In other areas, where broadband access is scarce, neighbors pool money to buy a T1 or other business-class high-speed Internet line and then share it wirelessly.

We think that both of these concepts make a lot of sense, but we do have a warning. Many ISPs don't like the idea of people sharing an Internet connection without paying (you may, for example, have to pay for a more expensive commercial ISP line). Check your ISP's terms of service, or look at the listing of wireless-friendly ISPs on the Electronic Frontier Foundation's Web page (www.eff.org).

Some folks provide other security recommendations that aren't that effective (we've been guilty of this in the past ourselves). Specifically, you'll hear recommendations to "hide" your network by turning off the base station's broadcast of your network's *SSID* (Service Set Identifier) — the "name" of your network. Although this might keep honest folks off your network, it won't do a thing to keep a malicious user off because they can download dozens of tools that will find your network even with SSID broadcast turned off. An additional bit of not-so-effective advice is creating a closed network that allows only specific MAC addresses to connect to your network. (The MAC address is a unique alphanumeric ID assigned to each NIC ever created.) This sounds like a great idea (only allow your own MACs to connect to the network), but it's simple for a malicious user to clone one of your MACs and get around this roadblock. To secure your wireless network, turn on encryption, preferably WPA or WPA2. Don't bother with these other steps, because they will simply give you a false sense of security.

Putting together a wireless LAN

Putting together a wireless LAN is simple because you don't have to spend any time running new wires or punching down UTP cables. If your house isn't too big, just plug the access point into your broadband modem or into an

Ethernet jack fed by your home router, and turn it on! You'll need to go through a few additional steps, such as naming your network (the SSID) and assigning passwords. Keep the following in mind:

- **Assigning IP addresses:** Every computer (or handheld or whatever) connected to your wireless network needs to have an IP address to talk on the Internet. The overall architecture of your network (all wireless, mixed wired and wireless, and so on) plays a big part in how you do this, as does the kind of access point you're using.

    - If you have a broadband connection connected to a home router and LAN (as discussed in Chapter 15), you need to set up your access point to be a *bridge* connection. In this case, the router assigns an IP address to your wireless computers, and the access point just provides a connection between the wired and wireless networks (a bridge — get it?). You can plug your access point into any outlet in your wired network, set it to bridge mode, and start computing.

    - If you're using a wireless access point incorporated into a router, the access point *is* your router. In this case, you will most likely set up the DHCP functionality of the router (we talk about this in Chapter 15), and use it to assign IP addresses to your wireless computers (as well as those attached to your wired LAN).

- **Finding a good spot:** Wireless LAN signals can travel through walls, doors, and the like, but some things are not nice to wireless signals. Huge chunks of metal (think full-sized filing cabinets) or really dense walls (such as the 18-inch-thick brick walls in Danny's house in Maine) can kill the strength of a wireless signal — which either keeps you from connecting or lowers your speed if you do get connected. Most access points include software that displays how much signal strength you're getting and provides tips for placement of the base station. Access points vary a bit model to model, because they have different antenna systems and the like. We recommend that you place your access point somewhere in the middle of the main floor of the house (or the floor on which you'll be most often using the wireless network), in a high location. (Pat has placed his high up on top of a shelf in his home office, after much trial and error.) Keep the access point away from potentially interfering devices (such as microwaves, power outlets, TVs, and stereos).

After trying different locations, you might find that you just can't get by with a single access point. For example, Danny couldn't get a signal upstairs. This situation can be easily resolved if you have a wired network infrastructure; just get a second (inexpensive) access point and plug it in on a different floor or on the other side of the house. If you don't have a wired infrastructure, you may want to try connecting a remote access point using a phone line or power line technology (discussed later). This works great if you want an access point outside on the porch or covered patio.

✔ **Securing the network:** We recommend that you plug in the network and find a spot for your access point *before* you turn on all the security features. This is exactly why most access points ship with security turned off by default — what you might think is a defective access point or an impenetrable wall is just a mistyped password. So begin with security features turned off, get the network working and the computers talking to each other and to the Internet, and then go back and turn on WEP and do the rest of the security stuff we mentioned.

We put together two diagrams of a wireless network. Figure 16-1 shows a wireless network added to a wired LAN infrastructure, and Figure 16-2 shows a wireless-only network.

In-wall CAT-5e/6 UPT
back to home router

PC with wireless NIC

CAT-5e/6 LAN
outlet

Radio wave

Figure 16-1:
Plugging
wireless
into your
wired LAN.

CAT-5e/6 →
UTP

Radio wave

Wireless access point

PC with wireless NIC

Extending a wireless LAN with WDS

The folks who have developed Wi-Fi systems are aware that many folks — particularly those who have bigger homes — run into problems getting Wi-Fi coverage everywhere in the home. Although Wi-Fi can theoretically extend up to 300 feet (and even further with the MIMO systems found in 802.11n), the real world range is usually much shorter, sometimes as little as 50 feet.

Figure 16-2:
Going totally
wireless.

Cable/DSL modem

Radio wave

PC with wireless NIC

CAT-5e/6 →
UTP

Radio wave

PC with wireless NIC

Wireless access point

The construction of your home, other radio systems, and even the objects in your home (such as appliances and furniture) can all conspire to reduce your Wi-Fi range. One approach to extending your Wi-Fi footprint is to install additional access points using your wired CAT-5e/6 Ethernet network. This works well if you have that network, but what if you don't?

Well that's where the Wi-Fi engineers were thinking ahead; they developed a system called *WDS* (wireless distribution system). WPS allows you to install additional Wi-Fi *repeaters,* or *extenders,* which receive the signal from your main access point or wireless router and rebroadcast that signal to reach farther into your home.

In a WDS system, you have a main access point (connected to your wired network or directly to your home router and cable/DSL modem) and a remote access point that extends the signals to your wireless clients (such as a laptop computer). You can even get sophisticated and install a *repeater* access point between the main and remote access points to extend your network even farther.

To get into WDS, you need the following:

> ✔ **A main access point (or wireless router) that supports WDS,** such as models from Linksys, D-Link, and Apple. You may also be able to upgrade the *firmware* (essentially the system software of your access point) to allow WDS features.

✔ **A remote access point.** This can be an identical access point as your main access point or a stripped-down AP developed for Wi-Fi extension.

✔ **The proper software configuration.** You need to configure your APs for WDS. Using the software or Web configurator built into your APs, you'll need to "turn on" WDS. How you do this varies from AP to AP — often it will be explicitly called WDS, but it may go by another name such as Wi-Fi extension or Wi-Fi repeater.

When considering using WDS, keep the following in mind:

✔ WDS slows your connection. Because WDS is essentially receiving and then retransmitting your wireless signals, the speed of your network connections are effectively cut in half. This is no big deal for Web surfing, e-mail, and voice calls, but may be a problem for video.

✔ WDS isn't implemented exactly the same way by different vendors. There's no Wi-Fi Alliance testing and logo for WDS and no guarantee that, to make up an example, your Apple AirPort Express will act as a WDS remote AP for your D-Link router (even though both support WDS). Our advice here is to stick with a single vendor if you're going to be messing around with WDS.

But wait — there's more to wireless networks

The technologies we've talked about so far in this chapter have been wireless LAN technologies. There are some complementary wireless technologies known as wireless PANs, or personal area networks. PANs, the most prominent of which is called *Bluetooth*, are shorter in range and typically lower in speed than LANs (which, in turn, have a shorter range than WANs, or wide area networks, such as the Internet). A LAN is designed to cover an entire home or business (or at least most of one), but a PAN is designed to connect devices within a few feet or yards of each other.

Most PANs are covered under the 802.15 standard. The initial version, 802.15.1, was adapted from the Bluetooth specification and is fully compatible with Bluetooth. Other short-range, in-home wireless standards that focus on very short-range mesh networks to interconnect home devices are on the way.

Following are some uses for PAN technologies:

✔ Connecting peripherals (such as printers, mice, and keyboards) to a PC

✔ Connecting a digital audio source (such as an MP3 player) to a wireless speaker or headphone system

✔ Connecting handheld computers and PDAs to a desktop computer for syncing and file transfer

✔ Connecting PDAs and mobile phones, to share Internet connections or contact lists

✔ Connecting voice-enabled PDAs or mobile phones to wireless headsets or to hands-free systems in cars

The bottom-line distinction between LANs and PANs tends to be blurry. If something connects to a computer by a network cable today, its wireless connection is a LAN. If it connects by a local cable (such as USB), its wireless connection is a PAN.

As mentioned, by far the most common PAN technology is Bluetooth. This isn't what you get when you eat too many blueberries or blue-dyed Popsicles. Instead, Bluetooth is a wireless PAN technology developed by big mobile communications companies (including Nokia and Ericsson) to expand what their mobile devices could do and to make their devices easier to use. Today, Bluetooth is controlled by an industry consortium called the Bluetooth SIG (special interests group) at `www.bluetooth.com`, which also includes companies such as Microsoft and Intel.

You're going to ask, so we'll tell you: Bluetooth is named after Harald Blåtand ("Bluetooth"), King of Denmark from 940 to 981, who was responsible for uniting Denmark and Norway.

Bluetooth uses the same 2.4-GHz radio spectrum that Wi-Fi LANs use (though most tests have shown that they don't interfere with each other too much) and is designed to be a low-power (good for battery-powered devices) and low-cost (good for everyone) alternative to a LAN. Bluetooth radios are embedded in cell phones, PDAs, and laptop computers, as well as a range of peripheral devices such as headsets and keyboards. Bluetooth has been around since the late 1990s and took a long time to take off, but the advent of those tiny (and geeky-looking) Bluetooth headsets and in-car Bluetooth hands-free phone systems for cell phones has finally made Bluetooth a Very Big Thing.

These days, most new mobile phones include Bluetooth, as do many laptop computers and a growing number of printers, keyboards, mice, and other PC peripherals.

A couple of types of Bluetooth systems are on the market:

✔ **Bluetooth 1.1:** This is the older, slightly slower variant of Bluetooth, with a maximum data rate of 721 Kbps.

✔ **Bluetooth 2.0:** The current version of Bluetooth, 2.0 adds an *EDR* (extended data rate) mode that supports speeds of up to 2.1 Mbps. This faster mode comes in handy when you're using Bluetooth to connect your laptop computer to the Internet through a 3G smartphone. (See Chapter 13 for more on 3G.)

Bluetooth 1.1 and 2.0 devices can connect to and talk with each other with no problems, so you don't have to worry about mixing and matching Bluetooth 1.1 and 2.0 devices. If you want the higher EDR speeds, however, you need to ensure that both ends of the connection support Bluetooth 2.0.

Making the Most of Your Phone Lines

Another alternative to using CAT-5e/6 Ethernet cabling or wireless LANs is to leverage your home's existing telephone wiring to carry Ethernet data. *Phone line networking* (the term for this networking technique) is a relatively mature technology — the first systems were shipped in the mid-1990s. An industry group called HomePNA or sometimes HPNA (Home Phoneline Networking Association — www.homepna.org) provides standards and product certification. As of 2007, there were three variants of HomePNA networking systems:

- **HomePNA 1.0:** This is a slower speed protocol (1.3 Mbps), and is essentially obsolete.

- **HomePNA 2.0:** This is a faster protocol (advertised as 10 Mbps, though the maximum speed is actually 16 Mbps), which is used in just about every HomePNA product on the market. HomePNA 2.0 is backwards compatible with HomePNA 1.0, so newer products can talk to older ones. The bad news about this backwards compatibility is that having even one HomePNA 1.0 device connected to your phone lines slows *all* the HomePNA 2.0 devices down to 1.3 Mbps. As we write, a few HomePNA 2.0 products are still on the market, but the number is dwindling as the new HomePNA 3.0 version hits the streets.

- **HomePNA 3.0:** The current version of HomePNA, now shipping from several vendors, is HomePNA 3.0. This is HomePNA on steroids, with a maximum speed of up to 240 Mbps.

Currently, no vendors are offering HomePNA 3.0 gear designed to be sold directly to consumers. Instead, they are focusing on the IPTV market (see Chapter 5 for more on IPTV) and are selling HomePNA solutions to phone companies and IPTV set-top box manufacturers. The goal here is to use HomePNA over existing phone lines to connect the set-top boxes in your home. With a HomePNA solution, the phone company can install one big, high-powered set-top box in your media room or home theater and then use cheaper remote set-top boxes in other locations. The main set-top box does the IPTV decoding and then sends your TV programming to the inexpensive satellite boxes over the phone lines. After HomePNA is installed in the millions of homes that may potentially become IPTV customers, we expect that additional devices will be developed to allow you to hop onto the HomePNA network for more traditional home LAN purposes.

I'll have a MoCA please

In the IPTV world, the biggest competitor to HomePNA 3.0 is a technology called *MoCA* (multimedia over coax — www.mocaliance. org). MoCA uses the coaxial cables that carry TV signals around the home as its media for high-speed Ethernet connectivity. MoCA can carry data at speeds exceeding 100 Mbps. Like HomePNA, MoCA technology isn't something you can go out and buy off the shelf. Instead, it is embedded into set-top boxes for TV services and is primarily used to send TV signals to remote set-top boxes from an Internet-connected main IPTV set-top box.

The company behind MoCA's technology, Entropic Communications (www.entropic. com) sells the same technology as an *Internet access* system as well as a home-networking system. Many high-rises and apartment and condo complexes are wired to the gills with coaxial cable but don't have CAT-5e/6 cabling for Internet access. Service providers can use (and are using, particularly in Asian markets) the coax and Entropic's technology to provide Internet service to each unit in the complex or building, without having to rewire.

The HomePNA system operates on different frequencies than analog or DSL telephone services, so you can simultaneously use a single phone line for your computer LAN and for all the other things you currently use it for — such as making phone calls, sending and receiving faxes, or connecting to the Internet.

Powering Your Network

Using electrical power lines for something more than sending juice to your appliances is not a new concept. If you read Chapter 19, for example, you know all about X10, LonWorks, and Insteon — home-automation protocols that use electrical wires to send control signals to lights, appliances, and more. For decades, people have been using X10 and other low-speed power line networking systems, but attempts to use power lines for high-speed networking have largely failed. In 2002, a bunch of networking companies (including Linksys, NETGEAR, and D-Link) began releasing high-speed power line networking products based on a system known as HomePlug.

To set up a LAN in your home under the HomePlug specification, you use a HomePlug-supporting device that runs an Ethernet cable to your computer and an electrical cord to the electrical outlet. That electrical cord *is* your LAN connection — along with all the rest of the electrical cabling in your house. Cool, huh?

Like the HomePNA group, HomePlug is an industry consortium designed to develop standards and promote products using HomePlug technology. Development of the HomePlug standard took several years, mainly because networking on power lines is a technically challenging task. Power lines are noisy, electrically speaking, with surges in voltage level and electrical interferences introduced by all sorts of devices both within and external to the home. The state of the electrical network in a home is constantly changing as well, as devices are plugged in and turned on. Because of this, the HomePlug standard adopts a sophisticated and adaptive *signal-processing algorithm* — the technique used to convert data into electrical signals on the power wiring. Because HomePlug uses higher-frequency signals than low-speed power line communications systems such as X10, the technology can avoid some of the most common sources of noise on the power line.

Following are the three variants of HomePlug devices:

- ✔ **HomePlug 1.0:** The initial HomePlug standard, HomePlug 1.0 devices provide connections at a maximum speed of 14 Mbps.

- ✔ **HomePlug Turbo:** Not actually an official HomePlug standard, HomePlug Turbo uses a proprietary chip that allows faster connections — up to 85 Mbps.

- ✔ **HomePlug AV:** The current version of HomePlug, HomePlug AV can provide speeds of up to 200 Mbps across your home's power lines. HomePlug AV is still basically brand new as we write in early 2007 — the first 14 products were certified in January 2007.

Like most home-networking systems, HomePlug advertises itself based on maximum theoretical speeds. Real world speeds are lower, due to both overhead and the vagaries of the power lines themselves. You should expect actual throughputs of no more than half the rated maximum speeds. This isn't that big of a deal with HomePlug AV, but tends to make HomePlug 1.0 and even Turbo devices less than ideal for high-bandwidth network applications such as video. There's a reason HomePlug AV has *AV* (audio/video) in the name!

Besides the speed, there are a few other neat things to consider about HomePlug-based networking systems:

- ✔ Power outlets are the most common and ubiquitous jacks in the home. Even if you heavily wire your home with CAT-5e/6 cabling for an Ethernet network, chances are you won't have more than two LAN jacks in the majority of rooms in your house. With HomePlug, every one of the dozens or even hundreds of power outlets in the house becomes a data-networking jack.

✔ HomePlug can be built right into many networked appliances. The almost legendary Internet refrigerator that we've discussed in several places in this book is a cool concept, but even we don't have a CAT-5e/6 outlet in the dark nook behind our fridges. We do have a power jack, and so do you.

✔ HomePlug automatically crosses phases in your electrical system. (The majority of homes have two-phase electrical power — where the 220-volt power line coming into your house is split into separate 110-volt phases or circuits.) As we discuss in Chapter 21, systems such as X10 may require a bridge device installed in the main electrical panel so that different parts of your electrical system can see each other and so that signals can reach all parts of your home. Because of the higher frequencies that HomePlug uses, it can cross these phases without a bridging device.

✔ HomePlug can reach beyond the limits of your home (and at lower signal levels) right into your neighbor's house. Although the signal levels are attenuated at longer distances, you could use HomePlug to create a community network with your neighbors, like the ones we describe in the "Opening up to your neighbors" sidebar. This works as long as you share the same power transformer with your neighbors as well as your encryption key, so it might not be the best thing to do.

✔ HomePlug has a built-in encryption system. Because HomePlug can reach beyond your house and you may not want to share your LAN with your neighbors, you can turn on HomePlug's encryption. In that way, only devices that have your password can be on the network.

Like the wireless systems we described previously, most HomePlug systems come with encryption turned off by default, or use a default password that anyone with Internet access can find on the manufacturer's Web site. We recommend that you get your network up and running first, and turn on encryption (with a new, strong password) after you've proven to yourself that your network is working.

✔ HomePlug is compatible with other power line communications systems. Because it operates on such high frequencies, HomePlug doesn't interfere with X10 and other low-speed power line systems, so you can use your LAN and your home-automation system at the same time.

HomePlug products are available in a variety of devices — you can buy HomePlug routers and switches (which often include wired Ethernet ports as well). As we write this, there aren't any HomePlug NICs. Instead, the most common application for HomePlug is Ethernet or USB bridges. These devices look and act a lot like the external USB Wi-Fi NICs we discussed earlier. You'll need two of them: one to connect to an Ethernet port on your router (or any LAN jack in your home) and another to plug into the wall outlet where you need LAN access.

The bridge typically has a power cord on one side of the box and an Ethernet or USB connector on the other. Plug the power cord into any wall outlet, and plug the Ethernet or USB into the computer or other networked devices, and you have a connection. Pat has been using a NETGEAR power line Ethernet bridge like this for a spot in his house that has neither Ethernet nor good wireless coverage — and he loves it. Danny has a NETGEAR bridge connecting his office (where the cable modem is) to the kids computing area (where all the screaming is). Figure 16-3 shows a typical use of HomePlug bridges.

Figure 16-3:
Plugging
your
computer
into the
wall — and
that's all.

Another interesting use of HomePlug is in the Wi-Fi extension arena. Several manufacturers (most notably NETGEAR — www.netgear.com) sell HomePlug Wi-Fi access points. These devices connect to a HomePlug-equipped home router (or to a HomePlug Ethernet bridge connected to an existing router) and provide a local Wi-Fi signal in whatever room they're plugged into.

We think power line networking through HomePlug is great, but we probably would never use it to replace our wired networks or even our wireless LANs. But HomePlug is quick, cheap (bridges cost about $80 a piece, with prices dropping rapidly), and perfect for spots you never thought you'd need to wire.

We hinted at this already, but let's just come right out and say it. We think HomePlug will have a huge effect in the noncomputer market — stereos, TVs, gaming machines, Internet fridges, and other pieces of electronic equipment that might benefit from an Internet connection. And as HomePlug becomes incorporated into new generations of appliances, you'll need just the power cord to make it work.

Mixing and Matching

Although many vendors will try to push you into one solution ("You need Wi-Fi," "No, you need HomePlug"), you might find that these various no-new-wires networks can complement each other. You know that we think a wired CAT-5e/6 network should be the basis of your computer-LAN infrastructure (and phone network, and maybe even your audio and video network), but we think also that all four of these technologies can be used in concert when you build a whole-home network.

Just for fun, here are a few examples:

- ✔ Build a wired Ethernet LAN, but plug a Wi-Fi access point in your living room for cordless sofa-based Web surfing.

- ✔ Use Wi-Fi as the basis for your home-computer LAN, but use HomePlug or HomePNA (or SercoNet's phone line solution) to extend your network to access points in distant locations out of reach of your primary base station (such as by the pool).

- ✔ Use wired Ethernet for your computers, but use a HomePlug AV system to connect your Xbox to the broadband Internet connection for online gaming.

We could keep this list going and going, but we think you get the picture. Think creatively, and use wired and unwired technologies together to get your LAN wherever you need it to go.

Part V
Keeping the Bad Guys at Bay — Security

The 5th Wave   By Rich Tennant

"So, someone's using your credit card info to buy stylish clothes, opera tickets, and exercise equipment. In what way would this qualify as 'identity theft?'"

In this part . . .

Most people are familiar with some of the core concepts of home security and safety. Smoke detectors, fire extinguishers, and shrieking alarms tend to come to mind, but a smart-home security system is much much more.

In this part, we talk about how to protect and prevent. We introduce you to a home-security infrastructure that goes beyond just setting off an alarm when someone opens a door. We tell you about sensors galore that not only run your home-security subsystem but also lay a foundation for later use in your home-automation environment. We also tell you about how some security services can utilize a broadband Internet service to make your home-monitoring system more interactive.

Chapter 17

Home Security Boot Camp

*E*ven though you have to plan for all sorts of scary disasters — robbery, fire, carbon-dioxide poisoning, floods, and so on — you don't need to be afraid of your alarm system. You may find that your alarm system is one of the more fun systems to plan because you can do so much with sensors and control panels. For example, you can configure an alarm system to detect when someone is standing on your front doormat and have the system turn on a light or even call you at work and let you know that you have a visitor.

An alarm system should fit your style and tastes. The system design should work around your daily schedule, your kids and pets (if you have any), and the overall way you live your life. For instance, the design should take into consideration whether you have valuable possessions in your home — a stash of jewelry, mattress money, gold, silver, baseball cards, or a wine cellar. The system can also contain a medical alert capability if you have the need for one or a pool alarm if young people live in the house. A smart-home alarm system simply reflects you.

Security systems entail a great deal of planning to make sure that you literally cover every angle. Just one glaring hole in your system makes you vulnerable. Still, the security component of your home network is probably one of the easiest to understand and plan because it's familiar and intuitive. And, because you'll likely have someone else wire your security system, you have to only think about where all those sensors need to be.

In this chapter, we show you how to batten down the hatches on security. Specifically, we describe what security systems can do for you and how they work. We also talk about the components that make up a security system and how they sense conditions that might be cause for alarm.

Deciding That You Need a Security System

People install security systems for three main reasons:

- ✔ To protect their home when they aren't around
- ✔ To protect their home when they are around
- ✔ To protect both their home and its occupants — different sensors and sensor arrangements are necessary to protect your home and to protect occupants, and many people want both

Protecting your house when you're not home typically serves as a baseline goal. If this goal is your only concern, you can take the minimalist approach — apply contact sensors on the doors, install a few passive infrared scanners on the interior of the house, and throw in a siren and control panel.

To protect your house when you are at home requires a more intense approach. Beyond what we just described, you have more to cover, especially the windows on the basement and first-floor levels. Security experts have determined that nearly 90 percent of break-ins involve a door. That is to say, 90 percent of the time, the burglar either enters or leaves the house using a door. When all you want to do is determine that a break-in has occurred, a simple perimeter defense like we just described is considered adequate. If you want a more thorough system that can detect the presence of an intruder and immediately sound an alarm, you need additional sensors.

You may want to consider glass-breakage detectors along with contacts (contacts only detect whether a window has been opened, but glass-breakage detectors can tell whether someone has smashed a window). If you don't want to see the devices for cosmetic reasons, you can install *stress detectors* — which are mounted to support beams under the floor and can register an individual's weight and activate the alarm. Stress detectors are often used in historic homes. You can also add other sensors, as we discuss in the "You fill up my sensors" section.

Security Basics

Before you head out shopping for a security system, you should know what these systems are designed to do. A smart-home security system has at least three goals:

- **Detection:** Your system should be capable of sounding an alarm when something triggers a sensor (though you may choose *not* to sound an alarm for certain types of events).

- **Emergency response:** Your system should be able to call for appropriate help, depending on the circumstances.

- **Prevention:** Your system should help prevent problems — such as scaring away potential intruders by automatically turning on outside lights at night. Well-built doors and windows and quality locks help determine whether a criminal attempts to break into a home, whether or not you have an alarm. Bringing prevention into the equation means connecting your security system with your home-automation system (see Part VI).

Your alarm system accomplishes its goals in three steps:

- **Input:** The system can't act if it isn't aware of a problem. The sensors in your system alert your security subsystem when something deserves attention.

- **Processing:** Something has to interpret these inputs to determine whether the system needs to do something. Your security system is constantly analyzing real-time inputs from all its tethered sensors, monitoring the status of your home's health.

- **Output:** After your subsystem decides what to do, it reaches out and runs through its preprogrammed checklist of to-do items. Sirens, flashing lights, silent alarms, and more are possible with a smart system.

Although every manufacturer has variations on the pieces and parts that make up a security system, your system should include at least the following basics:

- A control panel

- A keypad and corresponding key

- Basic sensors, such as an inside motion detector, door and window contact sensors, glass-breakage detectors, and a smoke alarm

- A siren or flashing strobe light

You should also link the system to a central monitoring station (a security company, in other words) for around-the-clock coverage.

Getting control of your security panel

You usually find the control panel — your security system's brain — in your home's wiring closet. This room also houses your telephone and home-automation subsystems. The control panel is basically an electronic box that serves as the core interconnection point for all the wiring (and wireless connections) in your subsystem. A sophisticated control panel has outputs that allow you to interface with X10, Z-Wave, or ZigBee home-automation systems (which we talk about in more detail in Chapters 19 and 20) to control lights, for instance, and with RS-232 serial ports for more proprietary and custom-programmed automation systems. The control panel also has ports for interfacing with telephone systems. In addition, the control panel has an internal battery for battery backup in case of a power failure.

Control pads range in size — some are the size of a telephone keypad, and others utilize several separate boxes mounted out of sight. In small systems that require only one keypad (perhaps for a small apartment), the keypad and control panel are often integrated into one unit.

Don't panic — use your keypad!

You can use different systems to activate and deactivate your security system. The most common interfaces for residential applications are *keypads,* which resemble telephone keypads, and *key switches,* which take a physical key. The majority of new installations use keypads because they offer a lot of flexibility.

Most people use a four- to five-digit code to activate and deactivate their alarm system and to gain entry for maintenance. Different systems record this activity in different ways. Higher-end systems track which codes are entered at which times; lower-end ones merely record that the system was activated or deactivated on a particular date and time.

You can also program your system directly from the keypad. A quick glance at the keypad's status display immediately tells you whether your system is armed, ready-to-arm, and so on (for example, if you've disabled sensors in a certain zone). You can change your system pass codes at any time, giving additional users temporary entrance. For instance, you can give out-of-town guests temporary codes that are automatically erased when you return.

If something triggers one of the sensors, the system has many options, including sounding the alarm, notifying remote monitoring services, paging you, or calling you on the phone and alerting you to the problem. The most common quickly activate an audible panic alarm, fire alarm, or medical emergency alarm.

Some alarm systems have a module that turns any Touch-Tone phone into a fully functional keypad. This saves you money because you don't have to distribute wired keypads all over the house. And if you're on vacation, you can check the status of your system for greater peace of mind. You can also dial in and activate the system if you forgot to turn it on when you left.

You fill up my sensors

You can use all sorts of sensors and detectors to drive your security system. And although some security-system purists try to make a strong technical differentiation between sensors and detectors, everyone that we know uses the terms interchangeably.

Sensors are the central part of your security architecture because your security subsystem operates solely on the inputs of the sensors — it can't act on something that it can't sense. You can surmise what most detectors do, so we won't take up your time detailing how each one works. Later in this section, however, we cover the main sensors you're likely to encounter in a base system: contact sensors, passive infrared sensors, and smoke detectors.

You can use the following sensors in your smart home:

- **Break sensor:** Mounted near windows to detect the specific high-frequency sounds of glass being shattered

- **Carbon monoxide detector:** Used inside a home to detect hazardous levels of CO gas

- **Contact sensor:** Mounted in doors and windows to detect when doors and windows are opened or closed

- **Flood sensor:** Mounted in basements or other flood-prone spaces, often used to trigger sump pumps

- **Freeze sensor:** Mounted outside to detect freezing temperatures for plant protection

- **Gas detector:** Detects the presence of gas fumes

- **Heat detector:** Part of a smoke- and fire-alarm system, detects high temperatures

- **Ionization detector:** The actual smoke detector in a smoke detector

- **Magnetic sensor:** A kind of contact sensor, determines when a door or window is opened

✔ **Moisture sensor:** Mounted indoors to determine humidity, often used to trigger air-conditioning or dehumidifier systems

✔ **Motion sensor:** Mounted in halls and stairways to detect the movement of unwanted intruders

✔ **Photoelectric sensor:** Shines a beam of light across a hall or doorway to detect motion (activates when a person walking by interrupts the beam)

✔ **Plunger switch:** A contact sensor that uses a small plunger (which looks like a refrigerator or car door light switch) to determine when a door or window is opened

✔ **Power status sensor:** Detects power outages and then possibly starts a generator

✔ **Pressure sensor:** Often mounted in doormats or under driveways to detect weight

✔ **Rain sensor:** Mounted outdoors to trigger or cancel sprinkler systems

✔ **Smoke detector:** Used for fire protection, but *smoke detector* is a bit of a misnomer because most include a heat detector

✔ **Snow sensor:** Mounted outside to detect snow and then activate, for example, a heated driveway

✔ **Tamper switch:** Mounted in vulnerable areas of alarm systems to sound in case of tampering

✔ **Temperature sensor:** Unsurprisingly, used to detect temperature

✔ **Vibration sensor:** Mounted under floors or elsewhere in a home's structure to detect people walking above

✔ **Water disturbance sensor:** Used in a swimming pool or hot tub to determine when someone or something has entered the water

✔ **Weather sensor:** Mounted outside to detect a number of weather conditions

Not only do these sensors drive your security system, but many can drive your home-automation capabilities as well. For instance, you can use the magnetic detector along your driveway to note that a car has pulled in and use an infrared motion detector to note when someone walks to the door.

Contact sensors

Some 90 percent of all break-ins involve outside doors — whether going in or going out. So only 10 percent of the time will someone come in and leave through windows. Clearly, protection for your doors is probably the single most important element of security-system planning.

Prepare to repel boarders!

Security systems work great on burglars — but did you know that they can protect your tomatoes too? A smart security system can help you with unwanted animals in your yard day or night. How about a motion-detector-based animal repeller that keeps wildlife and neighbors' pets out of your garden by spraying them with water? One model, the Scarecrow Water Spraying Animal Repeller by Contech Electronics Inc. (http://www.contech-inc.com//), has a range of up to 35 feet with a spray head adjustable from 10 to 360 degrees.

Magnetic switches are one of the most popular ways to protect doors. You put a magnet on the edge of the door itself and then, with the door closed, place a switch across from it in the doorjamb. When you open the door, the magnet loses contact with the switch, causing it to change electric states. The control panel recognizes this change and, if appropriate, triggers an alarm or other course of action.

Passive infrared receivers

Passive infrared receivers (PIRs) are another popular security-system item. These devices see heat in the infrared spectrum. A series of lenses on the receiver's cover guide a PIR's vision (which is fixed in one direction). PIR technology has been refined to the extent that false alarms are minimal.

You can get different coverage areas by using different lenses on the front of the PIR. A good security team can further aim or restrict this vision by placing opaque tape over portions of the lens to reduce the opportunity for false alarms from roving dogs and other unintended motion.

Many PIRs are pet immune and designed to keep Rover from setting off your alarm.

PIRs are relatively cheap and small (about the size of a light switch), can mount on a wall or ceiling inconspicuously, and go a long way toward protecting your home. The idea with PIRs is to guard your most sensitive areas, while attempting to catch a criminal early in an intrusion. A PIR covering the stairway to the second floor is always a great plan — you don't want the bad guys to get upstairs. Hallways leading to family rooms where electronics and saleable items are kept make sense, too.

Many PIRs offer different zones in the sensor's vision so that you can create events based on the sequence in which the sensor's zones are tripped. One of the neat things about sensors is that you can team them together for unique applications. Because software drives and enables sensors, you can attach additional detectors, such as active IR beams or magnetic contacts, to trip only in special combination circumstances.

For instance, with certain manufacturers' sensors, such as Optex America's VX-40A (www.optexamerica.com), you can wire two PIR detectors together and use different software modes to do different things:

✔ Set a mode that lets the two PIRs work together to double the size of your detection area

✔ Set your PIRs to activate alarms directionally — so they trip an alarm if they detect a person walking in a certain direction in your home

✔ Select a sequential mode to generate an alarm only if two detectors activate sequentially and separately

You can combine the VX-40A is with a voice-warning feature. When the system is armed, the voice-warning feature (a weatherproof speaker is inside the sensor) delivers one of two types of voice messages to anyone entering the protected area. This warning is designed to deter a would-be intruder from continuing toward the protected area.

A wireless annunciator system, such as the wireless Voice Alert system from Cross Point Industries (www.voicealert.com), alerts you with a custom voice message based on PIRs. You record your own alert messages. It has an extensive reach — up to 1000 feet in open space and up to 300 feet through walls. For high-traffic areas, it has a sleep mode that will wait three minutes before waking up and triggering again, so all your guests arriving at a party don't hear, "Hey, thanks for coming!" over and over. The sensor/transmitters can be used indoors and outside and can notify you of just about anything. "Alert, Pat's in the cookie jar!"

Smoke detectors

Battery-powered smoke detectors (you know, the little jobbies that you stick to the wall or ceiling) help you get clear in an emergency, but they don't do much to protect your home when you're not around. Neither a control panel nor a central station can monitor these detectors. If no one is around when the alarm goes off, the alarm beeps, buzzes, and whirs until, well, it melts. You need to ensure that your security system monitors for fire and automatically calls for help when necessary.

These smoke detectors are hardwired back to the alarm control panel and typically offer several levels of protection — a temperature sensor that sounds the alarm at a preset temperature, a temperature sensor that measures the rate of rise of a room's temperature and sounds the alarm when it meets its preset minimum, and an ionization detector that "smells" smoke and sounds the alarm.

In some parts of the country, these detectors may not meet your local fire regulations for hardwired smoke detectors because the security control panel itself (which powers the detector) may not be hardwired. Instead, the panel is attached to a transformer.

Tying in to home automation

One of the great things about these security devices is that they have multiple uses. A sensor just senses something — how the system acts on a trigger event is a different issue. If you tie these sensors into a home controller, you can set different states for these sensors. For instance, if someone trips an infrared beam across your lawn while you're working at home, you may see a display video on a monitor in your office. If the same trigger occurs when you're away on vacation, the system may instead phone your alarm-monitoring station.

As you think about automating your home, be careful when replacing nonautomated devices with automated ones because the results will not always be to your liking. If you don't like the effect of an X10 adapter, for example, you can simply unplug it. Other devices, however, might require that you climb a ladder or call the electrician or plumber. For example, people often leave floodlights on when guests are arriving. If you replace these with motion-sensitive floodlights, you might need to make other adjustments, such as adding sensors to your driveway to turn lights on when people arrive. Think twice about why your device works that way at the start and how it would work differently after being adjusted.

Sirens

You should complement your alarm system with visible and audible outputs, such as external sirens and flashing strobe lights. Your alarm system will probably allow different tones for different situations, such as an intermittent tone for fire but a steady tone for burglary.

Position your visible alarms in as high and as obvious a place as possible so that people coming to your aid can easily locate the beacon. Firefighters, police, and so on all look for these visible alarms first as they speed to your rescue. Remember, their siren is likely going off too, so being an obvious target can work to your advantage.

Monitoring

You have to make the key decision of whether or not to have a central monitoring station monitor your alarm. Because this option offers the bonus of professional security response, we highly recommend that you choose it. For a minor cost of $20 to $25 or so per month, you can give yourself peace of mind — and possibly save your life.

Most of the 12,000 plus alarm companies in the U.S. don't have their own central monitoring station. Rather, they bundle someone else's monitoring service — businesses that do nothing else but monitor systems for alarm companies — with their own installation and maintenance service. Your control system calls out to this monitoring station when an emergency or other problem situation arises; the central station interprets the information coming from your alarm system and calls the appropriate parties.

Traditional alarm-monitoring services use a standard (POTS) telephone line, with the alarm panel connected to your phone using a special jack (called an RJ-31x, discussed in Chapter 18). This solution has worked well for years, but the advent of broadband connections and phone services using VoIP (services such as Skype or Vonage) has changed the equation. For anyone with a broadband connection, *broadband alarm monitoring* provides an opportunity to save money and get a more interactive service that lets you control your alarm system from anywhere in the world (as long as you have an Internet connection). And for folks who have cut off their phone lines to use VoIP (or cell phones) exclusively, broadband monitoring may be the only way to get your alarm system monitored. We talk more about monitoring connections in Chapter 18.

Gathering Your 007 Security Equipment

Your security system can get quite extensive, depending on what you choose to place under the master control panel's domain. You can program your system to respond automatically or manually to almost any type of sensor or input device. One popular application for security systems — in fact, an area of considerable growth within the industry itself — is in video surveillance.

In Chapters 6 and 7, we talk about distributing video throughout the home by using modulators to send video from one room to every TV in the house. You are effectively doing the same thing here. You can buy security and safety products that transmit video signals so that you can see front, side, and back doors, garages, driveways, pool areas, play areas, valuables, babysitters, cleaners, and other people helping in sensitive areas of your home.

In fact, you can record video signals to VHS tape to review at your leisure. Have you hired a new nanny? Want to see whether your cleaning person is really cleaning all day long, or just eating your food? This technology lets you see what's happening at home — whether you're inside your home or 500 miles away.

Video surveillance

Many alarm, intercom, and telephone systems have an extension capability that includes video distribution for monitoring applications, such as checking out who's at the front door or how the baby is doing in the nursery. This area is one where the lines between security, telephones, and intercom subsystems blur because any of them can provide video distribution throughout your smart home. It's also an area where you can find solutions ranging from really cheap to really expensive — those guys in Las Vegas don't use X10 to monitor the craps tables, you know.

It's important to note the difference between surveillance and security. *Surveillance* products tend to require some sort of active involvement on your part. You have to watch something or take part in something for it to have a full effect. *Security* tends to be more passive — it does the watching for you. However, not all vendors adhere to this distinction.

You'll want to consider two forms of video surveillance: still image and live picture. Although you may love to have live, detailed, color pictures as part of your video-surveillance system, you have to determine whether the feature is worth the cost. A number of inexpensive systems that are either black and white or still image may do the trick, and they're easier on your budget. As you go up to color and faster frame-refresh rates, the cost of the product increases substantially.

Video-surveillance products have seen a lot of development in recent years. Prices have dropped for off-the-shelf consumer solutions, and more robust professional-grade cameras (for consumer applications) have likewise become much cheaper. Most consumer-oriented imaging products for surveillance are stand-alone, closed-circuit style cameras or are tethered to a local PC. Many newer products have networked cameras, which means they connect directly to a network without a host PC. This is the way to go if you can afford it because you can place these cameras just about anywhere, and you don't need to have a PC running for them to work.

The size of today's cameras and how secretive their locations can be is amazing. SecurityandMore (`www.securityandmore.com`) carries a line of hidden cameras that look like thermostats, tissue boxes, radios, books, PIRs, and even fake plants. These devices pick up video as well as audio signals. And at a few hundred dollars per camera, they're not that expensive an add-on to your system.

CCTV options

You used to see closed-circuit television (CCTV) only in movies and convenience stores. This technology is ideal for surveillance — you can monitor and record CCTV to stop theft, limit liability exposure, maximize productivity, and protect yourself and your property. You can get CCTV products at a range of prices and functionality. They start out at the low-end, black-and-white, low-frame-rate models and move up to color, multi-camera, high-frame rate models.

An example of a traditional wired CCTV system is Smarthome's 4 Color Camera Kit with 80GB DVR (find it on www.smarthome.com). This system includes four wired and waterproof cameras that operate in either color or black-and-white mode (depending on available light) and communicate back to the DVR (digital video recorder). You can view your cameras on a TV, or simply let them record to the DVR to save up to two weeks' worth of footage. The system uses standard NTSC composite video, so any standard definition or HDTV can display it.

If running a coaxial cable for your video-camera signal distribution is out of the question, you can use a *video balun* (basically a cable converter) to convert the signals for transmission over CAT-5e/6 cabling. You use two of the eight conductors in the telephone/data cabling for each signal. Surprisingly, line noise, cross talk, and attenuation are low, approaching the performance of shielded coaxial cable. You need one balun for each of the receiving and the sending devices.

Many warehouse clubs (such as Costco and Sam's Club) and office product stores (such as Staples and Office Depot) carry CCTV kits.

PC options

Another option for viewing and storing video in a home video-surveillance network is to leverage your PC investment. You can do so in two ways:

✔ **Use special-purpose PC video cameras that connect to the video capture card installed in your PC:** Most of these cameras are designed for other uses, such as videoconferencing, and can't get too far away from your PC (the average cord doesn't get much beyond 12 feet), but a few companies have wireless systems that will let you connect several cameras spread throughout your house. (See Chapter 12 for more info on these cameras.)

✔ **Install a TV card inside your PC and then connect your video-surveillance cameras to your home's video network:** Using devices called modulators (see Chapter 7), you can put these cameras on unused television channels and watch them on your PC or any TV.

Network options

By far the best option — and one of the most expensive — is a network camera, which is a camera with the internal parts of the computer to give it a presence on a LAN or on the Internet. In other words, you don't need the camera enslaved to a PC for it to work. All you need is a regular Web browser to access the cameras to set up the parameters; all other required software, including control software and e-mail software (for automatic e-mailing of images) is inside the camera.

Like the other cameras, wireless and wired options are available. Panasonic has both in its Network Cameras product line (www.panasonic.com/ consumer_electronics/gate/cameras.asp). Panasonic's cameras have built-in software to record data to a Web site using the FTP protocol (which you may be familiar with if you download or upload software on the Internet). You can use its subscription-based service at www.viewnetcam.com to view your images from anywhere in the world. The service basically creates a personal Web address for you. Or you can use the same FTP interface to record to the hard drive of a local computer. The cameras can be mounted on walls, tripods, a desk stand, or even the ceiling.

The Panasonic software allows you to view images from up to four cameras at once, and each image is a link to the control Web page for that camera. These cameras transmit up to 15 frames per second of live motion video with resolutions of up to 640 x 480 pixels. The Panasonic wireless models are compatible with standard 802.11b wireless devices, allowing the flexibility to install and operate the camera without running network wires. These products can cost up to $1000 for the most expensive models, but the price of indoor cameras is coming down rapidly, at about $200 for cameras that connect to your wired computer LAN (using Ethernet) and about $300 for cameras that use 802.11 Wi-Fi wireless technology.

Audio surveillance

Audio surveillance hasn't taken off in most home-security installations, but it's pretty neat nonetheless. By adding a device called a *two-way audio module* into your alarm's central panel, you can send and receive audio to and from your alarm company's central monitoring station. Most two-way audio systems communicate through a microphone and speaker installed in the alarm keypad. After an alarm is triggered, the alarm system notifies the central station, and the two-way audio system automatically kicks in.

Using the same telephone line that connects you to the monitors, you can have hands-free conversations with the monitors, which could be very handy in the event of a medical emergency. (See the "I've fallen and I can't get up!" section in Chapter 3.) If you're not home, the monitoring station can record all the sounds that your uninvited visitors make while they're in your home — not that you'd probably want to listen to their take on your home-decorating skills.

Finding and Installing the Right Security System

Security systems are easily expandable, provided that you have the right foundation. To choose a security system, look at both hardwired and wireless systems and determine how these systems will interface with your other smart-home subsystems, such as home automation.

Hardwired systems

We've heard one company compare wiring a wireline security system with wiring a train set. If you can do one, you can do the other. (If you don't have a train set, buy one, install it, see whether the installation was hard, and then come back to reading this book.)

Wireline systems are

- **Reliable:** There are no batteries to worry about; wires are hidden reliably in the walls. Control panels routinely have battery backup in case the power fails.

- **Sophisticated:** Because the alarm industry has its roots in wireline installations, wireline systems are by far the more sophisticated systems. Most of the innovations have taken place with the wireline as a foundation.

- **Supervised:** Wireline systems are constantly in touch with their endpoint devices, querying them to check their health and availability. Doing so ensures that your system is at peak efficiency at all times.

On the other hand, wireline systems are much more complicated to install and are permanent after you install them.

Wireless systems

Wireless systems are easier to install than wireline systems, particularly if you're doing the work yourself after your house has been built.

Wireless systems are

- ✔ **Portable:** If you move, simply unplug the wireless system and take it with you to your next home. You can get monitoring services from anywhere in the U.S. All you need is electricity and a phone line.

- ✔ **Easy to use and install:** The only tool you need is a screwdriver. Some systems come in a nice tidy do-it-yourself package, such as Visonic's PowerMax+ (www.visonic.com) or X10's Protector Plus Wireless Security System (www.x10.com). These systems are shipped to you with simple instructions and 24-hour customer support (for all of those 2 a.m. installations!).

- ✔ **Private:** No strangers come into your house, drill holes in your walls, or know your home's layout or system password.

Wireless systems require you to change batteries, so if you're the type who hates to change the batteries in your smoke detectors, you may want to opt for a wireline system.

You may hear people say that wireless systems are less reliable and more prone to false alarms. Years ago, wireless systems were inferior to wireline systems (and lower-end wireless systems are still inferior to wireline systems), but manufacturers of wireline systems are feverishly bringing high-quality, reliable wireless interfaces to market today.

Wireless systems used to be totally unsupervised — meaning that the central control panel did not know whether the sensor batteries were running low or whether the sensors had some problem. Now, however, some of the more professional wireless systems (such as the Visonic product mentioned previously) include a supervision capability that makes them increasingly accepted as part of a wireline implementation. More than 25 percent of all alarm systems installed professionally are now hybrid wireline/wireless. We give you more information on supervision issues in Chapter 18.

Getting someone to do the job

You have two options when installing a home-security system — do it yourself or hire a professional contractor to do it for you. Most do-it-yourself projects are wireless in nature. You can buy a range of sensors and control panels from home-improvement stores or electronics stores.

You can also choose a kit that offers everything in one box. Most of these kits come with a control box, an alarm siren, and various combinations of wireless contact and keychain remote controls. One such vendor is X10 (www. X10.com), which sells several systems over the Internet. They also sell all sorts of add-ons for surveillance, appliance control, and more.

Few homeowners install wireline systems themselves (although they could do so easily during a remodel or new home construction). Rather, most homeowners hire professionals to install wireline security systems designed explicitly for their homes. Professional security installers provide a proposal and make recommendations on the type and location of each sensor. They may have promotional deals that provide you with a starter system.

The choice between putting in a security system yourself and hiring a professional is a matter of budget and preference. We recommend that you seriously consider hiring a professional to install this system. Messing up the cabling of your stereo system is one thing, but messing up your security system could be life threatening. Don't scrimp on your security system.

Some companies install a basic system in your home for free if you sign a long-term (usually five-year) agreement with them for monitoring services. The upside of these deals is a low initial cost. The downside is inadequate coverage and higher fees as you go along. Most of these secure-now, pay-later packages include coverage for only four doors or windows and a single motion sensor. If you want to expand your coverage, you have to pay high additional costs. Moreover, you lease the system rather than own it. Monitoring fees are higher, and you have to agree to a long-term contract with a hefty early-termination fee. Be sure to check out comparable deals with non-free systems and figure the costs over time; you're generally better off just paying for a system up front.

The National Burglar & Fire Alarm Association (http://alarm.org/info_ctr/consumer.htm) offers advice on how to shop for a security system as well as the names of contractors who have qualified for their Installation Quality certificate.

Chapter 18

Wiring a Security System

*H*ome-security systems are better suited for installation by professionals than by do-it-yourselfers. Too much is at stake, whether you think in terms of your family's safety or the potential troubles that an improperly installed system can cause (such as false alarms, which drive the police and fire departments crazy and can result in fines to the homeowner). If you're using a wireless system, do-it-yourself is feasible, but for a full-up wired security network, hire a professional.

That said, we think it's important to have an idea about what kinds of wiring and equipment make up a home-security system so that you can have an intelligent conversation with potential installers. This chapter discusses these wiring and architecture issues and explains how security systems work.

How to Prewire

The best place to start thinking about a home-security system is to look at how you can prewire your home to meet your short- and long-term security needs. In this section, we discuss the layout, or architecture, of a security system and the types of wire (or wireless systems) that connect the components of a security system.

Running a security loop

Your home-security system is based on the star architecture, in which every cable meets at a central wiring control panel (see Figure 18-1). Locating your wiring control panel in the central wiring closet that we describe in Chapter 2 makes sense; your control panel should be near the point where your telephone service comes into the house so that you can configure the system to call for help in an emergency. We cover this connection in the "Super supervision" section later in this chapter.

The cables that connect to the sensors and other elements of your security subsystem extend from the control panel. Although you can daisy-chain sensors — adding an extra sensor sometime after the initial installation to the line that runs to a nearby sensor — the control panel can't differentiate between devices that share a line to the control panel.

The cable that connects security devices generally contains two or four smaller wires called *conductors*. Half the wires cover the circuit that delivers information to the sensor; the other half delivers information back to the security control panel. The signals form a loop between the control panel and each sensor. These loops enable the control panel to tell whether the sensor is functioning correctly.

Wiring choices

You use the following main types of wire in typical alarm installations:

- **Normal telephone wire:** This is 22-gauge, four-conductor telephone wire.

- **Fire-alarm cable:** You must connect fire alarms with special fire-alarm cable that rates to 105 degrees centigrade so that it doesn't easily burn. You see this wiring strung as bright red cabling in your basement.

- **Intercom cable:** Some intercom systems allow you to add intercom-monitoring stations to the security system. If you decide on such a system, make sure that your installer uses special 22-gauge stranded and shielded wiring and grounds on every run. Failure to do so exposes the intercom system to electrical interference, which generates an annoying hum.

PIR motion detector

Alarm siren

Window sensor

Central
control
unit

Four-conductor wire

RJ-45   RJ-31X

Keypad

CAT-5e/6
UTP

Door sensor

Two-conductor phone wire

Figure 18-1:
A star-wired
security
loop.

Home data
network

Home phone
network

Telephone NID

Wiring for wireless

Prewiring for wireless systems may sound weird, but it makes sense. Few professional installations are totally wireless; you usually install some sort of hybrid system. Wireless systems don't require prewiring at each point where you install the wireless endpoints, but you need to be careful about where you install your phone line interfaces (as we discuss later in the chapter in the "Phone line interfaces" section) and how you tie your central system into your other wireline assets.

If you trip a wireless sensor, it sends a high-frequency coded signal to the central station, which interprets and acts on the signal as necessary. Wireless systems basically act just like wired ones, sending electrical signals to and from sensors, keypads, and central stations, but the wireless systems use radio signals instead of cabling to send and receive the signals.

Good news for basement dwellers

Unlike other subsystem wiring schemes, security systems are expandable because so much of the wiring runs through the basement ceiling and then up short distances to the first-floor terminations. (In most cases, you don't need many sensors on upper floors.) So, unless you use sheetrock or otherwise close off your ceiling in the basement, running an extra cable shouldn't be an issue if you decide to add another sensor or end device. As long as you have an unfinished basement or drop ceiling, you don't need to overbuild your system. You merely install what you need today and add on to the system when you want to expand.

Beware of all-in-one wireless security solutions. These systems are wireless designs for apartments and other smaller applications that combine a *passive infrared receiver,* or *PIR,* with a siren. (We explain how these passive units monitor the infrared spectrum in Chapter 17.) When the PIR detects a burglar, the siren sounds to alert the family or frighten the burglar away. In practice, however, these systems are questionable because many issue a beeping tone if you trip them, which enables you to disarm the unit with a user-entered code. This time delay gives a burglar a chance to locate the alarm device and smash it before the siren goes off.

All Zoned Out

The central security control panel tracks each circuit as a separate *zone,* and ideally, each circuit connects to only one sensor or device. So if you have a room with three window contacts and a passive infrared receiver, you have four zones here, not one. Typical security control panels for home applications can monitor 6 to 48 zones.

Zones enable the control panel to query the status of each device and interpret the inputs from each device. By tracking triggers sequentially from three related zones, for example, you can interpret that someone is walking a specific direction down a hallway.

Still, in some cases, you may need to run multiple sensors on the same circuit, known as dividing a zone into *subzones.* The drawback to the subzone approach is that all the sensors that connect to the same circuit appear as a single sensor to the control panel. If you connect a door, a window sensor, and a PIR to the same circuit, you can't tell which is causing the alarm.

Phone lines — the weak link

The most vulnerable part of your security system is your phone line interface. Your phone line isn't monitored. The alarm system relies on that phone line to call the monitoring station and implicitly assumes that it's always there. And the monitoring service, which may be located hundreds of miles away, also assumes that the line is there and working.

As a result, many phone-line-based alarm systems are vulnerable if someone cuts the phone line before entering the house and tripping the alarm. As you're building your house, think about hardening the access to your telephone lines. In new subdivisions, the builders usually bury many of these lines, which is great. Many other homes, however, have exposed NIDs (network interface devices) on the outside of the

house, and the telephone line is in plain view. If your telephone company requires an outside interface, work with them to protect it as much as possible with a lock box and hardened conduit.

You can also buy a special alarm line called a *derived channel* from your local telephone company. The phone company puts a little black box in the central telephone office serving you and another box where the line from your house ends. This second box creates a subaudible two-way communication that provides a channel for your alarm's supervision. If the signal trips open, the central station gets a signal signifying that the phone line is down. Because of its cost, which is about $45 per month, the derived-channel approach has never taken off.

Wireless systems work by zones, too. Each wireless device that's part of a professional installation has its own port on the control panel, just like on the wireline devices. The wireless devices typically communicate in the 300- to 900-MHz frequencies, which are highly reliable — unless a lot of radio activity is nearby.

Super supervision

A key element of your security subsystem is the concept of *supervision,* which is the capability of an alarm system to sense the status of any attached device.

The control panel continuously monitors its attached devices — how often and which things it monitors vary from panel to panel. Among the things that most systems monitor for are power failure, telephone line trouble, loss of internal clock, trouble in any part of the system, low-battery conditions, attempts to tamper with systems, and other internal faults.

Typically once a week, the alarm system sends in test signal to the central monitoring station. You'd be amazed at the number of customers whose systems aren't functional. People install computers on telephone lines, and the telephone installer may reroute or cause problems with the same phone line that your subsystem is on. People put additions on their houses and mess up wiring. Lots of simple things can conspire to throw part of your security system into chaos, which is why supervision is so important.

Wireless supervision

Wireless systems need supervision to be successful, too. Control panels that support wireless systems should also enable you to supervise these devices. Unsupervised wireless systems can detect whether a sensor circuit opens. This sort of system can tell you whether someone opens the front door, for example, but can't tell you the state of the remote sensors at any particular time. It can't, for example, tell you that its batteries are low.

Supervised wireless systems mimic wireline systems. Typically, the system sends each wireless zone a supervisory round every so often. If the receiver hears from the wireless device at least once during that query, it doesn't report a problem. If it doesn't receive a response, it treats the situation just as it does any other fault and reports a problem with the system to the monitoring station.

Within the supervisory transmission, the system usually queries the device about the status of the battery. If the battery is low, the system reports a fault.

Connecting to Other Systems

The power of your security system is measured not only by its inherent capabilities but also by what subsystems you can add to it.

Phone line interfaces

If you can afford it, a monitoring service should remotely monitor your security system. Your control panel then dials the alarm-monitoring service if any event that you programmed into your system occurs.

To dial out, your system needs access to an outside phone line. In most cases, it accesses the phone line that you use as your home telephone number, unless you opt for derived-channel service. (See the "Phone lines — the weak link" sidebar.)

The alarm system must be *inline* with your service, meaning that the telephone line physically runs through the panel on its way to your in-home telephone network. If something trips a sensor, the system seizes the telephone line to make an outbound call. The alarm system uses a piggybacked jack with a shorting bridge that disconnects the rest of the home-phone network. In doing so, the system effectively disconnects all the phones in the house while it makes that outbound call for help.

Stand-alone wireless systems, such as those you find at the do-it-yourself outlets, enable you to merely plug them into the nearest phone outlet in the house. But if someone leaves a phone off the hook or if the phone is in use as the alarm trips, the wireless system can't seize the line and make the emergency call for help. For this reason, we recommend that you don't install a wireless system from a normal telephone extension in the house. Instead, run a phone line to the inline jack at the control box where your phone line enters the house.

Don't connect the alarm-panel communicator to telephone lines that you use with a fax machine. Fax-machine lines may incorporate a voice filter, which disconnects the line if it detects anything other than fax signals. This filter can result in partial transmissions to the monitoring center.

Your central security control panel connects with your home-phone lines with an *RJ-31X connection.* This interface — called the digital communicator — transmits the signal from the control panel to the central monitoring station. The connection is straightforward; the conductors from the local telephone line connect to the panel and then route back out of the panel to connect with the in-home telephones. One of the big advantages of the RJ-31X interface is that it enables you to dial into your system from a phone to do stuff such as turn the system on and off or turn up the temperature inside the house.

You can add enhanced phone functionality to your house through your alarm system. Sounds backwards, doesn't it? But because the alarm system is in-line with your phone connections, it can act as a gatekeeper to all the phones in the house. For instance, ADEMCO (www.ademco.com) has a TeleSmart module for its VISTA security systems that adds a digital answering machine to your alarm system. With TeleSmart, homeowners can arm or disarm their security system, check messages, screen calls, block calls, and more. Additional features include caller ID, memory and repeat dial, customized mailboxes for up to four family members, and a family message center that lets users record, play back, and retrieve voice memos.

Alternative phone line interfaces

Having the control panel send alarm signals to a remote monitoring station is not the only way to accomplish your goal of getting help if an emergency arises. Other possibilities are the focus of this section.

One alternative to having a phone line connection to the central security control panel is to use wireless communications — cellular phone technologies, for example — to dial into the remote monitoring station. You can use wireless technologies as an alternative to a phone line connection or as a supplement (in case someone cuts the phone line). At least two national networks are vying to get your wireless monitoring business: Uplink (www.uplink.com) and Honeywell's Alarmnet (http://www.security.honeywell.com/hsce/solutions/alarmnet/index.html), both of which use cellular and wireless data networks to carry signals between your local control panel and the monitoring station. These networks enable two-way wireless alarm communications to any monitoring station. Your alarm installer should be familiar with both of these services and can provide you with details about equipment requirements and pricing.

Home-control interfaces

Various control panels sport X10, ZigBee, Z-Wave, or other home-control modules that can also turn your lights on and off through the addition of programming and timers. By using such modules, you can program your security system so that if the fire alarm goes off, for example, you can turn on specific lights to guide you out of the house.

You can program more sophisticated systems, such as those that we discuss in Chapter 20, to utilize the inputs from your sensors to perform all sorts of tasks. You can use a driveway sensor that you connect to your security panel to issue home-automation commands that turn on the garage and porch lights, for example, or sound a chime in the home office.

X10.com (www.x10.com) has keychain-fob interfaces for its Monitor Plus security system that work from up to 40 feet away. You can arm and disarm the system with the press of a single button as you pull into the driveway! Modes on the remote include arm (instant mode), disarm, control of lights, and a panic feature to trip the system immediately. Each remote effectively has a unique code that is identified to the alarm panel so that only the remotes that the user has set up can be used to control the system. Napco (www.napcosecurity.com) has a fob unit with eight intuitive icons for system status that show up on an LCD display. Additionally, corresponding beep sequences on the min-isounder confirm commands. BellSouth (www.bellsouth.com/security/) issues these as standard on its security services. So much for having to remember a code or special siren sequences.

TECHNICAL STUFF

Serial port connections via RS-232?

A few home-security systems, such as those made by Napco (www.napcosecurity. com), provide an electronic interface known as *RS-232*. This connection is basically the same kind that the serial port on most PCs use. If you install a security panel with an RS-232 interface and you also have a home-automation controller with its own RS-232 input, you can connect them to get even more sophisticated sensor-to-automation relationships.

Why doesn't everyone use RS-232? Well, that involves a big problem. Although the RS-232 interface itself is standardized and common, the programming code that works the alarms and home-automation controllers is proprietary. So a security panel from manufacturer X may not be capable of talking to a home-automation controller from company Y. This lack of compatibility can be a major pain in the neck, although some companies are beginning to open up their programming to ensure interoperability.

Right now, security and automation interfacing is iffy. Unless you're a serial-programming expert, you need to leave this kind of system integration to a professional installer who's trained on both alarm and automation systems.

Audio interfaces

Some alarm systems enable you to connect a number of standard interior and exterior intercom stations or sensors to your alarm system. You can use these for listening in on the baby, playing background music, seeing who's at the door, answering incoming phone calls, and paging people around the house. A neat feature of such systems is that the central station can also access these intercoms, so monitoring agents can listen and talk through these systems.

Broadband interfaces

The Internet interface is a natural extension of the security subsystem, and some of the more progressive firms are making use of it. With a constant broadband connection to the Internet, you can have constant connections to your monitoring center and not have to rely on grabbing a dial-up phone line to communicate your status. You can also set up Web-based interfaces to control various aspects of your security system, including real-time video.

Two things about this connection are critical: the speed of the connection (how much information can be crammed up and down your access line) and the fact that the connection is always on, meaning that your home is always connected to the Internet. These systems use two-way communications that confirm your system is online and working, and the sheer size of the bandwidth available means you can do all sorts of neat things to provide service.

An example of a broadband security-monitoring service comes from a company called NextAlarm (www.nextalarm.com). NextAlarm's service uses a specialized version of VoIP (Voice over IP) hardware (we discuss VoIP hardware in Chapters 11 and 12) to connect a standard alarm panel to the central monitoring station. (The Web site lists the many panels that work with the service.)

Broadband alarm services provide all the standard alarm-response services you'd expect from any alarm-monitoring service, but use the always-on nature of the Internet connection to add additional features. For example, NextAlarm provides an extra layer of security assurance by pinging the alarm panel to confirm the connection every five minutes (traditional phone line systems do this only once a day). The Internet-based system also provides additional alerting and control mechanisms that are effectively real time — you can receive alerts or check your system's status by logging onto a Web page, through e-mail or SMS (text messages) to your cell phone, or by dialing into an IVR (Interactive Voice Response) unit from any phone.

The coolest part of services like NextAlarm's are that they cost less to operate than traditional phone line services — in fact, NextAlarm's most basic service is free!

Make sure that you have a UPS, or *uninterruptible power supply,* connected to your broadband modem, router, and the broadband alarm adapter itself. Unlike conventional phone lines (which get their power from the phone company), broadband connections go out when the power goes out. A UPS will keep things up and running typically for 30 to 90 minutes while the lights are out.

Part VI
Putting It All Together — Home Automation and Control

The 5th Wave   By Rich Tennant

"The kids are getting up right now.
When we wired the house we added
vibrating pager technology to
their bunkbeds."

In this part . . .

In a sense, we're reaching the climax of the book! This part is where it all comes together, where your home network really hums (but your wiring doesn't). This is where your house reaches the status of a smart home.

We describe two closely interrelated topics: home-control and home-automation systems, and remote-control systems for your home's entertainment networks. Both topics help you interconnect and take advantage of all the other subsystems — audio, video, telephony, computer LAN, security, and so on. We discuss traditional methods of automating and controlling the devices in your home (such as X-10) and get you up to speed on a new generation of controlling protocols such as ZigBee, Z-Wave, and LonWorks. Finally, we talk about the systems used to control your controllers, using touchscreens, PCs, and other devices.

Chapter 19

Home Automation Extravaganza

*I*n other chapters, we describe how to create a backbone that enables you to distribute various kinds of signals around your smart home. The next step — one that can make things more useful and more fun — is to install a home-control and home-automation network that can help you take charge of your smart home's subsystems.

You can get an amazingly wide range of home-control and home-automation systems — everything from simple X10 powerline controls that cost in the tens of dollars to custom-built proprietary networks that cost in the tens of thousands of dollars. In this chapter, we give you a taste of what's on the market and what these devices can do. We also talk a bit about some emerging standards that can make home automation and control easier, cheaper, and better than what's available today.

Where an Automated Home Begins — and Ends

An automated home can be a simple grouping of controls, such as a few lamps that turn themselves on and off, or it can be an extravaganza, where just about everything electrically powered is remotely controlled. The great thing is that you can start small and grow over time.

Any home-automation and home-control system includes the following basic elements:

- **Protocol:** The common language that all the devices in the home-automation network understand. X10 is the predominant protocol in home automation today, but it's being rapidly supplanted by new protocols such as ZigBee, Z-Wave, and INSTEON.

- **Wiring infrastructure:** The wires that carry signals to each automation or control device in the network. Many home-automation systems (including X10) use the existing electrical wiring to transmit signals, but a few require special wiring. Other systems (such as ZigBee or Z-Wave) use wireless technologies so you need no wires at all.

- **Controller device:** A device that sends signals over the infrastructure in a way that conforms to the protocol. The signals tell specific pieces of equipment what to do.

  Some of the newer home-automation systems can work in a *peer-to-peer* environment, where you don't need a centralized controller. In these cases you can let individual devices send commands to your equipment; for example, a Z-Wave light switch could communicate with a bunch of other switches to send elaborate commands without the use of a stand-alone centralized controller. You may still want to add a centralized control device so you can use the controller's interface (which often uses a TV or computer screen and is designed for ease of use) or to get involved in more complex automation tasks (such as integrating access from outside the home).

- **Device controllers:** Because most appliances and electronic devices aren't designed from the factory to be automated or remotely controlled, you need individual controllers that can respond to signals from the main controller device and make individual components do what you want them to do — such as turn on and off.

The big difference among the various implementations of home networking comes in the realm of controllers. You can start off with a small, stand-alone controller that costs about $40, or you can go with a high-end PC-type controller that runs into the thousands of dollars. (You can find much cheaper PC controllers, however.) These PC-type controllers can be software and hardware interfaces for a general-purpose PC in your home, or they can be stand-alone PC-like hardware devices purpose-built for home-automation control.

Understanding the Protocols

Just as data networks in your home use a *protocol* (Ethernet for wired networks and Ethernet plus Wi-Fi for wireless networks), home-automation systems use their own networking protocols to facilitate communications over powerlines, wireless systems, or even special proprietary cables. The first decision you'll need to make when you're considering a home-automation system is which of the several protocols you'll want to use.

There's no reason why you can't have more than one protocol in your home — perhaps some devices controlled over the powerlines using X10, LonWorks, or INSTEON, and others controlled wirelessly using ZigBee or Z-Wave. You just need to have a controller that can "speak" both protocols. However, we don't recommend that you mix and match protocols on the same *physical media* — meaning we wouldn't use, for example, both ZigBee and Z-Wave in the same home.

Six major home-automation and home-control protocols are on the market as we write:

- ✔ **X10:** X10 is the granddaddy of home automation, having been around since the 1970s. X10 uses your home's powerlines to communicate its commands around the home and can control up to 256 different devices. Each X10 device is configured with a *house code* (A through P) and a *unit code* (1-16) — 16 letters times 16 numbers equals the 256 devices that can be controlled. X10 devices can be *one-way* or *two-way* (many of the least expensive are one-way); one-way devices receive commands but can send no confirmation that they did so, which means your controller may think it has turned a light on when it hasn't. X10 is the cheapest of all systems but also the least reliable (powerlines are tough to communicate over) and the slowest (you can control only one device at a time, and it takes several seconds to issue a command). You can find X10 equipment at most home automation stores and online at suppliers such as www.x10.com or www.x10pro.com.

- ✔ **Universal Powerline Bus (UPB):** This standard was developed in the late 1990s by a company called Powerline Control Systems (PCS, www.pcs lighting.com) and is designed to be a faster and more reliable alternative to X10. Like X10, UPB uses powerlines (which you probably guessed by the name!) for communications. UPB is a two-way, peer-to-peer system with data rates up to 20 to 40 times faster than X10, so a command can be sent and received in a tenth of a second, instead of multiple seconds in an X10 environment.

- ✔ **INSTEON:** The folks at SmartLabs (www.smartlabs.com) run one of the biggest online stores for home-automation gear. They also have a big engineering team that develops their own equipment and devices. One outgrowth of that has been the development of the INSTEON home-automation protocol, SmartLab's replacement for X10. INSTEON-enabled devices can communicate either over powerlines or using wireless communications (modules are wireless only, powerline only, or use both media), and can work in a peer-to-peer or centralized environment.

INSTEON's main advantages over X10 are increased reliability and a much faster data rate (about 13Kbps versus X10's 20 bits per second). SmartLabs has licensed the technology to a number of companies, and the best place to find INSTEON equipment online is at `www.smarthome.com`.

✔ **ZigBee:** ZigBee is wireless automation networking standard based on an international standard (called IEEE 802.15.4 — similar to the 802.11 standards used for Wi-Fi networks). ZigBee systems use a peer-to-peer networking infrastructure, and furthermore use something called *mesh networking* to extend their reach. In a mesh network, a module or other ZigBee-enabled device not only communicates with other devices and controllers for its own commands but can also be used to relay commands on to devices elsewhere in the home. So the more devices you have in a mesh network, the better your coverage. ZigBee provides a much higher data rate than X10 (at 250 Kbps, it's more than 1000 times faster), while using chips that are very inexpensive to manufacture. A group called the ZigBee Alliance (`www.zigbee.org`) — similar to the Wi-Fi Alliance — is helping manufacturers bring ZigBee products to market and to ensure that they work well together. As we write, only a few ZigBee products are on the market, but dozens of manufacturers have joined the Alliance.

✔ **Z-Wave:** A Danish semiconductor company called Zensys (`www.zen-sys.com`) has developed a competitor to ZigBee called Z-Wave. Z-Wave is a wireless mesh peer-to-peer automation networking protocol that's similar to ZigBee. Z-Wave systems operate at speeds of up to 9.6 Kbps (slower than ZigBee, but still more than fast enough for home automation and control). Z-Wave products are still new to the market, but several major manufacturers, such as Leviton (`www.leviton.com`) and Wayne Dalton (`http://www.waynedalton.com`), are shipping products using Z-Wave.

✔ **LonWorks:** Outside of the home, LonWorks is perhaps the most successful automation networking protocol of all — and most home owners and builders have never heard of it because LonWorks is used in millions of *commercial* applications (not in *residential* applications). Like X10, LonWorks uses the powerline, but it does so in a much more robust and reliable fashion and at much faster speeds. The folks who developed LonWorks (Echelon Corporation, `www.echelon.com`) are beginning to bring the LonWorks system to the smart homes market. Tens of millions of LonWorks chips are already installed around the world, and this volume has allowed the company to create low-priced chipsets, which will soon be marketed to homeowners and builders for residential automation applications.

A bit more about X10

X10 actually refers to two things: a protocol and a company name. (We lied — it refers to *three* companies' names.) X10 is the dominant protocol for controlling (turning on and off) electrical devices such as lights and appliances through your home's electrical lines. Three X10–named companies are involved in the X10 automation industry: X10 Limited bought the original patent for X10 technology back in the 1980s and held the patent until it expired in 1997; X10Pro is a subsidiary of X10 Limited and builds X10 equipment for the professional installer market; and X10 Wireless Technologies is a manufacturing and marketing partner of X10 Limited that sells X10 equipment directly to consumers.

Confused yet? Most people type `www.X10.com` in their Web browser and find the third one, X10 Wireless Technologies. If you want to find X10Pro on the Web, type `www.X10pro.com`. X10 Limited doesn't sell anything to consumers under that name, so don't bother trying to find that one.

X10 is now an open standard, sold by the two X10 companies mentioned, as well as by other companies, such as Leviton and Stanley. We use the term *X10* to refer to the protocol or to mean a device that's compatible with the X10 protocol because thinking of X10 in this way reminds you that you don't need to buy from one of the X10 companies to get X10. All compatible products display an X10-compatible logo on their packaging or on the product itself; when you see this logo, you know that the product works with other X10 products regardless of manufacturer.

Understanding the Components

Regardless of which protocol you choose, the controller devices you'll use are similar. The basic building block of a home-automation system is a *module* or *switch* designed to control the state (on/off, dim, and so on) of an electrical or electronic device. These modules (we'll use that term generically to cover the entire spectrum) communicate with a controller or even amongst each other using one of the automation protocols discussed in the preceding section, and translate the commands communicated by the protocol into actions.

Modules

If you look in a home-automation catalog or go to a place that carries home-automation gear, such as Radio Shack or Home Depot, you'll find home-automation modules ranging from generic lamp modules to specialized devices that control specific pieces of equipment. The main distinctions among modules are as follows:

✔ **The kind of device they control:** Modules that control devices such as lamps are cheaper (and handle less electrical current) than those that turn on and off such high-powered devices as electrical dryers.

✔ **The control signals they can understand:** The simplest modules know how to turn things on and off in response to a control signal. More sophisticated modules can perform additional functions, such as lamp dimming or brightening or ceiling-fan speed adjustments.

✔ **The automation protocol they use:** It probably goes without saying, but we're saying it anyway! Another important characteristic of any module is which of the many home-automation protocols (discussed in the preceding section) the module uses for communications around the home. You've got to choose a protocol and stick with it!

✔ **Whether they're one-way or two-way:** Most X10 modules are one-way — that is, they receive control signals but don't respond back to the central controller to tell it that the module has performed an action. The least expensive modules don't offer a confirmation signal back to the controller, but a new breed of two-way modules provides this status confirmation. Newer protocols are inherently two-way, which is a great advantage because your system will always know the true *state* of devices being controlled, instead of "hoping" that your commands went through.

If you're using X10, keep in mind that sometimes (oftentimes in some homes), electrical noise and interference on a home's powerlines can prevent an X10 module from understanding or receiving the X10 signals. The new two-way modules tell you (or your controller) whether a command worked, which is a handy feature for such important commands as starting the coffee pot in the morning. Most of the modules that we discuss in this chapter are available in both one-way and two-way configurations. You can use them interchangeably in an X10 network, but only two-way modules send confirmation signals back to a two-way compatible controller.

The following sections describe some of the modules available for your use.

Lamp modules

The simplest and most common modules are *lamp modules*. These modules simply plug into any standard 110-volt AC outlet, between the lamp cord and the outlet. You can use these modules only with incandescent bulbs, usually up to 300 watts. (Check the labeling as you're choosing a module to make sure that it can handle the type of bulb involved.)

Lamp modules respond to on and off commands for the particular house and unit codes that you assign to the module. They respond also to all-on/all-off commands from your controller — commands that turn on or off (you guessed it) all the lights in the house that the modules control. In addition, many lamp modules respond to dim/brighten commands that a controller issues, so you can set the mood for dinner or a movie — or whatever you have in mind.

There's a big push afoot to have folks swap out their incandescent bulbs for *CFL* (compact fluorescent lights), due to the great energy savings these bulbs offer. When you are controlling fluorescent lights, you need to use lamp modules specifically designed to work with these types of bulbs for the following reasons:

✔ Most fluorescent bulbs can't be dimmed, so you need a module that doesn't try to dim them! A few dimmable CFLs are on the market (at about $18 a bulb) but the vast majority are not dimmable.

✔ Fluorescent bulbs can interfere with powerline signals. If you're using X10, UPB, or Insteon, you may get "noise" on the line that keeps your signals from being properly transmitted around the house. Special fluorescent lamp modules can filter out most of that noise — you may also want to consider a wireless automation protocol if you're planning on controlling a lot of fluorescents.

Appliance modules

For all the stuff in your house that uses a bit more juice (electrically speaking), you want *appliance modules.* These modules can handle the higher draws of electric current required by devices such as coffeemakers, portable heaters, and other household appliances.

You don't find dim/bright commands on most appliance modules, which makes sense because you can't really dim a coffee pot. You also don't find an all-on function on these modules, which is for safety reasons — some devices that connect to appliance modules are things that you *don't* want to turn on if you're just trying to light the house by turning on all of your *lamp modules.* You do usually find an all-off command — if you want everything off, you generally want *everything* off.

You can find appliance modules in both 110-volt AC and 220-volt AC versions. Heavy-duty stuff, such as hot tubs, window air conditioners, and clothes dryers, may require the 220-volt versions.

Universal modules

Universal modules (sometimes called *low-voltage modules*) are special-purpose appliance modules that control the electrical and electronic devices in a home that a *relay* (or remote switch) turns on and off. These devices include garage-door openers, electric drapery controls, sprinkler systems, and low-voltage lighting systems (such as yard lights and some track lighting).

You can set the universal module to provide a *momentary* or *continuous* relay closure. You might use the momentary mode for the garage-door opener (which creates the equivalent of pressing the open/close button) and the continuous mode for sprinklers and other devices that you want to remain on until you turn them off.

Universal modules don't receive all-on or dim/brighten signals (for the same reason that appliance modules don't) but do receive all-off commands.

Receptacles

Most modules are small and discrete, but for a truly invisible appearance, you can have your electrician install in-wall receptacles. These outlets are the same size and shape as conventional power receptacles but function the same as appliance modules. The main consideration in installing receptacles is whether you want the automation system to control one or both outlets in the receptacle. Some models have a controlled outlet on top and an always-live regular outlet on the bottom.

Duplex automated wall receptacles offer control over both outlets. We often see companies marketing these kinds of receptacles to parents who want to ensure that their kids aren't watching TV beyond certain time limits. After TV time is over, the controller can turn off the outlet and disable the TV set in the children's room. Boy, will *that* make them mad!

Switches

Another way to make automation connections less visible in your home is to have your electrician install automated *wall switches* to control hardwired lights, fans, and other devices. These switches enable both local and automated control of the devices that the electrician wires to them — so you can have your controller turn a light on or off, or you can just walk over to the switch and do it yourself.

If you use two-way automated switches, they can inform your intelligent controller that you manually changed the state of the switch (from on to off or vice versa). If you don't have two-way switches, you can end up getting your control system out of whack by manually controlling a switch. This system confusion arises when the switch is manually set to a different position (on or off) than the controller thinks it is set to.

You need to consider the following points when purchasing wall switches:

- ✔ Special switches (known as three-way *master* and *slave* switches) are necessary for applications in which more than one switch controls a particular light. Regular switches can't handle this job because they can't keep track of the light's status when another switch turns the light on or off. Three-way switches can communicate with each other to keep track of this status.

✔ Switches with dimmer functions work only with incandescent light fixtures — not with fluorescent lighting systems.

✔ Ceiling fans and low-voltage lighting sources (such as halogen track lighting) require a specific *inductive* switch — which by design specifically controls fan speeds or dims and brightens low-voltage lights.

✔ Certain 220-volt devices — such as pool pumps, hot-tub heaters, and some air conditioners — require special heavy-duty switches because of the large amount of electrical current they draw.

With the newer peer-to-peer automation systems such as Z-Wave and ZigBee, wall switches can take on the role of controller (discussed in the next section). You can program one switch in a room or section of your house to send commands to multiple modules or switches.

Controllers

All the automation modules, receptacles, and switches in the world aren't useful without some means of controlling them remotely. Luckily, you have at least as many options for controlling automation systems as you have module options.

Standard controllers range from $10 X10 minicontrollers, which provide remote control (but not automation) of a number of modules, to $500 touch-screen controllers that provide a more sophisticated means of controlling your network. Throw into the mix wireless controllers, specialized lighting controllers, telephone-activated controllers, timers, controllers that activate by light (or darkness), controllers that your security system triggers, voice controllers, and even controllers that use your PC to run your home network, and you have quite a selection to peruse. And that's not even considering some of the high-end, proprietary systems that control X10 systems, HVAC systems, alarms, and other controllers.

The sheer number of choices in the controller world can be a bit bewildering, but we have some good news: You don't need to limit yourself to just one controller. You can start small and then supplement your controller inventory with more sophisticated models as you expand your automation network — while keeping the original controllers active in the network.

You could begin with just a simple minicontroller, for example. Then as you expand your network, use a PC-based controller system to automate your entire house. You don't need to throw the minicontroller out; transfer it to the master bedroom and use it to control certain lights or appliances that you want to turn on and off from the comfort of your bed.

As we discuss controllers, whenever we use *module*, we're also including automation receptacles and switches. We just figured that you didn't want to read *module or receptacle or switch* a whole bunch of times.

The following sections describe some of the various controllers available.

Stand-alone controllers

The simplest and most inexpensive controllers are *stand-alone* controllers. These devices don't need a PC — or anything else — to operate. Just plug them into a wall outlet, program them to match the house and unit codes, and you're ready to go.

Minicontrollers and tabletop controllers

Among stand-alone controllers, the cheapest and easiest to install and set up are *minicontrollers*. These small boxes simply send on/off, all-on/all-off, and dim/brighten commands to a small number of X10 devices (usually eight). The minicontroller doesn't do any automation — that is, it requires input from a person to perform a task — but it does provide you with remote control from anywhere in the house.

Tabletop controllers do basically the same thing as minicontrollers — the only real difference is that they can control a larger number of modules (and they're bigger).

Programmable controllers and timers

The next step up in controllers — *programmable,* or *timer,* controllers — begins to offer a degree of home automation to complement the home-control functions of minicontrollers. These devices, which you mount on a wall or place on a desk or table, enable you to control a number of automation modules (usually eight or sixteen) manually or automatically.

To make the controller work automatically, you simply need to program the controller to perform a command or sequence of commands at a particular time. So you can, for example, tell your controller to turn on modules A1 (the kitchen lights) and A2 (the coffee pot) at 6:30 a.m. every Monday through Friday. This kind of automation isn't the end-all in sophistication, but it's a good way to get started down the road to an automated home.

Telephone interfaces

You don't need to be in the house to control your automation modules. By installing a *telephone interface,* you can dial into your network from any Touch-Tone phone and turn on the lights or get the hot tub warming up before you get home from the office.

Telephone interfaces plug into a phone line (using a telephone cord with a standard RJ-11 jack) and into any power receptacle in the house, and use Touch-Tone keypad tones to perform various control actions in your home. Prices for these devices range from about $70 for a simple unit that controls ten modules up to about $300 for units that can control one hundred or more modules.

When choosing a phone interface for your X10 network, look for the following features:

- ✔ **Local control:** Some phone interfaces enable you not only to dial in remotely, but also to pick up any phone (on the same line) in your home and enter commands.

- ✔ **Voice enunciator:** More expensive models have built-in *voice enunciators,* which confirm your commands (a handy feature if you're not sure whether you just turned on the porch light or the hot tub).

- ✔ **Answering-machine mode:** Some models enable you to put an *answering machine* on the same phone line as the controller, an important feature if you have only one phone line in the house. To use the controller, you just ignore the beep on your answering machine and punch in your commands. This feature doesn't work with telephone-company-provided voice-mail services, however, and may not work with every answering machine.

Sensor controllers and interfaces

Although programmable and timer controllers add some degree of automation to your home network, they're basically dumb devices. A certain time passes, and they initiate commands that you previously programmed into them. That's handy, but what happens if you want a command to activate under circumstances that don't adhere to a predictable schedule? What if, for example, you want the lights in your hallway to come on whenever your children walk to the bathroom in the middle of the night? (And believe Danny when he tells you that no predictable schedule exists for that.)

For these kinds of scenarios, you may want to use sensor-initiated controllers, such as those described in the following list:

- ✔ **PIR controllers:** These controllers send out a control signal whenever a passive infrared (PIR) motion detector picks up someone walking into a room (or past your back door in the middle of the night).

- ✔ **Photo sensors:** These controllers send out control signals as it gets dark outside (or, alternatively, as the sun rises).

- ✔ **Alarm interfaces:** These controllers use an input from your security system and sensors from the alarm system to trigger control commands.

Wireless controllers

After you start getting an automated home up and running, you're likely to find that you have less and less inclination even to get up and walk over to the controller sitting on the table across the living room from your comfy couch. Luckily, automation manufacturers have exactly the answer you need if you face this problem: *wireless controllers.*

For wireless automation protocols such as ZigBee and Z-Wave (and some INSTEON devices), the wireless controller is a self-contained unit. Put batteries in it, program it (typically using a USB connection to your PC), and you're ready to go. For automation protocols that use powerlines, wireless controllers consist of two parts — an *RF (radio frequency) receiver,* which plugs into the wall (and sends the actual commands over the powerline), and the handheld or tabletop *RF transmitter.* Some of these handheld remotes also serve double duty as IR remote controls, so you can use a single remote to control the TV and audio systems as well as the lights.

You can find wireless controllers in all sizes and shapes, ranging from sixteen-device controllers for the living-room table to small three- or four-module controllers that can hang on your keychain. (These smaller devices are great for controlling the modules that open your garage door or turn on your porch lights.)

The fanciest of these wireless controllers — such as those sold by Monster Cable (www.monstercable.com) and Leviton (www.leviton.com) in partnership or those sold by Logitech Harmony Remotes (www.logitech.com/harmony) — have advanced programmability and are essentially slightly less expensive versions of the touch panels we discuss next. There's a thin line between high-end wireless controllers and touch panels.

Touch panels

The fanciest controllers are the programmable *touch-screen panels* made by companies such as SmartHome Manufacturing (at www.smartlinc.com) and Control4 (www.control4.com). For about $500, these controllers enable you to control and automate hundreds of modules by using a touch-sensitive LCD screen.

You can use these systems also to create *macros,* or sequences of actions that you want to trigger through a single touchpad command or a timed, programmed command. Most touch-panel controllers are also compatible with two-way modules, so you can see an on-screen confirmation that your action has been performed.

The combination of two-way modules and macro capability also enables these controllers to set devices to certain levels of brightness. If you want to set a light to a medium level of brightness, for example, this type of controller can turn on the light, send a dim signal a certain number of times (to reach your desired level of brightness), and then confirm remotely that the light is set where you want it.

If you're going to shell out a significant amount of money for a touch panel or other high-end controller, get one that is two-way compatible and buy modules that can do two-way communications. These systems will make sure that your control signals get to modules in your home and are carried out.

PC interfaces

If you want to get fancy with an automation network, you can supplement or replace your stand-alone controllers with a *PC-based control system.* These controllers use the horsepower of your PC and the familiar graphical interface of Windows (or the Macintosh) to enable you to set up and control all automation modules in your home.

The majority of PC-based controllers are two-way capable, so they control and monitor the status of two-way modules. Many also provide inputs from external sensors such as temperature monitors and photo sensors and use these inputs to trigger commands.

Following are the two key components of a PC-based controller:

- ✔ **Control software:** Lets you program and control your automation network using a graphical interface on your PC.

- ✔ **Interface unit:** Connects your computer to the home's control network, using the home-automation protocol you've chosen.

Most interface units connect to one of your PC's USB ports, but you can find other interfaces, such as internal PC cards. You may think that you can just use your computer's own powerline connection to the wall to do your controlling, but the internal design of a PC doesn't allow this. That's why you need this interface unit to create and send control signals over your home's powerlines.

Most PC interface units download and save your preferred settings in their internal memory, so you don't need to keep your PC running for your automation system to work. Some systems, however, require a PC that's always on (and always has the home-automation software running). Unless you have an extra PC that you can dedicate to your home-automation network, think long and hard about this requirement. On the other hand, if you have an old computer sitting around, this sort of setup may be a great use for it.

You can interface with your PC home-automation software in the following ways:

✔ **Keyboard:** The simplest and most common way to set up and control PC-based automation software is to use your keyboard and mouse. Using a graphical interface, you can sit in front of your computer and program timed and macro events for your controller to perform, or you can manually control modules.

✔ **Telephone:** By using your computer's modem, you can dial into your home controller or PC from remote locations and trigger automation commands using Touch-Tone key commands.

✔ **Internet:** With a broadband, always-on Internet connection (such as DSL or a cable modem) and the right software, you can access your automation software from anywhere in the world using a Web browser. Your PC turns into a Web server, creating remotely accessible Web pages displaying the status and controls for your house.

✔ **Voice:** The neatest way to utilize PC control of your automation network is by voice command. Systems such as HAL2000 (check out www.automatedliving.com for information) enable you to use a telephone connection or a microphone connected to your PC to speak commands into your computer to trigger automation commands. These systems not only listen to (and obey) you but also answer back to provide confirmation of your spoken commands.

Lights, AC (Powerline), Action

One of the most important areas of home automation is control over your lighting systems. When we say *control,* we mean more than just turning lights on and off (though that can be useful). With a true lighting-control system, you can move beyond on and off and into the world of *scenes,* which allow you to control groups of lights in a room or throughout the house to set the mood for various occasions.

For example, you might have a scene programmed into your lighting controller to dim the lights in your home theater when you want to watch a movie, and another to dim all but your reading lamp when the TV is off and you just want to catch up on your current favorite novel. Many people like to create special scenes for the sleeping parts of their homes, so that the hall light can remain on at a very dim setting, for example, and the bathroom lights can be turned on to a nonblinding brightness when needed at night.

Although many general-purpose programmable controllers can be programmed with macros to create scenes to control lighting, we like to use a purpose-built lighting system to create and control our scenes.

Internet-controlled electric usage

Energy companies are launching a range of variable-rate pricing plans for consumer electricity, such that the rates during peak demand times are higher than those during off-peak times. Because no consumer wants to have to memorize energy rate tables, Internet-connected thermostats, such as those from market leader Lightstat, Inc. (www.lightstat.com), provide consumers with a user-friendly way to program their thermostats to do certain things during specific rate periods. You log onto a Web site that enables you to set your temperature preferences for sleeping at night, when you're away at work during the day, and so on. And you set your preferences for what to do when the prices hit certain thresholds, such as turning off one of your two water-heater elements to save energy.

Some of the smarter thermostats go beyond just the heating and cooling in the house. These have a discrete output (like a relay) built into the thermostat to control the water heater, for instance. There has to be a relay on the water heater, and the signal gets to the water heater from the thermostat either by a low-voltage cable or a wireless transmit/receive signal (Bluetooth or similar). In the same way, the thermostat could also turn off an electrical load such as a pool pump (until the rates are cheap again). In one implementation, Lightstat turns on a natural-gas-fired emergency generator with the thermostat and takes the whole house off the utility grid when the price is high enough! Houses that have alternate power-storage capability, such as solar cells, can tap this power in peak periods.

Leading home-automation programs, such as HAL2000, are starting to link to the utility energy databases to do the same thing for other devices around the home, including appliances such as dishwashers. Suppose a dishwasher uses around 58 kilowatt-hours per month. In one real-life example, the electricity rates range from 4.2 cents a kilowatt-hour on nights and weekends to 10 cents on weekday afternoons — more than double the cost. Add in air conditioning, the washer, the dryer, and other devices, and you can save a lot of money.

Traditionally, lighting-control systems have been the province of the very rich and have required extra wiring, switches, and control panels. Big lighting and wiring manufacturers, however, have brought high-end scene lighting to the mass market using X10 powerline controls or wireless systems (ZigBee or Z-Wave).

A good example of the X10 approach to scene control is the Toscana Deluxe controller from Leviton. This system uses Leviton's Intellisense-enhanced X10 protocol and can control up to 256 devices (the maximum allowed by any X10 system) and be programmed for up to 64 scenes. The Toscana controller can be controlled and programmed by a Windows PC and a standard RS-232 serial port, and can be controlled also using an IR remote control. (We talk about these later in the chapter.) The Toscana system is mounted in a standard wall outlet — but it's wider than a regular wall switch so it uses a four-gang outlet box. The system is two-way X10 compatible, so we recommend that you use two-way modules with it. And if you want to get the benefits of the Leviton Intellisense AGC (automatic gain control — which improves performance in "noisy" powerline environments), you'll need to use Leviton modules (although any X10 module will work with the system).

Getting fancy with home automation

For home automation and control that goes beyond even the functionality of most PC-based control systems, you may want to consider a high-end, proprietary home-automation system. These are stand-alone systems that you usually mount in a panel in your home's wiring closet. They have their own central-controller unit (usually a PC-based computer), controllers, and interfaces to a large number of other systems, such as security systems, audio and video networks, telephone and intercom systems, and external sensors.

If you walk into a really high-end A/V dealership (the kind of place with $50,000 speaker systems and the like), chances are you'll see Crestron's systems on display next to the megabuck A/V gear. Crestron is *the* choice for expensive smart homes, and it's not for the shallow of pocketbook: A typical Crestron installation in a residential setting costs about $50,000.

If you can afford it, Crestron is a cool way to go. The keys to Crestron's system are a series of touchpad controllers and a centralized computer-based controller. With these pieces in place (along with a wiring infrastructure of CAT-5e/6 and Crestron's own powered CrestNet cable), you can use the system to control just about everything in your home — HVAC systems, lighting, security, audio and video systems, and more. Crestron is more than just a control network. The combination of CAT-5e/6 and CrestNet cable is used also as a distribution backbone for audio, video, and even computer LAN networks throughout the home.

If you're looking for the ultimate in smart homes, check out Crestron's systems at www. crestron.com.

If you're looking for much of the same functionality at a slightly lower price, we recommend that you check out Control4 (www.control4. com). Control4 was started by some smart guys who had previously worked with some of the super-high-end, Crestron-style automation companies, and their goal was to bring the same kind of automation to a broader market. A full Control4 system for a typical whole-home installation runs between $5,000 and $10,000. You get essentially the same thing as you'd get from a Crestron system for a *lot* less. Control4 systems include ZigBee-based lighting controls, integration into home-security systems, whole-home audio systems (including a neat iPod dock), home-theater control, and more, with a great interface and some cool touch-panel controllers. How does Control4 do it more cheaply than their competitors? Mainly by leveraging standardized, mass produced components and technologies — such as Ethernet and Wi-Fi and ZigBee — instead of building everything from scratch. Although you can't install a Control4 system yourself (they sell through custom installers, which is one of the cost elements), and the programming takes some expertise, they are much more widely available in the kinds of stores "regular" people shop in, such as Magnolia A/V stores, Ultimate Electronics, Circuit City, and even Home Depot (in some markets).

On the wireless side of the coin, Leviton has recently launched a new Z-Wave-powered solution called Vizia RF. (As we write in early 2007, this is brand new.) This system consists of a range of plug-in modules, switches, and dimmer switches that can be installed throughout the home and communicate with each other wirelessly. Leviton also has a range of in-wall controllers (light switches with built-in controller functionality) and handheld wireless controllers. And they've also partnered with the folks at Monster Cable for the development of a universal remote control that works with ViziaRF lighting/control systems and *also* controls all of the components in your home theater or entertainment system. Very cool stuff.

We think that both the powerline (X10 or other powerline system) approach and the wireless (Z-Wave or ZigBee) approach are valid ways of controlling lighting in the home. Both work well and the cost is about the same. As with the rest of your home, you'll likely use some of both approaches, albeit probably within one manufacturer's product line. We do recommend that you buy a good quality product because the higher-end products tend to have more robust capabilities to deal with interference from other devices in the home.

Control Networks for Entertainment Systems

Home-audio and -video systems present a special case for home automation and control because you probably want to do a lot more with a VCR or CD player than just turn it on and off. In fact, you need a whole host of commands that lighting and appliance-focused automation standards don't even begin to address, such as start and stop, pause, and fast forward.

In a single room, you can take care of these functions using an infrared (IR) remote control — either the control that came with your equipment or a programmable universal remotes. Unfortunately, IR remote controls are line-of-sight and can't carry signals between rooms. So unless you can somehow suspend the laws of physics, pressing repeatedly on the pause button of your VCR's remote doesn't do you a bit of good if you're in the bedroom and the VCR is downstairs in the living room. You have the following three common ways of getting around this problem:

- Use a *radio frequency (RF) remote system,* if your equipment supports it.
- Use an *RF repeater* system to expand the reach of your IR remote.
- Use a *wired IR repeater system* to send the remote-control signals from one room to another.

Using RF remotes

Radio waves have one big advantage over light waves (including those of the infrared variety): They can get through and around obstacles such as walls, furniture, and large house pets. This particular trait makes radio waves ideal for whole-home remote-control systems. Unfortunately, because they cost more, RF remote controls are rarely part of the consumer-electronics package. If your entertainment-network needs are simple (for example, you just want to watch the output of your DBS satellite dish from a different TV), you may be able to find components fitted with an RF remote. Sony, for example, sells a DSS receiver system with an RF remote for just this purpose.

If your network becomes a bit more complicated, or if you already have the components and are stuck with IR remotes, you do have a solution. Several manufacturers offer wireless RF-repeater systems for IR remotes. Setting one of these systems up is a piece of cake. Most consist of just two parts: a *transmitter* that converts IR signals from your remote control to radio waves and beams them out throughout your home, and a corresponding *receiver* that reverses the process and sends the reconverted IR signals to your audio and video equipment. All you need to do is plug the receiver into a wall near the equipment that you want to control and do the same with the transmitter in your remote location. Some transmitters even come in a small, battery-powered package — all you need to do is slip such a transmitter over the end of your IR remote control and carry it to wherever you want listen or watch. We've seen another variation on this theme as well. Consisting of the same transmitter/receiver duo, some systems plug into a wall outlet and carry your remote-control signals over your home's AC powerlines instead of using RF signals.

Both these systems should work reasonably well, but they do have the following downsides:

- ✔ RF signals are better than IR at getting through and around obstacles, but as anyone with a cordless phone can tell you, they're not foolproof. Long distances, thick walls, and interference by other RF sources can cause problems.

- ✔ Powerline solutions can also suffer from interference and electrical noise in your electrical wiring.

- ✔ RF and powerline repeater systems aren't sophisticated enough for use in elaborate, multizoned audio- and video-distribution systems — they can't distinguish between zones or discriminate between multiple pieces of audio or video source equipment.

Using a wired IR repeater system

The best way to distribute audio and video control signals throughout your home is to install a hardwired, IR-signal-distribution network. In this kind of system, the IR signals from a standard handheld remote or wall-mounted keypad convert to electrical signals. These signals then travel to your entertainment center over in-wall wiring that runs to your audio or video equipment room and, by using devices known as *emitters,* are converted back into IR signals that can control your systems.

You can wire an IR network in one of the following three ways:

✔ You can run dedicated IR cables along with your audio and video signal-distribution wiring.

   Using IR cables is the *old* way of doing a whole-home IR control network. You can still find and buy this stuff, but most people have moved onto the next solution, using CAT-5e/6 cables.

✔ You can use an IR repeater system that uses CAT-5e/6 UTP cabling to carry the signals. Many of the CAT-5e/6 video and audio systems that we discuss in Chapters 7 and 9 carry IR control signals along with your audio and video source signals, so you can carry everything on a single CAT-5e/6.

✔ You can piggyback the IR signals on the RG6 coaxial cabling that you use for video distribution (as we mention in Chapter 7).

The third option, using existing coaxial video-distribution cables, requires you to have audio- and video-network outlets in the same locations. If you have some audio outlets (or wall speakers) in places where no video outlet is present, you can't control the system in that location.

The following components are common to any IR network:

✔ **Infrared sensors:** These devices convert the IR signal from a handheld remote into a DC electrical signal that you can distribute over your IR wiring. IR sensors come in a variety of shapes and sizes, including wall-mounted units, tabletop units, and even minisized sensors that you can hide in a small hole in the wall.

✔ **Infrared emitters:** At the other end of an IR network (next to your audio and video equipment), you install devices known as emitters. An *emitter* converts the DC electrical signal back into an IR signal and beams this signal to your equipment. Some companies call these devices *IR blasters.*

✔ **Emitter-connecting blocks:** These devices enable you to connect IR sensors in different rooms to single or multiple emitters. If you have a multizone audio system, an emitter-connecting block is an essential component of the IR control network because it enables you to separate IR signals by zone — so the signals from a particular zone go only to equipment that serves the same zone. For a system that uses CAT-5e/6 cabling instead of IR cabling, you can use a standard CAT-5e/6 patch panel to connect cables and route IR signals to and from your media room.

✔ **IR keypad controllers:** You can use a keypad controller in place of a handheld remote and IR sensor. Keypads are not required and cost more than simple sensors, but they're cool. Mounted on the wall like a light switch, the keypad controller can learn the IR commands that your system uses and send them back to your emitters at the push of a button.

Chapter 20

Making Home Automation a Reality

I n Chapter 19, we talk about all the things that make up your automated home. In this chapter, we talk about wiring and design strategies for putting it all together. Specifically, we talk about home-automation networks and IR control networks. Neither of these networks requires much in the way of special wiring — especially the powerline and wireless networks for home automation and control, but certain IR networks do require the installation of control wiring.

Installation is only half the battle in these kinds of systems, however. The real trick is to configure all the sensors, modules, emitters, keypads, and so on to make sure that they work together correctly. For simple networks — such as X10 lighting controls or IR controllers for single-zone audio networks — this configuration isn't too difficult, but more complicated systems can test your patience, diligence, and skill at reading manuals. We can't simply tell you how to get your Xantech IR controller keypad, for example, to turn on and off your Toshiba HD-DVD player and Harmon Kardon amplifier — just too many variables exist for us to cover everything. What we can do, however, is give you a good jumping-off point for getting a home-automation and control infrastructure in place and provide you with some useful tips.

In the first half of this chapter, as we talk about automation systems, we talk about ways you can create an automation system using any of the protocols we discuss in Chapter 19. We have a slight focus on the powerline systems (particularly X10) only because these have long been the most popular options, but our advice here applies equally to systems using any of the (many) home-automation protocols on the market. We aren't focusing on any one protocol because there's simply no telling at this point (early 2007) which of the competing protocols will become most popular. For example, three newer protocols are vying to replace X10 as the default powerline communications method for home automation, and ZigBee and Z-Wave are still in the early days of battling it out in the wireless market. Our advice here is a bit generic, but — just to repeat ourselves — it will apply regardless of which protocol you choose.

If you are using a wireless protocol such as Z-Wave or ZigBee, you can disregard all of the discussions about how to overcome the issues facing powerline communications.

X10 Marks the Spot

The wonderful thing about X10 (and other home-automation standards that use powerline communications) is that the installation's effects on your home's wiring infrastructure are minimal. However, you should consider having an electrician do a few things to optimize your home's wiring for powerline control (and we describe such changes in the following sections). These optimizations aren't complicated or expensive.

After your powerlines are ready for control networks, setting up the components is the epitome of plug and play. Plug a module into a power receptacle, plug the light or appliance into it, and that part of your network is complete. This simplicity combined with the low cost of components are the main reasons why powerline continues to be the default recommendation for home-automation systems for many folks.

You can take a few additional steps and precautions to ensure that everything works together in happiness and harmony: install bridges, noise blocks, signal amplifiers, and X10-, Insteon-, UPB-compatible surge protectors, as well as make sure that all your receptacles have three wires rather than two.

Building bridges

Depending on the state of the electrical wiring in your house, your electrician may need to install a device known as a *signal coupler* in your electrical service panel. This handy-dandy little unit — which costs about $50 — enables the powerline signals to get around the house even if the electrical system is split into two circuits.

The powerline that comes into your home from the utility company usually consists of a two-phase, 220-volt powerline (two 110-volt phases). After this line connects to your service panel or breaker box, the two phases split from each other to provide 110-volt powerlines to all standard outlets, switches, and hardwired fixtures. (A few outlets in your home, such as those for electric clothes dryers, use both phases for 220-volt circuits.) Because of this separation, powerline signals in some homes have a hard time getting across from one phase to the other. So a controller connecting to an electrical circuit in one room may not "see" a module in another room that runs on the other phase of the circuit. The signal coupler forms a bridge that enables the commands to jump across to the other phase.

A good way to tell whether a powerline problem is caused by this phase issue is to turn on an electric oven or dryer (these devices typically use 220-volt AC and effectively create a temporary bridge between the two legs when they're on). If your problem goes away when the oven is on, you need a coupler to correct the problem permanently.

Keep those nosy (or noisy) neighbors off your powerline

Powerline signals aren't powerful — you don't need to worry about one traveling back up your powerlines and sending your local nuclear reactor into meltdown. Powerline signals could, however, go from house to house in the small local area served by the local transformer for your house (that round thing on the telephone pole), disrupting your carefully planned powerline system.

Other powerline signals aren't the only thing that can make powerline signals act a bit funky. Electrical interference of all kinds finds its way into powerlines, giving you a noisy power supply, which can disrupt command signals.

If your powerline network is behaving weirdly or if you're just the cautious type, you may want to have an electrician install a *noise block* inline to your electrical power feed, just before the circuit-breaker box. This device should stop any incoming interference and keep the neighbors' controllers from triggering your modules.

Most of the noise blocks we've seen (ranging from $70 cheap ones to fancy $500 models) include signal-coupling functionality as well. So the electrician can make only one trip to kill these two birds (the noise block and the coupler).

Dozens of items in a typical home — for example, fluorescent lights, air conditioners, fax machines, and even computers or audio equipment — can interfere with powerline signals by creating noise on the electrical powerlines. In some cases, the circuits and chips within these devices send unintended electrical energy back into the power infrastructure that can confuse your X10 (or other powerline system) into thinking they are control signals — or block your signals from getting through at all. In these cases, you can install an inline noise filter (that plugs in between the noisy device and the wall) or a hardwired filter (for devices that are hardwired into the electrical system, such as air conditioners).

Noise-blocking filters are easy to install (especially the plug-in inline filters). The hard part is figuring out which of the dozens or hundreds of electrical devices in your house are causing the problem. You can buy an X10 signal-testing device, which may help you track down problems, but the best approach for most people is good old-fashioned trial and error. (We've not yet seen similar testers for other powerline protocols, probably because they are less susceptible to problems.) When you have issues with a certain powerline module not receiving signals, start turning off electrical devices until your module works again. Nope, it's not rocket science, but it does work! When you find the offender, simply install a noise filter and get back to your powerline-automated lifestyle.

The newer powerline systems (such as Insteon, UPB, and LonWorks) are much more *robust* — meaning their protocols are better at discerning control signals from the background noise on the powerlines. If you're starting from scratch, we highly recommend that you use one of these protocols or a wireless protocol (such as ZigBee or Z-Wave) rather than going with X10. If you're wedded to X10 (because of an existing installation or because certain components of your automation system aren't available with the newer protocols), we recommend that you choose an *enhanced* X10 solution using AGC (automatic gain control), such as the Leviton Intellisense system we discuss in Chapter 19.

Boost that signal

In an average-sized home, X10 signals coming from controllers (or back over the network from two-way modules) are usually strong enough to reach any spot in the house — as long as there's a signal coupler in place. Like many other things (cars, packs of toilet paper, and supersized fries, to name a few), houses are getting bigger. After a house hits about 3000 square feet, X10 signals start having a hard time reaching distant nooks and crannies. The solution here is to install an X10-signal amplifier/repeater in the main electrical panel.

There's no big mystery about what a signal amplifier/repeater does (this is definitely a case where the name fits). X10 signals entering the electrical panel pass through the signal amplifier/repeater, and the signal is boosted (amplified) and repeated to ensure that it reaches remote modules with sufficient strength to be understood by the module.

Even in smaller homes, a signal amplifier/repeater can come in handy as a way of getting around noisy electrical lines because the stronger signal is easier for modules to pick out from background noise. In fact, Leviton recommends that you always install their signal amplifier/repeater whenever you install their DHC X10 systems.

Signal amplifier/repeaters almost always have a built-in signal coupler, so you won't need a separate coupler.

Although the newer powerline systems are better at reaching every outlet in your home, they're not perfect. You can buy amplifiers/repeaters for these systems as well, if your home needs them.

Surge protectors kill powerline signals

Surge protectors, devices that protect your sensitive electronic equipment from transient voltages (such as lightning strikes on utility poles), can be real lifesavers. Ask people who have had a power surge zap a computer or television, and they'll tell you how much they wish they'd invested $30 or $40 on a decent surge protector.

Unfortunately, many surge protectors not only filter out bad stuff such as lightning but also remove or disable powerline signals. So you're left with an unpleasant choice: Protect your equipment from surges or automate it?

Luckily, you have the following two ways of getting around this problem:

- ✔ Install X10-compatible (or other powerline protocol compatible) surge protector strips (which don't cost any more than good-quality conventional ones) and plug your appliance modules into the strips.

- ✔ Take a whole-home approach to surge protection and have an electrician install a whole-home surge suppressor at your breaker box. These suppressors cost about $200 (the same as five or six good-quality strips), and they protect every circuit in your home.

When lightning strikes, no one can predict where it will hit. Your powerline (safely protected behind a surge protector) may not be the thing that gets struck. There are plenty of other electrical paths to your home's other sensitive electronics — antenna and cable TV cables, phone lines, or even satellite dishes and their cables. It makes good sense to install surge protectors on all these systems, just in case.

Wire those switches right

As your electrician is installing junction boxes and wiring for light switches in your home, tell him or her to do the following (and you'll *really* sound like you know what you're doing!): *Run the neutral wire to the light switch's junction box instead of bypassing it.*

Having all the wires run to the switch rather than running some to the switch and some directly to the light gives you more freedom to install powerline automated switches in the future.

Each of the 110-volt electrical circuits in a house consists of three separate wires: a *hot* wire (usually black), which supplies the current to the circuit, a *neutral* wire (usually white), which provides a return path for the current, and a *ground* wire (usually green), which grounds the circuit for safety. The conventional way to install light switches is to connect the hot wire to one side of the switch and run another wire, called the *load* (usually blue), from the switch to the light (or other device) itself. The neutral and ground wires often bypass the switch and run directly to the light. So the switch just interrupts the flow of the hot wire's current to the light: The light itself completes and grounds the circuit.

In an X10 environment, the wiring scheme for switches limits what you can control with an X10 light switch. X10 switches can control only incandescent light fixtures if you wire the switches this way — because the light bulb filament itself provides a path for the X10 signals, something that fluorescent and low-voltage lights can't do. If you want to use a switch to control fluorescent lights, low-voltage track lighting, or appliances, you need to use a special inductive dimmer or appliance switch that connects all the wires: the hot wire, the load wire, and the neutral wire. So all these wires must be available at the junction box.

For more information on how to wire electrical switches and how not to fry yourself while working with them, please check out *Home Improvement For Dummies,* by Gene and Katie Hamilton and the editors of HouseNet (published by Wiley Publishing, Inc.).

Some of the fancy X10-controllable mood-lighting switches also require this neutral wire connection, even for incandescent lights.

Controlling Your Home-Automation Systems

You can use X10, INSTEON, Z-Wave, and other home-automation protocols and equipment in one of the following two ways:

✔ As a simple home-control system that enables you to perform actions in one part of the house while you're in another part of the house

✔ As part of a true automated system that performs actions on its own, based on a schedule or on events that it detects

The modularity of automation systems and the fact that they're based on common standards that ensure that each manufacturer's equipment works with another's (within the bounds of that protocol — X10 modules won't talk to ZigBee modules, for example) make it easy to start with a simple home-control network and gradually build your way up to a fully automated system. You just add new components to the network as you go. So if you're not convinced that an automated home is for you, you can start with a few components and — if the automation bug bites — go crazy with it later.

Keeping it simple

If you just want to get your feet wet in the home-automation world, we recommend that you start with a simple plug-in module-based home-control network. You probably don't need to worry about electrical-wiring considerations or how to connect your computer to the network. All you really need to do is to plug a few lamp or appliance modules and a controller of some sort into your AC powerlines.

We can't promise that you aren't going to experience some electrical-wiring difficulties, even in a simple X10 network, but most people don't.

For a total investment of less than about $75 (about $11 for the controller and $8 for each lamp or appliance module), you can set up a simple network that controls eight lights or small appliances from a central location. Expanding this network is as simple as adding more modules and controllers as your needs expand. You may want a controller in the living room to set the right lighting levels for movie watching and another in the master bedroom to turn on a bunch of lights if you hear something go bump in the night.

Linking your car and home with HomeLink

More than 140 new car models are now available with a remote-control system called HomeLink. For most folks, the main selling point for this system is its capability to operate most garage-door openers; you don't need to search under the seat for the door-opener remote. HomeLink is integrated into your car's interior — usually in the headliner above the rearview mirror — and usually consists of two or three pushbuttons (each of which controls a single device). Some cars include HomeLink controller buttons on the car's remote entry key fob.

In a smart-home environment, however, you can also use one or more of the HomeLink's RF channels (most versions have three) to trigger wireless X10 controllers to send commands to such devices as lights and even X10-compatible security systems — from the warmth and comfort of your car. HomeLink isn't sold as an after-market add-in — instead, it's sold as a built-in, integral part of the car (although some automakers sell HomeLink as a dealer-installed accessory that you can have installed in certain car models after the fact). To find out more about HomeLink, look on the Web at http://www.homelink.com.

You can also expand your control network by using wireless controllers (perhaps as part of your home-theater universal remote control) that enable you to trigger controls without leaving the comfort of your couch or the front porch.

If you want to add a degree of automation to your control network, simply plug a programmable controller into the system. Doing so enables you to create simple timed programs to activate or turn off various modules.

Adding a computer for more control

Adding a personal computer to the mix enables you to bring a new level of sophistication to a home-control and home-automation network. The addition of a home-automation protocol interface (in other words, a device that plugs into your computer and "speaks" your chosen protocol) and graphical-interface software on your PC enable you to create complicated on/off schedules quickly and easily. The ease of using a computer interface for this purpose — instead of trying to fiddle with a small, somewhat unintuitive programmable controller — is worth the price of admission.

But wait — there's more! (We loved those old Ginsu knife commercials.) By using the computer software, you can program your PC's home-automation interface box to perform *macros* — sets of consecutive commands, such as turn on the kitchen light, start the coffee pot, and open the curtains. After you create a macro, you can save it and use it again. For example, you could create a lighting macro for TV watching, and then schedule it for whenever your favorite shows are on. You can even download macros from the Internet and apply them to your system.

Making your home interactive

Remotely controlling and scripting your home-automation systems are pretty cool ways of automating your home, but you can bring an automated home to a higher level by making it interactive and intelligent. By combining sensors with your X10 control systems, you can program your home to react to certain events by turning on lights, alerting you with a chime, or even muting your TV.

You can integrate sensors into a home-automation system in the following ways:

✔ You can keep things within the realm of your automation system, utilizing sensors with built-in automation controllers to trigger events.

✔ You can integrate an alarm system with your home-automation network and use the alarm's sensors to trigger home-automation events.

✔ If you have a sophisticated PC-based or stand-alone home-automation controller, you can directly connect sensors to the controller.

Put your network on the Net

Suppose that you control your home's X10 network with a PC and also have an always-on cable-modem or DSL connection to the Internet. Why not put the two together and use the Internet connection to control your PC from work or even from your laptop's wireless Net connection wherever you are? Well, you can do just that with HAI's Omni controller system and WebLink II software (check out www.home auto.com). The total package (the high-end hardware controller and the Web-based software) costs about $1500, which includes the professional installation of a system that controls not only lights but also the thermostat and a security system. HAI can also integrate touch-pad controllers for remote control of your audio/video network.

WebLink II uses a standard Windows PC as a Web server. The WebLink II software creates a series of interactive Web pages that can give you the current status of your home and control of any devices in your home that are connected to the Omni controller. You can turn lights and appliances on and off (individually or by using lighting scenes as discussed in Chapter 19), adjust the thermostat, and arm or disarm the security system. You can even use the software to remotely view video surveillance cameras that you've connected to the PC. The WebLink II software can also be set up to send you e-mail alerts or messages when certain conditions have occurred (such as an alarm condition or the kids returning home from school).

The following sections elaborate on these three methods.

Automation sensors

The simplest way to integrate sensors into a home-automation network is to install sensors that use your chosen automation protocol in your home. These sensors combine the sensor itself (a photocell or passive infrared detector, for example) and a controller that can send automation and control commands to several addresses. You don't need to go through a central controller for these devices — just assign some command actions to them (such as turning on certain lights) and plug them into a powerline receptacle. It's that simple.

Among the automation sensors that we've seen are the following:

- ✔ **Photocells:** Unless you live way up North, you can plan on the sun coming up and going down every day. By using a photocell, your home can distinguish the light from the dark and automatically turn lights on at dusk and off at dawn.

- ✔ **Motion detectors:** By using a PIR, these wall-mounted sensors can send several automation commands if they detect motion. You might want to install one in the upstairs hallway, for example, and set it to automatically turn on the hall lights if someone walks by.

  Many motion detectors also have a built-in photocell so that you can set them to turn on lights only as darkness falls.

- ✔ **Motion-detector floodlights:** These outdoor lights function just like the standard motion-detector lights that guide your path down the front walk after your dog forces you into yet another late-night walk. By using a PIR, these lights turn themselves on if someone (or something — such as that pesky dog from next door) walks into their detection field. After they turn on, the floodlights also send out a number of control signals and trigger other modules such as those controlling inside lights or chime modules.

- ✔ **Low-voltage sensor module:** This type of module accepts the output of almost any stand-alone sensor — such as a magnetic door-closure sensor, a doorbell, a driveway sensor, or even a nonautomated burglar alarm — and sends a command if something activates the sensor.

Using an alarm with built-in automation functionality

As we discuss in Chapter 17, a typical home-security system is chock full of sensors — door-contact sensors, window-contact sensors, glass-breakage

Voice control, the ultimate in interactivity

A few home-automation control software packages include voice activation as the primary means of controlling your home's systems. Using recent developments in speech recognition, these systems (most notably the HomeVoice system by Applied Future Technologies and the HAL2000 from Home Automated Living) enable you to speak in plain English to initiate X10 or IR commands. So you can boss your house around, *Star Trek* style, turning on lights or opening drapes without lifting a finger.

A discreet, omnidirectional microphone (or a telephone, for remote access) picks up the sound of your voice and feeds it into the microphone input of your PC's sound card. The speech-recognition software then translates your commands and correlates them with stored X10 or IR commands and sends the appropriate control signals out over your home's powerline or IR network. These products can also use speech synthesis to talk back to you — giving you a confirmation that your command was heard and carried out. Neat stuff.

Connecting a microphone to the sound card of your PC and getting the system up and running in the same room that contains your computer and computer-to-X10 interface are simple tasks. The job becomes a bit trickier, however, if you

want to use voice control throughout the house. To do so, you need to install microphones in each room and run microphone cable back to the controller location. Because most sound cards have only one microphone input, you need to combine all incoming microphone leads into a microphone mixer, which sends a single signal into the PC. (On the horizon is a method that uses distributed microphones built into light switches or other distributed devices that can process the sound at the origin and send over X10 only the actual command inputs.)

Both systems are software-based and run on most Pentium-class PCs. They're compatible with most computer-to-X10 interfaces, so you can easily add voice control into an existing system. Microphones cost about $90 each, but the mixers we've seen are expensive. (The Home-Voice mixer kit, which also includes a limiter/gate device to help filter out background noise, costs nearly $700.) The software itself isn't too expensive — $239 for HomeVoice and $169 for HAL2000.

We think that voice control is a logical next step for home-automation and home-control networks and something you're going to see more of in the future.

detectors, PIRs, pressure-sensitive doormats, and many more. The primary function of these sensors is, of course, to monitor your house for bad guys and trigger the alarm if necessary. By using an automation-protocol-equipped alarm system (or by adding an automation controller expansion module to certain brands of existing alarm systems), you can make these sensors serve double duty.

The simplest of these alarm systems activate X10 commands (such as All On) in an alarm condition — in other words, they turn on your lights if the alarm siren sounds. This setup isn't really the kind of home automation we're talking about, but it does add a nice security feature. (Being able to see where you're going sure would be nice after you peel yourself off the ceiling during a middle-of-the-night alarm.)

More sophisticated systems take a subtler approach in that they offer levels of reaction to various sensor inputs. In other words, these security systems are smart enough to know that certain sensor inputs don't necessarily spell doom. A pressure-sensitive doormat or a driveway sensor, for example, tells the system that someone is there, whether a burglar or the UPS delivery person. Obviously, the system's reaction to these sensor inputs should be something less than a full alarm. (No need to call out the cavalry if it's just the pizza guy.)

These security systems can interface with your automation network in the following ways:

✔ A sensor input can trigger a random automation output to create a "lived-in" look. An outdoor PIR motion detector, for example, may cause your alarm control panel to send control signals to lights in several different rooms, turning them on and off at seemingly random intervals.

✔ In the most advanced of these systems, you can program specific sensor inputs to trigger specific control outputs. So the motion detector in the backyard can turn on the rear porch lights, or the driveway sensor can turn on the carriage lights running from the driveway to the front door.

Combining sensors with a central controller

The biggest drawback to having an alarm trigger automation events is that most alarm systems are limited in their capabilities. You can think of these systems as alarms with some automation control added on, not as full-blown controller systems.

If you want to create a sophisticated, interactive home-automation system — one that combines a large number of sensors with a whole bunch of potential corresponding commands — consider using a high-end PC-based or stand-alone home-control system.

These systems directly accept the inputs of a number of sensors and can control hundreds of automation modules and even nonautomated hardwired systems (such as heating, ventilation, and air-conditioning systems and sprinkler controls), based on the settings you enter into the system's control interface.

Many of these central controller systems include an alarm system component or can integrate with many nonautomated alarm systems.

These intelligent home controllers can accept the following two types of sensor inputs:

 ✔ **Analog inputs:** These sensors can detect a range of measurements, such as temperature sensors or moisture/humidity detectors.

 ✔ **Digital inputs:** These sensors either detect a condition or don't detect one, such as motion/no motion sensors.

The wiring for these sensors varies — depending on the individual sensor type and manufacturer — but most use wiring similar to what you use for wiring alarm sensors (two- or four-conductor wiring, although some temperature sensors use three-conductor wiring). The key to integrating sensors into such a system is to anticipate as much of your sensor needs as you can upfront so that you can have your installer run the right wires ahead of time.

After you connect the sensors to your controller, you can program them (using a computer or a television and the system's graphical-interface software) and even create event-driven macros that map sensor inputs to specific control outputs. The sky's the limit here — if a system is controllable, you can match it to a sensor input. We'd like to find a way to turn on the lawn sprinklers if a salesperson comes to our door, but we haven't yet been able to find a sensor that can differentiate between the Fuller Brush man and the next-door neighbor.

Getting IR Around the House

As we mention in Chapter 19, automation systems are a great way of controlling all sorts of devices in a home, but they're not ideal for taking care of the complicated commands that you need to control audio and video systems. You can rig up something like an X10/IR converter system to perform this task, but doing so is complicated and a case of reinventing the wheel.

We make that last statement because you already have a great way of controlling audio and video systems — by using IR remotes. The only problem with IR remotes is that IR signals don't pass through walls and floors. You can solve this problem by using a radio frequency IR-extender system — this is the cheap and easy solution. Unfortunately, the RF method isn't quite up to the job of controlling multiple systems in multizone networks. To do that, you need a wired IR-repeater network.

If you're sending audio and video signals around your house using one of the next-generation CAT-5e/6 systems, such as Leviton's Decora Media System or ChannelPlus's SVC-10, you probably don't need an extra network to handle your IR networking needs. Most of these systems (including the two mentioned) use spare conductors on the CAT-5e/6 cable that carries the audio and video signals around the house to also carry IR signals. This is a neat, integrated way of creating an A/V network — you don't need separate audio, video, and IR control infrastructures. Remote control of these network systems is usually accomplished with a touchpad or an IR sensor built into the remote CAT-5e/6 faceplate (or sometimes both — a touchpad with a built-in IR receiver).

Similarly, wireless (Wi-Fi) entertainment systems (such as the Sonos Music System) can handle all of the control of your source materials over the wireless link, so there's no real need for an IR control network in these cases either!

Making your coaxial cable work overtime

If you have a coaxial cable network to distribute video signals throughout the home *and* if the endpoints of this network correspond with the endpoints of your audio network (or you don't have a whole-home audio network), you can avoid running extra wires throughout the home by running IR signals over that coaxial cable.

To do so, you need to install devices known as *IR signal injector/splitters,* which perform two tasks. In remote locations, the signal injector/splitter combines the electrical signal that an IR sensor sends with the video signals running over your coaxial network. In your media equipment room, another signal injector/splitter splits the same signal out from the coaxial cable and feeds it to an IR emitter to control your equipment. Figure 20-1 shows how these devices fit into a coaxial network.

Many newer audio/video devices, such as receivers and DVD players, are built with the home networker in mind and come with a jack on the back for connecting to remote IR systems. In these cases, you don't need to use an IR emitter. Instead, you connect the IR cable directly into this jack, usually using a stereo miniplug like the one used for headphones on iPods and portable CD players. Makes for a neater appearance and usually works better — we like this trend a lot.

The signal injector/splitter needs electrical power to do its thing because it's creating an electrical signal from an IR sensor output. You have the following two ways of providing this power to the devices:

Figure 20-1:
Piggy-
backing IR
signals on
a coaxial
network.

Note: Some RG6 coax lines omitted for clarity

✔ You can install a *remote power injector* near your coaxial distribution panel. One of these devices provides power for the entire network.

✔ You can use a video-distribution panel (discussed in detail in Chapter 7), which has a built-in power injector. ***Note:*** Some coaxial panel makers call this feature an *IR engine* (and no, it doesn't burn high-octane fuel) because it powers all remote IR sensors.

You can configure the guts of this IR network — where the IR signal splits off the coaxial network and goes to IR emitters — in one of the following ways:

✔ If you're controlling only one or two devices (such as a single VCR or an audio receiver and a CD player), simply connect the IR output of the signal injector (it has both an RF output and an IR output) to a single or dual IR emitter. The emitters themselves usually stick right onto the IR sensor of the equipment they control, so you need one per piece of equipment.

✔ If you're controlling more than two pieces of A/V equipment in one location, you can connect your signal injector/splitter to an IR expansion block, which enables you to connect multiple emitters to a single injector/splitter.

You can find IR-over-coax gear from most vendors of coaxial video network equipment. We like the stuff from ChannelPlus (www.channelplus.com).

Multizone IR considerations

If the roster of devices that an IR network controls includes a multizone audio system, you need to use a connecting block specifically designed for multiple-zone systems. This requirement stems from the fact that some of the components in this system are zone-specific, and others are common to the entire system. The amplifier that powers the speakers in a particular zone, for example, is used (and controlled) only in that zone, while all zones share the CD or DVD player.

A multizone connecting block separates the common and shared IR signals by providing

separate sets of emitter connections: common emitter signals and zone-specific emitter signals. This separation is especially important if, for example, you use the same type of amplifier in several different zones. By using the zone-specific emitter signal, you can direct *which* amplifier you actually want to turn up (or turn off).

Getting a multizone system up and running can prove a difficult and frustrating process — and one best left to a professional. Trust us on this one.

Being dedicated

Using coaxial cable is a perfectly adequate method of IR distribution, but the optimal way of carrying IR signals throughout a house is to build a separate IR control network using its own wiring. This setup provides the most flexibility and reliability and makes controlling several components in a multizone audio system easier.

In this section, we discuss two ways of creating a dedicated A/V control network in your home: using the traditional approach of dedicated IR control wires, and using the newer approach of using CAT-5e/6 cabling. We prefer the CAT-5e/6 method, and most manufacturers are moving (or have already moved) their product lines to support this approach.

The traditional approach

Traditionally, hardwired IR-distribution networks use simple three-conductor shielded cable (sold as IR cable in most catalogs and stores) to connect remote locations back to your audio and video network equipment. You wire this cable in a simple star architecture, with an individual run coming from each control point back to the audio/video equipment room, as shown in Figure 20-2. You can also run your IR cabling in a daisy-chain fashion, with a single cable running from room to room, connecting all your sensors and keypads. This type of wiring works only with a single-zone audio network, and we recommend that you don't try to save money on IR cable (which costs only about ten cents a foot) by running your cabling this way.

Figure 20-2:
A hardwired
IR network.

Even if you start with a single-zone speaker wire audio system, you may want
to upgrade to a multizone system some day. A star-architecture speaker wire
system used for a single-zone audio network can be easily upgraded to multizone with some additional equipment in the network. Don't get caught with
an IR system that has to be completely reworked — wire your IR network the
same way, with individual cabling runs to each remote location.

Plugging in the PC

As the PC becomes more integrated into your
home's audio and video networks, you'll find
that having a way to control audio equipment
while sitting in front of the computer (or having
your computer do this automatically) can come
in handy. For example, if you're using your PC as
a PVR and recording TV shows on the PC's hard
drive, it's necessary to give the PC (and your
PVR software on the PC, such as SnapStream's
Personal Video Station) the capability to tune
your TV, cable set-top box, or DSS receiver to
the channel you want to record. Most of these

solutions use an IR emitter with a USB interface
to the PC. The PVR software on the PC then
sends an IR signal out through this USB interface, which can control the channel changing.
If your PC isn't in the same room as the video
source equipment (and it probably won't be),
you can aim the IR emitter from this USB interface at an IR receiver installed in the room
where the computer is located, and use your
wired IR infrastructure to carry the commands
back to your media room.

Connecting the endpoints of this network — the IR sensors and keypads and IR emitters — to the IR cabling infrastructure is easy. Sensors and keypads connect directly to the end of the IR cable in remote locations — nothing complicated about that. On the equipment end of the network, all your IR cable "home runs" terminate on a connecting block, which then provides a number of outputs for IR emitters. The IR emitters simply plug into these outputs and physically sit right in front of the IR receivers on your audio/video equipment.

Like the IR-over-coaxial network that we discuss in the "Making your coaxial cable work overtime" section, the hardwired IR network needs a power supply to make the sensors sense, the emitters emit, and the keypads . . . er . . . key. Providing this power is a secondary job of the connecting block.

Using emitters, sensors, keypads, and connecting blocks from a single manufacturer ensures that everything works together smoothly. Major manufacturers of these systems, such as Niles Audio (www.nilesaudio.com), Nuvo (www.nuvotechnologies.com), and Xantech (www.xantech.com) make all these parts in matched sets.

The new approach

Throughout this book, we've mentioned lots of ways to use CAT-5e/6 cabling in your house. Phone networks and data networks use CAT-5e/6; audio and video networks can use it. There's really not much you can't do with CAT-5e/6 cabling. It's useful stuff.

So it probably won't surprise you to learn that you can use CAT-5e/6 cabling in place of three-conductor IR cabling in your home. There are two ways this can work for you:

✔ You can use three of the eight conductors in CAT-5e/6 cabling as a direct replacement for the three conductors in IR cabling. This is a simple process; just use the same three conductors on each end of the connection, and leave the others unterminated.

✔ You can use IR receivers and keypads designed to work with CAT-5e/6 wiring. Many of these keypad-based systems (such as Leviton's Chopin Volume control, or Nile's Audio's Intellicontrol ICS keypad system) need more than two conductors to do their job and are built from the start to accept only CAT-5e/6 cabling to send control signals back to the media room.

Most new audio/video control systems are built on the concept of using CAT-5e/6 cabling — rather than traditional three-conductor IR wire. CAT-5e/6 cables can carry all of the control signals, power, and more using a standard type of cabling that many more folks are familiar with and experienced at installing.

Our recommendation for a new installation of an audio/video control network is to — whenever possible — install *two* runs of CAT-5e/6 cabling to each room where you'll want to have a local control point (such as a wall volume control or touchpad). At first, you'll probably use only one of these CAT-5e/6 cables (to attach the controller itself). Over time, however, you'll find that more and more systems will be able to use the CAT-5e/6 cabling for carrying the audio/video signals themselves. By installing that extra CAT-5e/6 cable, you've created a future-proofed installation that will provide you with the flexibility to upgrade your entire A/V network as components change and evolve.

Part VII
The Part of Tens

The 5th Wave   By Rich Tennant

Okay—you were right, I was wrong. F5 opens the garage door, and F6 backs the car out.

In this part . . .

Top ten lists! You love 'em — we love 'em. We won't claim to top David Letterman's daily list in terms of humor, but we do try to be useful.

In this section, we give you some tips on things to avoid as you network and automate your home. These are big "uh-ohs" that we did ourselves (back in the early days) or that we've seen others do. We want to spare you the pain.

When it comes to smartifying your home, it's all about the toys, right? We discuss ten of the coolest new toys on the block — things that make your smart home a fun home.

Chapter 21

Ten Common Pitfalls When Building Your Smart Home

. . . .

In This Chapter

▶ Missing the basics of automation

▶ Not reading the manual

▶ Thinking that AC and low voltage are friends

▶ Using the weakest link

▶ That PPPPPP thing

▶ Thinking that wiring is a dirty word

▶ Falling into the proprietary pitfall

▶ Falling into the all-in-one trap

▶ Forgetting to add conduit

▶ Not bothering to use labels

. . . .

*T*hroughout this book, we try to point out potential gotchas that we've run into when building a smart home — things we've seen other people do, horror stories our friends in the smart-home industry have told us, and even a few dumb things we did when we were first getting started.

Building a smart home isn't rocket science or brain surgery. It's a common-sense approach to home building and wiring that makes your house more valuable to you now and more useful in the future. But we all know that common sense ain't all that common, so here are ten things we think are important to remember not to do as you get going.

Missing the Basics of Automation

Powerline (such as X10, INSTEON, or UPB) automation is simple. Plug a module in one outlet and a controller in another, and you're ready to go. But (as we mention in Chapters 19 and 20), these systems rely upon communications over your home's electrical powerlines, which were never designed to be a communications network. So your electrician, the power company, and companies that make electrical lights, appliances, and devices that connect to your AC power spent little time making sure you'd have a nice, noise-free power network over which you could automate and control your house.

You need to keep the following in mind:

- ✔ In the United States, the electrical main line coming into your house consists of two 110-volt phases, which are split off at the main distribution panel. Some outlets in your house are connected to one of these phases, and the other outlets to the other phase. To get X10 signals to cross over to different phases, you need to install a signal coupler in your main distribution panel. This is serious, high-voltage, zap-yourself-and-don't-live-to-tell-about-it stuff, so hire a qualified electrician to do it for you.

- ✔ Low-powered electrical signals such as X10 get weaker as they travel over long distances. If you have a big house, consider installing a signal coupler that also includes a signal amplifier/repeater to boost your signal strength.

- ✔ The surge protectors that you should (and probably already do) have connected to electronic gear in your home will not let automation signals through. Instead of buying a bunch of individual surge protectors, have your electrician install a whole-home protector at the main electrical panel. This will keep the noisy stuff out and let your automation signals work inside your home.

Not Reading the Manual

There are hundreds of different kinds of home-automation modules on the market. Some are designed to turn regular incandescent lights on and off, some are designed for dimming, and some can control fluorescent lights. Pay attention when you buy and install modules (or switches for that matter).

Our friends at companies who make automation products tell us that the number one reason for returned products and calls to their tech support lines isn't defective modules or noisy electrical systems, but rather people trying to do things that the equipment they bought just won't do, such as trying to dim a light with an X10 module that handles only on and off signals or trying to use a dimming switch on a fluorescent light. No matter how many times you hit that switch on your controller, you're not going to get a module to do something it simply can't, by design, do.

Thinking That AC and Low Voltage Are Friends

With the exception of the powerline home-automation systems that we discuss in Chapters 19 and 20 (and the HomePlug data-networking system we discuss in Chapter 16), everything we talk about in this book is a low-voltage system. AC power is high voltage; CAT-5e/6 , RG6 coax, IR cable, and the rest are low voltage. High-voltage systems, because they carry so much power, emit stray electromagnetic fields. Low-voltage systems, because they use very little power, are easily interfered with by these stray fields. It's not a marriage made in heaven.

If you install low-voltage lines too close to the high-voltage ones, the interference can cause major havoc with the networks in your home running over the low-voltage wiring. Have your installers keep low-voltage lines at least 18 inches from high-voltage lines. Try to not run these lines parallel to each other whenever possible. And when crossing high- and low-voltage wiring, do so at a right angle to minimize the length of cables that are near each other.

Using the Weakest Link

We hope that we've convinced you that it's worth the small amount of extra money to use CAT-5e/6 cabling wherever you run cable for telephones, computer networks, and the like. Even if you don't plan on having a phone or a LAN outlet in a room, the sheer usefulness and flexibility of CAT-5e/6 makes running a length or two to every room worthwhile. Every day, we see new systems that let you run audio, video, surveillance cameras, IR controllers, and more over CAT-5e/6.

The problem many folks run into doesn't have anything to do with the cable — most people accept the need for CAT-5e/6 cable. But what they don't realize is that all the pieces and parts of the CAT-5e/6 network are just as important as the cabling in the walls. The outlets, the jacks and plugs, the patch panel in the wiring closet, even the patch cords used to connect a device to an outlet all have to be rated CAT-5e or CAT-6 as well. Having even a single $1 piece of equipment that's not CAT-5e/6–rated connected to the network lowers the rating of the overall network.

It's not hard to find CAT-5e/6 equipment; most connectors, cords, and cables qualify for the rating. But there's still plenty of stuff on the market that looks exactly like CAT-5e/6–rated equipment, but isn't.

Now, to be honest, this really isn't going to matter much for some things you do on CAT-5e/6 networks. Phones, for example, don't require CAT-5e/6 (or even lower-rated CAT-3 cable) — heck, they'd probably work over a string and two tin cans. But as you start looking towards the future and doing things such as installing gigabit Ethernet LANs and high-definition video networks over your UTP cables, you absolutely need CAT-5e or CAT-6.

That PPPPPP Thing

Nope, we're not coming up with a new networking acronym for you. PPPPPP, or *proper planning prevents pretty poor performance*, means you get out of your home network what you put into it. In Part I, we emphasize the planning aspect of building a smart home. Think through what you want to accomplish, what you can afford, and what kind of help you need to make your smart home happen. These are vital steps. Skip them at your own peril.

Don't think you need cable in the nursery? Well you might not, if the kids stay toddlers in perpetuity. But when they're in school and need a computer, wouldn't you like to have an Ethernet LAN port next to the desk? We would.

You can do a pretty good job of prewiring your home by following the basic formula of two CAT-5e/6 and two RG6 coax cables to every room in the house (four and four in your home office and media rooms). There's not much you can't do with this setup. Plan well, and remember: You can't prewire too much.

Thinking That Wiring Is a Dirty Word

We absolutely LOVE wireless technologies. Love as in can't live without. Wireless LANs for our laptops, cordless phones, Bluetooth mobile phones — even Wi-Fi phones for making calls over the Internet. But despite all the hype, wireless networking technologies don't take away from the basic usefulness and necessity of wired connections in your walls.

Compared to wireless networks, purpose-built, wired networks using CAT-5e/6 and RG6 are cheaper and more capable than these wireless alternatives. For example, wireless LANs today top out at about 100 Mbps; wired LANs that cost no more can reach speeds of 1000 Mbps. That's an astronomically high difference.

Now, if you live in an apartment or historic house or for some other reason you can't run new wires, by all means take advantage of wireless and no-new-wire technologies. And in any case, use them where appropriate as an adjunct, companion network to your wired networks. Just don't think they're somehow better or more capable than a wired network.

Falling into the Proprietary Pitfall

Some cool home-networking and home-automation and control systems are built on a specific vendor's proprietary protocols. These proprietary systems often have tangible benefits. For example, they may offer tighter integration between different subsegments of the network than systems built on industry standards, or they may have a special feature (such as the capability to distribute component video) that standards-based systems don't yet have.

The downside of these proprietary systems is that you'll often find yourself locked into them — if you want to expand, upgrade, or otherwise modify your system, you need to go back to the same vendor who provided the rest of the system. Worse, if the vendor suddenly goes out of business, you may find yourself without any future support.

Sometimes you just can't avoid a proprietary system. For example, if you want to send audio and video over CAT-5e/6, you need to use some particular vendor's own equipment on all endpoints in the network. (This is the main reason we still recommend that you at least consider using speaker wire and RG6 coax for these networks.)

You may find that the benefits and features of a particular proprietary system are too compelling for you *not* to use it. That's a perfectly valid decision. Just make sure that you go into such an installation fully aware of the consequences.

Oh yeah — even if you do use one of these proprietary wiring systems, we still recommend that you put in some CAT-5e/6 and RG6 cabling. It will probably come in useful someday.

Tumbling into the All-in-One Trap

A close relative to the proprietary systems mentioned previously are all-in-one packaged solutions that some vendors sell. A single vendor offers all the cabling, all the wiring-closet hardware, all the outlets and receptacles, as well as active electronic equipment such as audio amplifiers, Ethernet switches and routers, and speakers.

We differentiate these approaches from the proprietary approach because typically you don't get locked in — these systems just use standards-based equipment from a single vendor. We're not really opposed to people using them. There's nothing wrong with going this route.

But (you knew there'd be a *but*, didn't you?) we prefer the best-of-breed approach. That's the beauty of standards: You can choose the equipment that best meets your price and performance requirements from a host of vendors and be assured that it will fit in with the rest of your network. So if you think that XYZ Company's amplifier or router or whatever is the best one for you, buy it! The same goes for the rest of your smart home; use standard infra-structures and choose the endpoints you like best.

Forgetting to Add Conduit

In Chapter 2, we mention adding conduits (PVC piping with pull wires) in your walls so that you can easily run new cables in the future. Someday there may be home-networking technologies and related wiring requirements that no one has even dreamed of yet. For example, networks running over fiber-optic cables hold much promise, but so far no one has figured out how they would be configured in a residential setting.

Having conduits in your walls makes it much, much, much easier to run new cables later. Ripping open walls is dirty, destructive, and expensive — accessing a conduit and pulling a wire through it isn't.

Not Bothering to Use Labels

Having a wiring closet is really handy. When you need to reconfigure your network, you just go in the closet, change the connections of cables on the patch and distribution panels, and you're finished. If you've ever peeked into a wiring closet, however, you'll notice one thing about wires. They all look the same. As in identical. As in "uh, I wonder where this one goes?"

So take a little time when you're doing your initial wiring (or have your installer take a little time) and label every single cable. Label both ends: in the wiring closet and at the outlet or receptacle in the remote location. Do this for your electrical panel too. Be obsessive about it (you might even want to print labels on your PC printer or a labelmaker if, like Pat, you can't read your own writing). Secure the labels to the cables well.

You can buy special-purpose labelmakers from companies such as Dymo or Brother for labeling cables. These use special label "tape" that's sturdier than the stuff you put on file folders and have built-in graphics designed for the needs of cabling labels. You certainly don't need one of these, but if you're willing to part with about $70, you can get professionally labeled cables and feel like the ultimate smart homes geek!

Chapter 22

Top Ten Toys of the Future

Smart homes never want for innovation. People are constantly inventing new gadgets and gizmos. Something that is niche-oriented and expensive today may be a high-volume consumer product tomorrow. In this chapter, we introduce you to some neat new toys, from robots to buttkickers. If you're like us, you'll want to mortgage your home to get at least one of these toys! We have more to say about these gadgets and ones like them, but we ran out of room. Check out our www.digitaldummies.com for more information as well as reviews of smart home gear.

Robotic Servants

On TV, it all started with robots like Klaatu in *The Day The Earth Stood Still*, Rosie on *The Jetsons*, and Robot on *Lost In Space*. It's progressed to Data on *Star Trek*, Max Headroom, and Simone. Whether on a screen or in person, robotic personalities offer the opportunity to create a life of leisure for us, while plotting to take over the world, apparently.

Although there are academic trials of various types of android-style robots — Honda's ASIMO robot among the leading examples — the robots that will be available commercially soon are focused on specific tasks, so we call them *taskmasters*. Something as simple as a breadmaker (which takes ingredients, mixes them, kneads the bread, and then bakes it automatically) can be considered a robotic kitchen aid, says Colin Angle, CEO and co-founder of iRobot, Inc. From cooking meals to cleaning windows, robots are on the way.

A dishwasher washes our dishes, a washing machine washes our clothes, and answering machines answer our phones. Here are some of the neater toys on the market now:

- ✔ **Robotic lawnmowers:** Cutting the grass is a repetitive and basic task, so it's a logical jumping-off point for robotics in the home. Products such as Friendly Robotics' Robomower (www.friendlyrobotics.com), Husqvarna's Automower (www.automower.us), Zucchetti's Ambrogio (www.roboticazucchetti.com), and Kyodo's Lawnbott (www.lawnbott.com) have hit the streets. Typically costing about $1500 street price, if you add up all those lawn mowing charges (or hours if you do it yourself), you'd probably find these a bargain!

- ✔ **Robotic vacuum cleaners:** Okay, we admit it, we're lazy when it comes to cleaning the house. (And we're constantly reminded of it by our spouses.) So when a product such as a robotic vacuum cleaner comes along for only $139, we get excited. iRobot (www.irobot.com) was first to market with a mass-production model that uses intelligent navigation technology to automatically clean all household floor surfaces. This machine, dubbed Roomba, looks like a squat little space saucer that can roam around the house sensing obstructions and switching floor modes automatically. iRobot also has a floor-scrubbing model now, the Scooba, as well as models for cleaning the pool or your workshop. Other robot vac vendors include Infinuvo, www.infinuvo.com/) has the CleanMate family of personal cleaning assistants, Yujin Robot (www.iclebo.com) has iClebo, AB Electrolux has its Trilobite (www.electrolux.com)... heck, there's even a race car robot vacuum, the Vesture NASCAR TrackVac Robotic Floor Vacuum (www.vesture.com).

Networking the Family Sedan

You may not realize this, but your car contains a massive computer network that touches many of its most critical parts, such as brakes, airbags, and monitoring systems. You don't see most of that stuff, so it's more useful than fun.

The focus on enhancing a car's internal smarts is driven mostly by the convergence of a number of add-ons, such as mounted cell phones, in-car video systems, and laptop wireless access devices. These previously unrelated items are starting to be linked to similar devices and services outside the car. For instance, the music you want to play in your car is probably much the same that you play at home.

Much of the focus thus far has centered on a few key areas, such as network connectivity (being able to communicate with things outside the car), the inherent computing capability of the car (being able to load new software to enable new functionality), and integration with the dashboard and steering wheel. If it sounds like we're talking about a computer, a network, and a user interface, we are: a network for your car, linking various endpoint devices to a central computer with the smarts to do a lot of things, in a fashion that's easy to use.

The key technology for cars is Bluetooth, which we talk about in Chapter 16. Bluetooth connects (or will connect) laptops, cell phones, PDAs, watches, and other such devices to interact with the car. Today, Bluetooth is mainly used for handsfree phone calls. You can also find in-car GPS navigation systems, such as those from TomTom (www.tomtom.com), which connect to your cell phone via Bluetooth and use your mobile broadband (Internet) connection to download information such as real-time traffic, weather reports, and detailed city maps.

Losing Weight on the Internet

There's something about riding an exercise bike to nowhere. It just doesn't work for us. Danny has a computer monitor, keyboard, and wireless mouse mounted just above the front of his treadmill to take in the best of the Web each morning. It's easy to do — just add a keyboard, video, mouse (KVM) switch that allows you to switch a single keyboard, video display monitor, and mouse between two computers (works when you want to interact with only one computer at a time).

But the folks at Icon Fitness (www.ifit.com) have taken it a step further by linking your exercise equipment, the Internet, SD cards, live personal coaches, and a library of audio and video slide tours that make each day's exercising a new adventure.

You can hike the hills of San Francisco or explore Hawaii's volcanoes, take in the Canadian Rockies or climb in Yosemite National Park. You can be berated by a drill-sergeant-like trainer or soothed with a firm voice. You can choose background music, your level, your pace, and more. Icon Fitness not only provides you with something to watch, but they can remotely control more than 100 models of treadmills, elliptical trainers, stationary bikes, and incline trainers — from Icon's NordicTrack, Pro-Form, Reebok, HealthRider, and Image divisions (www.iconfitness.com).

iFIT has many other products with an "exercise and entertainment" component: treadmills with built-in flatscreen TVs (cable-ready), ellipticals and treadmills with 3.5mm audio jacks for your iPod or other MP3 player, and ellipticals and bikes with built-in games in the console.

Figuring Out Which CD to Play

Do you have a few hundred CDs? Lots of MP3? Want to listen to them around the house? What are you to do? There's been a flurry of activity in recent years about opening up the stored content on an iPod, on CDs, and in MP3s. Making this info available elsewhere will depend on your budget and planning. In Chapter 9 we discuss media adapters and how to get info off your PCs and onto your stereo. These are relatively inexpensive extenders that give you remote access to your music. But suppose you want something specifically crafted to handle a music aficionado's need? What you want is a CD server! And here's the one you want: Request, Inc.'s AudioReQuest system (www.request.com). Capable of storing as many CDs as you have (you can add additional storage by their swappable hard drives or getting higher capacity units), this is the ultimate in CD listening pleasure.

You can use your TV screen or any Web browser as the interface to your music collection. You create playlists from albums and artists stored in the system. Loading (ripping) a CD into the system is as easy as opening the tray and closing it. The system determines whether the CD is already in your system and then looks up the name of the album and artist in its internal database of almost a million albums; if the system can't find the CD, it checks a master database on the Internet.

It's truly the future of music in the entertainment center. An entry-level N Series system costs about $1500 and scales up from there depending on storage capacity and features. This is the box you put in your home if you're serious about music!

Serving Up Video on Your Screen

Video is a different animal when you are trying to make it available all over the house. Digital rights management (copy protection) has more of an impact, files are larger, and let's face it, there's something cool about having 500 DVD cases all lined up on your bookshelves. Still, a video server is in your future, we're sure of it!

The ideal solution is to do the same thing you do with the Request N Series audio server — load your discs into the tray, scan them, and voila, they're available throughout the home. However, your Hollywood friends are not as keen on this as you'd think, and so most video servers are designed around the idea that you have large DVD carousels that spin around to the movie you've selected and start playing the DVD.

Again, we've looked to the serious consumer electronic vendors to tackle this problem. ReQuest, Inc. has a great video product, VideoReQuest (`www.request.com`), that is paired with up to four Sony DVP-CX777ES 400 disc DVD changers to give you on-screen access to 1600 movies. An on-screen TV menu lets you quickly find your DVDs through visual pictures of the movie posters and through search options such as Recently Added and Recently Played. You may also access your DVDs by MPAA rating, actor, director, or changer. Request's main product, the VRQ-1, retails for about $2500. A CD-changer will run you about $300.

Giving a Concert

Entertaining tonight? Why not treat your guests to a stylish in-home concert of Mozart's Piano Sonatas K. 310, K. 333, and K. 533? Don't play the piano? No problem, try Baldwin Piano's (`www.baldwinpiano.com`) ConcertMaster.

Your smart home can plug into your Baldwin, Chickering, or Wurlitzer piano and play almost any musical piece you can imagine. ConcertMaster works in several ways: as a standard piano, as a player piano that utilizes special digital data instead of the rolls used by old-fashioned ones, as a playback system (with built-in amplified speakers) for your own CDs, and as a karaoke system. You can even plug it into your home network's VCR and watch the pianist creating the music your piano plays back for you. If you play the piano a bit yourself, you can use ConcertMaster to record your own performances. You can use your smart home's Internet connection to download the latest operating system software from Baldwin's servers, too. Encore!

Gazing on a Starry, Starry Night

You want your child to see the space shuttle zooming across the sky, so you grab your trusty telescope and wait for it to appear across the horizon, right? Lots of luck. The space shuttle is moving at more than 17,500 miles per hour, and keeping an object moving that fast in focus is nearly impossible — unless you have a smart home. Imagine sitting on your couch and watching the night sky through your home-network-fed telescope.

Start with one of the finer telescopes, such as a Meade ETX, LX200GPS, or high-end RCX400 series (www.meade.com). With its super-high-tech motorized system for rotating the lens across the sky, the LX200GPS is a wonderful platform for satellite observing and tracking. As you use a handheld control to select specific planets or galaxies, the telescope slides over to that area of the sky. (The Meade telescopes start at about $500 and go up to more than $16,000 for the true sky enthusiast.)

Meade telescopes can be controlled remotely using AutoStar Suite software. Telescopes can be connected through serial or USB ports to a computer and operated from the warm comfort of your home. If you want to get star-crossed, you can add a Meade Deep Sky Imager Camera to your telescope and the images of celestial objects can be viewed directly on the computer screen. Point and click to any celestial object on the PC display and watch as the telescope moves to the object and places it in the field of view. Check out the International Space Station that's under construction as it passes by your field of vision!

Hook up a computer to a big screen TV and enjoy celestial wonders from your living room's plasma screen! Command the telescope to show you the night sky with "Tonight's Best" guided tour. Some models of Meade telescopes include extensions that allow the scope to be remotely controlled from any Web browser, so you don't need to install any software to control the telescope from your PC, Mac, PDA, or even a cell phone. This makes it ideal for kids to operate the scope without extensive software training.

3D Home Theater

3D has always meant something out of the ordinary for most folks — "Santa versus the Snowman" in IMAX, or the *T2: 3D* "ride" at the Universal Studios theme park, or the *Honey I Shrunk the Kids* exhibit at EPCOT in Disney World. Well, watch out, because 3D is coming to the mainstream.

A number of competing solutions will be vying for your 3D dollars. For years, the most common 3D technology has used *anaglyph* encoding. The anaglyph method creates a single image from two superimposed color-coded images — providing a sense of depth or 3D. Those red/blue cheap cardboard glasses you get at the theater are anaglyph-based. However, we're moving out of the age of cheap and into the age of super technology. One approach is to create a high-quality version of these cheap paper glasses. Sensio (www.sensio.tv, $2995), a Canadian firm, created glasses with electronic LCD shutters that alternately image on the left and right, allowing each eye to view the screen every other sixtieth of a second. Each eye only sees its corresponding image (left eye only sees the left angle images) on the screen. The base unit, Sensio S3D-100, is connected between your DVD player and your TV display. You play a special Sensio-encoded DVD in your DVD player; the S3D-100 reads the signal coming from the DVD player and translates that into alternative (left and right) progressive images that are sent to the screen. It also sends a signal over an IR emitter to the wireless IR-driven glasses that you wear.

The Sensio approach yields great results. Some cautions:

- ✔ You need a special DVD that carries the Sensio encoding — at the time of this writing a dozen movies were in their library, but more are coming.

- ✔ You need a TV or projector that can take a VGA connector — which is common on most video projectors. If you don't have VGA, you can use a VGA-to-component converter from companies like Key Digital.

- ✔ You can't use the Sensio with a plasma TV because the plasma screens emit a great deal of infrared, which interferes with the glasses' sync signal.

- ✔ Because the glasses shutter on and off rapidly, folks prone to seizures should avoid wearing the glasses.

A second major way that 3D is coming to a wall near you is the advent of 3D televisions. That's right, the television itself is capable of displaying a 3D image *without* the eyeglasses. You can just look at the screen and see depth of images. This is done by polarizing the display. A processor in the TV generates nine slightly different views fanning out in front of the display. From almost any location in front of the monitor, a viewer catches a different image in each eye. It enhances standard 2D content, as well as exploits 3D content.

Before you think this will take a while to roll out, the NBA has already broadcast a game in 3D — the 56th NBA All-Star Game. Standard broadcast cameras were replaced with a 3D HD setup that sports two HD cameras that work together to create one visual experience. On the viewing side of the equation, NBA fans watched on 3D television displays in special viewing areas set up just for the experience. Also, most recently made video games generate three-dimensional objects internally, and then flatten the images into 2D representations for standard monitors. 3D TVs can read the original depth information from the game engine and use it to create 3D images on their displays.

So where can you view all this great imagery? Philip's 42-3D6W01 WOW is a good example of a TV offering 3D enhanced depth performance with out-of-screen effects. Like the first generation of 2D plasmas, this unit is expensive; this 42" 3D TV costs about $15,000.

Putting the "Motion" in Motion Pictures

Are you ready to RUMBLE! We are, and there's lots of great toys to help us do this. There's nothing like the bone-shaking feeling of that low bass frequency humming from the speakers in a real theater. Now you too can have that at home, in some inexpensive or pricey ways — whatever suits your budget.

You can start with a set of audio transducers from companies such as Clark Synthesis (www.clarksynthesis.com) and The Guitammer Company Inc. (www.thebuttkicker.com). The grapefruit-sized units are screwed onto the bottom of your furniture or into the frames of your floorboards and take their cues from the special effects (LFE) channel of your home's sound system. They are better than the more generalized subwoofer-based effects because they can be localized — only your couch shakes, for instance, if they are attached to the couch's underframing.

You'll hear transducers by many names — *bass shakers*, *tactile transducers*, or even, *buttkickers.* They are inexpensive — you can buy a version that bolts to your chair for less than $100, and a multi-unit couch version is less than $300.

But for those who want to go the extra mile (or shall we say inches?), there are the motion simulator systems from D-Box (www.d-box.com). Where bass shakers vibrate and shake in response to the audio track and are in reality merely transducers that vibrate rather than move air, the D-Box motion simulator is a sophisticated three-axis motion simulation system driven by actuators that physically lifts you according to action in the film.

When a car crests a San Francisco hill in a car chase scene — or that F-14 screams into a tight turn — you jump or turn with it. The D-Box controller directs the translation of motion cues from the DVD to the motion of the actuators. The controller's microprocessors direct the vertical and horizontal movement of the actuators. Unfortunately, not all movies come with D-Box codes. Indeed, codes must be programmed for each specific movie by D-Box. Hundreds of movies and TV shows (such as *Lost* and *24*) are supported now (see the list at www.d-box.com/en/codes/index.html), with more coming each month.

D-Box systems are pricey — a full system will run you $15,000, but you can get individual chairs for far less. The high price is in the high-quality actuators.

Playing with LEGO, the 21st Century Way

Even toys can be made smart by your smart home. Driven by your PCs, LEGO's MINDSTORMS kits are the traditional LEGO building bricks on robotic steroids.

The LEGO MINDSTORMS kit ($250), targeted at kids 10 and over, lets you design, build, and program real robots using the standard LEGO brick system, a microcomputer core, and special bricks with light, touch, sound, and supersonic sensors. You can create light-sensitive intruder alarms, line-tracking rovers, robotic soda-can retrievers, or even robots with collision and edge detection.

The brain is the NXT brick, an autonomous microcomputer that looks like a big LEGO brick with an LCD screen in it. The NXT uses sensors to take input from its environment, process data, and signal output motors to turn on and off. You can also download the system's upgradeable firmware to your PC over your smart home's Internet connection, and then send it by Bluetooth to the NXT.

You build your robot by using the NXT and LEGO elements. Then you create a program for your invention by using NXT-G (a simple programming language for controlling your robot). Your creation can now interact with the environment, fully autonomous from the PC. Want to get other programs? The LEGO MINDSTORMS Web site http://mindstorms.lego.com/ has scads of advice and downloadable software.

Index

• *B* •

• J •

• N •

• O •

• P •

• X •

• Y •

• Z •

Notes

Notes

BUSINESS, CAREERS & PERSONAL FINANCE

 0-7645-9847-3

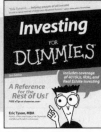 0-7645-2431-3

Also available:
- Business Plans Kit For Dummies
  0-7645-9794-9
- Economics For Dummies
  0-7645-5726-2
- Grant Writing For Dummies
  0-7645-8416-2
- Home Buying For Dummies
  0-7645-5331-3
- Managing For Dummies
  0-7645-1771-6
- Marketing For Dummies
  0-7645-5600-2
- Personal Finance For Dummies
  0-7645-2590-5*
- Resumes For Dummies
  0-7645-5471-9
- Selling For Dummies
  0-7645-5363-1
- Six Sigma For Dummies
  0-7645-6798-5
- Small Business Kit For Dummies
  0-7645-5984-2
- Starting an eBay Business For Dummies
  0-7645-6924-4
- Your Dream Career For Dummies
  0-7645-9795-7

HOME & BUSINESS COMPUTER BASICS

 0-470-05432-8

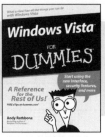 0-471-75421-8

Also available:
- Cleaning Windows Vista For Dummies
  0-471-78293-9
- Excel 2007 For Dummies
  0-470-03737-7
- Mac OS X Tiger For Dummies
  0-7645-7675-5
- MacBook For Dummies
  0-470-04859-X
- Macs For Dummies
  0-470-04849-2
- Office 2007 For Dummies
  0-470-00923-3
- Outlook 2007 For Dummies
  0-470-03830-6
- PCs For Dummies
  0-7645-8958-X
- Salesforce.com For Dummies
  0-470-04893-X
- Upgrading & Fixing Laptops For Dummies
  0-7645-8959-8
- Word 2007 For Dummies
  0-470-03658-3
- Quicken 2007 For Dummies
  0-470-04600-7

FOOD, HOME, GARDEN, HOBBIES, MUSIC & PETS

 0-7645-8404-9

 0-7645-9904-6

Also available:
- Candy Making For Dummies
  0-7645-9734-5
- Card Games For Dummies
  0-7645-9910-0
- Crocheting For Dummies
  0-7645-4151-X
- Dog Training For Dummies
  0-7645-8418-9
- Healthy Carb Cookbook For Dummies
  0-7645-8476-6
- Home Maintenance For Dummies
  0-7645-5215-5
- Horses For Dummies
  0-7645-9797-3
- Jewelry Making & Beading For Dummies
  0-7645-2571-9
- Orchids For Dummies
  0-7645-6759-4
- Puppies For Dummies
  0-7645-5255-4
- Rock Guitar For Dummies
  0-7645-5356-9
- Sewing For Dummies
  0-7645-6847-7
- Singing For Dummies
  0-7645-2475-5

INTERNET & DIGITAL MEDIA

 0-470-04529-9

 0-470-04894-8

Also available:
- Blogging For Dummies
  0-471-77084-1
- Digital Photography For Dummies
  0-7645-9802-3
- Digital Photography All-in-One Desk Reference For Dummies
  0-470-03743-1
- Digital SLR Cameras and Photography For Dummies
  0-7645-9803-1
- eBay Business All-in-One Desk Reference For Dummies
  0-7645-8438-3
- HDTV For Dummies
  0-470-09673-X
- Home Entertainment PCs For Dummies
  0-470-05523-5
- MySpace For Dummies
  0-470-09529-6
- Search Engine Optimization For Dummies
  0-471-97998-8
- Skype For Dummies
  0-470-04891-3
- The Internet For Dummies
  0-7645-8996-2
- Wiring Your Digital Home For Dummies
  0-471-91830-X

* Separate Canadian edition also available
† Separate U.K. edition also available

Available wherever books are sold. For more information or to order direct: U.S. customers visit www.dummies.com or call 1-877-762-2974.
U.K. customers visit www.wileyeurope.com or call 0800 243407. Canadian customers visit www.wiley.ca or call 1-800-567-4797.

 WILEY

SPORTS, FITNESS, PARENTING, RELIGION & SPIRITUALITY

0-471-76871-5

0-7645-7841-3

Also available:

- Catholicism For Dummies
  0-7645-5391-7
- Exercise Balls For Dummies
  0-7645-5623-1
- Fitness For Dummies
  0-7645-7851-0
- Football For Dummies
  0-7645-3936-1
- Judaism For Dummies
  0-7645-5299-6
- Potty Training For Dummies
  0-7645-5417-4
- Buddhism For Dummies
  0-7645-5359-3

- Pregnancy For Dummies
  0-7645-4483-7 †
- Ten Minute Tone-Ups For Dummies
  0-7645-7207-5
- NASCAR For Dummies
  0-7645-7681-X
- Religion For Dummies
  0-7645-5264-3
- Soccer For Dummies
  0-7645-5229-5
- Women in the Bible For Dummies
  0-7645-8475-8

TRAVEL

0-7645-7749-2

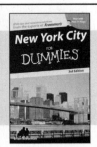

0-7645-6945-7

Also available:

- Alaska For Dummies
  0-7645-7746-8
- Cruise Vacations For Dummies
  0-7645-6941-4
- England For Dummies
  0-7645-4276-1
- Europe For Dummies
  0-7645-7529-5
- Germany For Dummies
  0-7645-7823-5
- Hawaii For Dummies
  0-7645-7402-7

- Italy For Dummies
  0-7645-7386-1
- Las Vegas For Dummies
  0-7645-7382-9
- London For Dummies
  0-7645-4277-X
- Paris For Dummies
  0-7645-7630-5
- RV Vacations For Dummies
  0-7645-4442-X
- Walt Disney World & Orlando
  For Dummies
  0-7645-9660-8

GRAPHICS, DESIGN & WEB DEVELOPMENT

0-7645-8815-X

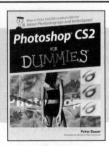

0-7645-9571-7

Also available:

- 3D Game Animation For Dummies
  0-7645-8789-7
- AutoCAD 2006 For Dummies
  0-7645-8925-3
- Building a Web Site For Dummies
  0-7645-7144-3
- Creating Web Pages For Dummies
  0-470-08030-2
- Creating Web Pages All-in-One Desk
  Reference For Dummies
  0-7645-4345-8
- Dreamweaver 8 For Dummies
  0-7645-9649-7

- InDesign CS2 For Dummies
  0-7645-9572-5
- Macromedia Flash 8 For Dummies
  0-7645-9691-8
- Photoshop CS2 and Digital
  Photography For Dummies
  0-7645-9580-6
- Photoshop Elements 4 For Dummies
  0-471-77483-9
- Syndicating Web Sites with RSS Feeds
  For Dummies
  0-7645-8848-6
- Yahoo! SiteBuilder For Dummies
  0-7645-9800-7

NETWORKING, SECURITY, PROGRAMMING & DATABASES

0-7645-7728-X

0-471-74940-0

Also available:

- Access 2007 For Dummies
  0-470-04612-0
- ASP.NET 2 For Dummies
  0-7645-7907-X
- C# 2005 For Dummies
  0-7645-9704-3
- Hacking For Dummies
  0-470-05235-X
- Hacking Wireless Networks
  For Dummies
  0-7645-9730-2
- Java For Dummies
  0-470-08716-1

- Microsoft SQL Server 2005 For Dummies
  0-7645-7755-7
- Networking All-in-One Desk Reference
  For Dummies
  0-7645-9939-9
- Preventing Identity Theft For Dummies
  0-7645-7336-5
- Telecom For Dummies
  0-471-77085-X
- Visual Studio 2005 All-in-One Desk
  Reference For Dummies
  0-7645-9775-2
- XML For Dummies
  0-7645-8845-1

HEALTH & SELF-HELP

0-7645-8450-2

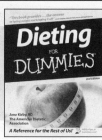

0-7645-4149-8

Also available:

- Bipolar Disorder For Dummies
  0-7645-8451-0
- Chemotherapy and Radiation
  For Dummies
  0-7645-7832-4
- Controlling Cholesterol For Dummies
  0-7645-5440-9
- Diabetes For Dummies
  0-7645-6820-5* †
- Divorce For Dummies
  0-7645-8417-0 †

- Fibromyalgia For Dummies
  0-7645-5441-7
- Low-Calorie Dieting For Dummies
  0-7645-9905-4
- Meditation For Dummies
  0-471-77774-9
- Osteoporosis For Dummies
  0-7645-7621-6
- Overcoming Anxiety For Dummies
  0-7645-5447-6
- Reiki For Dummies
  0-7645-9907-0
- Stress Management For Dummies
  0-7645-5144-2

EDUCATION, HISTORY, REFERENCE & TEST PREPARATION

0-7645-8381-6

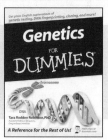

0-7645-9554-7

Also available:

- The ACT For Dummies
  0-7645-9652-7
- Algebra For Dummies
  0-7645-5325-9
- Algebra Workbook For Dummies
  0-7645-8467-7
- Astronomy For Dummies
  0-7645-8465-0
- Calculus For Dummies
  0-7645-2498-4
- Chemistry For Dummies
  0-7645-5430-1
- Forensics For Dummies
  0-7645-5580-4

- Freemasons For Dummies
  0-7645-9796-5
- French For Dummies
  0-7645-5193-0
- Geometry For Dummies
  0-7645-5324-0
- Organic Chemistry I For Dummies
  0-7645-6902-3
- The SAT I For Dummies
  0-7645-7193-1
- Spanish For Dummies
  0-7645-5194-9
- Statistics For Dummies
  0-7645-5423-9

Get smart @ dummies.com®

- **Find a full list of Dummies titles**
- **Look into loads of FREE on-site articles**
- **Sign up for FREE eTips e-mailed to you weekly**
- **See what other products carry the Dummies name**
- **Shop directly from the Dummies bookstore**
- **Enter to win new prizes every month!**

* Separate Canadian edition also available
† Separate U.K. edition also available

Available wherever books are sold. For more information or to order direct: U.S. customers visit www.dummies.com or call 1-877-762-2974.
U.K. customers visit www.wileyeurope.com or call 0800 243407. Canadian customers visit www.wiley.ca or call 1-800-567-4797.

Do More with Dummies

**Instructional DVDs • Music Compilations
Games & Novelties • Culinary Kits
Crafts & Sewing Patterns
Home Improvement/DIY Kits • and more!**

Check out the Dummies Specialty Shop at www.dummies.com for more information!